UNEXPECTED CONSEQUENCES OF COMPENSATION LAW

This book explores the performance of compensation law in addressing the needs of the injured. Compensation procedure can be dangerous to your health and may fail to compensate without aggravation/creating other problems. This book takes a refreshing and insightful approach to the law of compensation considering, from an interdisciplinary perspective, the actual effect of compensation law on people seeking compensation. Tort law, workers' compensation, medical law, industrial injury law and other schemes are examined and unintended consequences for injured people are considered. These include ongoing physical and mental illness, failure to rehabilitate, the impact on social security entitlements, medical care as well as the impact on those who serve – the lawyers, administrators, medical practitioners etc. All are explored in this timely and fascinating book. The contributors include lawyers, psychologists, and medical practitioners from multiple jurisdictions including Australia, the Netherlands, Canada, Italy and the UK.

Volume 34 in the series Hart Studies in Private Law

Unexpected Consequences of Compensation Law

Edited by
Prue Vines
and
Arno Akkermans

•HART•
OXFORD • LONDON • NEW YORK • NEW DELHI • SYDNEY

HART PUBLISHING

Bloomsbury Publishing Plc

Kemp House, Chawley Park, Cumnor Hill, Oxford, OX2 9PH, UK

1385 Broadway, New York, NY 10018, USA

HART PUBLISHING, the Hart/Stag logo, BLOOMSBURY and the Diana logo are trademarks of Bloomsbury Publishing Plc

First published in Great Britain 2020

A catalogue record for this book is available from the British Library.

Library of Congress Cataloging-in-Publication data

Names: Unexpected Consequences of Compensation Law (Conference) (2018 : University of New South Wales) | Vines, Prue, 1956- editor. | Akkermans, A. J., editor. | University of New South Wales. Faculty of Law, host institution.

Title: Unexpected consequences of compensation law / edited by Prue Vines and Arno Akkermans.

Description: Oxford, UK ; New York, NY : Hart Publishing, 2020. | Series: Hart studies in private law ; volume 34 | "This book arose out of a symposium held at the University of New South Wales, Sydney, Australia in March 2018"—ECIP introduction. | Includes bibliographical references and index.

Identifiers: LCCN 2020015559 (print) | LCCN 2020015560 (ebook) | ISBN 9781509927999 (hardcover) | ISBN 9781509928019 (ePDF) | ISBN 9781509928002 (EPub)

Subjects: LCSH: Damages—Social aspects—Congresses. | Compensation (Law)—Social aspects—Congresses. | Personal injuries—Law and legislation—Congresses. | Workers' compensation—Law and legislation—Congresses.

Classification: LCC K923.A6 U54 2020 (print) | LCC K923.A6 (ebook) | DDC 344.01/21—dc23

LC record available at https://lccn.loc.gov/2020015559

LC ebook record available at https://lccn.loc.gov/2020015560

ISBN: HB: 978-1-50992-799-9
ePDF: 978-1-50992-801-9
ePub: 978-1-50992-800-2

Typeset by Compuscript Ltd, Shannon

CONTENTS

PART III
APOLOGIES

PART IV
RESPONSIBILITIES OF LAWYERS

CONTRIBUTORS

Arno Akkermans is Professor of Private Law and Director Amsterdam Law and Behavior Institute and of the Amsterdam Centre for Comprehensive Law, Faculty of Law, Vrije Universiteit, Amsterdam, Netherlands.

Nicola Brutti is Professor of Comparative Law in the Department of Political Science, Law and International Studies at the University of Padua, Italy.

Kylie Burns is Associate Professor and Deputy Head of School (Learning and Teaching) Griffith Law School, Griffith University, Nathan, Queensland, Australia.

Ian Cameron is Professor of Rehabilitation Medicine, Faculty of Medicine and Health, and Head of the John Walsh Centre for Rehabilitation Research, at the University of Sydney, Australia.

Robyn Carroll is Professor of Law and Deputy Head (Community and Engagement), University of Western Australia Law School, Perth, Australia.

Alex Collie is Professor and Director of the Insurance Work and Health Unit, School of Public Health and Preventive Medicine, Monash University, Melbourne, Australia.

Genevieve Grant is Associate Professor, Director of the Australian Centre for Justice Innovation and a Convenor of the Law, Health and Wellbeing Group, Faculty of Law, Monash University, Melbourne, Australia.

Rosamund Harrington is Lecturer in Occupational Therapy at the School of Allied Health, Faculty of Health Sciences, Australian Catholic University, Banyo, Queensland, Australia.

Christopher Hodges is Professor of Justice Systems and Head of the Swiss Re Research Programme on Civil Justice Systems, Centre for Socio-Legal Studies, University of Oxford. He is a supernumerary Fellow of Wolfson College, Oxford.

Katherine Lippel is Canada Research Chair in Occupational Health and Safety Law, Civil Law Section, Law Faculty, Professor, University of Ottawa, Ottawa, Canada.

Ellen MacEachen is Associate Professor and Associate Director of the School of Public Health and Health Systems, University of Waterloo, Ontario, Canada.

Jennifer Schulz Moore is Associate Professor and Director of Learning and Teaching, Faculty of Law, and Associate of Faculty of Medicine, University of New South Wales, Sydney, Australia.

Christine Parker is Professor in the Faculty of Law, Melbourne University, Australia.

Clare Scollay is a PhD candidate, Faculty of Law, Monash University, Melbourne, Australia.

Sonja Senthanar is Postdoctoral Research Fellow, The Partnership for Work, Health and Safety, University of British Columbia, Vancouver, Canada.

Prue Vines is Professor of Law and Co-Director Private Law Research & Police Group in the Faculty of Law, University of New South Wales, Sydney, Australia.

PART I

Introduction

1

An Overview of Some Unexpected Consequences of Compensation Law

PRUE VINES AND ARNO AKKERMANS*

I. Introduction

Compensation law concerns the legal recognition of wrongs which cause harm and the giving of compensatory awards in recognition of the wrong and the harm. The area of personal injury is particularly significant and is often thought of as the primary area of compensation law, with a focus on negligence, workers' compensation and other schemes; but other areas of private law are also significant where personal injury and/or economic loss may arise. Thus compensation law may encompass a range of causes of action and a large range of systems, all of which are aimed at compensating persons for their harms. Unfortunately, it has become clear that even where the aims of the compensation systems are met, there are often unintended and unexpected consequences of compensation which may badly affect the person who is supposed to be compensated.

Knowledge of these unintended and unexpected consequences has been in existence since the 1970s and earlier, but until recently there was very little systematic discussion of these issues outside Law Commission and Law Reform body[1] reports. Amongst legal academics, the work of Patrick Atiyah in Britain, including *The Damages Lottery* and *Accidents, Compensation and the Law*[2] is one example of

* Prue Vines is Professor and Co-Director, Private Law Research and Policy Group at the Faculty of Law, UNSW Sydney. Arno Akkermans is Professor of law at Vrije Universiteit Amsterdam and director of the Amsterdam Law and Behaviour Institute (A-LAB).

[1] For example, *Royal Commission on Civil Liability and Compensation for Personal Injury: Report* (Pearson Report) (London, HMSO, 1978) and its earlier counterparts; *Compensation for Personal Injury in New Zealand: Report of the Royal Commission of Inquiry* (Woodhouse Report) (New Zealand, 1967); *National Rehabilitation and Compensation Scheme Committee of Inquiry* (Woodhouse Report Australia) (Canberra, AGPS, 1974).

[2] P Atiyah, *The Damages Lottery* (Oxford, Hart Publishing, 1997); *Accidents, Compensation and the Law*, written by Patrick Atiyah and first published in 1970. He wrote the first four editions and Peter Cane then took over. It is now in its 8th edition, (Cambridge, Cambridge University Press, 2013). See also T Ison, 'The Therapeutic Significance of Compensation Structures' (1986) 64(4) *The Canadian Bar*

significant attention being paid to the actual workings of the compensation system and its real impacts on the people involved in it. Dutch academics have been interested in this for some time.[3] Others have begun to pay attention to the issues which may be 'under the radar', such as how costs affect this area, how insurance affects it and how the structure of legal systems may affect it.[4] Academic discourse on unexpected consequences is only beginning to become systematic and to involve more than legal academics. We are now beginning to see the development of systematic empirical work evaluating the 'side-effects' of compensation law coming from not only legal academics but also from academics in medicine, epidemiology, psychology and sociology. One of these new interdisciplinary research fields is Compensation Health Research, studying the anti-therapeutic effects of legal arrangements and procedures on the victims of accidents who have suffered injury. It is the mission of Compensation Health Research to provide more detailed understanding and higher quality evidence of what exactly causes the detrimental effects of compensation procedures and how they can be restrained, in order to enable informed changes in policy, case law, the modus operandi of the legal profession and relevant institutions, and to inspire legislative change. Australia has been a leader in this field and there is a significant development of international research and collaboration of which this book is a part.

This book arose out of a symposium held at the University of New South Wales, Sydney, Australia in March 2018. It included a range of researchers from the various fields of law, medicine, epidemiology, psychology and sociology and included Australian, Dutch and Italian participants, and research carried out in those countries and in the USA and New Zealand. In this book we have also been able to include an English and Canadian perspective on the field. Much of the discussion

Review; T Ison, *The Forensic Lottery: A Critique on Tort Liability as a System of Personal Injury Compensation* (London, Staples, 1968).

[3] NA Elbers et al, 'Do Compensation Processes Impair Mental Health? A Meta-Analysis' (2013) 44:5 *Injury*, 674, doi.org/10.1016/j.injury.2011.11.025; NA Elbers et al, 'What Do We Know about the Well-being of Claimants in Compensation Processes?' (2012) 33:2 *Recht der werkelijkheid* 65, ssrn.com/abstract=2562343; AJ Akkermans, 'Reforming Personal Injury Claims Settlement: Paying More Attention to Emotional Dimension Promotes Victim Recovery' (2009) *Torts & Products Liability eJournal*, dx.doi.org/10.2139/ssrn.1333214; NA Elbers et al, 'Procedural Justice and Quality of Life in Compensation Processes' (2013) *Injury* 1431, doi.org/10.1016/j.injury.2012.08.034; AJ Akkermans and KAPC van Wees, 'Het letselschadeproces in therapeutisch perspectief: hoe door verwaarlozing van zijn emotionele dimensie het afwikkelingsproces van letselschade tekortschiet in het nastreven van de eigen doeleinden' (2007) *Tijdschrift voor Vergoeding Personenschade* 103; SD Lindenbergh and AJ Akkermans (eds), *Ervaringen met verhaal van schade. Van patiënten, verkeersslachtoffers, geweldsslachtoffers, burgers en werknemers* (Civilologie / Civilology, 7) (Den Haag, Boom Juridische uitgevers, 2014).

[4] R Lewis, 'Insurers and Personal Injury Litigation: Acknowledging "The Elephant in the Living Room"' (2005) 1 *Journal of Personal Injury Law* 1; R Lewis, 'The Influence of Insurers upon the System of Compensation for Personal Injury' (2005) 20(2) *Insurance Research and Practice* 16; R Lewis, 'Litigation Costs and Before-the-event Insurance: The Key to Access to Justice?' (2011) 74(2) *Modern Law Review* 272; R Lewis, 'Strategies and Tactics in Litigating Personal Injury Claims: Tort Law in Action' (2018) 2 *Journal of Personal Injury Law* 113; J Morgan, 'Tort, Insurance and Incoherence' (2004) 67(3) *Modern Law Review* 384.

concerns issues which are common to not only most common law jurisdictions, but also to civil law jurisdictions.

II. Promising More than Law Can Deliver?

Taking tort law and personal injury law as the paradigm of compensation law, we are all very much aware that the law often promises more than it can deliver. The harm that compensation law sometimes wreaks on the people involved in it ranges from the mental and physical injury caused by stress to the parties who are in the compensation system – which might be relatively unsurprising but, as becomes abundantly clear from several chapters of this book, is to be considered a central factor for negative health impact on claimants – but also to the vicarious harm done to lawyers and administrators acting for plaintiffs, and occasionally defendants. For parties, long delays and their associated uncertainty may create stress, which can create significant psychological or physical injuries separate from the original injury that led to the claim or suit. Sometimes this may also lead to addictions or other unhelpful outcomes. Other unexpected consequences include the creation of a situation where lawyers advise their clients not to apologise following some kind of adverse incident. This was not an intended outcome of the law, but remains a significant issue in civil liability. Other unexpected consequences include situations where the law falls short – for example, where damages awards are insufficient to support an awardee for the time they were expected to last. The consequences of administrative processes used to carry out compensation law in systems such as workers' compensation and motor accidents systems can also be unexpected and unintended. The processes of insurance and the operation of compensation law in interacting with insurance is another area where sometimes unexpected consequences arise.

The actual area in which the compensation law is operating may have significant effects on the dynamics, which might create unexpected consequences. Personal injury caused by a traffic accident and that caused by medical malpractice may be experienced very differently by the parties concerned – for example in medical malpractice there will often be a previous relationship which may affect the view of what the best outcome is. Particular areas may also be differentially insured, so that sporting injuries might be treated very differently from traffic accident injuries. There may be different approaches in relation to individuals affecting outcomes and systemic effects. Different expectations and different personnel and different institutions and systems may interweave to create quite different outcomes. In this book we attempt to scrutinise the warp and weft of this weave in order to illuminate the issues.

Two very significant issues concern the identification of what should be compensated for and the identification of what amounts to, or can be regarded as, compensation. The law has been slow to identify emotional issues as part of the discourse of law. The traditional view of damages, in common law and civil law jurisdictions alike, has been that monetary damages are given to compensate for wrongs, and that the damages are awarded in recognition mostly for physical harm which has created deficits in a person's life which can be made up for by money. This is not to say that legal systems have not recognised emotional harm, but they have been slow to recognise even catastrophic psychiatric illness, and slower yet in most jurisdictions to recognise emotional harms of lesser seriousness. Non-economic loss or general damages has traditionally been awarded in a way which de-emphasises them, and recent tort reforms in the United States and Australia in particular, have placed thresholds and caps on such damages. The reality of emotional harm is only beginning to be recognised,[5] both as a matter of the harm the law recognises and compensates for, but also in respect of the unintended harms that the legal system inflicts. These, of course, may be physical, economic and emotional.

III. This Book

This book aims to consider in some detail the range of issues that may arise unexpectedly from the ordinary processes of compensation law. It is divided into several parts. There is an Introduction, then a section on current shortcomings of personal injury compensation systems. Part III concerns apologies, and Part IV considers the responsibilities of lawyers.

A. Some Current Shortcomings of Personal Injury Compensation Systems

Part II starts with Chapter 2, 'Achieving Justice in Personal Injury Compensation: The Need to Address the Emotional Dimensions of Suffering a Wrong' by Arno Akkermans. He outlines the psychological consequences of suffering a wrong and the ensuing emotional and moral needs of personal injury victims, and argues that compensation procedures generally fail to address these needs but instead often exacerbate them, leading to the experience of injustice and considerably increasing the risk of secondary victimisation. As a growing body of evidence suggests that perceived injustice plays a central role as a predictor of worse health and recovery outcomes, this failure is not only problematic from a justice point of view, but should also be addressed to mitigate the anti-therapeutic effects of compensation procedures. Akkermans submits that these issues go beyond the differences between fault-based and no-fault compensation regimes, and elaborates on possibilities to

[5] See H Conway and J Stannard, *Emotional Dynamics of Law and Legal Discourse* (Oxford, Hart Publishing, 2019).

make claims resolution psychologically more responsive and intelligent regardless of what kind of system is involved, fault-based or no-fault. He identifies adversarialism as a common noxious element, and suggests proactive claims resolution as an antidote, and changing the roles in the game by having assessments carried out by neutral third parties as the most thorough countermeasure. Other suggestions are to provide a broader scope of services than monetary compensation only, to promote personal contact between those involved in the harm-causing incident, and to promote restorative and procedural justice.

The point of view of a medical researcher considering the relationship between compensation and health is taken in Chapter 3, 'Compensation and Health' by Ian Cameron. He discusses an extensive range of the literature on the subject, setting out the approach taken by the World Health Organization and its sub-organisations. He notes that it is well known that participation in injury compensation schemes may be associated with limited recovery after injuries sustained in motor accidents and other settings. He discusses the empirical data which suggest that this is likely to be a causal relationship rather than a mere correlation. In his chapter he synthesises the findings of all available Compensation Health Research and considers the mechanisms which may underlie the negative effects. Cameron concludes that health and recovery after injury can be improved by appropriate injury insurance scheme design, and suggests some possible useful interventions.

Alex Collie's Chapter 4, 'Apples, Oranges and Bananas' considers a range of Australian compensation schemes from the standpoint of psychology, drawing on a number of empirical studies which show that aspects of the particular design of a compensation scheme really matter to the outcome for the claimant and that no-fault schemes appear to produce superior health or recovery outcomes compared with fault-based schemes. His investigation considers the individual within the context of the complex social system we all live in. Work disability is affected by all the interactions in this social system and the 'control' in the system may be highly dispersed or not in an expected place. This can make the relatively simple analyses which are envisaged by the legal system wholly inadequate. The rapid rate of change of legislation in Australia's workers' compensation systems contributes to a situation which is extremely complex. The chapter reports the results of a major study of participants in workers' compensation schemes across Australia. The results themselves show that often the changes to workers' compensation schemes suffer from a lack of understanding of the extent of the complexity involved and may not achieve the correct goals, or only one of a multiple number of goals – for example, reducing costs as a goal is quite often achieved, but it is often at the expense of rehabilitation or return to work, despite legislative attempts to do both. The research summarised in this chapter suggests that there is substantial scope to improve workers' compensation schemes through more effective practices and policy settings, leading to better health outcomes and significant economic and productivity gains.

Katherine Lippel, Ellen MacEachen and Sonja Senthanar in Chapter 5, 'Workers' Compensation in Canada: Experiences of Precariously Employed

Workers in the return to Work Process after Injury' bring us a view from Canada of workers' compensation schemes across different provinces. They discuss the experiences of precariously employed workers in the return to work process after injury, which is an interesting comparison to Alex Collie's chapter on Australian workers' compensation systems and return to work patterns. In Canada each province has its own workers' compensation system. They compare the systems in Quebec and Ontario which differ in relation to the requirements for return to work. In Quebec the employer has the right but no obligation to offer modified work, whereas in Ontario both parties are required to cooperate so that theoretically an employer could be penalised for failing to offer work (although this appears to rarely happen). In Ontario much litigation occurs in relation to the modified work process. Particular aspects of each regime give rise to obvious differences in what happens to workers. For example, in Quebec, benefits are higher than those in Ontario, which meant that sometimes it was not worthwhile for claimants in Ontario to make a claim for what would be a very low benefit. For Quebecois claimants benefits are higher and last longer than in Ontario and this gives the Quebec employer a clear incentive to take the worker back. The picture is extremely complex, which is part of the problem: lawyers may not know who is entitled without extensive investigation in Ontario, workers may be confused, and complex systems may allow employers to duck their obligations, or indeed may create a situation where they are not able to understand their obligations. Lippel et al find that the economic incentives in both systems seem to become finalities in themselves, regardless of the aims of the workers' compensation system itself.

What happens to lump sum compensation when the plaintiff spends their money on housing? In Chapter 6, 'Safe as Houses? Lump Sum Dissipation and Housing', Kylie Burns and Ros Harrington look at this aspect of the effects of lump sum dissipation, This is a very common way for people to use a lump sum, but it is very likely to lead to the person having insufficient resources to manage ordinary living and as many of these people are denied social security, they may become destitute. The authors' research involved a detailed study of the impact of spending lump sums on housing by analysis of social security appeal cases in the Administrative Appeals Tribunal in Australia. They first critique the justifications for lump sum damages, showing how seriously impeded these are by social security rules of various kinds. Lawyers' support for lump sum damages should not be dismissed as (entirely) self-interested – many factors create the desire for lump sums, including people's sense of autonomy and the wish to be free of unwarranted state interference. These are also reasons people spend money on housing. Burns and Harrington show that the social security response to people doing this is to argue that they are 'double-dipping' because their lump sum was supposed to be used for income support and spending on housing is characterised as not income support. This narrow characterisation ignores the cultural and emotional value of housing and the fact that income is often ultimately spent on housing.

Chapter 7 is by Christopher Hodges. It is entitled 'Achieving a Just Culture that Learns and Improves' and it tackles a number of the barriers to open justice in relation to compensation law, particularly in relation to medical malpractice. Hodges regards this as a situation where there are two clashing institutional cultures: the medical and legal systems. The legal system is focused on individual wrongs, and deals with those after the event, often on the (wrong) assumption that this will deter poor behaviour in future, while the medical system is a *systems* culture where things may go wrong not because of one individual, but because of the nature of the system and where investigation of the *system* is more often what is required. Hodges discusses the evidence of what patients want and various approaches from NHS and other systems, and from behavioural sciences to argue where the possibilities of creating a culture that actually *learns* from its mistakes might lie. His analysis makes clear that both a fault-based system and an adversarial process present strong barriers both to openness of clinical staff with patients about what happened and why, and to medical learning so that future mishaps can be avoided on a wide scale. Hodges submits that 'fault and adversarial systems are old technology', and discusses more efficient mechanisms for delivering compensation to those who qualify, and for delivering further functions, especially caring responses, explanations and apologies, aggregating data on adverse events and feeding back information on how to improve both practice and culture in healthcare. He concludes that the traditional legal system is incapable of delivering these objectives.

B. Apologies

The next part, Part III, concerns the treatment of apologies. As an unexpected consequence of compensation law, apologies are a particular issue deserving of investigation. The unexpected thing is the common advice of lawyers to clients not to apologise, which is a consequence of the fear of liability. The compensation systems rarely mention apology and indeed may ignore the subject altogether, but this treatment of apologies comes out of the legal arrangements constituting the compensation system. The fear is always that an apology might mean that liability has been admitted. That is an evidential matter which is not considered particularly here. However, it is well known that apologies in certain circumstances may reduce litigation, or at least increase the likelihood of early settlement. One unexpected consequence of compensation systems which is considered in the chapters on medical and psychological consequences is the failure to pay attention to the extra harms suffered by people who suffer personal injury – these include humiliation, hurt to their sense of justice, and so on. Apologies may operate as remedies in these situations.

Chapter 8, 'An Incentive Based Approach to Apologies and Compensation' by Nicola Brutti, considers whether apologies could be regarded as having any real relevance to a legal system such as Italy's. He points out that apologies come from the moral domain and are almost never referred to in the Italian Civil Code. As a comparative lawyer he suggests that the fact that common law countries have recognised apologies in various ways may allow the Italian legal system to allow the gradual emergence of similar recognition. Can they be remedies? And if so, on what legal basis? He uses the work of Guido Calabresi to consider the possibility that apologies might be used to impact the consequences of an unlawful act. Protecting apologies may create an incentive to do this and this might be preferable to mandatory or commanded apologies in civil law systems. Despite the risk that incentivising apologies like this might commodify them, there may still be a value in using apologies in this way, and Brutti argues that cultural and legal system differences should be taken into account in determining what the particular legal system or society considers is the proper subject of an apology.

Taking a different tack in Chapter 9, 'Compensation for Intangible Loss: a Closer Look at the Remedial Function of Apologies', Robyn Carroll argues that apologies should be considered as a non-monetary way to compensate for personal injury. The recognition of apologies as matters of morality and of emotional compensation might give apologies an extra role in healing as compensation, allowing a greater recognition in the law of the need for healing the emotional impact of a wrong. She considers whether fault and intention are both relevant to the possibility of using apologies as remedies, whether it is helpful to think of the law relating to apologies as providing incentives for self help in compensation systems, and whether either of these is preferable. In noting that it is fault rather than intention that is relevant, and that apologies do provide incentives for self-help, she argues that there may be concerns if those incentives lead to reduction in the amount of compensation in response to apologies – because under-compensation is a constant problem in the law – but that apology-protecting laws seem to remain the best response to allow parties autonomy in respect of both compensatory and remedial functions.

C. The Responsibilities of Lawyers

Part IV concerns the professional responsibilities of lawyers. A first question of interest is the extent to which personal injury compensation systems use or allow lawyer representation. Clare Scollay, in Chapter 10, 'Exploring the Dynamics of Legal Use in Compensation Systems', explores the influence of compensation schemes and legal services market factors on how claimants use legal services for compensation issues. She notes that most international evidence has focused on person-level factors but little attention has been paid to systemic factors that shape legal use. For example, how do market factors affect claimants' use of legal services for compensation law? How much are lawyers embedded in compensation systems? Some are highly routinised and it is expected that there will be little use of lawyers – indeed lawyers may be banned – while in others lawyers are regarded as 'angels' (as in Chapter 13 by Jennifer Moore). Scollay notes that factors in system design which increase stress and complexity may lead to more lawyer use by complainants. Her chapter is an extremely useful view of the systemic factors which are often ignored in considering how compensation processes affect claimants. She concludes that there is a need to increase the accessibility of legal services and alternatives to legal services, but also a need to look beyond the engagement of legal services and support claimants to select the most appropriate method of problem resolution: this might not be legal services, as lawyers are not always the most appropriate source of guidance for claimants.

In Chapter 11, 'Addressing the Problem of Lump Sum Compensation Dissipation and Social Security Denial: The Lawyer Contribution', Prue Vines considers what lawyers can do to address the situation described in chapter 6 by Kylie Burns and Ross Harrington, where people who have been awarded lump sum compensation run out of money. This is seemingly an egregious example of unexpected consequences of compensation law, since the rule for awarding compensation is to put the plaintiff back in the position he or she would have been in had the wrong not occurred. Vines notes a number of systemic issues which could be addressed by lawyers, including changing settlement processes, altering how costs are created and explained to clients, and changing the way lump sum compensation amounts are communicated to social security. Given that many of these people run out of money but are denied social security, this is a significant issue that deserves serious attention.

In Chapter 12, Genevieve Grant and Christine Parker consider the ethical implications of findings from empirical research linking compensation systems with major personal stress and poor health outcomes amongst injury claimants. How should lawyers respond to the knowledge that the compensation process may do harm? The authors draw on Parker and Evans' four ethical approaches to lawyering to analyse the potential responses lawyers might make: The Adversarial Advocate, the Responsible Lawyer, the Ethics of Care and the Moral Activist. They suggest that, in addition to implementing aspects of the canvassed ethics of care approach, lawyers need to take responsible lawyering and moral activist responsibility for justice of the existing system and its accompanying institutions. A key focus for their work should be the opportunity to work collaboratively with schemes, insurers and regulators to implement improved cultures and practices. While attention is often drawn to the lawyer as advocate for the individual client, lawyers also contribute to system design, change, reform and evaluation, through advocacy by peak bodies, liaison and reference groups, having input into policies and protocols that shape how claims are managed and processed and the compensation system is implemented as a matter of practice. These opportunities could be used to promote initiatives such as dispute resolution systems that are about a more integrated and holistic sense of justice – including restorative justice and apology where appropriate.

Ending this book with a most encouraging note, Jennifer Moore in Chapter 13 discusses empirical research about New Zealand and American patients' and family members' experiences of the role of lawyers in non-litigation approaches to medical injuries. This shows that lawyers can play an important role in facilitating resolution after medical injury. In contrast to the overwhelming literature which depicts lawyers as 'devils', this chapter reveals that competent lawyers, who approach resolution after medical injury as a collaborative process, may play a vital role in facilitating fairness, creating opportunities for injured patients to be heard, and restoring trust between injured patients and health care providers. This might be epitomised by the description by injured patients and family members of their lawyers as 'angels'. This narrative is encouraging for lawyers, injured patients, family members, and health care providers. The discussed research highlights the valuable role of lawyers who promote resolution and restore trust in the therapeutic relationship. As health care organisations strive to provide care that meets patients' needs, an opportunity exists to include competent and collaborative lawyers in resolution processes after medical injury.

IV. Conclusion: Not So Unexpected?

We hope that this book will serve to alert lawyers, medical practitioners and legislators who develop the policies and laws which manage compensation in the various legal systems, that these systems are hugely complex and have a very significant impact on their participants. A person applying for compensation seeks what seems to be a simple goal – to make their situation better by being given compensation to help them lead their life. But very often the compensation system itself becomes the problem that the injured participant has to solve. Many people have non-pecuniary goals as well in engaging compensation systems, and the failure of these systems to address those needs seems to be an important factor for falling short in achieving their restitutionary goals. We would hope that these situations would become not so unexpected as this research might suggest, and that people become better aware of the multiple unexpected consequences that can materialise. This involves an assignment for professionals from several different disciplines. By conducting research that zooms in more detail on to compensation trajectories and the experiences of those who navigate them, psychologists and health researchers might shed more light on how compensation systems can be made more successful in achieving their mission in restitution, recovery, and rehabilitation. Compensation Health Research seems to have only just begun to gain more insight into the complex relationship between compensation systems and health outcomes. This relationship needs to be unravelled in more detail to allow the evidence found to be given the weight it deserves for the operation and design of compensation systems. But as Chapters 10–13 in particular illustrate, it is above all lawyers in various roles who have a major responsibility to improve the functioning of existing compensation systems and to contribute to the design of better ones. And of course, planners and policy makers, and legislators should also consider the complexity of compensation systems and their consequences thoroughly when creating systems and changing them. In a speedy world this is obviously a difficult matter, but this book should establish how important it is for the people these systems are aimed at, that the consequences of the compensation law are known, thought about and become not so unexpected.

PART II

An Agenda for Change? Some Current Shortcomings of Personal Injury Compensation Systems

2

Achieving Justice in Personal Injury Compensation: The Need to Address the Emotional Dimensions of Suffering a Wrong†

ARNO AKKERMANS*

Research shows that perceived injustice is an important predictor of worse health and rehabilitation outcomes after injury. Fault-based injury compensation schemes are considered to be generally more anti-therapeutic than no-fault schemes. This chapter starts from the submission that the fault or no-fault basis of schemes is not necessarily decisive for the level of adversarialism of claims handling procedure, and that a more detailed knowledge is required of the mechanisms that lie behind the negative correlation of adversarialism with recovery and health outcomes. It recounts some findings in empirical studies on reconciliation and the elements and effects of apologies, to extrapolate these to the process of the resolution of injury claims. The emotional and moral impact of suffering harm as a result of a committed wrong as identified in these studies, is compared to the properties of the process of the out of court resolution of injury claims. After it is concluded that these properties generally do not address this impact but instead often increase it, several options are identified to tackle these anti-therapeutic effects. These options involve several aspects of the process of the resolution of injury claims, such as taking responsibility by taking and keeping the initiative, providing recovery-focused services, promoting personal

† I am deeply indebted to Liesbeth Hulst, and must also acknowledge the contribution of Susanne van Buschbach, as this chapter consists to a considerable extent of further thoughts on earlier collaborative research, published in AJ Akkermans and JE Hulst, 'De niet-financiële impact van schadetoebrenging en hoe daaraan tegemoet te komen' (2014) *Tijdschrift voor Vergoeding Personenschade* 102, and JE Hulst et al, *Excuses aan verkeersslachtoffers. Een onderzoek naar baten, effectiviteit en methode van het bevorderen door verzekeraars van het aanbieden van excuses aan verkeersslachtoffers* (Den Haag, Boom Lemma uitgevers, 2014). I also wish to acknowledge the support of Alfred Allan, professor of psychology at Edith Cowan University in Perth (WA), who reassured me of my fears of being on thin ice here and there in my extrapolation of the outcomes of psychological research.

* Professor of law at Vrije Universiteit Amsterdam and director of the Amsterdam Law and Behavior Institute (A-LAB).

contact between the person responsible for the harm-causing event and the victim, promoting participation of the victim in the resolution process, having assessments carried out by neutral third parties, and more in general promoting the experience of procedural justice.

I. Introduction

A growing body of evidence of the impact of justice-related appraisals on recovery trajectories following injury, shows that perceived injustice is a powerful predictor of worse outcomes.[1] It seems to be increasingly likely that perceived injustice is an appraisal process that is central to physical and psychological outcomes in the context of rehabilitation after injury.[2] Perceived injustice is of course also undesirable in itself. It has been suggested that fault-based injury compensation schemes are generally more burdensome and anti-therapeutic for the individuals that have to resort to them than are no-fault schemes.[3] This is generally attributed to the fact that fault-based schemes involve more adversarial interactions, as claimants have to prove liability, causality and financial consequences. I have no reason to question these assumptions,[4] but I think that in order to contribute to the improvement of compensation systems a more detailed understanding is required of the experiences of injured claimants and of the mechanisms that can make those experiences

[1] MJL Sullivan et al, 'Perceived Injustice and Adverse Recovery Outcomes' (2014) 4 *Psychological Injury and Law* 325; C Orchard et al, 'How Does Perceived Fairness in the Workers' Compensation Claims Process Affect Mental Health Following a Workplace Injury?' (2019) *Journal of Occupational Rehabilitation* 1; NA Elbers et al, 'Differences in Perceived Fairness and Health Outcomes in Two Injury Compensation Systems: A Comparative Study' (2016) 16 *BMC Public Health* 658; NA Elbers et al, 'Procedural Justice and Quality of Life in Compensation Processes' (2013) *Injury* 1431; A Collie et al, 'Injured Worker Experiences of Insurance Claim Processes and Return to Work: A National, Cross-sectional Study' (2019) 19 *BMJ Public Health* 927; E Yakobov et al, 'The Role of Perceived Injustice in the Prediction of Pain and Function after Total Knee Arthroplasty' (2014) 155 *Pain* 2040; MJ Sullivan et al, 'Pain, Perceived Injustice and the Persistence of Post-traumatic Stress Symptoms during the Course of Rehabilitation for Whiplash Injuries' (2009) 145 *Pain* 325; MJ Sullivan et al, 'Perceived Injustice: A Risk Factor for Problematic Pain Outcomes' (2012) 28 *The Clinical Journal of Pain* 484; MJ Sullivan et al, 'Perceived Injustice is Associated with Heightened Pain Behavior and Disability in Individuals with Whiplash Injuries' (2009) 2 *Psychological Injury and Law* 238; KR Monden et al, 'The Unfairness of it All: Exploring the Role of Injustice Appraisals in Rehabilitation Outcomes' (2016) 61:1 *Rehabilitation Psychology* 44.

[2] Monden et al, above, n 1.

[3] Elbers et al (2016), above, n 1; K Lippel, 'Therapeutic and Anti-therapeutic Consequences of Workers' Compensation Systems' (1999) 22 *International Journal of Law and Psychiatry* 521.

[4] Which is not to say that these assumptions are generally accepted. Shuman has pointed out that in theory, the adversarial system has the potential to perform better in promoting procedural justice than first-party insurance and no-fault systems. See EW Shuman, 'The Psychology of Compensation in Tort Law' (1994) 43 *Kansas Law Review* 39. He also notes that 'How well the process in fact fulfills that idealized goal in each case may be a matter of some dispute' (ibid, p 64). Indeed. It seems to me that in the reality of everyday life, the adversarial process more often than not completely fails to fulfil that idealised goal. Yet Shuman's interesting observations certainly deserve more consideration than space permits me to give here.

so negative.[5] This involves going beyond the fault/no-fault divide. Whether a system is fault-based or not is, strictly speaking, only a difference in the legal basis of the substantive rights of claimants to compensation – the payment trigger, so to speak. The extent to which this is necessarily also decisive in terms of the kind of procedure by which claims are handled is an interesting question. I would like to submit that it is not. It is only tradition that might make us suppose otherwise. There are plenty of claims and entitlements that are not based on anyone's fault which are resolved in a most adversarial way. One only has to think of private disability insurance, but of course there are many other examples.[6] And conversely, it seems perfectly possible – at least in theory – to resolve a fault-based claim in a non-adversarial manner, while fully honouring all the requirements intrinsic to fault-based compensation, such as the establishment of fault, causality and damage. For example, an interesting – although probably too feeble – legislative effort to this effect has recently been made in the Netherlands with regard to the resolution of medical malpractice claims.[7] That, for instance, fault has to be established, does not necessarily imply that the relevant facts have to be established on the basis of a process of submission and refutation in which both the initiative and the burden of proof lie with the plaintiff, whose claim will be rejected if he does not present sufficient facts to support it or fails to present sufficient proof. It is perfectly possible for an insurer or an agency actively to investigate all aspects relevant to the claim, take the initiative in the discovery of facts, and to complement or even correct in good faith the presentations made by the claimant. I must add, however, that I think that in any system, fault or no-fault, it can be problematic to establish that the claimant is continuing to experience significant disability.

Once one is willing to open up to the possibility that there is nothing inevitable in the way claims are to be handled, either in a fault-based or in a no-fault system, many questions come to the fore. If non-adversarial procedures produce better outcomes in terms of perceived justice, recovery and health, why do we have adversarial ones at all? What particulars determine the level of adversarialism of a procedure, and what mechanisms lie behind the negative correlation with recovery and health outcomes? What does it take to change claims handling procedure for the better?

[5] See eg E Kilgour et al, 'Interactions between Injured Workers and Insurers in Workers' Compensation Systems: A Systematic Review of Qualitative Research Literature' (2014) 25:1 *Journal of Occupational Rehabilitation* 160.

[6] Another example is workers' compensation. According to Lippel et al is the promise of no-fault workers' compensation systems for non-adversarial relations between workers, employers and the systems themselves in many cases 'a chimera'. See K Lippel et al, 'Workers' Compensation in Canada: Experiences of Precariously Employed Workers in the Return to Work Process after Injury', Ch 5 of this book. See also K Lippel, 'Preserving Workers' Dignity in Workers' Compensation Systems: An International Perspective' (2012) 55:6 *American Journal of Industrial Medicine* 519; Kilgour et al, above, n 5.

[7] BL Laarman and AJ Akkermans, *Compensation Schemes for Damage Caused by Healthcare and Alternatives to Court Proceedings in the Netherlands. The Netherlands National Reports to the 20th General Congress of the International Academy of Comparative Law, Fukuoka, Japan, 22–28 July 2018*, available at dx.doi.org/10.2139/ssrn.3143320.

I can, of course, not even begin to discuss all these questions in this chapter, but there is one particular issue that I would like to elaborate on here, and that is the emotional and moral impact of suffering harm as a result of a wrong being committed, the possible ways to address this, as identified in empirical studies on reconciliation and apologies, and what these insights could possibly tell us about the process of the resolution of injury claims. As this brings together apology research and research on compensation and health, I think it is an appropriate perspective for this book.

II. The Impact of Suffering Harm as a Result of a Wrong Being Committed

It should be noted that not all injury claims result from being subjected to a wrong, as in no-fault contexts one can also be eligible for compensation when no other party was involved in the incident that caused the injury, and it might even be that the injured person blames himself severely for occasioning his injury and the ensuing predicament of his loved ones. Nonetheless, also in a no-fault system, many claims will originate in an incident for which someone else is to blame,[8] and my estimate would be that they generally constitute the vast majority.

It is a constant outcome of research into the motives and experiences of injured persons pursuing a claim for damages, that financial compensation is often not reported as their sole or even primary motive. Research has revealed a variety of non-financial needs and motives, such as for clarification of what has happened, acknowledgement of fault, the taking of responsibility for the incident and its consequences, the offering of apologies, seeing justice done, and preventing the same incident from occurring again.[9] Depending on the circumstances, these aspirations need not be less significant than the objective of receiving a fair and honest

[8] See LJ Ioannou et al, 'Traumatic Injury and Perceived Injustice: Fault Attributions Matter in a "No-fault" Compensation State' (2017) 12:6 *PLoS ONE*: e0178894, doi.org/10.1371/journal.pone.0178894; NA Elbers et al, 'Does Blame Impede Health Recovery after Transport Accidents?' (2015) 8(1) *Psychological Injury and Law* 82, doi.org/10.1007/s12207-015-9215-5.

[9] T Relis, 'It's Not about the Money, A Theory on Misconception of Plaintiffs' Litigation Aims' (2017) *Pittsburgh Law Review* 1; AJ Akkermans, 'Reforming Personal Injury Claims Settlement: Paying More Attention to Emotional Dimension Promotes Victim Recovery' (2009) *Torts & Products Liability eJournal*, dx.doi.org/10.2139/ssrn.1333214; C Vincent et al, 'Why Do People Sue Doctors? A Study of Patients and Relatives Taking Legal Action' (1994) 343:8913 *Lancet* 1609; T Relis, *Perceptions in Litigation and Mediation. Lawyers, Defendants, Plaintiffs, and Gendered Parties* (Cambridge, Cambridge University Press, 2009); JK Robbennolt and VP Hans, *The Psychology of Tort Law* (New York, New York University Press, 2016) 17 ff; AJ Akkermans and KAPC van Wees, 'Het letselschadeproces in therapeutisch perspectief: hoe door verwaarlozing van zijn emotionele dimensie het afwikkelingsproces van letselschade tekortschiet in het nastreven van de eigen doeleinden' (2007) *Tijdschrift voor Vergoeding Personenschade* 103; JL Smeehuijzen et al, *Opvang en schadeafwikkeling bij onbedoelde gevolgen van medisch handelen* (Amsterdam, Vrije Universiteit Amsterdam, 2013); SD Lindenbergh and AJ Akkermans (eds), *Ervaringen met verhaal van schade. Van patiënten, verkeersslachtoffers, geweldsslachtoffers, burgers en werknemers (Civilologie / Civilology, 7).* (Den Haag, Boom Juridische uitgevers, 2014).

compensation. In the Netherlands, this is sometimes summarised by the metaphor that an injured person is also 'overdrawn on his emotional bank account'.[10] The suggestion made here is that compensation is required not only on the monetary level but also on the emotional one.

It is stating the obvious to say that suffering injury from an accident can have a serious psychological impact. No research seems needed to establish that. But if one asks oneself how to best understand these psychological consequences and how they could be addressed, there is quite some empirical psychological research on the impact of suffering a wrong and the effects of apologies that could be useful. I do not present anything of a proper review of this research here,[11] but in a collaborative study I conducted with a research psychologist some time ago,[12] we concisely summarised existing theoretical perspectives on the psychological consequences of suffering a wrong roughly as follows.

A. Relational: Restoration of Status

First, psychological research suggests that a harm-causing event disturbs the balance between victim and perpetrator, which is accompanied by moral and emotional discomfort for both parties. An important notion is that a victim feels affected in his 'status' by a damage-causing event.[13] This status is also described as social power or relative value of the victim in relation to the perpetrator. A harm-causing event affects victims in their perception of being an autonomous, respected, significant social player who is treated fairly and whose rights and identity are respected. Victims feel inferior regarding their power, honour, self-esteem, and perceived control, and may experience feelings of victimisation or anger. According to the needs-based model of reconciliation of Shnabel and Nadler, victims must restore their sense of status and power.[14] Shnabel and Nadler submit that victims want perpetrators to acknowledge their responsibility for the

[10] This metaphor, widely used in a variety of contexts, derives from the concept of 'emotional bank account' coined by the American author Stephen Covey, see www.stephencovey.com.

[11] Overviews are offered by: D Slocum et al, 'An Emerging Theory of Apology' (2011) 63:2 *Australian Journal of Psychology* 832; A Allan and R Carroll, 'Apologies in a Legal Setting: Insights from Research into Injured Parties' Experiences of Apologies after an Adverse Event' (2016) 1 *Psychiatry, Psychology and Law* 10; A Allan et al, 'Interpersonal Apologies: A Psychological Perspective of Why They Might Work in Law' (2017) 7:3 *Oñati Socio-Legal Series* 390, ssrn.com/abstract=3003880.

[12] AJ Akkermans and JE Hulst, 'De niet-financiële impact van schadetoebrenging en hoe daaraan tegemoet te komen' (2014) *Tijdschrift voor Vergoeding Personenschade* 102 and JE Hulst et al, *Excuses aan verkeersslachtoffers. Een onderzoek naar baten, effectiviteit en methode van het bevorderen door verzekeraars van het aanbieden van excuses aan verkeersslachtoffers* (Den Haag, Boom Lemma uitgevers, 2014).

[13] N Shnabel and A Nadler, 'A Needs-based Model of Reconciliation: Satisfying the Differential Emotional Needs of Victim and Perpetrator as a Key to Promoting Reconciliation' (2008) *Journal of Personality and Social Psychology* 116. Shnabel and Nadler use the terminology of resources theory, which classifies the resources that are exchanged in social interactions into six categories (love, status, services, goods, information and money) and suggest that the resource that is threatened in victims falls into the category of status (ie the need for relative power).

[14] Shnabel and Nadler, above, n 13.

injustice that they have caused, and thus meet the victims' need to have their status restored. Perpetrators, too, experience psychological discomfort for having caused harm to someone. They suffer from moral inferiority and may feel guilt, shame or repentance. Being a perpetrator threatens one's image as moral and socially acceptable. Perpetrators want to restore their moral image and would actually hope for a friendly gesture from the victim. One major way the emotional needs of both parties can be met is through the offering and accepting of apologies. I will return to the healing power of apologies later.

B. Moral: Confirmation of the Violated Norm

A second implication of suffering a wrong presented in psychological studies is that victims would need (re)confirmation of the values that underlie the violated norm. This may sound somewhat abstract, but in fact is easy to imagine: anyone who apologises for his behaviour confirms that what he did was wrong; anyone who does not apologise could be perceived as not recognising that it was wrong. The most immediate satisfaction of this need might be the confirmation of the violated norm by the perpetrator himself, but confirmation from elsewhere can also be effective. This second implication of suffering a wrong seems to be in line with the first, as confirmation of the violated norm will generally contribute to the restoration of the victim's status.

C. An Example to Illustrate these Effects

A simple example may illustrate these effects. Imagine that in the hall of a railway station you are knocked over by someone running to catch his train. You hurt yourself, damage your clothes, and for a moment you lie on the floor in the sight of all onlookers before you manage to get up. Now imagine two scenarios for the events which follow: (1) the person who knocked you over continues running without any signs of caring about anything; (2) the person who knocked you over halts immediately, turns around, acts as embarrassed as you are, assists you in getting up, apologises, inquires whether you are hurt, and offers to reimburse costs in case of any damage to your clothes. It seems quite clear that scenario 1 will be much more offensive to you – even humiliating – than scenario 2. This may illustrate both the element of loss of status, and the suitability of apology to restore that status. In scenario 1 an element of 'denial' of the violated norm is also clearly recognisable: a person who just continues running seems to suggest that there is nothing abnormal about what happened. In scenario 2 the element of the confirmation of the violated norm is equally perceptible: a person who responds in that way clearly acknowledges that what occurred is something that was not supposed to happen.

III. Apologies

A. The Healing Power of Apology

It seems rather obvious that apologies can make a lot of difference. This is sometimes summarised by speaking of 'the healing power of apology'.[15] This chapter is not the place for an extensive discussion of the research literature on the healing effects of apology and forgiveness. Apologies express responsibility, as well as confirmation of the violated norm, and thus meet the psychological needs of victims mentioned above.[16] A principal result is the increased willingness to reconcile. Research literature offers many empirical indications for the assumption that in the case of personal injury also, apologies will have positive effects. Apologies can reduce negative emotions and perceptions of the injured party about the event that caused his injury and the responsible person, and create more room for a constructive, conciliatory attitude. Reducing negative emotions and attitudes will also mean that injured persons will be less inclined to seek justice through litigation.[17] In particular, Jennifer Robbennolt's empirical studies offer clear indications that apologies contribute to a more constructive attitude of injured parties with regard to claims settlement and to a smoother claims resolution process.[18] There are also ample indications that by diminishing the experience of injustice, apologies will promote recovery.[19]

B. The Content of Apologies

Research literature indicates that there is no formula for a 'perfect' apology. An apology is effective when it is considered 'good enough' by the injured party. Whether this is the case depends on several aspects identified in the literature, such as the sincerity, the content, and the focus of the apology, and multiple variables relating to the parties involved and the circumstances in which the apology takes place.[20] As for the content of apologies, researchers have differed considerably as to the specific number and names of its components. A concise

[15] Eg A Lazare, *On Apology* (Oxford, Oxford University Press, 2004).

[16] This is an enormous simplification. For a comprehensive overview see Allan et al, above, n 11.

[17] P Vines, 'Apologising for Personal Injury in Law: Failing to Take Account of Lessons from Psychology in Blameworthiness and Propensity to Sue' (2015) 4 *Psychiatry, Psychology and Law* 624.

[18] JK Robbennolt, 'Apologies and Legal Settlement' (2003) 102 *Michigan Law Review* 460; JK Robbennolt, 'Apologies and Settlement Levers' (2006) 3 *Journal of Empirical Legal Studies* 333; JK Robbennolt, 'Apologies and Medical Error' (2009) 467 *Clinical Orthopaedics and Related Research* 376.

[19] MJL Sullivan et al, 'Perceived Injustice and Adverse Recovery Outcomes' (2014) 4 *Psychological Injury and Law* 325.

[20] Allan and Carroll, above, n 11.

classification distinguishes between three elements, which can be summarised as affirmation, affect and action:[21]

1 affirmation: recognising responsibility for the transgression and its consequences;
2 affect: expressions of remorse and sympathy for the injured party;
3 action: to actually take remedial measures.

The most powerful is a 'full' apology containing all three elements but each of them separately has an autonomous effect. The first element seems to be the most important, and all three elements reinforce each other. Recognising responsibility is more effective than merely showing sympathy. Apologies that acknowledged responsibility led to less negative and more positive perceptions and emotions about the perpetrator and the incident than when only sympathy was expressed. Only an expression of sympathy was generally better than no apology at all. It seems, however, quite possible that, when sympathy is expressed but the wrongfulness of the behaviour is not acknowledged, injured parties might for example consider recurrence of the transgression more likely. Taking remedial measures (in our context: the offering of compensation) reinforces the other elements by adding to their credibility. Victims form impressions of the character and sincerity of the perpetrator on the basis of both his actions and his statements. A perpetrator who takes remedial measures seems to be accepting responsibility and/or feel remorse and sympathy not only in words but also in deeds. In our context, apologies will have to be offered in addition to – and not instead of – compensation. The offering of only compensation or only apologies was found to be less effective than the combination of the two.[22]

IV. Procedural Justice

There is one particular element of perceived justice that has been researched extensively over recent decades, and that is procedural justice. Procedural justice literature shows that people form a subjective opinion about the justice and fairness of procedures and rules (in our case: of claims resolution) and are particularly sensitive to whether they are treated in an honest, respectful manner (in our case: primarily by the agency or insurer).[23] The key constructs that are considered to be decisive for the experience of procedural justice are: voice, trustworthy motives, dignity and respect, and neutrality in decision making. An abundance of evidence demonstrates that the subjective judgement people make

[21] Slocum et al, above, n 11; Allan and Carroll, above, n 11.

[22] TG Okimoto and TR Tyler, 'Is Compensation Enough? Relational Concerns in Responding to Unintended Inequity' (2007) 10:3 *Group Processes & Intergroup Relations* 399.

[23] JW Thibaut and LJ Walker, *Procedural Justice: A Psychological Analysis* (New York, Wiley, 1975); TR Tyler, *Why People Obey the Law* (New Haven, CT, Yale University Press, 1990).

about proceedings being fair and just has significant effects on their subsequent behaviour and attitudes towards the decision and the authority that took it (the so-called 'fair process effect').[24] In the resolution of injury claims as well, the positive effect that people's fairness perceptions have on their subsequent reactions will be greater the more they experience the process as fair and just. As mentioned above, a growing body of evidence shows that perceived (in)justice is a powerful predictor of health and rehabilitation outcomes after injury.[25] The effect of perceived procedural justice on the responses of injured persons might be all the more considerable in lump-sum systems, as the outcome only comes at the end and is difficult to judge on its merits. In any system it seems plausible that injured persons will be extra-susceptible to perceived procedural justice, as research literature shows that people are extra-sensitive to procedural justice under 'alarming circumstances' and when they are in a state of personal uncertainty.

V. Some Characteristics of Claims Resolution in the Light of the Emotional Dimensions of Suffering a Wrong

If one considers the conventional process of resolution of injury claims in the light of the psychological consequences of suffering a wrong and the ensuing emotional needs of victims outlined above, it seems clear that certain characteristics of this process are likely to frustrate satisfaction of those needs, and may even increase them.

A. The Initiative Lies with the Victim

In any compensation system, be it fault or no-fault based, it will be up to the injured party to take the initiative to file his claim. It is more typical for fault-based than for no-fault systems that information relevant to the claim has to be brought forward by the plaintiff, yet both systems may vary in the extent to which the agency or insurer actively makes inquiries. In both types of system, claimants will experience a substantial power imbalance between themselves and the agency or insurer, and may experience suspicion due to the agency/insurer's responsibility to identify and reject spurious claims. The agency or insurer will

[24] K van den Bos, 'What is Responsible for the Fair Process Effect?' in J Greenberg and JA Colquitt (eds), *Handbook of Organizational Justice: Fundamental Questions about Fairness in the Workplace* (Mahwah, NJ, Lawrence Erlbaum, 2005); K van den Bos et al, 'On the Role of Perceived Procedural Justice in Citizens' Reactions to Government Decisions and the Handling of Conflicts' (2014) 4 *Utrecht Law Review* 1.

[25] See references above, n 1.

have more bargaining power in negotiating settlement offers, and issues that are in dispute will often be decided on the basis of a process in which the initiative and the burden of proof lie with the claimant. All these features will presumably evoke the impression among victims that they themselves are the 'owners' of the problem that damage has been inflicted upon them, which now has to be limited and assessed, and for which they have to seek compensation. To the victim, the agency or insurer may seem to be dragging their feet or passive, the resolution process may appear to be slow, laborious, and taking too long. Since, from the victim's perspective, the responsibility for acknowledging wrongdoing and for rectifying its consequences lies with the perpetrator, the merely reactive or even passive behaviour of his agents (agency or insurer) will be experienced as morally inappropriate and cause further grievance. This will contribute to the victim experiencing injustice and thereby hamper recovery.

B. The Responsible Party Disappears Out of Sight

Second, depending on the context of the case, there may be no, or only a limited amount of, personal contact between the victim and the person responsible for the incident. In case of traffic accidents, the responsible party often disappears out of sight right after the accident and the victim is referred to the insurer or the compensation agency. In case of adverse medical events, the extent to which the patient initially has personal contact with the doctor or other healthcare professional may vary, but for the resolution of financial issues the patient will invariably be referred to others. Victims who have sought representation often no longer participate in person in interactions with the other party. The perpetrator does not personally compensate the victim for his damage and costs, and will usually no longer have any personal contact with him. From the perspective of victims, the perpetrator is not taking responsibility for having caused the damage: either in words or in deeds. The perpetrator is often not even aware of the consequences for the victim and does not undertake to be informed about them.

C. No Symbolic Confirmation of the Violated Norm

Third, the vast majority of personal injury claims are resolved out of court. Fortunate as that may be for a variety of reasons, it implies that there will not be an authoritative proclamation that a norm was violated and that the incident and the ensuing damage are the responsibility of the transgressor. Practices will no doubt vary, but it seems safe to assume that when at a certain point in time an insurer or agency accepts liability, this step will normally be merely a matter of routine, just one of the boxes to be ticked – albeit an important one – and will not involve any explicit or implicit recognition of the legitimacy of the violated norm. It seems plausible that merely ticking the box of liability will neither serve to confirm the violated norm, nor to restore the status of victim.

D. 'Taboo Trade-off'

Finally, the following mechanism may also be at play. The resolution of personal injury claims is almost exclusively focused on assigning monetary value to the victim's losses. Research shows that people regard money and impairment of health as qualitatively very different entities, which are not interchangeable. There is empirical evidence that the comparing of non-interchangeable quantities such as money and impairment is perceived as morally inappropriate and produces emotional and cognitive discomfort: especially anger and negative appraisals of persons who make such 'inappropriate' comparisons. This is referred to as an 'taboo trade-off'.[26] Lawyers, insurers and other professionals involved in claims resolution are of course quite aware that money cannot really make up for physical or psychological injury, but reason that monetary compensation is the only remedy available. In the research literature it is, however, assumed that the psychological discomfort about this inappropriate comparison will diminish if the violated norm is symbolically confirmed.[27]

E. An Example to Illustrate these Aspects

Some of these aspects may be illustrated by an example. Imagine that you take your car to work every day, backing out from your carport to the street. On a bad day, when you return from work, your partner explains that you hit a child that morning without noticing, and that it lives a few blocks away in your neighbourhood. There was some crying and possibly some blood, but it is unclear how serious the consequences are, because the child was immediately taken home. What would be your immediate reaction – as a morally sound person? What would you do at that moment? I will tell you what you would do. You would *go* there. You would not send a letter or write an email. You might try to call them first but you would want go there in person. The normal reaction would be to immediately get in touch with the family to inquire about the child's condition, to explain that you did not see it and really didn't notice the incident, to apologise, to offer compensation of any damage, and so on. You would take responsibility and you would do it in person. It is a morally 'normal' reaction like this that injured victims and their families consciously or unconsciously expect from any fellow member of society.

The aftermath of most injury-causing events is often very different. Those involved in a traffic accident, for instance, often do not know what the consequences are for the other party, do not always have personal contact, and after the initial

[26] AP Fiske and PE Tetlock, 'Taboo Trade-offs. Reactions to Transactions that Transgress the Spheres of Justice' (1997) 44 *Political Psychology* 255; PE Tetlock et al, 'The Psychology of the Unthinkable: Taboo Trade-offs, Forbidden Base Rates, and Heretical Counterfactuals' (2000) 78 *Journal of Personality and Social Psychology* 853.

[27] Tetlock et al, above, n 26.

shock there is only contact with the insurer or agency. And for that insurer or agency, however empathic they may be, a victim is simply the umpteenth file. They may communicate as professionally as can be (or not), but they were not personally involved in the incident. In this light, it is not surprising that the usual course of events does not fit well with the moral experiences of personal injury victims, and can be experienced as a denial of responsibility, even if the insurer or agency actually takes steps to compensate the financial damage. Many professionals working in compensation systems will have experienced the fact that, even years after the event, victims can still be upset about the fact that they never heard from the person responsible for the incident that caused their injury.

F. Why Secondary Victimisation Looms So Close

In view of the characteristics of the claims resolution process described above, it seems clear that this process generally will not contain sufficient elements that can accommodate victims' emotional needs, but will instead often increase their aggravation. Usually, neither the element of restoration of status, nor that of confirmation of the violated norm, will be met. These characteristics can greatly contribute to the experience of injustice. Victims who enter into the resolution process with an 'overdrawn emotional bank account' resulting from the original injury causing event, will not experience emotional compensation but will see their emotional deficit increased. The suffering of the original injury can easily be followed by additional moral and emotional affront. If relations are further stressed by a demanding – let alone a downright adversarial – resolution process, it is quite conceivable that the originally felt lack of recognition can become the starting point of a chain of interactions in which negative stereotypes are further confirmed. The insurer or agency can thus easily become 'the enemy'. The consequences of this are severe. You are injured at the fault of another. You are not at your best. To try to get what is due to you, you have to face an opponent much more experienced and powerful than you. The triumph of injustice. Bad outcomes all round.

VI. Making Claims Resolution Processes More Emotionally Intelligent

As submitted above, and as will be further illustrated below, the payment trigger of a compensation system – fault or no-fault – need not be decisive for the level of adversarialism of its claims resolution process. It should be added that neither is this the case for the moral and emotional experiences which personal injury victims are likely to gain when navigating the system. There are of course many different perspectives from which one could deliberate on better claims resolution processes.[28] Thompson, Elbers and Cameron have recently done so from a health system perspective, and I will come to one of their important considerations later.[29] In line with the argumentation developed above, I will discuss more optimal claims resolution processes from the perspective of the psychological consequences of suffering a wrong and the ensuing emotional needs of personal injury victims. How can the claims resolution processes be made more emotionally intelligent? However, I cannot pretend that the analysis outlined above will be my sole inspiration. Inevitably, considerations also come into play that are more or less generally known in the field of injury and compensation – many of them are discussed in other chapters of this volume – which I was not in a position to introduce explicitly above. The psychological consequences of suffering a wrong and the ensuing emotional needs of victims will nonetheless remain my main point of reference.

A. The Antidote to Adversarialism: Proactive Claims Resolution

If one is truly prepared to accept the moral inappropriateness of such a generally accepted and uncontested element of compensation procedure as the initiative being placed – and in many respects remaining – on the injured party, a new light is shed on a multitude of elements of claims resolution and the aftermath of accidents. The first thing that comes to mind is proactive claims resolution, already often advocated for expeditiousness and other virtues, but actually also indispensable to address the needs for justice of personal injury victims.

From the victim's perspective, the responsibility for acknowledging the wrongdoing and rectifying its consequences lies with the perpetrator. It seems plausible, therefore, that an explicitly active attitude on the part of his agents (insurer or agency) in claims settlement is essential to meet the victim's moral expectations, and in particular to address the core need that responsibility be taken for unjustly causing damage. A merely reactive or wait-and-see attitude on the part of the insurer or agency, let alone a dismissive one, could easily appear inappropriate and might well be perceived as an implicit denial of responsibility. The injured party has been the victim of another person's fault and it simply does not feel fair to have to go for it himself. Why should the victim be responsible for solving a problem that someone else has created? The victim should not be placed or left in the position of being the 'owner' of the problem that damage has been inflicted upon him, which must now be

[28] For instance from the perspective of the preservation of the dignity of claimants, see Lippel (2012), above, n 6.

[29] J Thompson et al, 'Optimising the Health of People in Road Injury Compensation Processes: What is the Role of Regulators and Insurers?' in A Craig and R Guest (eds), *Adversity after the Crash: The Physical, Psychological and Social Burden of Motor Vehicle Accidents* (New York, Nova Science, 2019).

identified, acted upon, limited, assessed, compensated and so on. The insurer or agency should deliberately position itself at least as the 'co-owner' of these problems and responsibilities, and express not only through its words, but also through its actions, that it (on behalf of the perpetrator) takes responsibility for the accident and its consequences.

One could object that such a role is irreconcilable with adversarial procedure. The defendant has the right to defend himself, hasn't he? It is true that a proactive approach goes to the heart of adversarialism. It should go there and kill it. In some of the most innovative and state-of-the-art compensation schemes this already seems to be on the horizon. In present-day practice, many claims resolution processes, or, depending on jurisdiction and compensation scheme, most such processes, including fault-based ones, do not start off in such an unmitigated adversarial way that the insurer or agency has no room to take and keep the initiative. Sensible claims resolution should simply never start off in an adversarial way. No scheme design requires it – not even when eligibility cannot prima facie be established, which is generally a minority of cases. There are no relevant facts that cannot be actively investigated by (the agent of) the party addressed. All the requirements, including those intrinsic to fault-based compensation such as fault, causality and damage, can be determined on an objective basis, with no or only a minimal burden of establishing relevant facts remaining on the applicant for compensation. The necessary cooperation of the applicant will normally be given when politely asked for, for instance in providing information that can only come from him. When problems arise, deliberate efforts can be made to mediate solutions and prevent conflict. The party whose actions have caused the injury (the 'defendant') need not worry. He just needs to be insured.

Such an approach may not always succeed. That resort is taken to adversarial procedures, in second instance or sometimes even from quite early on, will probably remain unavoidable in a minority of cases. That will be so, by the way, irrespective of the nature of the scheme – whether fault or no-fault. The default, however, should be that the agents of the responsible party take and keep the initiative. Not the other way around. Such is required by justice. Better outcomes all round.

B. Providing a Broader Scope of Services than Purely Monetary Compensation

There are many reasons why, in any compensation scheme, the agent or insurers should not limit themselves to providing financial relief, but also provide for, or facilitate the provision of, recovery and rehabilitation services. This chapter is not the place to elaborate on the wealth of reasons behind this. Let it suffice to say that even the most traditional tort or common law-based compensation system cherishes the purpose of restoring the victim as much as possible to his original state ('restitutio in integrum') and in case of personal injury this intrinsic restitutionary goal in proper analysis requires a clear priority to recovery and rehabilitation.[30] It is a big mistake to leave this entirely up to the victim's own efficacy. No-fault schemes often have a more explicit mission in promoting health, recovery, rehabilitation and return to work.

Actual support in overcoming the consequences of the suffered wrong, and not just the provision of money, will also be in line with the moral expectations of the victim. Apart from the element of 'taboo trade-off' referred to above, truly accepting responsibility for the consequences ('affirmation'), genuine sympathy for the injured party ('affect'), and taking appropriate remedial measures ('action'), all seem to call for some degree of practical engagement with the predicaments of the victim. In the example of the incident in the railway station hall, how much would you feel restored if the person who knocked you over wouldn't do anything more than pull out his cheque book – or give you the contact details of his insurance company? If, for example, you had difficulty moving around due to bruising, wouldn't you expect him to verify whether you can get home by yourself or offer to assist you in one way or another? The expectations victims have in this regard are, of course, highly context dependent. From a fellow citizen at a railway station who has created only a minor incident, one would probably indeed expect no more than assistance in bringing a quick end to an embarrassing situation. But when the transgressor is represented by a professional organisation whose core mission is to address the predicaments of injury victims, and the consequences are much more severe, diverse and long lasting, the moral expectations for actual support will probably be higher, more diverse and long lasting too.

An approach to the provision of recovery and rehabilitation services in line with the moral expectations of victims would, as a matter of course, take the victim's perspective as the guiding principle. Overviewing the wide array of difficulties victims can experience, it seems that a wider variety of services would be required than those for which responsibility is traditionally assumed. Practices differ considerably between different compensation schemes of course, but everywhere several kinds of needs remain unaddressed. This starts with the immediate practical needs of a household, especially one with children, when one of its members is suddenly put in hospital or in any other constrained state. Why should 'first aid' only involve medical treatment? Recovery from serious injury involves not just one's medical status, but also the practical, emotional, psychological and social. The immediate aftermath of an accident are the golden hours to show solidarity and engagement with the victim. Practical assistance in meeting immediate needs could psychologically make a decisive difference. Further services could involve general support for the injured party in everything he needs to get his life back on track, such as information, advice, guidance and

[30] Akkermans, above, n 9.

coaching. They may involve support in administrative matters, such as applying for facilities, tax deductions, benefits and surcharges, or in contacts with third parties, such as the employer, landlord, the rehabilitation centre, care providers and contractors. Sometimes it is about solving bottlenecks in everyday life, such as personal care, activities of daily living, household tasks, caregiving tasks and mobility. But more complex services could also be offered, such as the management of a complex medical care process, requesting facilities from the municipality, organising adapted housing, selecting suppliers of aid, putting the financial administration in order – everything up to arranging an adapted holiday. All this, of course, would depend on the circumstances of the case and the needs of the victim and his or her household.

C. Promoting Personal Contact between those Involved in the Incident

There is one 'recovery service' in particular that should be mentioned here, and that is the promotion and facilitation of personal contact between those involved in the event that caused the injury: between the 'victim' and the 'perpetrator' if you want to put it that way, although often one will find that on the emotional level there are in reality only victims. In view of the basic nature of the emotional needs of persons who have been injured at the fault of another, and the significant therapeutic value of addressing those needs, not just for the victim but for the responsible party too, it could actually be considered quite peculiar that routines have drifted so much away from what seems to be the morally obvious thing to do. Given the difficulties and obstacles that apparently hinder the parties in bringing about personal contact at their own accord,[31] insurers and compensation agencies could make a deliberate effort to promote and facilitate personal contact, or see to it that some other agency does.[32] The operationalisation of such an undertaking depends, of course, on the circumstances. In the context of medical errors, significant efforts are already being made to coordinate direct contact between patients and doctors as part of 'open disclosure' policies and the like.[33] In the

[31] One significant obstacle, extensively addressed in literature, is (the perception) that personal contact, and apologising in particular, would lead to the undue admission of liability or the loss of insurance coverage. See P Vines, 'Apologies and Civil Liability in the UK: A View from Elsewhere' (2008) 12(2) *Edinburgh Law Review* 200; P Vines, 'The Power of Apology: Mercy, Forgiveness or Corrective Justice in the Civil Liability Arena' (2007) 1 *Journal of Public Space* 1; P Vines, 'Apologising to Avoid Liability: Cynical Civility or Practical Morality?' (2005) 27(5) *Sydney Law Review* 483; AM Zwart-Hink, 'The Doctor Has Apologised. Will I Now Get Compensation For My Injuries? Myth and Reality in Apologies and Liability' (2017) 7:3 *Oñati Socio-legal Series* 497, available at ssrn.com/abstract=3029245.

[32] It should, of course, always be the choice of victims whether to participate or not.

[33] Australian Commission on Safety and Quality in Health Care, *Australian Open Disclosure Framework* (Sydney, ACSQHC, 2014); TH Gallagher et al, 'Disclosing Harmful Medical Errors to Patients' (2007) 356:16 *New England Journal of Medicine* 2713; Laarman and Akkermans, above, n 7.

context of traffic accidents, such a thing is still much more rare. In serious cases it seems obvious to aim for mediated contact, as for instance is being done in case of traffic offences or accidents resulting in death or serious injury in pilot schemes in Victoria, Australia,[34] Belgium, the Netherlands, Hungary and Ireland.[35] In addition, efforts may also be made to promote unaccompanied contact in all cases of road accidents, as is being done in a pilot in the Netherlands.[36] If the promotion of personal contact between the parties involved in an injury-causing event were to become standard practice in compensation schemes, also in no-fault ones, this would very likely facilitate improved experience of justice and better recovery and health outcomes.

D. Restorative Justice and the Importance of Participation

The initiatives to bring about personal contact in case of traffic accidents mentioned above are inspired by the ideas of restorative justice, and frequently use the label 'restorative justice conferencing' for the meetings they seek to promote and organise. In the context of medical errors too, restorative justice has recently been suggested as a valuable theoretical framework to achieve objectives such as open disclosure, patient safety and 'just culture'.[37] The ideas of restorative justice encompass much more than mediation between the parties involved in a transgression. Apart from the key value that 'because injustice hurts, justice should heal', restorative justice involves a process conception, described by John Braithwaite as 'a process in which all the stakeholders affected by an injustice have the opportunity to discuss the consequences of the injustice and what might be done to put them right'.[38] Restorative justice is about putting the affected parties as much as possible in control, and Braithwaite emphasises that their empowerment should be prioritised over other values.[39] There is a wealth of empirical evidence

[34] Centre for Innovative Justice, *It's Healing to Hear Another Person's Story and Also to Tell Your Own Story: Report on the CIJ's Restorative Justice Conferencing Pilot Program* (Melbourne, RMIT University, 2019).

[35] I Marit, *Restorative Justice in Road Traffic Offences. A Manual for Professionals and Victim-volunteers* (Kessel-Lo, Moderator vzw, 2018).

[36] At the Vrije Universiteit Amsterdam we are currently working on a pilot with banners placed on the webpages of third-party car insurers at which their insured report accidents online, leading to a dedicated website called Contact Helpt ('Contact Helps') where they are informed about and encouraged to take up personal contact with the other party involved. It features podcasts of narratives of those involved in traffic accidents, and all kinds of additional information. See contacthelpt.nl.

[37] SWA Dekker, *Just Culture: Restoring Trust and Accountability in Your Organization* (Boca Raton, CRC Press, 2017); SWA Dekker and H Breaky, '"Just Culture": Improving Safety by Achieving Substantive, Procedural and Restorative Justice' (2016) *Safety Science* 187; BS Laarman, 'Just culture en herstelrecht in de afwikkeling van medische schade' (2019) *Tijdschrift voor Vergoeding Personenschade* 65; J Carroll and D Reisel, 'Introducing Restorative Practice in Healthcare Settings' in T Gavrielides (ed), *Routledge International Handbook of Restorative Justice* (Oxford, Routledge, 2018).

[38] J Braithwaite, 'The Fundamentals of Restorative Justice' in S Dinnen et al (eds), *A Kind of Mending: Restorative Justice in the Pacific Islands* (Canberra, ANU Press, 2003) 35; J Braithwaite, 'Restorative Justice and Therapeutic Jurisprudence' (2002) *Criminal Law Bulletin* 244.

[39] Braithwaite, ibid.

of the beneficial effects of restorative justice, not only for the victim but also for the responsible person.[40]

Participation and empowerment of the affected parties seem to coincide largely with the element of 'voice' that is one of the key constructs of procedural justice, although the ideal of control obviously goes further than offering people the opportunity to tell their side of the story and to express their opinion on decisions to be taken by others. Voice, participation and control are not narrowly defined concepts, but can be seen as adjacent bandwidths on a sliding scale. It is interesting to notice that a development towards a stronger position for clients is taking place in various sectors of society that are relevant to compensation systems, not least in the field of health care. In a recent chapter on optimising the health of people in road injury compensation, Thompson, Elbers and Cameron point out that the concept of health system responsiveness, incorporating patient-centred and patient-oriented models, has moved to the centre of contemporary thought and practice, and that such models:

> require health care providers to become more participatory; traditional doctor-patient or administrator-patient power dynamics are therefore exchanged for a model of partnership, emphasising patient empowerment and information exchange between all players in the system. A more interactive, participatory environment affords injured patients the opportunity, within practical limits, to be involved in decision-making and direct their course of treatment. The patient must be provided with options to be engaged, consulted, effectively communicated with and informed of their options. In short, the patient has agency.[41]

In view of all the above, it seems very likely that more participation would not only serve people's health, but also their experience of justice. Compensation systems would be wise to follow suit. This too, need not be a matter of absolutes, but can best be seen as a matter of taking as many steps as possible towards an ideal.

One such step could be to optimise the opportunity for victims to give input to the claim resolution process and to express what is important to them, and to allow for the time it takes them to do so. Accommodating victims' participation in the claims resolution process seems to be perfectly feasible even in traditional fault-based compensation schemes, although if there is a lawyer involved or some other representative, much will of course depend on his approach and collaboration.[42] For instance in the Netherlands, where the large majority of injury claims are resolved

[40] J Latimer et al, 'The Effectiveness of Restorative Justice Practices: A Meta-analysis' (2005) 85:2 *The Prison Journal* 136; H Strang et al, 'Restorative Justice Conferencing (RJC) Using Face-to-face Meetings of Offenders and Victims. Effect on Offender Recidivism and Victim Satisfaction. A Systematic Review' *Campbell Systematic Reviews 2013/12* (Oslo, The Campbell Collaboration, 2013). See also Chs 9 and 13 of L Sherman and W Strang, *Restorative Justice: The Evidence* (London, The Smith Institute, 2007) and Chs 8–19 of T Gavrielides (ed), *Routledge International Handbook of Restorative Justice* (Oxford, Routledge, 2018).

[41] Thompson et al, above n 29 (references omitted).

[42] On the responsibilities of lawyers for claimant health and emotional wellbeing, see G Grant and C Parker, 'Lawyers' Responsibility for Claimant Health in Injury Compensation Systems', Chapter12 of

in sometimes long-drawn-out out of court negotiations, the Code of Conduct for Handling Personal Injury Claims[43] recommends the use of a plan of action, drawn up by mutual agreement between the parties at the beginning of the resolution process. This plan of action sets out the steps to be taken in order to achieve a settlement, contains arrangements on who will do what and targets in a regard for deadlines. During the resolution process, the plan of action is reviewed at periodic consultations and adjustments can be made. Such a plan of action not only better enables the victim to give input to the resolution process, it is also a tangible expression of the 'joint ownership' of the problem that the damage has to be identified, act upon, limited, assessed, compensated and so on, and for this reason alone serves to allow the victim to experience justice. A plan of action can be made up in various forms but it seems likely that an interactive action plan that is part of an internet application that allows for information, communication, case documents to be viewed and uploaded and so forth, would be the most powerful tool for victim participation.

E. Changing the Roles in the Game: Having Assessments Carried Out by Neutral Third Parties

There is a more fundamental way in which to address the risk that the injured party might experience his interaction with the insurer or agency as being forced into an unjust and unfair struggle with a more experienced and powerful opponent. This is by separating the two roles that are normally both fulfilled by the insurer or agency, namely, on the one hand, to bear (or to guard) the costs of compensation and services and, on the other hand, to carry out the necessary assessments to establish eligibility and to estimate amounts of compensation. Although it is a widely accepted feature of compensation procedure that these two roles are fulfilled by one and the same party, the fact that his opposite party is acting as a 'judge in his own case' does not feel right for the victim from a moral point of view, nor from the point of view of justice. Of course, the insurer's assessments can be disputed, whether in the context of negotiations or in some form of appeal, and ultimately also before a real judge. But not only is this hampered in reality by various serious obstacles, it also invokes exactly the kind of adversarialism that obstructs the victim's experience of justice. And, as an aside, it is also very cost-inefficient as it involves several assessments of the same issue.

This fundamental flaw in conventional claims resolution procedure can be addressed by having all key assessments carried out by a neutral third party.

this book; M Keet et al, 'Anticipating and Managing the Psychological Cost of Civil Litigation' (2017) 34:2 *Windsor Yearbook of Access to Justice* 73, wyaj.uwindsor.ca/index.php/wyaj/article/view/5023; NA Elbers et al, 'Exploring Lawyer-Client Interaction: A Qualitative Study of Positive Lawyer Characteristics' (2012) 5:1 *Psychological Injury and Law* 89, doi.org/10.1007/s12207-012-9120-0.

[43] *Gedragscode Behandeling Letselschade* (GBL), English translation available at deletselschaderaad.nl/wp-content/uploads/GBL-Engels-2012-def.pdf.

This could take the form of a neutral party advising on the case as a whole, as is being done by the Swedish Road Traffic Injuries Commission (RTIC),[44] the Irish Personal Injuries Assessment Board (PIAB),[45] and the Belgian Fund for Medical Accidents (FMA).[46] Or it could involve several separate assessments, such as eligibility for compensation, the estimation of certain heads of loss, eligibility for certain services, medical assessments and all other key decisions. The neutral third party could be a public body, such as the RTIC, PIAB and FMA mentioned above, but this role could also be fulfilled by for-profit loss adjustment or assessor companies. In the latter case, however, it does seem essential that the instruction should not be given by the insurer or agency alone, but by both parties together, otherwise there would still be an incentive in the system that could lead to the interests of the paying party being given a greater weight in the assessment than the interests of the receiving party. This also applies to independent medical assessments (IMEs).[47] What is essential is that all decisions that matter are not taken by the victim's counterpart, but by a neutral third party, so that the victim is not put in a position in which he is likely to feel that he has to fight as David against Goliath to get what is rightfully due to him.[48]

If pursued consistently, such an approach could allow for a change of roles, in which the insurer or agency is not so much in opposition to the victim, but rather alongside him, in a joint quest for equitable solutions to a common problem. In this respect, it seems to be the most thorough countermeasure against needless adversarialism, and therefore potentially very promising for achieving justice. Since the results of jointly prepared assessments are likely to be accepted more often than positions taken unilaterally, it may also be a more cost-efficient approach.

[44] The Swedish RTIC (www.trafikskadenamnden.se) reviews serious traffic injuries in order to ensure that compensation for bodily injury is fair and uniform. The Government designates the Board's chairman, and the remaining members represent employer and employee organisations and the insurance companies. The Board issues recommendations on claims adjustment in individual cases, private insurance companies pay for the damage.

[45] The Irish PIAB (www.piab.ie/eng/) is a statutory body set up under the Personal Injuries Assessment Board (PIAB) Act 2003. It provides independent assessment of personal injury compensation for victims of workplace, motor and public liability accidents. See J Ilan, 'Four Years of the Personal Injuries Assessment Board: Assessing its Impact' (2009) 1 *Judicial Studies Institute Journal* 54.

[46] The Belgian FMA was set up under the Medical Accidents Act 2010 (Wet 31 maart 2010 betreffende de vergoeding van schade als gevolg van gezondheidszorg, BS 2 april 2010, p 19913). It provides independent assessment of claims for compensation after adverse medical events. See T Vandersteegen et al, (2017) 'Advantages and Disadvantages of the Belgian Not-only-fault System for Medical Incidents' (2017) 72:1 *Acta Clinica Belgica* 36; T Vansweevelt et al, 'No-fault Law on Medical Accidents in Belgium: An Evaluation after Six Years' (2019) 10:3 *Journal of European Tort Law* 257.

[47] B Kilgour et al, 'Procedural Justice and the Use of Independent Medical Evaluations in Workers' Compensation' (2015) 8 *Psychological Injury and Law* 153.

[48] I do realise that, especially in no-fault systems, it might be that the executive agency itself is already explicitly instructed to act on the basis of objective and neutral criteria. However, it is the victim's perspective and experience, and not the formal mission of the agency, that is decisive here. Even if the agency takes its decisions solely on the basis of neutral and objective criteria, the objection remains that it is the victim's opponent who is taking unilateral positions, and not a neutral third party who is doing justice between the parties.

F. Promoting Procedural Justice

An obvious way to address the justice needs of personal injury victims is in the promotion of procedural justice in the claims resolution process. Several issues that were addressed above incorporate or coincide with one or more of the elements of procedural justice, which should not come as a surprise. The key constructs that are decisive for the experience of procedural justice are voice, trustworthy motives, dignity and respect, and neutrality in decision making. As mentioned above, participation and empowerment coincide largely with the element of 'voice'. Having assessments carried out by neutral third parties should greatly benefit the element of 'neutrality in decision making'. But also, apart from such more or less demanding undertakings, the promotion of procedural justice should be perfectly feasible. This chapter is not the place to discuss all possible modalities of the promotion of procedural justice in the context of the resolution of personal injury claims. I will confine myself to two issues where it seems both essential and relatively easy to achieve improvements, namely information and face-to-face contact.

An issue that is often reported by claimants and that should be relatively easy to address is the lack of adequate information.[49] Adequate information is of course a prerequisite for achieving more ambitious objectives such as participation, empowerment and agency, but will already in itself benefit perceived procedural justice. Information provided on a dedicated website alone has proved to be enough to improve the perceived fairness of the monetary outcome of claims resolution.[50] Given the fundamental importance of adequate information, it should be considered unacceptable that there are still so many deficiencies reported on this basic point. Insurers or agencies could be much more ambitious in this respect, which by no means implies that claimants' lawyers, when involved, do not bear the greatest responsibility in this matter.[51] But many claimants do not engage a lawyer, and even when they do, information provided by the insurer or agency remains to be of independent importance. Online information, preferably in the form of an internet application allowing for personalised information, communication, the consultation of a plan of action or any other overview of steps to be taken, case documents to be viewed and uploaded and so forth, combined with regular face-to-face communication, seems to have great potential, much more than any written information.

[49] Akkermans, above, n 9; Lippel (2012), above, n 6; Kilgour et al, above, n 5; Elbers et al (2013), above, n 1; NA Elbers et al, 'Factors that Challenge Health for People Involved in the Compensation Process Following a Motor Vehicle Crash: A Longitudinal Study' (2015) *BMC Public Health* 339, doi.org/10.1186/s12889-015-1694-5; GM Grant et al, 'Relationship between Stressfulness of Claiming for Injury Compensation and Long-term Recovery: A Prospective Cohort Study' (2014) 71:4 *JAMA Psychiatry* 446, doi.org/10.1001/jamapsychiatry.2013.4023; D Murgatroyd et al, 'The Perceptions and Experiences of People Injured in Motor Vehicle Crashes in a Compensation Scheme Setting: A Qualitative Study' (2015) 15:423 *BMC Public Health* 67.

[50] NA Elbers et al, 'Effectiveness of a Web-based Intervention for Injured Claimants: A Randomized Controlled Trial' (2013) 14 *Trials* 227, doi.org/10.1186/1745-6215-14-227.

[51] On the responsibilities of lawyers see the references in n 42 above.

It may seem paradoxical, but it is not: no matter how promising the future may be in terms of web-based information and support for the applicants of compensation, at the same time, personal contact should also be prioritised. These two means of information are actually strongly mutually supportive. Face-to-face communication between the victim and the claims or case manager of the insurer or agency also seems to be very important for the way in which victims view the accident and the other party.[52] This relates not only to the issue of being perceived as truly taking responsibility, as discussed above – in this case, not by the perpetrator, but by the party representing him – but also to the procedural justice elements of 'voice' and 'dignity and respect'. Claimants often report that they feel treated as though they are just a number.[53] A respectful and dignified treatment is much more than politeness and smiling. It is most of all about allowing someone the opportunity to express himself and listening carefully, asking what happened, how things are going, and allowing him the time he needs to give an answer (even when this involves issues that – strictly speaking – are not relevant to the steps that are to be taken), asking what he expects from the resolution process (and adjusting unrealistic expectations), and explaining in a careful and comprehensible way one's own position and the reason why certain information is necessary and certain steps have to be taken. Direct consultation, of course, is indispensable to do all of these things. Web-based information can add immensely to the comprehensibility of all this information – but it can never replace personal contact.

It would be a tragic misconception to think that face-to-face contact is only necessary once. If one considers what is known about the experiences of personal injury victims in compensation procedures,[54] it becomes clear that personal contact should take place with a certain regularity – depending of course on the duration of the process. In particular, when a representative is involved, one should not think that it is his responsibility to inform his client, and that there is no longer a role for personal contact. If there is a representative, he or she should, of course, be able to attend, but for the purposes in question, personal contact with the claim or case manager of the insurer or agency remains indispensable.

VII. In Conclusion

There are many possibilities for countering personal injury victims' experience of injustice by making claims resolution psychologically more responsive and intelligent, regardless of what kind of compensation system is involved, fault-based or no-fault. A system more responsive to the moral expectations of victims will actively acknowledge responsibility for the incurred harm and its redress, take

[52] Elbers et al (2013), above, n 1.

[53] Kilgour et al, above, n 5; Elbers et al (2013), above, n 1; Lippel (2012), above, n 6; Akkermans and van Wees, above, n 9.

[54] See the references in n 49 above.

action to promote recovery and participation, and involve sufficient personal contact, not only between the victim and the person responsible for the injury-causing event, but also with claims or case managers. As noted above, it could actually be considered quite peculiar that routines have drifted so much away from what seems to be the morally obvious thing to do. In particular, it seems high time to review the adversarial character of compensation procedures and to consider whether adversarialism is ready for the dustbin. I think it is. In his chapter in this book, Christopher Hodges concludes in pointed terms that 'fault and adversarial systems are old technology'.[55] I am not so sure about fault[56] – that is, as no more than a payment trigger – but I couldn't agree more about adversarialism. That is simply harmful, while the mission of justice can only be to heal. Under certain conditions, adversarial procedures may be unavoidable and, for the development of the law, sometimes even desirable. But adversarialism just should not be the default condition. Justice requires that we get rid of it. Responding to the moral expectations and justice needs of victims will promote recovery and health outcomes, reduce health care costs and promote return to work. It also seems a reasonable expectation that this will have a positive effect on the overall amount of damages, diminish transaction costs and increase customer satisfaction. The societal costs of personal injury are already more than high enough. Psychologically more responsive and intelligent claims resolution is in the interests of us all. Let us devote our efforts to developing the legal technology of the future.

[55] C Hodges, 'Achieving a Just Culture that Learns and Improves', Ch 7 of this book.

[56] This ultimately has to do with the difference between corrective and distributive justice. Space does not permit me to elaborate on this here.

3

Compensation and Health

IAN CAMERON*

It is well known that limited recovery after injuries sustained in motor vehicle crashes, and in other settings, is associated with participation in injury compensation schemes. Whether this association is causal is controversial. There are now a number of empirical studies that strongly suggest this is the case. This chapter synthesises the findings from research studies, analyses mechanisms that may underlie the negative effects, and suggests interventions that are likely to enhance health recovery in the context of compensable injury.

I. Introduction

There are a variety of injury compensation and treatment schemes operational in most higher and middle-income countries. They vary considerably but for the purposes of this chapter are considered to be motor vehicle injury, workers' compensation, and the law of torts. These are largely funded by various kinds of insurance: motor vehicle injury insurance (third party and first party), income protection insurance, total and permanent disability insurance, trauma insurance and public or private health insurance. The chapter will focus particularly on the first two types of schemes, motor vehicle injury and workers' compensation, but the discussion with reference to health is relevant to each of the listed types of scheme. However, public or private health insurance schemes are not commonly regarded as 'compensation' schemes because they provide only health-related interventions. This chapter also does not address 'injury' sustained as a result of medical or other health-related treatments.

* John Walsh Centre for Rehabilitation Research, Faculty of Medicine and Health, University of Sydney, Australia. Ian Cameron's salary is supported by an Australian National Health and Medical Research Council Senior Practitioner Fellowship.

Compensation systems can be divided broadly into fault-based schemes (which are also termed common law or tort law systems) and no-fault schemes.[1] The main difference is that in fault-based schemes the entitlements of the claimant are based on the fault of someone else for the incident, whereas in a no-fault scheme entitlements are based on the occurrence of the incident as such, regardless of anyone being at fault for it. Generally, fault-based schemes are regarded as being more adversarial and less therapeutic compared to no-fault schemes.[2]

The objective of this chapter is to explore the associations between participation in compensation schemes and the recovery and longer-term health status of people with injuries or health conditions related to motor vehicle crashes or work injury and their paid employment, if applicable.

II. Definitions

The perspective taken for this chapter is explicitly a health perspective. Health has been defined in a variety of ways from a very global concept by the World Health Organization (WHO) in 1948 which is 'a state of complete physical, mental and social well-being and not merely the absence of disease or infirmity',[3] to a more nuanced view in the recent past. The more recent view is that the WHO definition is unattainable, and a more reasonable aim is that adequate health allows participation in all aspects of personal, family and community life.

Alongside health is the concept of disability. The WHO has also conceptualised this and emphasises that disability is a somewhat different concept from health. However, it is explicitly related to health conditions and there are multiple other factors associated with it. This is exemplified in the WHO International Classification of Functioning, Disability and Health (ICF).[4] This model embraces a psychosocial view of health and adds it to the traditional biological models of health. It includes contextual factors which relate to the person as well as to the environment. Environmental factors are acknowledged to be complex and this is important in the context of compensation and health. The environment includes laws and the societal perspective, as well as the physical and built environment.

[1] K Armstrong and D Tess, *Fault versus No Fault – Reviewing the International Evidence* (The Institute of Actuaries of Australia, 2008) available at actuaries.asn.au/Library/Events/GIS/2008/GIS08_3d_Paper_Tess,Armstrong_Fault%20versus%20No%20Fault%20-%20reviewing%20the%20international%20evidence.pdf.

[2] K Lippel, 'Therapeutic and Anti-therapeutic Consequences of Workers' Compensation' (1999) 5 *Int J Law Psychiatry* 521.

[3] WHO, *WHO remains firmly committed to the principles set out in the preamble to the Constitution* (2019) available at www.who.int/about/mission/en.

[4] WHO, *International Classification of Functioning, Disability and Health (ICF)* (2018) available at www.who.int/classifications/icf/en/.

A related concept is health-related quality of life and this includes components related to symptoms, including pain, as well as disability and other aspects of daily life.[5] Both disability and health-related quality of life have been investigated by the WHO and scales developed by the WHO are available that assess these concepts.[6] It is useful to look at the scales to understand the concepts that they include. These are understanding and communicating, mobility, self-care, interacting with other people, domestic responsibilities, leisure, work and school and participation in community activities.

A final concept is of rehabilitation. This has also been addressed by the WHO and it currently sees rehabilitation as an essential concept of all services that aim to assist and promote health.[7] The goal of rehabilitation is to assist a person who has experienced injury or illness, to participate fully in all aspects of life.

III. A Theoretical Framework for Compensation and Health

This leads us to an examination of the theoretical frameworks that might underlie these issues related to compensation and health. It is difficult to know where to start, because of the complexity involved.

Perhaps the best way is to embrace the current internationally accepted and dominant model of health. This is the biopsychosocial model.[8] It recognises that there is an interaction of biological, psychological and social factors to produce an experience of health.

As a further framework the WHO ICF, as introduced above, can be invoked to characterise a complex range of issues in more detail in relation to this biopsychosocial model.

The ICF shows that there are factors related to the environment which, in this case, is the compensation system. These interact with personal factors such as education and health literacy and there are, in some people, issues related to the injuries sustained, although the nature and severity of the injury is less important than is generally understood.

The interaction of these factors impacts on the unwell or injured person. The result can be support for recovery (if the impact is a positive one), or disablement where the impact is negative. The latter causes restrictions in daily life 'activities'

[5] National Center for Chronic Disease Prevention and Health Promotion *Health-Related Quality of Life (HRQOL)* (2018) available at www.cdc.gov/hrqol/.

[6] WHO, *WHO Disability Assessment Schedule 2.0 (WHODAS 2.0)* (2018) available at www.who.int/classifications/icf/whodasii/en/.

[7] WHO Rehab-2030, *Rehabilitation: key for health in the 21st century* available at www.who.int/disabilities/care/KeyForHealth21stCentury.pdf?ua=1.

[8] S Inerney, 'Introducing the Biopsychosocial Model for Good Medicine and Good Doctors' (2002) *British Medical Journal* 324, 1537.

in the self-care domains or limitations in more complex socially and community or family-related activities which are termed 'participation'. An example is a person with neck pain (also termed whiplash associated disorder) who, after a motor vehicle crash may have a positive experience with the initial treating health professional who explains, encourages physical activity, and suggests maintaining a normal daily routine. Family members provide encouragement and note that they have recovered readily with similar symptoms. This person is able to return to work because they are able to make some modifications to their duties at work. The neck pain gradually lessens, and recovery is achieved after several weeks. The contrasting experience is to have contact with a health professional who expresses concern about a likely long period of symptoms, certifies the person unfit for work, and prescribes inappropriate analgesics. Family members also express concern and suggest that a compensation claim should be made. This latter scenario sets the scene for long-term reduction in activities and participation.

There is also a temporal component to these phenomena which is best exemplified by a concept from the injury epidemiology literature which is termed Haddon's Matrix.[9] This considers an injury experience with reference to pre-injury factors, factors related directly to the injury and post-injury factors. This well captures the dynamic interaction between pre-injury health, personal and environmental factors that are potent predictors of post-injury experience, direct injury-related factors (which can be important where there are severe injuries sustained). However, current research shows that direct injury-related factors, for example what part of the body is injured, is not directly relevant to recovery.[10] However, where the injury is severe, this does clearly slow recovery.

A simplified model that incorporates the temporal component and acknowledges other issues is shown in Figure 1.

Figure 1 Interventions to improve recovery – basic conceptual model

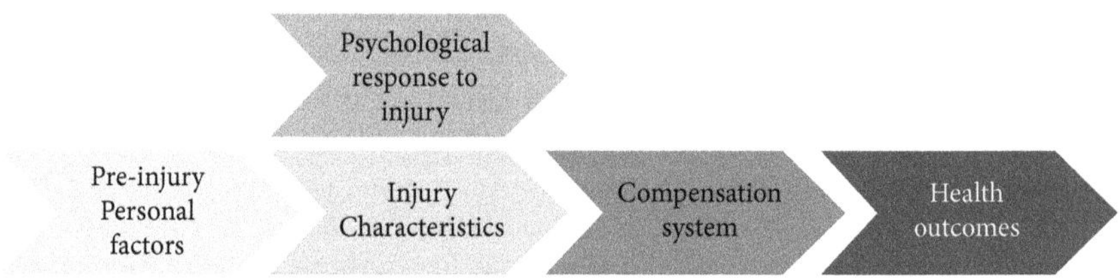

- Applies the Haddon Matrix – pre-event, event, post event
- Uses International Classification of Functioning Disability and Health (World Health Organisation) concepts

[9] CW Runyan, 'Using the Haddon Matrix: Introducing the Third Dimension' (1998) 4 *Injury Prevention* 302.

[10] B Gopinath et al, 'Overview of Findings from a 2-year Study of Claimants Who Had Sustained a Mild or Moderate Injury in a Road Traffic Crash: Prospective Study' (2017) 10 *BMC Research Notes* 76.

A further relevant area is the more recent investigation of secondary victimisation.[11] This refers to a process where there is further trauma caused to the victim by the follow up of the incident. This has been applied in the injury field after being developed elsewhere in research, particularly in legal studies. Given the audience for this book and the other chapters in this book, this is not explored further except to confirm that research in the injury field has established it to be a useful concept.[12]

There are a variety of other theories related to compensation and health that will not be discussed in detail except to dismiss them. The secondary gain theory, related to a view that injured people limit recovery while waiting for financial or other compensation, is generally not supported by experimental studies.[13] However, there is evidence that injured people may amplify or magnify their symptoms, and this is most developed with reference to psychological conditions.[14]

IV. Types of Injury and Types of Compensation – Does it Matter?

The longstanding debate about health and its physical and psychological components has largely been superseded by the biopsychosocial model in which physical (biological factors) interact with psychological and social factors to influence the health status of a person. The original and seminal papers of Engel provide excellent examples and explanations related to this.[15] His example of a man with a heart attack and the interaction of the three types of factors well illustrates their complex and detailed interplay.[16]

Injury compensation schemes have not embraced the biopsychosocial model, and attempt to define injuries (or health conditions) in physical or psychological terms. Furthermore, in some schemes claims for 'psychological injury' are partly or completely excluded. This generally means that people with injuries are encouraged to express their experience in 'physical' terms through pain complaints and disability with reference to daily life rather than in terms of a psychological condition. It can also be difficult to determine when psychologically based symptoms, such as anxiety or feeling unsettled, that are a universal experience, develop to an extent to become a 'psychological injury'.

[11] European Commission, *Member States' legislation, national policies, practices and approaches concerning the victims of crime: Final study* (2009) available at ec.europa.eu/info/policies/justice-and-fundamental-rights_en.

[12] N Elbers et al, 'Do Compensation Processes Impair Mental Health? A Meta-analysis' (2013) 44 *Injury* 674.

[13] DA Fishbain, 'Secondary Gain Concept: Definition Problems and its Abuse in Medical Practice' (1994) 3 *APS Journal* 3264.

[14] AJ Barsky et al, 'The Amplification of Somatic Symptoms' (1988) 50 *Psychosom Med* 510.

[15] GL Engel, 'The Need for a New Medical Model: a Challenge for Biomedicine' (1977) 196 *Science* 129.

[16] GL Engel, 'The Clinical Application of the Biopsychosocial Model' (1980) 137 *Am J Psychiatry* 535.

Another dimension is whether the part of the body injured, or the severity of the injury sustained, influences the potential effects of involvement in a compensation scheme. This is a contested area but the literature generally suggests that the part of the body injured is not important and the severity of injury (as long as it is not too severe) is also not important.[17] There are some caveats to express about this. There is some evidence that conditions in which the main identifying effect is pain, such as neck pain (whiplash associated disorder) or back pain, may be somewhat more sensitive to the effects of compensation systems. However, in general, generic tools that assess risk of poor recovery or return to work, work well across a range of injury types or health conditions[18] and work in the motor vehicle injury context as well as in the work injury context.

Within the limits of mild to moderate injury, severity of injury is not associated with effects of the compensation scheme.[19] However, this statement cannot be confirmed in more severe injuries. This may be due to severe injuries being associated with prolonged exposure to compensation schemes and their negative components.

As to whether the type of compensation scheme matters, the answer is that the type of scheme may influence health related outcomes. This overall answer is justified in subsequent parts of this chapter. For example a study from adjoining states in Australia with different motor vehicle injury compensation schemes showed significant differences, with the fault-based tort scheme being associated with poorer outcomes.[20] Compensation system design effects have also been investigated with reference to Australian workers' compensation systems and time off work.[21] For example, workers in Victoria had significantly longer durations of time off work (13 weeks' time off) when compared to workers in Tasmania (7 weeks' time off) and this was related to specific regulations within the differing compensation systems.

A possible exception relates to private health insurance, where that insurance will pay claims without question or dispute. This was illustrated in the curious paper of O'Donnell and colleagues[22] which exemplifies the Australian situation at the time when a private health insurer would never question the payment of a health (medical) expense. Subsequently, due to increasing costs of health insurance, this situation has changed, with insurers aiming to contain cost by limiting types of treatment for which they will provide limited benefit.[23]

[17] Gopinath et al, above, n 10.

[18] B Gopinath et al, 'Predictors of Time to Claim Closure following a Non-catastrophic Injury Sustained in a Motor Vehicle Crash: a Prospective Cohort Study' (2016) 16 *BMC Public Health* 421.

[19] Gopinath et al, above, n 10.

[20] NA Elbers et al, 'Differences in Perceived Fairness and Health Outcomes in Two Injury Compensation Systems: a Comparative Study' (2016) 16 *BMC Public Health* 658.

[21] A Collie et al, 'Does Time off Work after Injury Vary by Jurisdiction? A Comparative Study of Eight Australian Workers' Compensation Systems' (2016) 6 *BMJ Open* e010910.

[22] ML O'Donnell et al, 'Does Access to Compensation have an Impact on Recovery Outcomes after Injury?' (2010) 192 *Med J Aust* 328.

[23] C Schilling et al, 'Predictors of Inpatient Rehabilitation after Total Knee Replacement: an Analysis of Private Hospital Claims Data' (2018) 209 *Med J Aust* 222.

V. The Evidence from Research in Compensation and Health

This next section of the chapter explores the range of scientific studies related to compensation and health. For the purposes of this review studies in relation to motor vehicle crash injury are considered. It is recognised that there are also many relevant studies with reference to other forms of injury, particularly work injury compensation.

A. Qualitative Research Approaches

Qualitative research provides an exploration of issues from a personal perspective. This is useful in understanding the range of issues that are potentially relevant from the perspective of the injured person. These are helpful in understanding the overall experience of an injured person but are not able to quantify the importance of relative factors or whether it can be concluded that there is a causal relationship between aspects of compensation and poor health.

Qualitative research is quite instructive in this regard as it captures the range of viewpoints. It can be seen that in addition to negative experiences there are experiences that are either positive or neutral from the perspective of the injured person.[24] The key in understanding the compensation and health issue is to recognise that there will be a range of responses to injury and these will be determined by multiple complex and interacting factors. In general, people with less severe injuries raised fewer problems in the qualitative studies, with people with severe injuries who were participating in the compensation process reporting major problems.[25]

Similar results have been reported in qualitative studies in the workers' compensation insurance domain.[26] Negative interactions with insurance agency staff were frequently reported. Interactions with healthcare providers in this setting can also be problematic.[27]

[24] D Murgatroyd et al, 'The Effect of Financial Compensation on Health Outcomes following Musculoskeletal Injury: Systematic Review' (2015a) 10 *PLoS One* e0117597; D Murgatroyd et al, 'The Perceptions and Experiences of People Injured in Motor Vehicle Crashes in a Compensation Scheme Setting: a Qualitative Study' (2015b) 15 *BMC Public Health* 423.

[25] D Murgatroyd et al, 'Understanding the Effect of Compensation on Recovery from Severe Motor Vehicle Crash Injuries: a Qualitative Study' (2011) 17 *Inj Prev* 222.

[26] E Kilgour et al, 'Interactions between Injured Workers and Insurers in Workers' Compensation Systems: a Systematic Review of Qualitative Research Literature' (2011) 25 *J Occup Rehabil* 160.

[27] E Kilgour et al, 'Healing or Harming? Healthcare Provider Interactions with Injured Workers and Insurers in Workers' Compensation Systems' (2015) *J Occup Rehabil* 220.

Table 1 Summary of negative compensation related factors from qualitative studies from the injured person's perspective[28]

Injury factors	**Fault determination**
Early claim factors	Complexity of claims process
	Delays in approvals
	Questioning legitimacy of the claim
	Financial hardship
	Necessity for legal representation
Treatment factors	Limited access to treatment
	Treatment perceived not effective
	Health care professional role conflicts
Cumulative claim factors	Non therapeutic assessments – 'independent medical assessments'
	Sense of injustice
	– Difficult claim settlement processes

The negative effect of fault-based schemes on health is attributed to the fact that fault-based schemes involve more adversarial elements. The adversarial interactions mostly relate to the assessment of liability, medical examinations, determination of damages, and type of insurer (third-party or first-party; government or for profit). These adversarial interactions are elaborated upon below.

An extreme example is illustrated with reference to a newspaper article. This vividly shows the negative impact that participation in a compensation process can have.[29] It shows that multiple factors contribute to cause ill health, including severe psychological symptoms. It can be seen from this story that the injured person found himself enmeshed in a system. This labelled him a liar or malingerer because of his ongoing experience with pain. The result of this was clearly severe psychological distress, and almost certainly overt psychiatric illness.

B. Quantitative Research Studies

In quantitative research, data from groups of individuals are analysed to draw general conclusions, which can then potentially be applied to other people in similar situations with reference to health-related issues. Single case studies are also an area of quantitative research that can give insights into rare or unusual

[28] Based on three studies: Kilgour et al, above, n 26; Murgatroyd et al, above, n 25; Murgatroyd et al, above, n 24.

[29] J Power, 'They're Called Liars and Malingerers because They Face Pain You Can't See' *The Sydney Morning Herald* (2018), available at www.smh.com.au/lifestyle/health-and-wellness/they-re-called-liars-and-malingerers-because-they-face-pain-you-can-t-see-20180213-p4z06z.html.

circumstances. There are now established guidelines for reporting all types of health research.[30]

First, there are cross sectional associational studies in which the associations between factors, such as a motor vehicle or work injury, and other potentially explanatory factors, such as participation in a compensation scheme and outcomes (such as good health or return to work) are investigated. While this can be a helpful approach in some areas of health, it is a flawed method in the context of the issues examined in this chapter. The problems are many. There is the issue of whether it is A leading to B or B leading to A. As both A and B are measured at the same time, there is no way of knowing the correct answer. Furthermore, as illustrated in Haddon's Matrix (mentioned above) a number of factors are time dependent. Factors might be important at some times and not others, and some issues take time to develop, for example exposure to the compensation system.

Due to the likelihood of unrecognised factors influencing cross sectional studies in the area of compensation and health, they will not be examined further. There are better research approaches available and these are reviewed in subsequent sections.

C. Cohort Studies

The next area of relevant research is cohort studies, where a group of injured people are followed over time and their return to health is monitored. These studies can establish whether particular factors are associated with better or worse health outcomes. These are associations and, again, are not evidence of causality. Cohort studies are broadly used in health research and most famously the Framingham Heart Study has been used to define factors underlying heart disease and many other health conditions.[31]

Cohort studies are most useful when the cohort is defined prior to the health event of interest. This is clearly very difficult, or practically impossible, in the situation of a low frequency and largely unpredictable events such as motor vehicle crashes. With reference to work injury the challenges are not as great.

Where there has been a motor vehicle crash, the best cohort study designs are so-called inception cohort, where the group of people with injury are enrolled in the study as close to the time of injury as possible. This is because the person's experience will be influenced by a variety of largely negative factors from the moment of injury, and the effect of these can be limited if the baseline data is recorded close to injury. The problem with this approach is, as Haddon's Matrix suggests, that the

[30] UK EQUATOR Centre, *Enhancing the Quality and Transparency of Health Research* (Centre for Statistics in Medicine (CSM), NDORMS, University of Oxford, 2019) available at www.equator-network.org/.

[31] Framingham Heart Study, *History of the Framingham Heart Study* (2019) available at www.framinghamheartstudy.org/fhs-about/history/.

background health and personal factors related to the injured person may not be clear if this approach is taken. The pre-injury factors are best elucidated by record linkage studies where there is access to health and other information about the injured person prior to injury. These studies are very difficult and expensive to perform in most countries and may raise ethical issues related to privacy.

Cohort studies have assisted greatly in understanding the issues related to compensation and health. There are many studies available that have established that there are a vast number of interacting factors that influence recovery after injury. The dominant groups of these factors are personal factors which relate to intrinsic characteristics of the injured person such as age, education, past life experiences, income and family structure and support. The other large group of factors is related to the compensation system. The systems in which the injured person is required to prove that they have sustained significant injury or continue to experience significant disability, appear to be most damaging. However, it can be difficult to conclusively establish the effects and influences of the many factors that are operating.[32]

However, inception cohort studies, which are studies in which the cohort is recruited soon after injury, with stronger research designs, are confirming results of earlier studies. For example, a current study that includes people recruited after motor vehicle crashes from hospital emergency departments, has confirmed many of the findings. With reference to level of pain at 12 months after injury, its independent predictors were age, sex, education, claiming compensation, spine/back injury, being a bicyclist, physical well-being, pain-related catastrophising, pain-related disability and trauma-related and general psychological distress.[33] This means that after statistically adjusting for the effects of all the other measured factors, these were the ones that influenced pain. The influence on pain can be to reduce it (for example being a bicyclist or having better physical well-being) or to increase it by having pain-related catastrophising or being psychologically distressed. Clearly some factors are unmodifiable (such as age and sex) but a number are modifiable, including whether compensation is claimed. This last factor might seem strange as a modifiable risk factor, but it is well known that propensity to claim, meaning the percentage of people who actually claim compensation compared to the number that could, is much less than the percentage who actually do claim compensation. This percentage propensity to claim varies between insurance schemes. For motor vehicle injury insurance it is generally approximately 40–50%.[34]

This same inception cohort study also examined predictors of quality of life 12 months after motor vehicle crash injury. The key predictors of better quality

[32] SM Littleton et al, 'The Association of Compensation on Longer Term Health Status for People with Musculoskeletal Injuries following Road Traffic Crashes: Emergency Department Inception Cohort Study' (2011) 42 *Injury* 927.

[33] B Gopinath et al, 'Differential Predictors of Pain Severity over 12 Months Following Noncatastrophic Injury Sustained in a Road Traffic Crash' (2019) 20 *J Pain* 676.

[34] Motor Accidents Authority of NSW, *Annual Report October 2012–2013* (NSW Government publication, 2013), available at www.opengov.nsw.gov.au/download/13695.

of life were younger age, not lodging a compensation claim, lower body mass index, less pain severity, less pain-related disability and less general psychological distress.[35] It is interesting and important to again note that there are similar predictors for quality of life compared to persistent pain, and again a number of these factors are potentially reversible, including claiming compensation. With reference to another key health-related outcome for people with injury, which is disability, similar relationships exist.[36]

D. Systematic Review Studies

As health and medical research has advanced, the power of combining results from multiple similar studies has been recognised. This commenced with studies of treatments of various types (where individual studies were not large enough to provide specific answers to important questions about whether a particular type of treatment was effective). Subsequent advances have permitted the combination of results from cohort studies and also from qualitative research studies. Systematically identifying all relevant studies related to a particular research question, and then combining the results using established and validated methods, provides important information. Where the systematic review includes mathematically combined data, it is termed a meta-analysis.

In the area of compensation health there are two well-known and cited systematic reviews. The first by Harris and colleagues examined the influence of having a compensable injury on surgical outcomes.[37] This established that compensation was associated with much worse outcomes from surgical procedures. The second systematic review examined associations with compensation more broadly.[38] There is also a more recent systematic review that comes to similar conclusions with reference to the workers' compensation insurance realm.[39]

VI. Areas of Contention

In this health-related perspective there is a continuing narrative about the impact of legal involvement in compensation and the effect of it. Based on an extensive

[35] B Gopinath et al, 'Predictors of Health-related Quality of Life after Non-catastrophic Injury Sustained in a Road Traffic Crash' (2019) Nov *Ann Phys Rehabil Med* ii.

[36] S Derrett et al, 'Prevalence and Predictors of Disability 24-months after Injury for Hospitalised and Non-hospitalised Participants: Results from a Longitudinal Cohort Study in New Zealand' (2013) 8 *PLoS One* e80194.

[37] I Harris et al, 'Association between Compensation Status and Outcome after Surgery: a Meta-analysis' (2005) 293 *JAMA* 1644.

[38] Murgatroyd et al (2015a), above, n 24; Murgatroyd et al (2015b), above, n 24, 423.

[39] Y Fujihara et al, 'The Effect of Workers' Compensation on Outcome Measurement Methods after Upper Extremity Surgery: A Systematic Review and Meta-Analysis' (2017) 139 *Plast Reconstr Surg* 923.

systematic review, legal involvement is clearly associated with increased claim cost, longer duration of claim and less recovery.[40] Table 2 shows the levels of evidence for lawyer involvement, as a component of financial compensation, on health outcomes after musculoskeletal injury.

Table 2 Summary of level of evidence of effects of financial compensation on health outcomes after musculoskeletal injury[41]

Level of evidence (GRADE classification)*	**Factors associated with negative effects**		
	Physical function	**Psychological status**	**Pain**
Strong evidence	Lawyer involvement	Compensation claim	
Moderate evidence	Compensation claim	Lawyer involvement	
	Compensation at two years		
	Fault		
Limited evidence	Number of sick days in prior three years		Compensation claim
	Prior claim		Number of sick days in prior three years
			Prior claim

* GRADE Working Group, www.gradeworkinggroup.org/.

However, the extent to which this is a causal relationship, rather than an association, remains unclear. Others have argued that injured people with certain characteristics are more likely to consult a lawyer, and these people are likely to have less resilience and may have past negative experience that influences their decision to seek legal representation.[41] Seeking legal representation is also related to the severity of the injuries sustained in a number of jurisdictions, including accidents dealt with by compulsory third party motor vehicle insurance in the state of New South Wales. Finally, with reference to legal representation it is recognised that the systems of motor vehicle crash compensation generally do not have the injured person and the insurer with equal power and knowledge of the situation. Working in this area with injured people, it is the author's observation that insurance companies will operate to maximise their financial return rather than necessarily assisting the injured person appropriately to recover. Due to that power imbalance between the injured person and the insurer, legal representation is necessary in a number of situations, particularly where the injuries are more severe or where there are factors complicating the situation, such as people who

[40] Murgatroyd et al (2015a), above, n 24.
[41] Based on Murgatroyd et al (2015a), above, n 24.

have pre-existing disabilities or health conditions. These factors also operate in work injury compensation schemes.

It is important to note that not all research is in support of the summary and synthesis provided in this chapter. The findings of O'Donnell and colleagues have been noted above. There is also a view that the available cohort studies do not adequately address whether compensation is the direct cause of poorer health outcomes or whether it is factors related to the person who has claimed compensation that underlie this relationship. This has been termed 'reverse causality' by Spearing and Connelly.[42] In this conceptualisation it is background factors associated with the injured person (such as poorer pre-injury health or adverse socioeconomic circumstances) that cause the person to consult a lawyer and also influence whether the person claims compensation. These issues can be addressed with suitable research study designs (for example inception cohort design including details about pre-injury health status and including people who both claim and do not claim compensation). A further way of addressing these views is to conduct 'experimental' studies that consider changes to or participation in compensation schemes. That is the subject of the next section in this chapter.

VII. 'Experimental' Studies of Compensation and Health

This next section of this chapter focuses on the studies that provide experimental evidence related to the issue of compensation and health. These studies are quite rare because it is not possible to manipulate the situation to have some people being provided with compensation and some not. These are quantitative studies that include differing types of information about recovery, and what is associated with it, together with relevant information about compensation system changes.

These studies are possible when a 'natural experiment' occurs, and there is a change in compensation law and health that can be assessed before and after the change in law or regulation. Again, opportunities to do this are more common in workers' compensation settings because of the frequency of change in this legislation, but there are some examples related to motor vehicle crash injury.

There are some older studies that have provided a number of insights. One is a study in the state of Victoria which suggested that health, specifically related to whiplash associated disorder, was altered after a change in legislation. This is the study of McDermott and others.[43]

Research in this area, however, became much more prominent when Cassidy and colleagues published their study about changes in health following legislative

[42] NM Spearing and LB Connelly, 'Is Compensation "Bad for Health"? A Systematic Meta-review' (2011) 42 *Injury* 15.

[43] FT McDermott, 'Reduction in Cervical "Whiplash" after New Motor Vehicle Accident Legislation in Victoria' (1993) 158 *Med J Aust* 720.

change in Saskatchewan in Canada.[44] This study was published in the most prominent medical journal in the world and it has had a resounding effect. In Canada it provoked very great comment and anecdotally it appears that the first author moved to Europe eventually as a result. It showed that elimination of compensation for pain and suffering was associated with a decreased incidence and improved prognosis of whiplash injury as assessed by time to claim closure. The data were strong but the main criticism was that the primary outcome measure, which was time to claim closure, did not necessarily mean that the person with whiplash had recovered. Cassidy and colleagues subsequently asserted that their view, that time to claim closure was a reasonable proxy for recovery, was correct.

In New South Wales there was the opportunity to assess changes in health following a new Motor Accidents Compensation Act in 1999. The government regulator of insurance companies commissioned a study to assess whether changes in health to people with whiplash associated disorder occurred as a result of the new legislation. The legislation had multiple components which included provision for earlier treatment for people with whiplash associated disorder, and treatment guidelines, but the Act also effectively abolished access to non-economic loss for people with whiplash associated disorder. The results of the study showed that there was a substantial improvement in health of people sustaining a whiplash injury after the change in legislation.[45] Unpublished data shows that those changes are associated with substantial reductions in claim costs.

These types of 'natural' experiment study are ongoing and will increase knowledge in this area. Scheme changes, if designed appropriately, can be an important public health intervention to provide a benefit to a significant number of people across the jurisdiction of the scheme.

VIII. Actual Experiments Related to Compensation and Health

Another approach is to conduct research using experimental methods that change different aspects of the many factors that influence recovery after injury. These issues are complex, but many are amenable to scientific investigation. There are relatively few studies of this type.

One example is the use of an injury recovery clinic to try to assist people with motor vehicle related injuries to recover more effectively. The evaluation concluded that the clinic was not effective.[46] The authors of this study suggested

[44] JD Cassidy et al, 'Effect of Eliminating Compensation for Pain and Suffering on the Outcome of Insurance Claims for Whiplash Injury' (2000) 342 *N Engl J Med* 1179.

[45] ID Cameron et al, 'Legislative Change is Associated with Improved Health Status in People with Whiplash' (2008) 33 *Spine* 250.

[46] SM Littleton et al, 'The Health Status of People Claiming Compensation for Musculoskeletal Injuries following Road Traffic Crashes is Not Altered by an Early Intervention Programme: a Comparative Study' (2014) 45 *Injury* 1493.

that participation in a compensation process for a substantial number of participants may have negated the potentially beneficial effects of the clinic approach that encouraged early resumption of activities. The other possibility that the authors discussed was that the study was insufficiently large to have sufficient statistical power to be able to detect benefit.

Another example is of an intervention to reform insurance company claims management practices. This utilised a prospective design and aimed to communicate effectively with injured people, intervene early, screen for adverse prognostic factors and focus on early return to work and usual activities. As a result of this there were a few positive outcomes, including earlier return to usual activities.[47]

These actual experiments involving aspects of the compensation system can make important contributions. They can be small scale or large scale and provide the opportunity to manipulate aspects of the compensation system. These experiments are usually difficult to perform because they are operating in the real world and thus there are many relevant factors – not part of the experimental treatment – that can cloud issues. However, if relevant factors are recorded there are statistical techniques that can adjust for them.

IX. Conceptualising Compensation and Health

The dominant scientific paradigm in health and medicine is to explain health-related phenomena in mechanistic terms. The complexity of issues in the area of compensation and health make this very difficult and, some will argue, impossible. However, models that incorporate putative mechanisms are important because they can suggest high priority topics to allow better understanding of the issues. Models which incorporate mechanisms that have empirical evidence supporting them can also be used to influence the design and operation of compensation systems.

There are so many factors operating in the compensation and health domain that it can readily become so complex that appreciating the full picture can be very difficult. However, some simplification is possible and that can be a starting point.

That starting point is to accept that return to usual health and usual daily activities, including work if appropriate, is the goal. 'Usual health' can be defined in a variety of ways, as shown above. Usual health is the 'health outcome' and can be defined with reference to health-related quality of life (which incorporates physical, psychological, pain and other factors), or physical health or psychological health or pain or disability.

The next point is to understand that 'compensation' or the compensation scheme or system or regulations can have a multitude of effects that can influence the claimant directly (such as providing benefit on a fault based or no-fault basis) or indirectly. The indirect factors can be incentives or disincentives for recovery (for example

[47] F Schaafsma et al, 'Changing Insurance Company Claims Handling Processes Improves some Outcomes for People Injured in Road Traffic Crashes' (2012) 12 *BMC Public Health* 36.

providing compensation for 'pain and suffering' or positively encouraging early and appropriate treatment). A further effect can be on people or organisations interacting with the claimant. These effects can again be positive for health (for example using treatments that are established as beneficial), or negative for health, with the examples being paying health practitioners for excessive treatment or investigations.

It can be best to see these factors as an interconnected network where components have direct and indirect effects. Listing the components comprehensively can, however, be overwhelming.

Figure 2 Interventions to improve recovery – detailed conceptual model

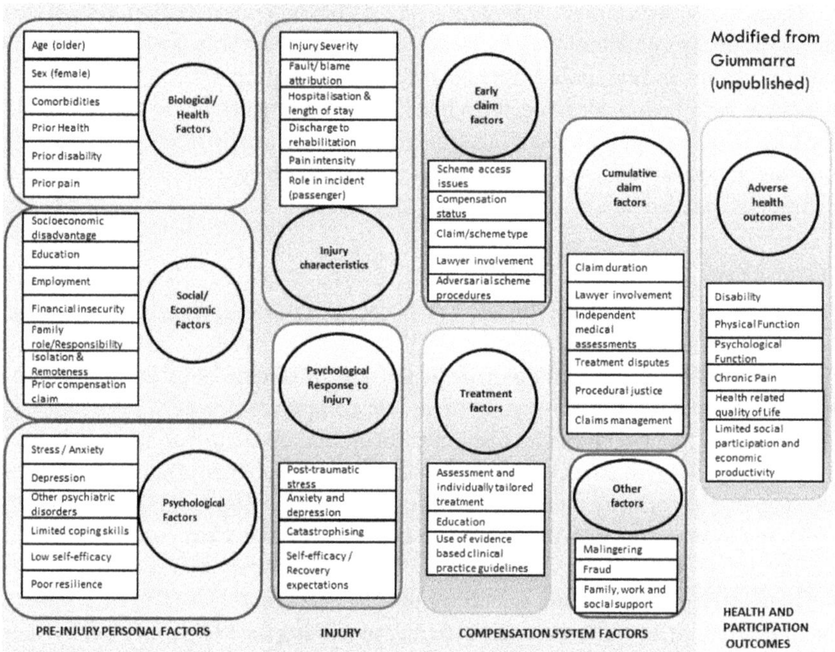

However, this comprehensive approach is useful when taking a broad view. This can be focused onto areas of interest where there may be greater possibilities of making change in some form. For example, there may be opportunities to change specific treatment protocols to recognise and help people with psychological distress at an early stage, while at another time the issue might be the possibility of a 'no fault' compensation scheme.

X. Reforming Compensation Systems to Improve Health

It is all very well understanding the relationships between compensation and health, but the ultimate outcome of this knowledge should be the reform of compensation systems to realign them as health-promoting schemes. Thus, one role of compensation schemes is to advocate and structure themselves for health improvement.

The opportunity to reform compensation schemes to improve health comes more often than might at first thought be expected. Compensation schemes may have a relatively short life expectancy because cost pressures become unsustainable in the short or medium term, or because of political factors related to change of government. As well as these changes providing opportunities for 'natural experiments', there are explicit or implicit processes whereby the changes to the compensation schemes can be influenced.

As compensation systems evolve and are changed frequently, this information potentially has important real-world consequences that can influence the health of thousand or tens of thousands of people. The previous example of reforming compensation arrangements for people with whiplash in New South Wales Australia is an example of this.

It is acknowledged that opportunities to reform compensation systems to reform health are limited, because it is unlikely that there can be a direct impact through advocacy to achieve a health-related goal. However, a number of examples can be provided to illustrate how these processes can operate.

The NSW Workers Compensation Act was amended in 2012 because of extreme cost problems. However, these reforms incorporated aspects that are likely to be associated with improved health. The reforms included thresholds that limited excessive healthcare interventions, limitations on 'lump sum' payments, and encouragement to return to work in a timely manner. These reforms were not made explicitly from a health basis, and a formal evaluation with reference to effects on health outcomes has yet to be published. The controversy associated with this is illustrated by whether a work injury[48] or 'justice' perspective is taken.[49] The latter perspective illustrates a complete lack of awareness of the health-related effects of the changes.

With reference to motor vehicle injury compensation, a recent example is the compulsory third party motor vehicle accident insurance reform initiatives. In response to a request for public submissions, an evidence-informed response to an issues paper was prepared.[50] This argued for a no-fault first party insurance system and defined benefits, with non-economic loss payments for major injuries only. It argued that the aim of the scheme should be to 'assist people to return to a productive life and good health'. It also stated that a greater proportion of funds should go to more severely injured people because their needs are greater. It suggested

[48] NSW Nurses and Midwives' Association, *Summary of the 2012 workers compensation changes* (2012), available at www.nswnma.asn.au/summary-of-the-2012-workers-compensation-changes/.

[49] R Markey et al, *The Impact on Injured Workers of Changes to NSW Workers' Compensation*, available at www.aph.gov.au/DocumentStore.ashx?id=b7f4f140-4724-4df8-9800-75773f4d3682&subId=412978.

[50] I Cameron et al, *Submission from John Walsh Centre for Rehabilitation Research on the CTP Reform Options Paper*, available at www.sira.nsw.gov.au/__data/assets/pdf_file/0004/102289/John-Walsh-Centre-for-Rehabilitation-Research.pdf.

reforming regulations to make scheme processes less adversarial, and also to limit legal fees to try to reduce the amount of lawyer involvement in the scheme.

While none of these changes was completely achieved, significant progress was made. The scheme became 'no-fault' for the first six months after injury. Excessive treatment for minor injuries was reduced, and disincentives for legal representation were introduced. There were also benefits introduced for people who were unable to work as a result of their injuries.[51]

Another example where similar principles of evidence-informed compensation scheme reform have been applied is in another territory of Australia, the Australian Capital Territory. This jurisdiction has had a tort-based system that was associated with poor health outcomes[52] and high costs. It is important to realise that high insurance premiums are a potent factor in influencing discussions about compensation scheme reform. Probably because it was clear that the topic was politically difficult, the government of the Territory initiated a Citizens' Jury approach to the issue of compulsory third party motor vehicle injury insurance scheme reform. Working with the jury demonstrated that they were able to consider and implement evidence-informed approaches to reform. The preferred model, which has been subsequently adopted by the government, is that everyone injured in a motor vehicle accident will receive up to five years' treatment, care and income benefits, regardless of who was at fault, while quality of life benefits, which provide compensation for non-financial loss, will be available for all people who meet injury thresholds. Early and appropriate treatment was prioritised. In addition, people whose injury was caused by someone else's negligence and who are more seriously injured will still be able to access additional benefits through common law.[53] Thus, a no-fault scheme was adopted but there were additional benefits for people not at fault subject to a level of impairment threshold. The final version of the new legislation is yet to be enacted and has been altered as a result of political compromises.[54]

However, it is acknowledged that interpretations of the issue vary. An extreme example of the polarisation of opinion between 'fault based' and 'no-fault' insurance schemes is a paper from economists that suggested that the operation of no fault schemes in the motor vehicle context was associated with

[51] State Insurance Regulatory Authority, *New Benefits for Injured People* (NSW Government) available at www.sira.nsw.gov.au/fraud-and-regulation/reforms/ctp-green-slip-reforms/new-benefits-for-injured-people.

[52] Littleton et al, above, n 44.

[53] ACT Government, *Citizens Jury on Compulsory Third Party Insurance – Final Report* (2017) available at www.yoursay.act.gov.au/application/files/6715/0925/8006/Citizens_Jury_on_CTP_Final_Report_29th_October.pdf.

[54] K Burgess, 'More People Able to Sue for Damages under Amended CTP Bill' *The Canberra Times* (18 March 2019), available at www.canberratimes.com.au/story/5992702/more-people-able-to-sue-for-damages-under-amended-ctp-bill/?cs=14229.

moral hazard.[55] These authors suggest that, because there was no-fault insurance available, people would deliberately cause motor vehicle crashes to obtain financial benefit and an increase in fatalities would result. Whether this risk exists outside the USA is not known, but there is no empirical evidence to demonstrate that this is the case.

XI. Conclusions

In closing, it is acknowledged that these are extremely complex issues. While observations and recommendations based on empirical studies can be made, there are always contextual issues that influence what can be achieved.

However, the general conclusion is that health and recovery after injury can be improved by appropriate injury insurance scheme design. There is empirical, as well as theoretical, evidence to support this, as has been presented in this chapter.

It is also the anecdotal experience of health professionals working with people who have had injuries, that there is a detriment to many patients who are enmeshed in compensation systems and processes with reference to their recovery and long-term health status. This particularly applies to people with long exposure to a compensation system. Taking the health perspective further, it might be preferable to see compensation as a drug with serious side effects that has to be used very carefully, or as a toxic chemical with important positive uses in addition to its negative effects.

[55] A Cohen and R Dehejia, 'The Effect of Automobile Insurance and Accident Liability Laws in Traffic Fatalities' *NBER Working Paper No 9602* (Bureau of Economic Research USA 2003) available at www.nber.org/papers/w9602.pdf.

4

Apples, Oranges and Bananas: Comparative Studies in Australian Workers' Compensation Systems

ALEX COLLIE*

Nearly one quarter of a million Australian workers experience a new episode of work disability annually and make claims for compensation through one of the nation's workers' compensation systems. A substantial evidence base demonstrates the scope to reduce the burden of work disability through more effective practices and policy settings. This chapter describes findings from a recent, four-year comparative study of Australian workers' compensation systems that sought to identify and characterise policy impact on work and health relevant outcomes in Australians with work disability. The Compensation Policy And Return to Work Effectiveness (COMPARE) project includes before-and-after comparisons of the impact of major policy changes such as legislative reform in the states of Tasmania, South Australia and New South Wales. The project also compares work and health and claim outcomes between jurisdictions, for example examining the rate of return to work planning amongst the state and territory compensation systems. The research summarised in this chapter demonstrates that legislative settings of Australian workers' compensation systems have a significant impact on work disability, and on processes and practices that are intended to support recovery and return to work following work-related injury and disease. The studies presented

* Professor, School of Public Health and Preventive Medicine, Monash University. The COMPARE study has been supported financially by Safe Work Australia and Worksafe Victoria, and by the Australian Research Council through a research grant to the author. This report uses data supplied by Safe Work Australia and has been compiled in collaboration with state, territory and Commonwealth workers' compensation regulators. The views expressed are the author's and are not necessarily the views of Safe Work Australia or the state, territory and Commonwealth workers' compensation regulators. The author gratefully acknowledges the contributions of multiple collaborators and advisors throughout the course of the COMPARE project including Dr Shannon Gray, Dr Tyler Lane, Mr Luke Sheehan, Dr Ross Iles, Ms Dianne Beck, Dr Behrooz Hassani-Mahmooei, Dr Jason Thompson, Assistant Professor Christopher McLeod, Mr Robert McPherson, current and former staff of Safe Work Australia and WorkSafe Victoria; representatives of the Commonwealth, state and territory workers' compensation regulatory authorities, the Australian Council of Trade Unions and the AiGroup; and the Social Research Centre.

use epidemiological and quasi-experimental methods to address questions of policy and legislative impact on health-related outcomes. The COMPARE study has begun to develop an evidence base to support future policy development in the field, and has at least demonstrated the need for long-term follow-up and evaluation of changes in law.

I. Work Disability in Australia

Work disability occurs when a worker is unable to stay at work or return to work (RTW) following injury or illness due to social, administrative, physical, psychological, or cultural reasons. Nearly one quarter of a million Australian workers experience a new episode of work disability annually and make claims for compensation through one of the nation's workers' compensation systems.[1] The total cost to society has most recently been estimated at $61.8 billion or 4.1 per cent of GDP,[2] and Australia's workers' compensation systems bear direct costs of $9 billion per annum in income support, treatment and rehabilitation and lump sum payments.[3]

Conditions that commonly cause work disability, such as back pain, depression and anxiety, represent three of the five leading causes of disability in working age Australians. One study by the author reported a loss of 189,000 productive working years in the state of Victoria alone between the financial years 1995 and 2008 in workers with accepted workers' compensation claims.[4] Return to work can support recovery from illness and injury, and reduce ongoing disability.[5] Work disability may have knock on social and economic consequences, such as increasing the risk of marital separation[6] and negatively impacting the health of family members.[7]

Prevention of work disability and promotion of return to work are central mandates of workers' compensation agencies worldwide. While the incidence of work-related injury and illness resulting in working time loss has decreased by up to 30 per cent over the last decade, the duration of disability of those injured has increased.[8] Several social factors have hindered efforts to reduce work disability.

[1] TJ Lane et al, *Work-related Injury and Illness in Australia, 2004 to 2014. What is the Incidence of Work-related Conditions and their Impact on Time Lost from Work by State and Territory, Age, Gender and Injury type?* (Melbourne, Institute for Safety Compensation and Recovery Research, 2016) 54.

[2] SafeWork Australia, *The Cost of Work-related Injury and Illness for Australian Employers, Workers and the Community: 2012–13* (Canberra, SafeWork Australia, 2016).

[3] Above, n 1.

[4] R Ruseckaite and A Collie, 'The Incidence and Impact of Recurrent Workplace Injury and Disease: A Cohort Study of WorkSafe Victoria, Australia Compensation Claims' (2013) 3(3) *BMJ Open*.

[5] S Rueda et al, 'Association of Returning to Work with Better Health in Working-aged Adults: A Systematic Review' (2012) 102(3) *American Journal of Public Health* 541.

[6] A Dembe, 'Social Inequalities in Occupational Health and Health Care for Work-related Injuries and Illnesses' (1999) 22(5–6) *International Journal of Law and Psychiatry* 567.

[7] A Asfaw et al, 'Incidence and Costs of Family Member Hospitalization Following Injuries of Workers' Compensation Claimants' (2012) 55(11) *American Journal of Industrial Medicine* 1028.

[8] Above, n 1.

For example, the ageing of the workforce poses particular challenges given our findings that older workers have longer durations of disability than younger workers, and are more likely to 'relapse' into a period away from work following an initial return to the workforce.[9] Similarly, there is a growing trend towards so-called precarious employment relationships (eg workers on short-term contracts). Workers with precarious job arrangements also take longer to RTW than those with secure employment relationships.

The presence and resolution of work disability occurs within a complex social system that involves people and organisations (actors) within, at a minimum, the person's immediate social/family environment, their workplace, the healthcare, and workers' compensation systems. The investigator team have examined interactions between these system actors.[10] These studies make it clear that work disability is influenced by the interactions between actors, and that these actors relate to each other in dynamic and non-linear ways. The features of interaction, non-linearity and dynamism are hallmarks of complex adaptive systems. In the past two decades complex systems approaches have been applied to several social policy areas including healthcare, education, economics, environmental science and, more recently, work disability prevention.[11]

Complex systems theory holds that the performance of workers' compensation systems (say, in their ability to return injured workers to work) is an emergent property of the numerous interconnected interactions between actors within the system. Efforts to reduce work disability will succeed or fail based on the non-linear inter-dependencies of system actors, rather than on pressure for improved performance applied by an external party or by a single actor. The 'control' of complex systems tends to be highly dispersed and decentralised. The model of workers' compensation in many developed nations invests the 'regulation' of the system in a government authority. In reality there are many other actors with influential roles in return to work and disability reduction. Policy and practice interventions informed by this understanding will be more likely to succeed than otherwise.

One implication of system complexity is that identification of effective policy and practice requires real-world evaluation and policy experimentation. Isolating policy or practice effects via controlled trials may provide a misleading indication of effectiveness. Instead, quasi-experimental methods, testing the impact of 'natural' policy and practice experiments on system relevant outcomes, are likely to provide a more meaningful evidence base.

[9] J Berecki-Gisolf et al, 'The Impact of Aging on Work Disability and Return to Work: Insights from Workers' Compensation Claim Records' (2012) 54(3) *Journal of Occupational and Environmental Medicine* 318.

[10] E Kilgour et al, 'Interactions between Injured Workers and Insurers in Workers' Compensation Systems: A Systematic Review of Qualitative Research Literature' (2015) 25(1) *Journal of Occupational Rehabilitation* 160.

[11] A Jetha et al, 'Return-to-Work within a Complex and Dynamic Organizational Work Disability System' (2016) 26(3) *Journal of Occupational Rehabilitation* 276.

II. Policy, Health and Disability

Current models of function, disability and health with respect to work disability recognise the important contribution of social and environmental factors to work-related injury and ability to function in employment. These models include, for example, the biopsychosocial model of disability and the International Classification of Functioning, Disability and Health.[12] These models present an alternative to the biomedical model that views recovery from injury and illness as primarily the product of treatment modalities. They explain the divergent outcomes that are commonly observed in people with similar conditions and receiving similar treatment, but in whom social circumstances and psychological processes may differ.

Within this broader context, there is also clear evidence that policy is a critical social determinant which exerts a powerful influence on the health of individuals and communities. The World Health Organization (WHO) sponsored Helsinki Statement on Health in All Policies recognised the importance of governments considering health as an outcome across all areas of policy making, and states that 'Health in All Policies is an approach to public policies across sectors that systematically takes into account the health implications of decisions, seeks synergies, and avoids harmful health impacts in order to improve population health and health equity'. One rather dramatic example of a policy impact on health is the effect of 2005 changes to the state of Florida's criminal laws to provide legal immunity to individuals using lethal force in self-defence. Evaluation of the impact of the so-called 'stand your ground' law on homicides reported that following introduction of the law the monthly homicide rate increased by 24.4 per cent and the rate of homicide by firearm by 31.6 per cent. These effects were sustained for more than a decade post-implementation of the law.[13]

While perhaps with less dramatic impacts, there is also evidence of policy effects in the field of work disability and workers' compensation. For example, one study across 49 states of the USA identified that waiting periods for wage replacement and policies on access to medical treatment were independently associated with duration of disability in workers with low back pain.[14] Comparative studies such as these provide powerful evidence of policy and practice effects, but remain rare in the work disability literature.

The current evidence suggests there is substantial scope to reduce the burden of work disability through more effective practices and policy settings, leading

[12] World Health Organisation, *How to Use the ICF: A Practical Manual for Using the International Classification of Functioning, Disability and Health (ICF). Exposure Draft for Comment* (Geneva, World Health Organisation, 2013).

[13] DK Humphreys et al, 'Evaluating the Impact of Florida's "Stand Your Ground" Self-defense Law on Homicide and Suicide by Firearm: An Interrupted Time Series Study' (2017) 177(1) *JAMA Internal Medicine* 44.

[14] M Shraim et al, 'Length of Disability and Medical Costs in Low Back Pain: Do State Workers' Compensation Policies Make a Difference?' (2014) 57(12) *Journal of Occupational and Environmental Medicine* 1275.

to significant economic and productivity gains. This chapter describes findings from a recent, four-year comparative study of Australian workers' compensation systems that sought to identify and characterise policy impact on work and health relevant outcomes.

III. Australian Workers' Compensation Systems

In Australia, compensation and rehabilitation for people with work disability is organised through workers' compensation systems established in state, territory and Commonwealth law. In total there are 11 main workers' compensation systems in operation across the nation. Each of the eight states and territories has developed its own workers' compensation system, and there are also three Commonwealth systems. All operate under an 'insurance model', with premiums collected from employers based on the risk of work injury. The benefits and services provided are, at a high level, similar between schemes and focus on medical treatment/healthcare, income support and long-term care for people with severe injury or complex health needs. The schemes also share common objectives, which include an emphasis on returning injured workers to work and maintaining the financial sustainability of the compensation schemes.

Despite these high level similarities, there is substantial variability in policy and practice between the Australian workers' compensation schemes. They vary with respect to their structure and administration (eg source of funding); the coverage and eligibility of workers (eg workforce coverage, waiting periods); the types of benefits and entitlements provided (eg level and duration of wage-replacement benefits) and the approach to case management (eg provided in-house by regulator or by private provider). The Australian approach to workers' compensation, including an overview of these similarities and differences between schemes, has been described previously.[15]

These systems are also dynamic, with policy and practice changes very common. For example, a recent study identified 60 instances of legislative amendment between 2004 and 2015, where the primary purpose was to amend or introduce schemes for compensation and/or rehabilitation of workers for work-related injury or illness.[16] These ranged from very large 'scheme transformations' following major reviews to very minor changes. Of these 20 per cent (12 in total) were characterised as major changes, in which there was a clear policy intent to modify worker outcomes, including return to work. These findings make clear that legislation is an instrument that is regularly used by governments across Australia to modify workers' compensation scheme performance.

[15] A Collie, 'Australian Workers' Compensation Systems' in E Willis et al (eds), *Understanding the Australian Healthcare System*, 3rd edn (Melbourne, Elsevier Health, 2016).

[16] A Collie et al, *The Impact of Legislative Change on Workers' Compensation Processes and Outcomes: Findings from the COMPARE Project* (Melbourne, Monash University, 2017).

In summary, Australia has a complex and fragmented approach to workers' compensation. The compensation schemes have common objectives but they vary with respect to how these objectives are achieved. Or, referring to the title of this chapter, they are all fruit, but some are apples, some oranges and others bananas. The policy frameworks of individual systems also change regularly, and at the same time, there have been substantial efforts to collect longitudinal data across most of the Australian schemes (see section IV). This landscape provides a strong foundation for the program of comparative research that will be described in following sections.

IV. The Compensation Policy and Return to Work Effectiveness (COMPARE) Project

A. Background

The COMPARE project was established at Monash University in 2014, following engagement and discussion with workers' compensation regulators across multiple states and territories regarding the lack of evidence around the impact of policy and practice. The overarching purpose of the project was to develop an evidence-base around the impact of policy and practice on return to work in Australian workers' compensation jurisdictions, and in doing so to support development of policy and practice in future. The specific research aims related to this were:

1 to determine the impact of workers' compensation scheme policy on return to work and duration of time loss;
2 to identify policies that have positive and negative impact on return to work and duration of time loss.

The study had a number of other important objectives that supported achieving these research aims. These included developing a national workers' compensation research data platform, extracting insights from two existing national datasets of relevance to the sector, developing and testing methods for assessing the impact of policy and policy change in Australian workers' compensation system, and developing an academic/government collaboration that enables two-way knowledge exchange and transfer of evidence into policy and practice.

The study was established in mid-2014 and the first phase was completed over a four-year timeframe. Funding was provided by the state of Victoria and the Commonwealth, with data provision by the eight state and territory workers' compensation regulators. A further three years of funding (for 2019 to 2021) has subsequently been secured through an Australian Research Council Discovery Grant.

B. Methods

The COMPARE project adopted a comparative research paradigm, utilising the unique features of the Australian workers' compensation system to conduct a series of 'natural experiments' to test the effect of policy and practice. Two sorts of comparison were made. First, through a series of sub-studies we compared worker and scheme relevant outcomes between groups. This could include, for example, comparing the duration of time off work between different states and territories. Second, in a second series of sub-studies comparisons were made before and after a policy event, for example examining duration of time off work before and after a change in legislation that was intended to have an impact on return to work. In both approaches attempts are made to isolate policy effects by accounting for the effects of other factors. This occurs in two ways: first, by selecting cohorts that are matched on certain features (eg age, occupation, injury type); and second, by including a range of co-variates related to the person, their workplace, their injury and their compensation claim in statistical analyses.

Using these high level principles, specific analytical approaches were developed for each individual sub-study. Details of these methods are contained in the articles and reports referenced and will not be repeated here. They broadly included descriptive methods, different forms of regression analysis and time series analysis. For each study our analytical objective was to move beyond description and wherever possible to conduct inferential analysis, examining relationships between measures, while taking into account the influence of other factors. We also applied analytical techniques that test causal inferences, such as Interrupted Time Series (ITS).

Throughout the study two main data sources were used. These were the National Dataset of Compensation Based Statistics (NDS) and the National Return to Work Survey (NRTWS). Each of these has been described in detail elsewhere.[17]

The NDS is case level claims administrative data that includes information on the claim, the worker, employer, and claim outcomes such as compensated time lost. For the COMPARE study data was available from the 2003/04 financial year to 2015/16 and was updated annually. At June 2018 the database included 4,363,267 cases with data from the New South Wales, Victoria, Queensland, Western Australia, Tasmania, South Australia, Australian Capital Territory, Northern Territory and Commonwealth (Comcare) workers' compensation schemes.

The NRTWS captures self-reported RTW outcomes plus a range of self-reported health, employer and claim indicators. The data accessed for the COMPARE study included the 2013, 2014 and 2016 waves of the survey. This included 14,501 cases of self-reported data from injured workers approximately

[17] Safe Work Australia, *National Dataset of Compensation Based Statistics*, 3rd edn (Canberra, Safe Work Australia, 2004); Social Research Centre, *Return to Work Survey: 2016 Summary Research Report (Australia and New Zealand)* (Melbourne, Safe Work Australia, 2017) 59.

4 to 24 months post claim, from the New South Wales, Victoria, Queensland, Western Australia, Tasmania, South Australia, Australian Capital Territory, Northern Territory and Commonwealth (Comcare & Seacare) workers' compensation schemes.

The research team also accessed a range of other data sources to support specific analysis, including labour force data from the Australian Bureau of Statistics (ABS), estimates of workers' compensation coverage data provided by Safe Work Australia, and summary data from the National Work Injury Survey conducted by the ABS.

C. Study 1 – Setting the Scene

The first study from COMPARE sought to examine differences in disability duration (time off work) between the major Australian workers' compensation jurisdictions. The objective of the analysis was to determine whether the jurisdiction in which a work-related injury compensation claim is made is an independent predictor of duration of work disability following injury, and if so, the magnitude of the effect.

Using the National Dataset of Compensation Based Statistics, the authors first selected a standardised cohort of compensation claims lodged during the 2010 year across eight different jurisdictions. Differences in disability duration were compared between these jurisdictions using a Cox regression model, with statistical adjustment for other factors that have been shown to impact on duration, such as age, gender, injury type, and occupation. Large and significant differences between the jurisdictions were observed. Compared with New South Wales, workers in Victoria, South Australia and Comcare had significantly longer durations of time off work and were more likely to be receiving income benefits at 104 weeks post injury, while workers in Tasmania and Queensland had significantly shorter durations of time off work. Western Australia was not significantly different from New South Wales. The differences between jurisdictions were substantial. The cumulative probability of still being off work at 20 weeks post injury was ~0.5 in the state of Victoria, whereas in Tasmania and Queensland the probability at this time point was approximately half that, at 0.2. These differences persisted throughout the 104-week follow-up period. The magnitude of these effects were as substantial as effects observed for injury type and larger than the effects observed for age, which is commonly accepted as one of the strongest predictors of disability duration.

The findings suggest that the design and management (ie policy and practice) of workers' compensation have a substantial effect on duration of work disability for injured workers. However, this says little about which policies are responsible for the differences. The authors argued that this justified future research that isolates specific policies to determine their effects. The report also demonstrates that it is feasible to conduct comparative studies in Australian workers' compensation systems using existing administrative data sets. This finding established the evidence to support the future studies in the COMPARE project.

D. Study 2 – Before-and-After Comparisons

In a series of studies using ITS designs, the COMPARE project team sought to determine the impact of legislative changes on worker and employer outcomes. ITS is considered one of the most powerful quasi-experimental designs for evaluating natural experiments like policy change or community interventions where data have been collected at regular intervals before and after a time-bounded event. ITS can be applied where randomised controlled trials are cost-prohibitive, impractical, or unethical, and is particularly suited to the evaluation of population-level impacts in real-world settings.[18] Unlike other before-and-after analytical techniques such as difference-in-differences, ITS accounts for secular trends, minimising the likelihood that observed differences due to pre-existing trends are misattributed to the event. Using the ITS approach it is possible to estimate causal effects using observational data such as that used in the COMPARE study.

i. Introduction of Employer Incentives in South Australia and Tasmania

This study investigated the impact of incentives for employers to report work injuries more quickly.[19] The incentives were implemented across two workers' compensation jurisdictions as part of larger legislative amendments. In July 2008 South Australia began offering employers a rebate on their two-week employer excess if they reported an injury within two working days of notification. Eighteen months later, Tasmania began penalising employers who reported work injuries more than three days after notification, requiring them to pay compensation for each day they were late. Both were designed to hasten access to workers' compensation benefits and services to improve recovery, reduce costs, and shorten time off work.

Using claim-level workers' compensation data in the NDS, aggregate datasets of the amount of time between several stages in the claim lodgement process were created. The key time periods were claim lodgement time, insurer decision time, and total time (see Figure 1). The dataset described the median number of days between each date within South Australia, Tasmania and a comparator that consisted of other Australian workers' compensation jurisdictions. An ITS analytic approach was used to examine level and trend disruptions in time series following the policy changes.

[18] J Lopez Bernal et al, 'Interrupted Time Series Regression for the Evaluation of Public Health Interventions: A Tutorial (2016) 46(1) *International Journal of Epidemiology* 348.

[19] TJ Lane et al, 'Effectiveness of Employer Financial Incentives in Reducing Time to Report Worker Injury: An Interrupted Time Series Study of Two Australian Workers' Compensation Jurisdictions' (2018) 18(1) *BMC Public Health* 100.

Figure 1 Key events and time periods in the claim lodgement process

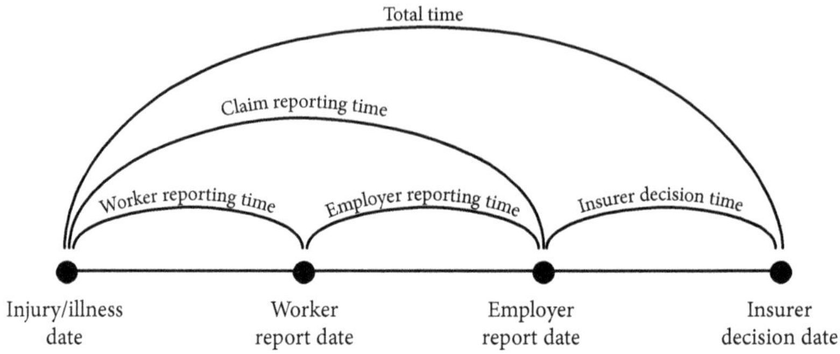

This study identified that the introduction of incentives was followed by reductions in claim reporting time in both states. However, in South Australia there was only a change in worker reporting time and not employer reporting time, which undermined the proposed causal mechanism (it was not possible to analyse these times in Tasmania due to a lack of worker report date data). There was also an increase in insurer decision time in Tasmania, and similar increases in South Australia following implementation of the different waves of the workers' compensation amendments, which suggested an effect due to administrative burden. Overall, total time did not immediately change, though there was a marginal but significant trend decrease in both states

The reduction in worker reporting time in South Australia was attributed to the introduction of provisional liability, which coincided with the reporting incentives. Provisional liability grants workers' compensation applicants' access to benefits and services before their claim is accepted. It was not possible to compare this effect in Tasmania, which had introduced provisional liability two decades earlier. Provisional liability also limited the potential negative effect of increased insurer decision times, since delays in insurer decision are less of an obstacle to treatment and related services where provisional liability exists. As claim reporting time decreased in both jurisdictions, this would suggest that injured workers were receiving services more quickly and the legislative amendments achieved their aim. However, there remain questions about the generalisability of findings, particularly for jurisdictions without provisional liability.

ii. Tasmanian Workers' Compensation Scheme Reform

On 1 July 2010, Australia's smallest state, Tasmania, introduced an amendment to its Workers Rehabilitation and Compensation Act 1988 in response to a major review in 2007.[20] Along with aiming to make the system fairer, the amendment's

[20] A Clayton, *Review of the Tasmanian Workers Compensation System* (2007).

objective was to provide 'prompt and effective management of workplace injuries in a manner that promotes and assists the return to work of injured workers as soon as possible'.[21] The amendments sought to increase benefit generosity and introduce a new Return to Work and Injury Management Model (IMM). The IMM established a framework for improving and streamlining the injury management processes in order to encourage and promote return to work, including the creation of an 'injury management coordinator' role to oversee the injury management process and introduction of a new claims form and medical certificate.[22] ITS analysis was used to determine the impact of this major scheme reform on the duration of disability.

No changes in claim volumes were observed. Following the legislative amendment, there was a decrease in the median duration of disability, however this was non-significant. Relative to the rest of Australia, which was used as a comparator condition, there was a statistically significant increase in the trend of time loss in Tasmania of 0.11 weeks per quarter following the legislative amendment. However, there were no statistically significant changes to the mean number of weeks lost. Assuming that duration of time on compensation income benefits is a reasonable proxy for RTW,[23] this finding indicates that the Tasmanian legislative amendments did not achieve their objective of returning injured workers to work faster.

One possible explanation for this null finding is that the two major components of the Tasmanian legislative package were acting in opposition. There is evidence that increased benefit generosity is associated with increases in disability duration.[24] As the Tasmanian amendments included more generous benefits, these effects may have 'cancelled out' any reductions in disability duration arising from the new injury management model.

iii. New South Wales Workers' Compensation Scheme Reform

In June 2012, the Workers' Compensation Legislation Amendment Act (2012) came into effect in New South Wales. The Act made multiple changes to the structure and operation of the state workers' compensation scheme. The primary objective of the reform was to improve the long-term financial sustainability of the workers' compensation scheme. This was intended to be achieved by reducing expenditure on benefits and services and restricting access to the scheme for

[21] WorkCover Tasmania and Workplace Standards Tasmania, *A Guide to Workers Rehabilitation and Compensation in Tasmania – For Injuries Occurring on or after 1 July 2010* (2010), cited 22 September 2016, available at worksafe.tas.gov.au/__data/assets/pdf_file/0005/541157/GB260-Guide-to-W-Rehab-and-Comp.pdf.

[22] S Gray et al, *Evaluating the Success of Legislative Amendments Designed to Reduce Work Disability, Policy Design and Practice* (2019) 2(3) *Policy Design and Practice* 291.

[23] N Krause et al, 'Alternative Approaches for Measuring Duration of Work Disability after Low Back Injury Based on Administrative Workers' Compensation Data' (1999) 35(6) *American Journal of Industrial Medicine* 604.

[24] BD Meyer et al, 'Workers' Compensation and Injury Duration: Evidence from a Natural Experiment' (1995) 85(3) *American Economic Review* 322.

certain groups of workers. A second objective was to improve return to work rates of injured and ill workers whose workers' compensation claims were accepted. The proposed mechanism to achieve this objective was to introduce financial disincentives for not returning to work where the worker has some work capacity. The reforms also provided the regulator and insurers with additional powers to make claims decisions that affect treatment and income benefits. Emergency service personnel and coal miners were exempted from the reforms to eligibility, income benefits and medical treatment.

The reforms had a significant impact on the finances of the scheme. A subsequent statutory review demonstrating a $5 billion improvement in the scheme's financial position, moving from a $4 billion unfunded liability that prompted the reforms, to a $1 billion surplus within two years of the reforms taking effect.[25] The COMPARE study team examined the impact of these reforms on access to benefits (number of compensation claims accepted) and on duration of disability (time off work) using an ITS analytical approach.[26]

Results indicated a 15.3 per cent reduction in monthly claims volume immediately following the legislative amendments, with a greater impact for workers making claims that involve income replacement (17.3 per cent). These effects were not uniform across the scheme, as there was a more substantial reduction in accepted claims for occupational disease (36.5 per cent) and for mental health conditions (25.9 per cent) than for workers with other conditions (13.1 per cent). Concurrent with these decreases in claim volume, there were increases in disability duration following the reforms. Median duration of disability across all accepted claims increased by 0.5 weeks (statistically significant at $p<0.01$), while the median duration of claims for mental health conditions increased by 4.0 weeks (20 days).

These findings demonstrate that the New South Wales reforms achieved their intended objective of improving the long-term financial sustainability of the scheme by restricting access to benefits. However these effects were not uniform and there appears to be a negative impact on disability duration, indicating slower returns to work in those workers accessing the New South Wales scheme post the reforms.

E. Study 3 – Between Jurisdiction Comparisons

In a further set of studies using epidemiological analysis methods, the COMPARE project conducted a set of analyses that focused on the relationships between modifiable employer and insurer practices and work disability. These studies

[25] Centre for International Economics, *Statutory Review of the Workers Compensation Legislation Amendment Act 2012: Final Report* (Canberra, Centre for International Economics, 2014).

[26] A Collie et al, 'Impact of Legislative Reform on Benefit Access and Disability Duration in Workers' Compensation: An Interrupted Time Series Study' (2020) 77(1) *Occupational and Environmental Medicine* 32.

focused on aspects of the workers' compensation claim management practices where there are clear expectations set in legislation. Analyses sought to characterise between-jurisdiction differences in these practices and relate these to disability duration.

i. Return to Work Planning

A RTW plan is a mandatory requirement for employers of injured workers in all Australian workers' compensation jurisdictions, although the specific requirements vary between jurisdictions (see Table 1). Having a RTW plan has been associated with improved RTW outcomes in previous studies, however these studies have been from single jurisdictions or have not focused on the RTW plan as a primary outcome. The NRTWS provides an opportunity to assess both: (a) how frequently a RTW plan was developed in multiple Australian workers' compensation jurisdictions; and (b) the association between having a RTW Plan and duration of disability.

Table 1 Overview of RTW plan policy in Australian workers' compensation legislation

Jurisdiction	Who is responsible for RTW plan?	Is plan compulsory?	Minimum expected injury time before a RTW plan becomes compulsory
Comcare	Employer	If required following a rehabilitation assessment	Rehabilitation assessment after 3 days
New South Wales	Employer	Yes	7 days
Northern Territory	Employer	Yes	28 days
Queensland	Insurer	Yes	Not specified
South Australia	Insurer	Yes	28 days
Seacare	Employer	Yes	28 days
Tasmania	Injury management co-ordinator	Yes	5 days
Victoria	Employer	Yes	Not specified
Western Australia	Employer	When required by treating doctor	Not applicable

Analysis of the 2013 and 2014 iterations of the National RTW Survey (N=5651 completed surveys) revealed that 47 per cent of injured workers with accepted workers' compensation claims reported having a written RTW plan, 9 per cent reported having an unwritten RTW plan, while 44 per cent of surveyed workers did not recall having a RTW plan. Multivariate regression models identified that female workers, those with musculoskeletal and neurological conditions and workers employed by self-insurers were all significantly more likely to have a RTW plan.

Using a binary logistic regression model, the odds of having any RTW plan was determined in each jurisdiction, using New South Wales as the comparator (see Figure 2). Workers with accepted workers' compensation claims under the Comcare scheme were 1.5 times more likely to report having had a RTW plan than those in New South Wales. In contrast, workers in Queensland and Seacare were significantly less likely to report having a RTW plan.

A further analysis testing the association between self-reported presence of a RTW plan and time taken to return to work identified that workers who reported having a RTW plan had increased odds of RTW. In the first 30 days after the claim, whether the plan was written or unwritten did not affect RTW, however it was significantly better than having no RTW plan. However, after 30 days, having a written plan was most effective, increasing the odds of RTW 3.4 times, while an unwritten plan increased the odds of RTW 2.2 times.

Figure 2 Adjusted odds of reporting a RTW plan by jurisdiction (relative to NSW)

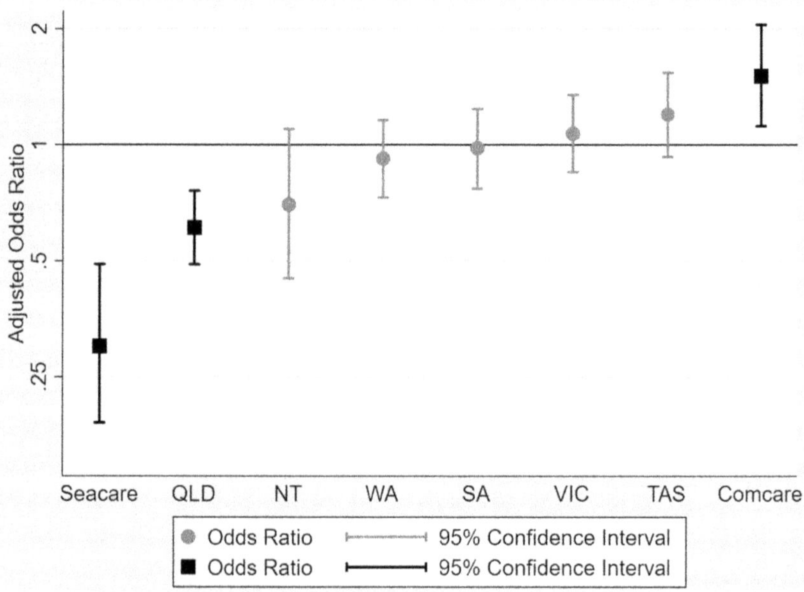

This study suggests both that legislative requirements to prepare RTW plans vary substantially between jurisdictions, and that rates of RTW planning varies. Further, having a RTW plan is significantly associated with increased odds of RTW. Nationally, 43 per cent of workers surveyed reported not having a RTW plan prepared during their workers' compensation claim. Provision of RTW plans is highly amenable to modification and thus represents an opportunity for intervention that may improve RTW outcomes.

ii. Benefit Duration and Commutation

As with RTW plans, workers' compensation legislation in Australia commonly sets time limits with respect to the duration for which income benefits can be provided, and the circumstances under which a claim can be commuted. A commutation commonly involves paying a lump sum to the worker to close the claim. There are multiple 'long-tail' schemes in which income benefits may be provided from date of claim acceptance until retirement age, and in which commutations or redemptions are only provided under limited circumstances. There are also 'short-tail' schemes that provide income benefits for defined periods of time (eg two years, 130 weeks), and some schemes in which claims can be commuted based on their duration or following negotiation with the worker and/or their employer. These policy settings are variously intended to encourage return to work and as a means of controlling the costs of providing workers' compensation. A summary of some relevant legislative settings is provided in Table 2.

Table 2 Overview of income duration and commutation policy in Australian workers' compensation legislation

Jurisdiction	Maximum Duration of Income Support	Commutation/ Redemption
Comcare	Retirement age	In limited circumstances
New South Wales	130 weeks (work capacity); 260 weeks (no work capacity)	In limited circumstances
Northern Territory	104 weeks (work capacity + suitable employment) 260 weeks (work capacity + no suitable employment) Until retirement age (>15 per cent WPI)	No time limit. Negotiated between worker and insurer/ employer.
Queensland	104 weeks; 104–260 weeks (>15 per cent permanent impairment)	After 2 years.
South Australia	104 weeks (most workers); retirement age (>30 per cent WPI)	No time limit. By agreement with worker.
Seacare	Retirement Age	In limited circumstances
Tasmania	9 years (<15 per cent WPI); 12 years (15–20 per cent WPI); 15 years (20–30 per cent WPI)	Within two years of date of claim (conditions have been met)
Victoria	130 weeks (most workers); retirement age (no work capacity)	In limited circumstances
Western Australia	Retirement age	After six months

Long periods of involvement in workers' compensation systems have been associated with, and may contribute to, poor health and quality of life outcomes for workers.[27] (Comparing jurisdictional patterns of long-term claims may provide some insight into the effect of these legislative settings on duration.)

This study used the NDS to examine jurisdictional differences in the frequency of long duration claims and the amount of working time lost to long duration claims, and changes in long duration claims over time. Each claim was categorised into one of four groups based on duration of paid income benefits (1) Group 1 = less than 6 months; (2) Group 2 = 6–12 months; (3) Group 3 = 13–24 months; (4) Group 4 = greater than 24 months. Claim duration was capped at a maximum of 260 weeks (five years) to ensure estimates were conservative and did not over-inflate the impact of very long duration claims. Pearson's Chi squared test was used to test for statistical differences in the proportion of claims and weeks compensated between each group. Statistical differences in the rate of long-term claims, weeks compensated and in the change in the rate of long-term claims and weeks compensated from 2004–2013 between groups were tested by modelling the incidence rate ratio with a Poisson distribution.

Analyses identified that 12 per cent of all included time-loss claims were of at least six months' duration, but that these accounted for 76 per cent of the total burden of disability as measured in weeks of compensated time loss. Almost half of all time compensated (47 per cent) was in those 3.9 per cent of workers whose claims lasted over 24 months. For every 1,000 workers who have workers' compensation insurance coverage in Australia, 2.5 per annum have a long-tail workers' compensation claim with income benefits provided beyond six months.

There were large differences between jurisdictions in the percentage who were long-term and in the rate and change over time of long-term claims. The number of claims and weeks compensated were similar between jurisdictions up to 24 months. After 24 months there was great variation between jurisdictions, as indicated in Figure 3. These differences are probably explained by different policies regarding the maximum duration of income support and access to commutations and redemptions, rather than reflecting different RTW outcomes. For example, short-tail jurisdictions in which commutations are common (such as Queensland) have a relatively small proportion of all income benefit compensation paid to workers with claims greater than two years' duration. Those in which the use of commutations is restricted have a much greater percentage (eg Victoria, South Australia and New South Wales).

[27] Kilgour et al, above, n 10.

Figure 3 Percentage of total weeks compensated in each jurisdiction

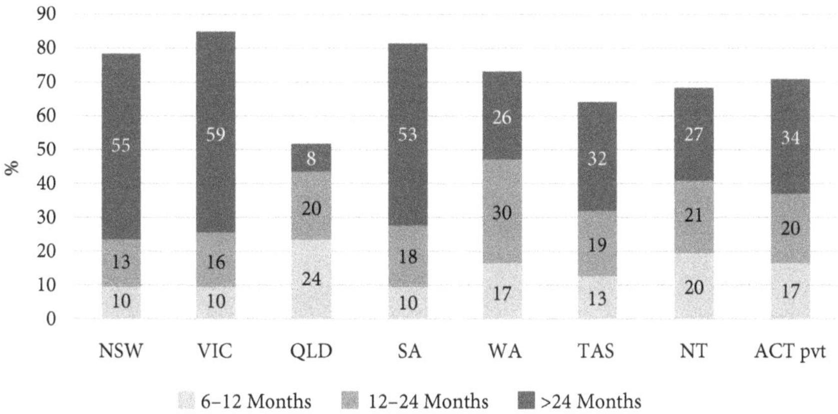

F. Strengths, Limitations and Data Gaps

The overarching strengths of the COMPARE study include the use of very large datasets, with population coverage in the case of the NDS. With the exception of the Defence and Veterans Affairs (DVA) compensation scheme, all of the major Australian workers' compensation schemes are represented in these databases. Both databases record multiple worker, injury, demographic, claim and employer characteristics which enable inclusion of multiple co-variates in statistical analysis, producing greater certainty in estimates. Standard injury and occupation coding schema are used in both datasets and these are consistent between datasets. In addition the national standard industry coding schema is included in the NDS. Combined, the datasets have enabled examination of multiple RTW relevant outcomes including duration of time loss (disability duration) and self-reported RTW. Both datasets include a time series. This was critical for evaluation of policy change using ITS and has enabled the development of causal inferences related to time-bound changes in policy (legislative amendments) using ITS analysis. Finally it was possible to source denominator data for most analyses, in the form of ABS labour force data or covered worker estimates at occupation and industry level. This has enabled calculation of rates of claims (per 1,000 working population or covered population, for example) in addition to raw counts.

The datasets also have some limitations. The NDS is administrative data collected primarily for the purposes of managing workers' compensation claims. The estimate of time loss derived from the NDS appears robust. However, prior research has shown that time loss data is not equivalent to RTW, particularly for longer duration claims where other factors can result in benefit cessation other than RTW. The NDS also has multiple gaps in data. These relate mainly to gaps in the claims process (for example very little information on disputation or legal system involvement during the course of a claim), lack of information on health-care provision which is a major feature of workers' compensation schemes in Australia and an important return to work tool, and relatively limited information on the psychosocial predictors of return to work. Through the course of the COMPARE project the research team identified multiple instances of differences in data entry between jurisdictions. For the most part analytic strategies were able to account for these, however in some cases we needed to develop modified coding approaches to account for these differences. For the NRTWS, the cross-sectional nature of the data limits our ability to make causal inferences.

G. Summary

The COMPARE study sought to establish a research evidence-base around the impact of policy and practice on return to work in Australian workers' compensation systems. The study has demonstrated that jurisdictional policy and practice has a major impact on duration of disability in workers with accepted workers' compensation claims, and has isolated the effects of some specific employer and insurer practices and processes such as RTW planning. The study has provided evidence that changes to scheme design through legislative amendment can have significant impacts on access to workers' compensation systems, claims processing times and duration of disability, but can also produce unanticipated effects in some groups of workers or where competing RTW incentives are introduced via legislation.

In summary the COMPARE study has provided a foundation of evidence which can support current and future workers' compensation policy and practice, and there is substantial potential to extend this knowledge base through future studies.

V. Other Comparative Studies in Injury Compensation

There are multiple other comparative studies conducted in injury compensations schemes within Australia and internationally. These include studies in motor vehicle accident compensation schemes, USA workers' compensation and even cross-national comparisons.

For example, one study across 49 states of the USA identified that waiting periods for wage replacement and policies on access to medical treatment were independently associated with duration of disability in workers with low back pain.[28] In another example, in 1999 the tort-based transport injury scheme in the Australian state of New South Wales introduced four key legislative changes:

[28] Above, n 14.

removing non-economic loss from common law (eg 'pain and suffering'); introducing clinical guidelines for whiplash treatment; ensuring earlier acceptance of compensation claims through regulation; and earlier access to treatment.[29] Cameron et al followed insured whiplash-afflicted individuals in NSW two years after their injury and found that those whose accident occurred after the legislative change had better health outcomes.[30]

Another study in Australian motor vehicle crash compensation schemes demonstrated that the Victorian no-fault scheme was considered fairer and was associated with superior health outcomes at 12 and 24 months post-injury than the NSW common law scheme.[31] This study surveyed 182 CTP claimants (N=98 in NSW; N=84 in VIC) at 12–24 months post injury regarding their self-rated health status and their perception of the fairness of the claims management process. Regression modelling showed a significant positive interaction between overall fairness perception of the compensation process and health post-injury (odds ratio = 2.78, p = 0.002). Adjusting the model for demographic and injury characteristics showed that the association between fairness and health was of the same magnitude after adjustment (adjusted odds ratio = 2.83, p = 0.004). Similarly, in a natural experiment conducted of the motor vehicle injury compensation scheme in Saskatchewan, Canada, it was found that whiplash-affected individuals had improved prognoses following a major policy change.[32] Here the scheme changed from a tort-based to a no-fault system, which meant that an individual could no longer access payments for 'pain and suffering', and income replacement and medical benefits were increased. It has subsequently been shown that these two sorts of systems are associated with differences in health outcomes,[33] and therefore improvements in health outcomes following this change were unsurprising. These studies further demonstrate the value of the comparative research paradigm in teasing apart policy impacts.

VI. Conclusions

The research summarised in this chapter demonstrates both that work disability is a significant public health and social policy issue, and that the legislative settings within the Australian workers' compensation systems have a significant impact

[29] ID Cameron et al, 'Legislative Change is Associated with Improved Health Status in People with Whiplash' (2008) 33(3) *Spine* 250.

[30] ibid.

[31] NA Elbers et al, 'Differences in Perceived Fairness and Health Outcomes in Two Injury Compensation Systems: A Comparative Study' (2016) 16 *BMC Public Health* 658.

[32] JD Cassidy et al, 'Effect of Eliminating Compensation for Pain and Suffering on the Outcome of Insurance Claims for Whiplash Injury' (2000) 342(16) *New England Journal of Medicine* 1179-1.

[33] NA Elbers et al, 'Differences in Perceived Fairness and Health Outcomes in Two Injury Compensation Systems: A Comparative Study' (2016) 16 *BMC Public Health* 658.

on the duration of disability, and on processes and practices that are intended to support recovery and return to work following work-related injury and disease. The studies presented use epidemiological and quasi-experimental methods to address questions of policy and legislative impact on health related outcomes. The COMPARE study has begun to develop an evidence base to support future policy development in the field, and has at least demonstrated the need for long-term follow-up and evaluation of changes in law. There remain substantial gaps in knowledge that future similar studies will seek to address. There also remain significant variations in policy and legislative design between Australian systems and as yet no consensus regarding the optimal scheme design for supporting recovery and return to work, and reducing the burden of disability following injury and illness in the workplace.

5

Workers' Compensation in Canada: Experiences of Precariously Employed Workers in the Return to Work Process after Injury†

KATHERINE LIPPEL,* ELLEN MacEACHEN**
AND SONJA SENTHANAR**

This chapter reports on findings drawn from a Canadian study empirically investigating the experiences of precariously employed workers in the provinces of Ontario and Quebec who attempt to return to work after work injury. Methods for these studies included classic legal analysis of legislation, policies and administrative tribunal decisions in both provinces. Parallel to the legal analysis, we interviewed 25 workers, five employers and 26 key informants to better understand effectiveness of the regulatory frameworks. We begin by comparing workers' compensation legislation in Quebec and Ontario, looking at coverage and reporting requirements, benefits, assignment of modified work, the right to vocational rehabilitation and support provided to workers seeking suitable employment or exercising their right to return to work. We then draw on the material generated by our interviews to illustrate applications of these provisions. We conclude by questioning the effects of the economic incentives embedded in these workers' compensation regimes, including aggressive claims management and workers' perceptions of injustice in systems where the power imbalance is palpable.

† These studies were part of a research program funded by the CIHR and the SSHRC in the Healthy and Productive Work Competition for the research program, SSHRC: 890-2016-3026; CIHR: HPW-146002. The authors wish to acknowledge the support of Camille Lanthier-Riopel, masters of law candidate at the University of Ottawa, who provided research and coordination assistance to the research team.

* Canada Research Chair in Occupational Health and Safety Law, Civil Law Section, Law Faculty, University of Ottawa, Ottawa, Ontario, Canada.

** University of Waterloo Faculty of Applied Health Sciences, Waterloo, Ontario, Canada.

I. Introduction

'No-fault' systems are compensation systems that provide income support for people disabled because of an injury or illness caused by specific circumstances.[1] Workers' compensation provides benefits to workers who are injured in the course of employment or who develop occupational diseases because of exposures at work. They are 'no-fault' systems in the sense that they replace tort remedies; in Canada, workers cannot sue their employers for damages regardless of the employer's negligence and, in principle, the workers' fault cannot reduce the level of benefits, although systems vary with regard to workers' negligence and eligibility for benefits.[2] Employers are the sole funders of workers' compensation systems, a price they pay in exchange for broad protection from liability.

Previous studies have shown that the promise of 'no-fault' compensation systems for non-adversarial relations between workers, employers and the systems themselves is, in many cases, a chimera.[3] Relations can be very adversarial in no-fault systems and this can have negative effects on workers' health and poison the employment relationship when it is time to return to work. Research has shown that the compensation process can affect health outcomes, and stress related to that process can contribute to disability and delay return to work.[4]

Few studies have focused on specific characteristics of the compensation systems that either promote or reduce claimant stress. A study that focused on the appeal process showed that the appeal hearing was actually a positive feature of the claims experience, allowing the workers to be heard and to better understand the reasons underpinning their frustrations.[5] In contrast, various dimensions of the rehabilitation process have been identified in studies both in Canada[6]

[1] K Lippel, and F Lötters, 'Public Insurance Systems: A Comparison of Cause-Based and Disability-Based Income Support Systems' in P Loisel and JR Anema (eds), *Handbook of Work Disability Prevention and Management* (New York, Springer, 2013).

[2] Quebec's workers' compensation system includes a provision that denies benefits to workers if their injury is not severe and it is attributable solely to their own gross negligence: An Act Respecting Industrial Accidents and Occupational Diseases, C.Q.L.R., c. A-3.001 (hereinafter AIAOD), s 27.

[3] K Lippel, 'Therapeutic and Anti-therapeutic Consequences of Workers' Compensation Systems' (1999) 22 *International Journal of Law and Psychiatry* 521; K Lippel, 'Workers Describe the Effect of the Workers' Compensation Process on their Health: A Quebec Study' (2007) 30 *International Journal of Law and Psychiatry* 427; E Maceachen et al, 'The "Toxic Dose" of System Problems: Why Some Injured Workers Don't Return to Work as Expected' (2010) 20 *Journal of Occupational Rehabilitation* 349.

[4] MJ Spittal et al, 'Development of Prediction Models of Stress and Long-Term Disability among Claimants to Injury Compensation Systems: A Cohort Study' (2018) *BMJ Open*, doi:10.1136/bmjopen-2017-020803; ML O'Donnell et al, 'Compensation Seeking and Disability after Injury: The Role of Compensation-Related Stress and Mental Health' (2015) 76 *Journal of Clinical Psychiatry* E-1000; G Grant et al, 'Relationship Between Stressfulness of Claiming for Injury Compensation and Long-term Recovery: A Prospective Cohort Study' (2014) 71(4) *JAMA Psychiatry* 446.

[5] K Lippel, 'L'expérience du Processus D'appel en Matière de Lésions Professionnelles Telle Que Vécue par les Travailleuses et les Travailleurs' in Barreau Du Quebec (eds), *Développements Récents en Droit de la Santé et Sécurité au Travail* (Cowansville, Éditions Yvon Blais, 2006); Lippel (2007), above, n 3.

[6] E MacEachen et al, 'The "Ability" Paradigm in Vocational Rehabilitation: Challenges in an Ontario Injured Worker Retraining Program' (2012) 22 *Journal of Occupational Rehabilitation* 105; K Lippel,

and Australia[7] as a source of humiliation for many injured workers. Return to work obligations under workers' compensation legislation have also been found to be a source of frustration for employers,[8] particularly small employers,[9] resulting in ill will between workers and employers, and contributing to the stigmatisation of injured workers.[10] Medical evaluations in the context of contested compensation claims have been found to be a source of anxiety in claimants,[11] and several studies have found that doctors have negative associations with the treatment of injured workers and in some cases refuse to treat patients who are also claimants in compensation systems.[12]

While there are many studies that have examined the role of compensation systems in promoting early and safe return to work,[13] the effectiveness of workers' compensation systems in supporting sustainable return to work for the precariously employed is rarely the subject of attention, and very few studies have looked specifically at workers' compensation applied to the precariously employed.[14]

This chapter reports on results of a comparative empirical study of two workers' compensation systems in Canada, looking at the effects of specific characteristics of those systems on the return to work experiences of workers who incurred a work-related injury while precariously employed. In our study the precariously employed included workers in a non-standard employment relationship with

'L'intervention Précoce pour Éviter la Chronicité: Enjeux Juridiques' in Barreau Du Quebec (eds), *Développements Récents en Droit de la Santé et Sécurité au Travail* (Cowansville, Éditions Yvon Blais, 2008).

[7] DC Roberts-Yates, 'The Concerns and Issues of Injured Workers in Relation to Claims/Injury Management and Rehabilitation: The Need for New Operational Frameworks' (2003) 25 *Disability & Rehabilitation* 898; R Guthrie, 'The Dismissal of Workers Covered by Return to Work Provisions Under Workers Compensation Laws' (2002) 44 *Journal of Industrial Relations* 545; L Sager and C James, 'Injured Workers' Perspectives of their Rehabilitation Process under the New South Wales Workers Compensation System' (2005) 52 *Australian Occupational Therapy Journal* 127.

[8] Guthrie, above, n 7.

[9] JM Eakin and E MacEachen, '"Playing it Smart" with Return to Work: Small Workplace Experience under Ontario's Policy of Self-Reliance and Early Return' (2003) 1 *Policy and Practice in Health and Safety* 19.

[10] JM Eakin, 'The Discourse of Abuse in Return to Work: A Hidden Epidemic of Suffering' in CL Peterson and C Mayhew (eds), *Occupational Health and Safety: International Influences and the 'New' Epidemics* (Amityville, NY, Baywood Publishing, 2005); Lippel (2007), above, n 3.

[11] K Lippel et al, 'The Structure and Process of Workers' Compensation Systems and the Role of Doctors: A Comparison of Ontario and Quebec' (2016) 59 *American Journal of Industrial Medicine* 1070; E Kilgour et al, 'Interactions Between Injured Workers and Insurers in Workers' Compensation Systems: A Systematic Review of Qualitative Research Literature' (2015) 25 *Journal of Occupational Rehabilitation* 160; E Kilgour et al, 'Healing or Harming? Healthcare Provider Interactions with Injured Workers and Insurers in Workers' Compensation Systems' (2015) 25 *Journal of Occupational Rehabilitation* 220; E Kilgour et al, 'Procedural Justice and the Use of Independent Medical Evaluations in Workers' Compensation' (2015) 8 *Psychological Injury and Law* 153.

[12] B Brijnath et al, 'Is Clinician Refusal to Treat an Emerging Problem in Injury Compensation Systems?' (2016) 6 *BMJ open* 1–7; MacEachen et al, above, n 3; Lippel et al, above, n 11.

[13] For an international overview see E MacEachen (ed), *The Science and Politics of Work Disability Prevention* (New York, Taylor & Francis, 2019).

[14] M Quinlan and C Mayhew, 'Precarious Employment And Workers' Compensation' (1999) 22 *International Journal of Law and Psychiatry* 491.

the employer[15] defined as such either because of temporal dimensions (part-time, on-call, temporary employment contracts), or because of the nature of the contractual relationship (triangular employment through a labour hire agency or a subcontractor, or self-employed). We also included workers working full time while earning minimum wage at the time of their injury, in their case because of economic precarity rather than direct contractual precarity.

In Canada,[16] workers' compensation falls under provincial jurisdiction and each province has its own law, regulation and policies. In all provinces the systems are managed by public, not-for profit, compensation agencies: in Quebec, the *Commission des normes, de l'équité, de la santé et de la sécurité du travail* (CNESST), and in Ontario, the Workplace Safety and Insurance Board (WSIB). In both provinces workers and employers may appeal decisions to a final appeal tribunal; in both cases appeal tribunal decisions are protected by privative clauses that prevent, or at least radically limit judicial review. In Quebec, the appeal tribunal is the Tribunal administratif du travail (TAT); in Ontario the Workplace Safety and Insurance Appeal Tribunal (WSIAT). Our study focused on Quebec and Ontario, the two most populous provinces in Canada. French is the official language in Quebec, the language of judgments and the language of work and of all but one of our interviews, while English is the official language in Ontario.

This chapter reports on findings from our pilot studies of return to work and precarious employment in Quebec and Ontario. The methods for these studies included classic legal analysis of legislation, policies and administrative tribunal decisions in both provinces. Parallel to the legal analysis, individual and group interviews[17] with workers, employers and key informants in each province allowed us to identify similarities and differences between the experiences of analogous informants and to link those experiences with the regulatory drivers of the experiences, a method previously labelled as 'inter-jurisdictional transdisciplinary analysis' used to tease out the effect of the regulatory environment on the experiences of people and institutions acting in the context of a regulatory process.[18] To better understand the role of specific legal rules we undertook qualitative studies in two jurisdictions focusing, in this case, on the experience of precariously employed workers and that of their employers in the return to work process. The parallel study, based on comparative law methods,[19] identifies in detail the similarities and differences between the relevant legal environment, in this case workers'

[15] M Quinlan, 'The Effects of Non-Standard Forms of Employment on Worker Health and Safety' in *Conditions of Work and Employment* (Geneva, International Labour Office, 2015).

[16] K Lippel, 'Strengths and Weaknesses of Regulatory Systems Designed to Prevent Work Disability after Injury or Illness: An Overview of Mechanisms in a Selection of Canadian Compensation Systems' in MacEachen, above, n 13.

[17] We received ethics approval for the empirical studies from the University of Ottawa's Office of Research Ethics and Integrity, File number 08-16 36 and the ethics board of the University of Waterloo. All names used in this chapter are pseudonyms.

[18] K Lippel et al, above, n 11.

[19] For a classic example of comparative law applied to disability and accommodation in the workplace see K Banks et al, 'The Lasting Influence of Legal Origins: Workplace Discrimination, Social

compensation[20] and human rights legislation[21] applicable to the workplace in Quebec and Ontario. In total we interviewed 25 workers, five employers and 26 key informants. When available, we read the legal decisions related to the appeals involving the workers interviewed, which provided additional details relating to the claims process.

We now turn to the results of our parallel studies, linking the experiences of the participants to the specific regulatory provisions in each province. To do so, we will first look at the legal environment in Quebec and Ontario and then turn to our findings based on our interviews.

II. Regulatory Comparison of Workers' Compensation Legislation Relevant to Return to Work

Many of the provisions are similar in both provinces, so here we will focus in particular on issues that we have identified as having specific impact on the experiences of our participants.

A. Coverage and Reporting

Quebec's workers' compensation legislation provides coverage for all employees except those that are explicitly excluded by the Act, ie domestic workers and sports professionals. Broader coverage is provided in Quebec than in most Canadian provinces[22] because some who are solo self-employed, regardless of their industry, are deemed to be workers under the Act,[23] a provision that does not exist either in Ontario or in any other Canadian province, although Ontario has specifically provided coverage for bicycle and foot couriers regardless of the

Inclusion and the Law in Canada, The United States and The European Union' in M Finkin and G Mundlak (eds), *Comparative Labor Law* (Cheltenham, Edward Elgar, 2015).

[20] In Quebec, AIAOD and related regulations, available at www.canlii.org/en/qc/laws/stat/cqlr-c-a-3.001/latest/cqlr-c-a-3.001.html; in Ontario, the Workplace Safety and Insurance Act 1997, SO 1997, c 16, Sch A (hereinafter WSIA) and related regulations and policies, available at www.canlii.org/en/on/laws/stat/so-1997-c-16-sch-a/latest/so-1997-c-16-sch-a.html.

[21] In Quebec, *Charter of Human Rights and Freedoms*, CQLR c C-12 (hereinafter Quebec Charter); in Ontario, *Human Rights Code*, RSO 1990, c H 19, (hereinafter HRCO).

[22] 93.17% of Quebec's workforce is covered, as compared to 74.48% of Ontario's workforce according to the most recent figures provided by the Association of Workers' Compensation Boards of Canada, awcbc.org/wp-content/uploads/2013/12/Industries_Occupations_Covered.pdf, last accessed 17 February 2020. This url leads to a document entitled 'Scope of coverage', which provides the information for each province.

[23] If the self-employed individual is deemed to be a worker under s 9 then it is the client who pays the premiums. Part of the deeming process presupposes that the client is responsible for a significant portion of the self-employed person's workload. If the self-employed individual is not deemed to be a worker under the Act, he or she may pay the premium if they choose to obtain coverage under s 18, but it is not mandatory.

nature of their employment contracts[24] and some independent contractors who work in construction.[25] In contrast to the broad scope of Quebec legislation, Ontario's workers' compensation legislation is one of the least comprehensive of workers' compensation systems in Canada: coverage is provided only when specified in legislation or policy, so a broad range of workers are effectively excluded from the regime, and as we found, the inclusion or exclusion of a given workplace is difficult to identify and the criteria for exclusion are not transparent, even for experts in the system.

Reporting of occupational injuries and diseases by the employer is obligatory in Ontario. Failure to report is punishable by a $C500,000 fine.[26] In Quebec, by contrast, employers have no obligation to report injuries to the compensation branch of the CNESST, and only the most serious accidents, leading to death, amputation or equivalent, or $C150,000 material damages, need be reported to the occupational health and safety branch of the CNESST. Failure to do so could result in a maximum fine of $C3,000.[27]

Finally, in both provinces, failure of the employer to pay premiums or to declare employees to the compensation board will be sanctioned by the board, however, this has no impact on the rights of the workers. Workers employed 'under the table' are eligible for workers' compensation benefits if the work they were doing should have been covered.[28]

B. Benefits

Workers with accepted workers' compensation claims receive 90 per cent of their net salary in Quebec and 85 per cent of their net salary in Ontario. Maximum insurable earnings are slightly higher in Ontario than in Quebec; however the most significant difference between the systems, for the precariously employed, is that Quebec's legislation guarantees a minimum insurable earning equal to minimum wage for a 40-hour working week, which represents, in 2020, an annual gross income of $C26,070. No minimum is guaranteed in Ontario.[29] Workers will receive temporary benefits while awaiting maximum medical recovery, unless they occupy modified work, in which case their salary will be paid in

[24] WSIAT Decision 866/16, 2016 ONWSIAT 3286. It is interesting to note that it is the insurer of the motor vehicle involved in the accident that sought protection from tort liability for injuries incurred by the bicycle courier, an argument that was successful.

[25] WSIA, s 12.2.

[26] WSIA, ss 21(3), 152(3), 158(1) 2.

[27] Act Respecting Occupational Health and Safety Act, CQLR, c S-2.1, s 62 and s 236(2); note the maximum fine is slightly higher today given that it is indexed to the cost of living since 2009.

[28] In Quebec, s 26 of the AIAOD is clear on this point. In Ontario policy is clear with regard to the worker's obligation to report regardless of whether the employer says there is no coverage: www.wsib.ca/en/businesses/claims/report-injury-or-illness, last accessed 25 February 2020.

[29] For a detailed analysis of the calculations of benefits and their link to return to work processes in Quebec and Ontario see Lippel, above, n 16.

lieu of benefits. When this happens, employers' experience rating will not be adversely affected, as we shall examine in due course. Other benefits are payable, including lump sum benefits for permanent impairment in Quebec, for example. However, our findings suggest that the important determinants in the benefit structure are the benefits paid for loss of earnings. Loss of earnings benefits will be paid until the worker is 65 in Ontario at which time the WSIB may provide retirement benefits,[30] and until age 68 in Quebec (AIAOD, s 57), although in the latter case benefits will start diminishing when the worker reaches the age of 65 (AIAOD, s 56).

C. Assignment of Modified Work Prior to Maximum Medical Recovery

Both systems provide the opportunity for early return to work prior to maximum medical recovery, however the mechanisms, rights and obligations associated with each early return to work process are very different.[31]

In Quebec the employer has the right, but no obligation, to offer modified work to the worker who is temporarily unable to return to pre-injury employment. The employer describes the requirements of the proposed modified work and the worker's treating physician determines whether the work is appropriate, given the legal requirements under s 179 of the AIAOD that the 'temporary assignment' 'is beneficial to the worker's rehabilitation', 'the worker is reasonably fit to perform the work' and 'the work, despite the worker's injury, does not endanger his health, safety or physical well-being'. If the 'doctor in charge of the worker' (the treating physician) refuses to approve the proposed assignment, the employer may submit as many new proposals as it wishes, however the employer cannot appeal the physician's refusal to approve the assignment, and the CNESST cannot intervene to influence the physician's opinion. There is hardly any litigation surrounding the approval of a 'temporary assignment'. If the worker's physician approves the assignment, the worker may appeal the decision requiring that they take up the assignment, otherwise benefits may be suspended if the worker fails to report for work. Although employers are not obliged to propose temporary assignments, experience rating of employer premiums provides a strong incentive to offer modified work; workers who have high incomes, particularly those whose incomes are superior to the maximum insurable earnings provided for in the legislation, have a strong incentive to accept those offers, as they lose money when they receive workers' compensation benefits as compared to their earnings at the time of the injury.

[30] See www.wsib.ca/en/injured-or-ill-people/claims/wsib-benefits, last accessed 25 February 2020.

[31] For a more detailed explanation of these mechanisms and the role of physicians in relation to early return to work see Lippel et al, above, n 11.

In contrast, in Ontario, both the worker and the employer have an obligation to cooperate in the early return to work process (WSIA, s 40). Theoretically an employer may be penalised for failing to offer modified work to an injured worker, however in practice our informants confirmed that employers were almost never penalised by the WSIB for failing to offer modified work. Two of our informants, who together cumulated several decades of legal practice in the field, one representing employers, had never seen an employer penalised in this context. A third informant was able to provide one example of a penalty being imposed, again after years of experience in the field. Workers, however, will lose their benefits if they fail to take up the modified work imposed by the employer, and the opinion of their treating physician as to the appropriateness of the proposed assignment is not solicited in the process. Doctors are asked only to detail the worker's residual functional abilities, not to determine in any way whether modified work is appropriate. In Ontario, a great deal of litigation surrounds the modified work process. In practice, experience rating mechanisms can also serve as an incentive to an employer to offer modified work, but if the cost of benefits for a precariously employed worker is very low, the incentive is proportionately low, and in triangular employment relationships it falls on the labour hire agency or the subcontractor, not on the primary contractor.[32]

D. Right to Vocational Rehabilitation

For a worker who suffers a permanent impairment as the result of a compensable injury, the workers' compensation board will determine a vocational rehabilitation plan for the worker, should the impairment prohibit return to work in pre-injury employment. In both provinces, the compensation board will evaluate the residual abilities of the worker, taking into account the work-related impairment as well as the worker's residual skill sets and abilities and will determine a vocational rehabilitation plan based, in most cases, on a cost benefit analysis comparing the cost of doing nothing with the cost of an eventual vocational rehabilitation program. There will be an evaluation of the cost of loss of income benefits payable during the life of the claim as compared to the cost of retraining, for example. The higher the cost of future benefits, the more the incentive to invest in retraining. The rehabilitation program has as its objective to permit the worker to obtain 'suitable employment', defined in s 2 of the AIAOD, in Quebec, as

> appropriate employment that allows a worker who has suffered an employment injury to use his remaining ability to work and his vocational qualifications, that he has a reasonable chance of obtaining and the working conditions of which do not endanger the health, safety or physical well-being of the worker, considering his injury.

[32] E MacEachen et al, 'Workers' Compensation Experience-Rating Rules and the Danger to Workers' Safety in the Temporary Work Agency Sector' (2012) 10 *Policy and Practice in Health and Safety* 77.

Policy under WSIA determines that the concept of 'suitable occupation',

> represents a category of jobs suited to a worker's transferable skills that are safe, consistent with the worker's functional abilities, and that to the extent possible, restores the worker's pre-injury earnings. The suitable occupation must be available with the injury employer or in the labour market.[33]

E. Support in Seeking Suitable Employment

During the rehabilitation process the worker receives full benefits for loss of earnings. Once the worker has completed the rehabilitation plan, in Ontario, the benefits will be reduced by the amount of income the 'suitable employment' is deemed to generate, regardless of whether the worker actually occupies a job. If the worker does occupy a job that generates income higher than that deemed to be earned in the 'suitable employment', the loss of earnings benefits will be reduced by actual income.

In Quebec, the deeming process is very similar, with one significant difference. Once the worker has finished the rehabilitation program, loss of earnings benefits are payable for up to 12 months after the rehabilitation program has been completed.

Loss of earnings benefits for most precariously employed workers are thus much higher in Quebec than in Ontario because on the one hand they cannot be lower than benefits based on a gross salary equivalent to full-time minimum wage, and on the other, once a worker is judged to be capable of occupying suitable employment, benefits are payable for 12 months or until the worker occupies a job, after which the salary earned will be subtracted from the loss of earnings benefits. If the worker does not return to the labour market after 12 months, the system will presume the worker is earning the equivalent of full-time salary associated with the 'suitable employment'. Thus, in both systems, loss of earnings for a worker earning minimum wage or less at the time of the injury will be equal to zero once the 'deeming' process kicks in; immediately after the vocational rehabilitation program in Ontario, and 12 months later in Quebec.

The cost of benefits has a significant impact on compensation board and employer behaviour for two reasons. The compensation boards use the estimate of these costs to evaluate the amount of money they are willing to invest in the vocational rehabilitation program. As to the employer, experience rating mechanisms are based in large part on the cost of benefits, as we shall see in the next sections.

[33] WSIB Operational Policy, Work Reintegration: Determining Suitable Occupation, Doc Number 19-03-03.

F. Right to Return to Work and Related Provisions

Legislation provides incentives for employers to reintegrate injured workers in their workplaces once they have reached maximum medical recovery. In Quebec, all workers except those in construction have the right to return to pre-injury employment if they are capable of doing so, although the duration of that right varies according to the size of the workplace and the nature of the contract.[34] Workers can file a complaint against an employer who fails to reintegrate a worker[35] and a legislative presumption (AIAOD, s 255) facilitates the worker's claim if the termination occurs within six months of the employment injury or the exercise of a right under the AIAOD. Experience rating provides a further incentive, as full benefits are payable to a worker searching for a new job for up to 12 months, and those benefits are experience rated. Finally, in Quebec, s 243 of the AIAOD states that 'No person may refuse to hire a worker because the worker has suffered an employment injury if the worker is able to carry on the employment contemplated'. Although this provision has existed since 1985 it has never been applied by any appeal tribunal. As of 3 March 2019, 151,801 decisions cited the AIAOD, of which 23 mention section 243. Section 243 has never been applied by the appeal tribunal.

While Quebec's Charter[36] prohibits discrimination on the basis of disability, it has – as we shall see – failed to effectively protect injured workers from discriminatory hiring practices.

Ontario legislation provides for weaker job protections: workers in workplaces with fewer than 20 employees do not have the right to return to pre-injury employment. If they work for a larger workplace, a right to return to work exists for up to 12 months after the injury, if the worker 'had been employed continuously for at least one year by the employer'.[37] Precariously employed workers are less likely to be protected by this provision, particularly temporary workers, including employees of labour hire firms. No presumptive legislative protections apply if the worker is sanctioned for exercising a right or making a claim under the WSIA. Experience rating also acts as an incentive in Ontario, as does human rights legislation,[38] which prohibits discrimination on the basis of disability.

[34] Sections 236ff AIAOD guarantee the right to return to work for two years for workers in workplaces with more than 20 employees, or in one year if there are 20 or fewer. For temporary employees, s 237 provides for the right to return to work if the worker can do so before the expiry of the contract. If the contract has expired, unlike workers with indeterminate contracts, temporary workers, according to certain appeal decisions, will not have the right to 12 months of benefits while searching for a job as provided for in s 48. See *Muhlbauer et Commission des normes, de l'équité, de la santé et de la sécurité au travail*, 2018 QCTAT 4191.

[35] AIAOD, s 32.

[36] CQLR c C-12, ss 10, 16, and 18.1.

[37] WSIA, s 41(1) and 41(2).

[38] HRCO, ss 5, 10(3) and 23; WSIA, s 41(6) also explicitly imposes on the employer the duty to accommodate the injured worker up to the point of undue hardship

G. Experience Rating and Related Incentives for Employers

Experience rating, mechanisms by which employers' workers' compensation premiums are affected by the claims numbers and costs of compensation for their employees, has become a primary tool of compensation systems in providing incentives to employers to reduce claims for injuries and illnesses in their workplaces and to reduce the duration of claims and severity of disability. In theory, this economic incentive encourages organisations to adopt best practices: primary prevention to avoid injuries that result in claims, and secondary and tertiary prevention to promote employer collaboration in reducing disability by supporting early return to work in appropriate work that reduces the danger of chronicity and in reintegrating workers disabled as a result of their work. Most studies on the effects of experience rating do not distinguish between reduced number of claims and reduced claims costs, on the one hand, and reduced injury or illness and reduced severity on the other.[39]

As Tompa and colleagues have shown in a comparison of workers' compensation experience rating in the Canadian provinces of British Columbia and Ontario, experience rating is not a binary variable, and the design of experience rating systems, the way they work in practice, can vary a great deal. They note that the Ontario system is more 'aggressive' than the British Columbia system, which means that 'premium adjustments have a larger association with claims cost performance'.[40] In Quebec, the experience rating system used by the CNESST is more extensive than that in Ontario, notably because small businesses may apply for membership in a *Mutuelle de prévention* which allows them to 'benefit' from experience rating, and the *Conseil du Patronat*, the largest employers' lobby group, states that Quebec's experience rating system is the most reactive in the country.[41] In Quebec, all types of expenses for a claim are experience rated, and in some cases one dollar spent on physiotherapy can have a five-fold impact on the employer's subsequent premiums.

The effects on number and duration of claims vary between systems, although Tompa and colleagues are careful to note that '[t]he different types of behaviour incentives created by [experience rating] is something that warrants further exploration, in particular the distinction between cost versus OHS management'.[42] The effectiveness of experience rating as an injury prevention tool – as distinguished from a system to prevent claims and claims costs – is unclear, and studies have

[39] E Tompa et al, 'A Comparative Analysis of the Financial Incentives of Two Distinct Experience-Rating Programs' (2016) 58 *Journal of Occupational & Environmental Medicine* 718.

[40] ibid, 721.

[41] *Conseil du Patronat du Quebec & Federation des chambres de commerce du Quebec* 2010. Mémoire du comité patronal consultatif soumis au groupe de travail présidé par monsieur Viateur Camiré, chargé de faire des recommandations au conseil d'administration de la CSST sur le régime québécois de santé et de sécurité du travail.

[42] Tompa et al, above, n 39, 727.

suggested that in some cases the goal of experience rating is to prevent costs, not necessarily injury or disability.[43]

Among negative behaviours that have been associated with experience rating incentives is the outsourcing of dangerous work, including outsourcing to labour hire agencies[44] and discriminatory hiring practices.[45] It has also been suggested that experience rating is a primary driver of disputed claims, and it is telling that employers in Quebec are responsible for over half the appeals to the final appeal tribunal, while in Ontario they are far less present in appeals. Quebec appeals are far more numerous than appeals in Ontario, and have increased significantly since experience rating became more aggressive,[46] and a large proportion of the Quebec appeals raise medical issues which involve multiple medical evaluations of workers.[47]

Of key importance to our results are the explicit legal mechanisms in the experience rating system that provide employers opportunities to offset costs of injuries affecting their employees in Quebec. In principle, all costs are imputed to the employer's account, however the employer can externalise those costs to other employers, or to the general compensation fund to which all employers contribute in various ways. If the worker was previously 'handicapped' at the time of injury, and the disability contributed to either the occurrence or the severity of the injury, costs can be transferred from the employer's account to all employers contributing to the compensation fund.[48] Under s 326(2) AIAOD the CNESST may also

> impute the cost of benefits payable by reason of an industrial accident to the employers of one, several or all units if the imputation under the first paragraph would have the effect of causing an employer to support unduly the cost of benefits due by reason of an industrial accident imputable to a third person or unduly burdening an employer.

This provision has been shown to reintroduce fault in the no-fault system, providing incentives to employers to lay blame on those responsible for the injury, including the worker in some cases. If the injury causes death or 'severe permanent physical or mental impairment',[49] regardless of the worker's negligence, compensation must be provided by the CNESST, but the employer can externalise these

[43] E Tompa at al, 'Financial Incentives in Workers' Compensation: An Analysis of the Experience-Rating Programme in Ontario, Canada' (2012) 10 *Policy and Practice in Health and Safety* 117; E Tompa et al, 'Update on a Systematic Literature Review on the Effectiveness of Experience Rating' (2016) 10 *Policy and Practice in Health and Safety* 63; T Thomason and S Pozzebon, 'Determinants of Firm Workplace Health and Safety and Claims Management Practices' (2002) 55 *Industrial and Labor Relations Review* 286; H Arthurs, 'Funding Fairness: a Report on Ontario's Workplace Safety and Insurance System' (WSIB Funding Review Toronto: Queen's Printer for Ontario, 2012).

[44] MacEachen et al, above, n 32.

[45] M Harcourt et al, 'The Impact of Workers' Compensation Experience-Rating on Discriminatory Hiring Practices' (2007) XLI *Journal of Economic Issues* 681.

[46] K Lippel, 'Preserving Workers' Dignity in Workers' Compensation Systems: an International Perspective' (2012) 55 *American Journal of Industrial Medicine* 519.

[47] Lippel et al, above, n 11.

[48] AIAOD, s 329.

[49] AIAOD, s 27.

costs if it shows it is unduly burdened. If the injury is less severe, AIAOD, s 27 can be used to deny a claim if the injury is attributable to 'the gross and wilful negligence of the worker'. In some cases, the appeal tribunal has found that the fact that a worker lied about their functional limitations at the time of hiring is a form of 'gross and wilful negligence', and workers injured on the job have been denied benefits in some cases.[50]

Key informants in Quebec, corroborated by the statistics of the appeal tribunal, were clear that disputing compensation claims was a pervasive practice for employers in that province, including small employers who delegated their rights of appeal to the '*mutuelles de prevention*', for profit organisations that are designed to reduce costs for their members. In Ontario, litigation generated by employers was mentioned much less often. The employers were seen to be represented by the WSIB itself; the organisation was perceived by some to manage the compensation system with a view to reducing costs whenever possible.

III. Living in a System: Stories from the Trenches

We have provided a summary review of the prevailing legal contexts in Quebec and Ontario in order to better understand the regulatory drivers affecting precariously employed injured workers, their employers and the compensation boards. Now we examine key findings of the qualitative studies in the two provinces.

A. Coverage

In the course of our study we found it far more difficult to recruit precariously employed workers who had applied or received benefits from the workers' compensation system in Ontario, while in Quebec it was relatively easy to recruit participants. In the end, the Ontario sample included several workers who were injured while they were precariously employed but who had not filed for workers' compensation. Subsequently, our interviews with Ontario key informants provided at least a partial explanation for our difficulties. Because there is no minimum benefit level in Ontario, the level of benefits provided to the precariously employed, who may have very low earnings at the time of their injury, is often so low as to discourage workers from claiming. A lawyer specialised in workers' compensation for claimants eligible for legal aid explained to us that they start a file by doing an economic calculation to decide whether it is better for their client to apply for the Ontario Disability Support Program (ODSP), a means tested program of last resort for the disabled, or whether applying to WSIB is worth their while. We were told that for a precariously employed worker with dependants, ODSP often provided better

[50] See for example *Cloisons Corflex inc et Maher* [2017] QCTAT 4306.

protections, because the whole family is covered for expenses such as dental costs and prescription medication, while WSIB only provides benefits related to the work injury, and salary replacement benefits that are often lower than the ODSP benefit. Several Ontario lawyers told us that their clients sought support from ODSP rather than WSIB because of the inadequacy of the benefits and the difficulties surrounding the compensation process itself. Thus, precariously employed workers who **do** have coverage do not necessarily claim under the WSIA, a situation that transfers the costs of their disability, that should be borne by employers, to taxpayers. It also affects the legitimacy of the statistics generated by the WSIB, so that information used to promote prevention in Ontario workplaces is skewed by effective exclusion of the poorest and most precarious workers.

In Quebec, because of the minimum level of benefits guaranteed to all claimants, the difference between workers' compensation benefits and 'welfare' benefits is very significant,[51] and neither the workers nor any key informants suggested that choosing social assistance benefits would be a sound economic choice. However, the absence of mandatory reporting obligations on employers in Quebec also affects the validity of compensation board statistics, particularly in a context of aggressive claims management, as we shall discuss in due course.

This said, when coverage was provided to a precariously employed worker we interviewed in Quebec, a school crossing guard working part time and on call who was hit by a car while working, was allowed the time to heal and was very positive about her experience with the CNESST. In her case, rapid access to physiotherapy, benefits actually slightly higher than her usual take home earnings paid for four months of temporary disability, smooth and rare interactions with the case manager all contributed to her positive experience. Her employer did not insist on providing her with modified work, which was not realistically available in her workplace, and after four months she returned to her pre-injury employment, where she was working at the time of the interview. Her story serves as a reminder that workers' compensation systems, when coverage is provided and the system works smoothly, can have a therapeutic effect.[52]

A second issue that arose related to the nature of coverage itself. As we have seen, coverage in Ontario is more selective than that in Quebec. An employee of a long-term care facility in Ontario informed us that she was not covered under workers' compensation. She still suffers from chronic pain five years after her

[51] In 2020, monthly payments for a single person with a temporary disability on welfare in Quebec totalled $C793 per month or $C9,516 per year. The website of the Ministère d'emploi et de solidarité sociale provides information on the current level of benefits: www.mani.mess.gouv.qc.ca/?sujet=42429, last accessed 25 February 2020. Minimum annual benefits for an injured worker with no dependants were equal to $C19,695.69 (90% of net based on minimum gross salary of $C26,070.00) AIAOD, Arts 6 and 65 and *Table of income replacement indemnities payable under the Act respecting industrial accidents and occupational diseases and indemnities payable under the Workers' Compensation Act for 2020*, CQLR c A-3.001, r 15 (2020).

[52] We reported on similar positive experiences in our previous study of the effect of workers' compensation systems on workers' health: Lippel et al (2007), above, n 3.

work-related injury, incurred when she fell while helping one of her patients who had limited mobility. When we asked several of our key informants if this was legally accurate, we discovered that even legal experts are not in a position to know whether a worker has coverage without fairly extensive research. Indeed, we undertook that research and finally understood that private long-term residential care facilities that provide care to elders who require less than two hours of nursing or personal care a day are not obliged to provide coverage to their workers under WSIA legislation and policies, although publicly funded facilities with the same clientele must provide coverage,[53] a distinction that cannot be rationalised on the basis of differential exposure to occupational hazards. This has meant that a worker has no right to economic support throughout the duration of her disability, although the employer can choose to provide private insurance, which, in the case of our worker, provided benefits for a limited time, shorter than WSIA would have provided. In her forties, she has moved back to live with her parents who are retired, and she receives benefits from the Ontario means-tested ODSP that provides minimum support for people with disabilities who are living alone or with families who meet the economic criteria for eligibility.

Finally, in both provinces we encountered workers who were working in undeclared work, working 'under the table' at the time of their injury. In Quebec, we interviewed a young construction worker, Simon, who had been seriously injured on a construction site where all of the workers, including the contractor, were working under the table, without the required construction permits and without declaring income to the tax authorities. Our interviewee was aware of the fact that he had coverage under workers' compensation law, even if the employer had not declared the worksite to the authorities. He threatened to submit a workers' compensation claim, and received cash payments from his employer at minimum wage for full-time work for 18 months, as he used the threat of declaring his accident to leverage economic support.

The workers we interviewed in Ontario appeared to be less aware of their rights and more easily manipulated. For example, Scott, an employee of a temporary employment agency, was told by his employer that on the day of his injury he was paid cash, and therefore was not eligible for workers' compensation, misinformation that was seemingly confirmed by his doctor, while another temporary worker, Peter, was simply told that temporary agency workers were not entitled to workers' compensation; this misinformation was provided by his employer.

In some cases, the documentation required by WSIB for a successful claim was impossible for workers to collect. For instance, Alice, a seasonal forestry worker, was asked to provide an eye-witness account of her back injury. However, her only colleague in the forest, a temporary foreign worker, had already returned to South America and could not be reached; her claim was denied.

[53] WSIB, Employer Classification Manuel, Nursing and residential care facilities, NAICS Code and Title 623310; available at safetycheck.onlineservices.wsib.on.ca/safetycheck/ecm/naics/623310?lang=en, last accessed 25 February 2020.

B. Why Benefit Levels Matter: It's Not Just about the Money

As we've seen in the first part of this chapter, in both provinces, when work injury results in permanent impairment, workers will be deemed to be able to earn a salary once they have completed a rehabilitation program. The cost of their claims is dependent on their presumed earnings at the time of their injury and their deemed earnings after the rehabilitation process. The higher the gap, the greater the justification for investment in the rehabilitation program. The determination of the vocational rehabilitation plan in both provinces will depend on a cost-benefit analysis: how much will benefits cost in the long term if the compensation board does nothing, as compared to the cost of the vocational rehabilitation program. The Quebec system is clearly far more favourable to low waged precariously employed workers than the Ontario system, because benefits are based on minimum wage for full-time work and last up to a year longer than the benefits payable in Ontario. Costs of the injury are thus more effective drivers of tertiary prevention in Quebec: an employer has a clear economic incentive to take the worker back, as well as a legal requirement to accommodate that worker up to the point of undue hardship under human rights legislation[54] and the CNESST has a clear economic incentive in insuring the worker can earn at least minimum wage in full time work. While the Quebec system is more supportive, this does not imply that workers feel they are treated fairly by the system.

We spoke with Ali during our interviews, who had immigrated to Quebec from a francophone country only a few years prior to his injury. He spoke perfect French, the language of work in Quebec, and had a doctorate in a field that was highly prized on the labour market. Yet the only job he could get to support his family was working for a labour hire agency as a security guard, and it was while he was doing that job that he was injured. The severity of his injury precluded return to work as a security guard, so he was admitted to a rehabilitation program by the CNESST, who referred him for evaluation to a career counsellor who recommended a short retraining course to allow him to improve his employability in his field of expertise by obtaining knowledge on the local practices in his field. The CNESST refused to fund the training course, and Ali, in the course of his interview, identified this exchange as one of the triggers for his mental health problem which has since been judged to be a compensable injury. He spoke to his rehabilitation case manager at the CNESST and asked:

> why did I work for three or four months with a woman YOU paid who tells you I should take a course and then you say NO. Why do you do that? She said 'listen … We're an insurance company …' (pause) 'insuring a Mercedes is not the same as insuring a Toyota …'. I don't cost the system much, I was earning $21,000, they don't have to spend

[54] Although this has always been the case in Ontario, in Quebec this has only become clear since 2018 when the Supreme Court of Canada held that the Quebec Charter applies to injured workers: *Quebec (Commission des normes, de l'équité, de la santé et de la sécurité du travail) v Caron*, 2018 SCC 3.

> money on me, but someone earning $60,000 or $70,000 … is expensive for the system. In that case they give training, they give everything, why? Because … that person will cost the system money without retraining. It's as if I'm a scrap heap … An old car ….

At the time of our interview Ali was still receiving full benefits because of his physical and psychological injuries, he had become what the compensation jargon would label a 'complex claim'.

C. Strengths and Weaknesses of Incentives for Early Return to Work

Ontario's legislation provides strong incentives to employers to bring workers back to work, and workers who fail to comply may lose their benefits. In our Ontario interviews with key informants it became clear that more sophisticated employers, such as temporary employment agencies (labour hire firms) do not hesitate to offer alternative employment to keep workers off benefits, even in contexts where the therapeutic benefits of the alternative employment were not obvious. We were told that sometimes the mechanisms by which workers were required to rapidly consult a physician to identify residual capacities were not easily complied with by these workers, and the work offered by the employer, while not physically harmful, was in some cases of dubious therapeutic effect. For example, a key informant described the situation of a construction labourer who was injured on a construction site where he had been placed by the labour hire firm. The 'true employer', the labour hire firm, was willing to offer him modified work to classify documents in their office, a practice that we have seen in many cases and in our previous studies.[55] As key informant Jennifer explains, the worker was deemed to have failed to cooperate, as he had not produced the required form and had not accepted the job of filing papers in the office of the labour hire firm. Employers were also disgruntled by the obligation of providing modified work to temporary agency employees who were in no way qualified to do clerical work. As one employer described modified work recipients to us: 'most of them you know, are cranky that they don't want to be here and, and yeah, it's just usually not a, a good environment'.

In Quebec we spoke with Mathieu whose early return to work program was a textbook example of good rehabilitation practice. Although he suffered from severe back problems that precluded return to work as a trucker, his employer provided him with alternative employment prior to maximum medical recovery and he and his wife explained to us how much better he felt doing something useful. He loved his temporary assignment, felt respected by his employer and his colleagues.

[55] K Lippel et al, 'Legal Protections Governing Occupational Health and Safety and Workers' Compensation of Temporary Employment Agency Workers in Canada: Reflections on Regulatory Effectiveness' (2011) 9 *Policy and Practice in Health and Safety* 69.

Unfortunately, Mathieu technically worked for a temporary employment agency, a shell corporation created for the exclusive use of the primary contractor. His supervisor from the temporary employment agency was supportive and played by the rules, but when the primary contractor's human resource department got involved, they told Mathieu that it was illegal to have brought him back before he was fully recovered (which was untrue), and they told him to go home and rest until he was fully recovered, an outcome which was very disappointing to him.

At the time of our interview he was starting to feel very discouraged. We've since learned that he was sent for a medical evaluation by the employer's doctor, who concluded he would no longer be able to work as a trucker. He's since been laid off and is now occupying 'suitable employment' for a different employer, earning a salary far below his previous earnings. In his case, the economic incentive for return to work fell on the labour hire agency, a shell company, while the real decision-maker, the primary contractor, was unaffected by experience rating.

D. Right to Return to Work: Protective Right or a Poisoned Chalice?

The right to return to work does not apply to workers with less than one year's seniority in Ontario, and that clearly has an impact on the possibility of retaining employment after injury. One young minimum wage worker was told she was no longer a good fit and she ultimately lost her job:

> She called and she was like, 'Oh, I heard … you got hurt. I just want to hear about that.' So, I told her … I just described [the child] coming lunging at me …. She is like, 'I am sorry to hear about all this. I was just taking a look over your files and I see that … you have been great for this kid … however we are going to have [to] determine whether you are still a good fit given the nature of the job'. (Louise (FT worker, on probation))

Brenda's employer, a retail store, was reluctant to file a claim for WSIB when Brenda incurred an eye injury at work. Because of the severity of the injury, Brenda went to her doctor and initiated the claim there, leaving the employer with little leeway except to file the required workplace form. Brenda's compensation claim was denied, but although she received some economic support from her employer while she recovered from surgery, she found that her work responsibilities changed and schedules became poorer and she ultimately decided to quit.

In Quebec, where the right to return to work applies to all employees, Paulo's employer took him back after his first injury – he had no choice. He took him back again after a second injury, but made his life miserable after that, providing him with a temporary assignment outside in the cold for eight hours a night, counting trucks going through the gate, a job that had never existed prior to his accident. His employer complied with the letter of the law, but not the spirit, and Paulo ultimately ended up quitting his job, believing he'd been retained by a new employer. The accident employer provided very negative references and as a result the new employer changed his mind and withdrew the job offer. The bitter relationship with his previous employer may well be attributable to the employer's frustration at having to comply with the law that translated into hostility, a situation not dissimilar to that observed in Ontario with regard to the 'early and safe return to work program'.[56]

The self-employed who have no protections under workers' compensation legislation in most cases have no job protection if they are injured, so they are known to cover up occupational injuries to ensure they remain marketable. As explained by an employer in mining we interviewed:

> I said, 'How come we haven't seen you for a while?' and one of them said, 'Because I hurt myself doing a job and I couldn't work for about 8 months. Now I am okay, so I am coming back.' I said, 'Why didn't you say anything?' He said, 'What is the good – if I had said … that I hurt myself … I would have lost all of my contracts around and … nobody will have given me any small contracts'. So, not only our mines but other places where you subcontract, so he just said that he was off for a while because of personal illness.

E. Experience Rating: Unintended Consequences of Regulatory Incentives

In both provinces we found evidence of aggressive management practices that undermined both the workers' compensation system and the return to work mechanisms prescribed. While claims were far more often disputed in Quebec, many of the workers in Ontario reported other forms of intimidation.

In a climate of anti-injured worker animus, precarious employees are sometimes afraid to file their claims, as explained by Shannon:

> She [family doctor] wanted me to [file a WSIB claim]. That's one thing I really, really, really regret not doing [because of ongoing health problems]. I didn't end up filling it out because I was in such fear about my company. I was worried that they might come after me. I was worried that they might fire me. I was worried that they might give me less shifts. Like I was just had so much anxiety. …. After my accident I started to develop … panic attacks … Because I had very little support from my company, I was so paranoid. Like they were going to fire me or they were going to report me, or they were going to like not give me enough shifts. I was just [so] constantly fearful that I basically didn't do anything.

Employers sometimes avoided financial responsibility for claims related to injured workers by submitting false information to WSIB, claiming that the injury was not related to work. For instance, in Ontario Seth, who worked for an auto assembler, found out that his employer had claimed his injury was due to his activity of lifting weights and professional boxing, despite his having never engaged in either activity.

[56] Eakin and MacEachen, above, n 9.

In Quebec, Medhi's supervisor told the compensation board that Medhi had lied when he said that he had informed his supervisor of his injury, saying that he, the supervisor, was on vacation on the date of the alleged injury. Fifteen months later, during the appeal hearing of the denial of Medhi's claim, under oath, the supervisor admitted he couldn't remember whether or not he was on vacation at the time of the injury, and the claim was accepted on appeal. Medhi's story helps to demonstrate the different ways that the compensation process, in an adversarial context, can undermine the worker's health and ability to return to work. At the time of our interview, six years after the injury, Medhi had been declared unemployable by the CNESST, yet this outcome could have been avoided by fair management of the claim. Here is his story, as told to us in the interview and as corroborated by the multiple judgments of the appeal tribunal relating to his claim.[57] Medhi worked over 60 hours a week holding two jobs at minimum wage at the time he injured his back. He immediately reported his injury to his supervisor and mentioned it to a colleague. The supervisor lied to the front-line adjudicator, so the claim was denied, which meant that Medhi had no access to physiotherapy and no income to support his wife and four children. He won the right to compensation in appeal, 16 months after his initial claim. Without access to adequate treatment he hadn't learned to manage his pain and by the time physiotherapy and psychological therapy were provided his pain had become chronic and he was clinically depressed. His employer, a large firm, continually disputed even minor decisions rendered in his file, often requiring medical evaluations by doctors chosen by the employer, until five years after the injury when experience rating provisions no longer applied. Unfortunately, the damage was done, and Medhi, according to medical evidence and the final decision in his file, will never work again, both because of chronic pain but also because of his fragile mental health. He is in his forties. He has full benefits and will do so until he is of retirement age, yet this is no victory for him: during his interview he talks of suicide, of a wasted life.

IV. Conclusion: Access to Justice in Workers' Compensation

Throughout our study we were confronted with examples by which economic incentives in both workers' compensation systems appeared to have become finalities unto themselves. The employers' goals were not to prevent injuries

[57] Over four years, nine judgments were rendered in appeal, one allowing his claim, a second revising his benefit levels to take into account revenue from both jobs he was unable to perform and seven denying the employer's various disputes of decisions including appeals relating to the right to psychological treatment, the acceptance of the claim for depression related to his chronic pain, the recognition of his right to rehabilitation and a decision relating to permanent impairment. Mehdi won all his appeals. The employer never contested the recognition of his unemployability because it didn't matter anymore.

or disabilities but to prevent costs; once costs were not an issue, the aggressive management practices ceased, as in the case of Mehdi. If costs could be transferred elsewhere, incentives to promote rehabilitation ceased, as in the case of Mathieu.

There is clearly a structural imbalance in these two workers' compensation systems, imbalance evocative of Galanter's description of one-shotters and repeat players.[58] Workers in both systems are one-shotters, while employers and the compensation boards are repeat players. Not only do employers have the economic advantage that allows them to hire lawyers and human resource managers to promote their best interests, the compensation boards have both the economic advantage and the better understanding of very complex systems that are difficult to navigate.

Being treated poorly and with disrespect is bad for a worker's mental health and, if it leads to delays in recognition of legitimacy of a claim, it is bad for physical health as well, as it delays access to treatment. Yet the workers' compensation systems studied, when accessible without conflict, are supportive of workers' health and return to work. If either the claims experience or the potential repercussions of claiming are so bad that workers do not claim, the acknowledged positive qualities of no-fault systems are lost. Finding incentives to put an end to aggressive claims management practices would be a first step in redeeming the compensation systems we studied.

[58] M Galanter, 'Why the "Haves" Come out Ahead: Speculations on the Limits of Legal Change' (1974) 9 *Law and Society Review* 95.

6

Safe as Houses? Lump Sum Dissipation and Housing

KYLIE BURNS* AND ROS HARRINGTON**

Lump sum damages payments for personal injury claimants who suffer serious and catastrophic injury are common across Australia. One of the benefits of lump sum compensation for personal injury is argued to be the ability of claimants to purchase housing with their lump sum. In this chapter, we focus on whether the expenditure of significant amounts of a lump sum compensation payment on the purchase of or payment for housing is desirable for personal injury compensation recipients, particularly considering the complex interaction between Australian compensation systems, the Australian social security support system and lifetime care and support schemes such as the National Disability Insurance Scheme (NDIS) and the National Injury Insurance (NIIS) schemes. We discuss our content analysis of Australian Administrative Appeal Tribunal (AAT) social security preclusion appeals between 2013 and 2017 to illuminate the potential consequences of compensation recipients expending compensation lump sums on housing. We argue that purchase of housing can contribute to compensation recipients prematurely dissipating lump sum funds meant to provide economic support for loss of earnings and lifetime care and support costs. This may result in preclusion from income and other support from the social security system for lengthy periods of time, with injured people then left in a precarious financial position. It may also result in poor health outcomes for compensation recipients, who may also be unable to access enough lifetime care and support through the NDIS or through a state or territory NIIS scheme. The use of lump sum compensation funds on purchase of property may not, in fact, be 'safe as houses'.

Lump sum damages payments for personal injury claimants who suffer serious and catastrophic injury are common across Australia.[1] Despite the introduction of

* Associate Professor and Deputy Head of School (Learning and Teaching) Griffith Law School, Griffith University, Nathan, Queensland, Australia.

** Lecturer in Occupational Therapy at the School of Allied Health, Faculty of Health Sciences, Australian Catholic University, Banyo, Queensland, Australia.

[1] H Luntz et al, *Torts: Cases and Commentary*, 8th edn (Sydney, Lexis Nexis, 2017) 526.

no fault lifetime care and support through the National Injury Insurance Schemes (NIIS) for catastrophic motor vehicle and work injuries,[2] damages for economic loss and general damages generally continue to be paid in a lump sum which is meant to last a lifetime.[3] This is said to allow those who suffer personal injury to have choice and control in the way they expend their compensation funds.[4] It is argued that there are psychological benefits to claimants being able to detach their lives from the 'drip feed' of periodic payment schemes administered by bureaucratic government compensation bodies and private insurers.[5] Claimants are said to have the most well informed view of what services they require and who should provide those services Finally, it is strongly argued – particularly by lawyer interest groups – that the provision of lump sums allows claimants to secure housing either through the purchase of a new property or through the contribution of the lump sum to payment or payout of an existing mortgage. Housing is viewed by both lawyers and claimants as both legitimate and necessary to enable long-term management of the health effects of severe or catastrophic injury, and to ensure the long-term financial security of those who suffer such injuries.[6] It is the Australian dream to own a 'home' and this is considered a legitimate expenditure of funds for those who receive a damages payment.

In this chapter, we focus on whether the expenditure of significant amounts of a lump sum compensation payment on the purchase of or payment for housing is desirable for personal injury compensation recipients, particularly considering the complex interaction between Australian compensation systems, the Australian social security support system and lifetime care and support schemes such as the National Disability Insurance Scheme (NDIS) and the National Injury Insurance (NIIS) schemes.[7] The provision of appropriate housing plays an important role in the ongoing health and injury outcome of those with significant disability[8] and may provide (at least in the short term) some financial security. However, lump sum damages are not generally calculated to include any provision for purchase of housing, which is considered a cost of ordinary life not attributable to the injury

[2] ibid, 66.

[3] ibid, 525. See *Todorovic v Waller* [1981] HCA 72, (1981) 150 CLR 402.

[4] See eg Australian Lawyers' Alliance, *Review of National Disability Insurance Scheme (NDIS) Costs: Submission to the Productivity Commission*, 24 March 2017, available at www.lawyersalliance.com.au/documents/item/803, 7–10.

[5] ibid.

[6] ibid.

[7] There is not a single NIIS scheme. It is a federated scheme. There are multiple state and territory motor vehicle and work lifetime care and support schemes. See also Productivity Commission, *Disability Care and Support: Inquiry Report* (August 2011), www.pc.gov.au/inquiries/completed/disability-support/report, Ch 18.

[8] C Wright et al 'What Housing Features Should Inform the Development if Housing Solutions for Adults with Neurological Disability?: A Systematic Review of the Literature' (2017) 46 *Health and Place* 234. See also Joint Standing Committee on the National Disability Insurance Scheme, *Accommodation for People with Disabilities and the NDIS* (May 2016), www.aph.gov.au/Parliamentary_Business/Committees/Joint/National_Disability_Insurance_Scheme/JNDIS-44th/NDIS_accommodation/Report.

caused by the defendant. Damages may contain an allowance for alteration to a property necessary to accommodate the specific needs of a disability or an allowance for the costs of permanent institutional care where a claimant cannot be cared for at home. We argue that purchase of housing can contribute to compensation recipients prematurely dissipating lump sum funds meant to provide economic support for loss of earnings and lifetime care and support costs. This may result in preclusion from income and other support from the social security system for lengthy periods of time, with injured people then left in a precarious financial position. It may also result in poor health outcomes for compensation recipients, who may also be unable to access enough lifetime care and support through the NDIS or through a state or territory NIIS scheme. The use of lump sum compensation funds on purchase of property may not, in fact, be 'safe as houses'.

In section I of this chapter we explore and critique the justifications for lump sum damages payments. Section II briefly outlines the complex interactions between 'common law' lump sum payments and the Australian social security system, NDIS and NIIS schemes. We demonstrate that the 'freedom' to spend lump sums on housing assumed by the common law is seriously impeded by the social security, NDIS and NIIS schemes. In Section III we explore the existing Australian evidence about how compensation recipients spend lump payments, including expenditure on housing. We also discuss the factors which appear to contribute to premature expenditure of lump sums. Section IV discusses our content analysis of Australian Administrative Appeal Tribunal (AAT) social security preclusion appeals between 2013 and 2017 to illuminate the potential consequences of compensation recipients expending compensation lump sums on housing.

I. Why Lawyers Like Lump Sums

Where an injured plaintiff obtains damages in negligence for a personal injury these are typically paid in a lump sum, once and for all, for life.[9] While various types of damage are considered in the calculation of the lump sum, once paid the plaintiff is free to spend their damages as they please. They are not generally restricted to spending only that portion of the lump sum allocated to a particular head of damage, on that kind of expense.[10] While courts throughout Australia are authorised to approve periodical payments or structured settlements, it appears most damages are paid as lump sums.[11] Most lump sums are obtained in settlement, rather than as a result of court judgment and, as Luntz et al note, there is a strong preference by both plaintiff and defendants alike for lump sum

[9] See above, n 3.

[10] Where funds management has been mandated due to the plaintiff's lack of cognitive capacity, there may be practical limitations on how a plaintiff chooses to spend funds.

[11] Luntz et al, above, n 1, 527.

settlement.[12] In some ways this is puzzling. There are many recognised limitations of lump sum settlements or judgments. These include: inability to accurately predict future economic damages such as loss of income; unexpected increase in medical expenses and care costs; erosion of lump sums by deductions for allowance for vicissitudes and discount rates; risks of plaintiffs or their financial advisers inappropriately managing the lump sum; and the impact of uncertain financial investment markets.[13] In addition, as we discuss in Section III, there is existing evidence that compensation recipients may prematurely (and sometimes very prematurely) expend their lump sum for a wide range of reasons. As we discuss in Section II, there is a complex interaction between social security, NDIS and NIIS legislation that negatively impact upon the ability of lump sum recipients to make their lump sum last. Major policy innovations in the area of injury and disability support, such as the NDIS and NIIS schemes (including long running life-time care and support schemes)[14] have been introduced at least partly on the premise that support for lifetime care and support for the injured is more efficiently and effectively provided on an ongoing, as required basis, rather than as a single point in time lump sum.[15]

Yet, despite existing evidence, lawyer interest groups have consistently favoured lump sum damages. Key lawyer interest groups, such as the Australian Lawyers' Alliance (ALA), have actively campaigned in recent years against reforms which would restrict lump sum common law damages.[16] This has been successful in some jurisdictions, for example in Queensland and Western Australia, where injured plaintiffs who can prove fault retain the right to claim ongoing care and support costs in a lump sum rather than through the state NIIS schemes.[17] Why do lawyers so strongly support lump sums? One possible answer to this question lies in potential lawyer self-interest. Personal injury litigation is, of course, fee producing for personal injury lawyers. Out of pocket legal fees will typically be paid out of lump sum payments. Lump sums are a secure fund to meet lawyer fees and it is in lawyers' financial interest to promote maximum lump sum payments over other ways of compensating claimants such as periodic payment or no-fault type schemes. While

[12] ibid. See also discussion in Ch 11 of this volume: P Vines, 'Addressing the Problems of Lump Sum Dissipation and Social Security Denial after Compensation: The Lawyer Contribution'.

[13] See Luntz, above, n 1, 29–49; Productivity Commission, above, n 7, Ch 17.

[14] For example, the Lifetime Care and Support Scheme in NSW and the Transport Accident Compensation scheme in Victoria.

[15] See Productivity Commission, above, n 7, Ch 17.

[16] The ALA has made a large number of submissions to both state and Commonwealth inquiries in recent years lobbying against attempts to limit lump sum common law damages. For eg see Australian Lawyers' Alliance, above, n 4. Further ALA submissions are available at www.lawyersalliance.com.au/resources/submissions. See also Law Society of New South Wales, *CTP Proposals*, www.lawsociety.com.au/advocacy-and-resources/advocacy/policy-submissions/CTP-proposals.

[17] For example, the Western Australian NIIS motor vehicle lifetime care and support scheme only covers claimants who cannot prove fault of another driver: see Motor Vehicle (Catastrophic Injuries) Act 2016 (WA). In Queensland, plaintiffs who are not at fault or less than 25 per cent contributorily negligent can elect to claim lump sum lifetime care and support damages rather than participate in the NIIS scheme: see National Injury Insurance Scheme (Queensland) Act 2016.

this answer is convenient and may provide a partial response to the complex question, we doubt lawyer self-interest (at least in a conscious sense) is the main reason that personal injury lawyers like lump sums. First, there are clear issues with funding actions for civil justice for many claimants, particularly with few legal aid resources available in this area. This is an area of often unmet legal need.[18] Consequently, lawyers cannot be blamed for utilising lump sums as a form of litigation funding for injured plaintiffs who could otherwise not access justice at all. Second, for personal injury lawyers lump sums represent and embody key inviolable values in the law: autonomy; personal freedom; individualism; formal justice; and freedom from unwarranted state interference.[19] Lawyer attraction to these values as sacrosanct has to be understood in light of the very limited training lawyers receive in empirical effects of the law in action or evidence-based policy making.[20] It also has to be understood in the context of personal injury law, including tort law, being primarily seen by lawyers as an instrument of corrective justice and deterrence.[21] This probably seems alien to health or compensation policy researchers, who are more likely to focus on matters such as the long-term health impacts of the tort compensation system on claimants.[22] Third, personal injury lawyers indicate dissatisfaction with the 'drip-feed' nature of periodic payment systems of support, which require injured claimants to continue to interact (potentially for a lifetime) with bureaucracies or insurance companies.[23] Submissions along these lines typically rely on anecdotal accounts of individual clients who have experienced difficulties through the claim process or who wish to completely finalise their interactions with the compensation system as a matter of psychological health. These claims have some validity. However, they tend to ignore evidence that the common law system of tort compensation through lump sum itself may have a propensity to cause psychological harm and inhibit health recovery.[24] In addition, these forms of claim downplay the risk of harm that occurs when lump sums run out, long after lawyers cease contact with claimants. Finally, lawyers like lump sums as they see lump sums as potentially providing a source of funding to purchase a suitable property, particularly where an injured claimant otherwise would not have the means to do so.[25] Again, this (on its face) is not an immediately absurd reason to like lump sums. Security of appropriate accommodation is an important aspect of injury recovery

[18] C Coumarelos et al, 'Personal Injury Problems: New Insights from the Legal Australia-Wide Survey' (2017) 22 *Justice Issues* 1.

[19] See eg above, n 4 and n 16.

[20] K Burns and T Hutchinson, 'The Impact of "Empirical Facts" on Legal Scholarship and Legal Research Training' (2009) 43 *The Law Teacher* 153; F Bell, 'Empirical Research in Law' (2016) 25(2) *Griffith Law Review* 262.

[21] Luntz et al, above, n 1, 77–83, 95–96.

[22] For example, see MJ Spittal et al, 'Development of Prediction Models of Stress and Long-Term Disability Among Claimants to Injury Compensation Systems: A Cohort Study' (2018) 8 *BMJ Open*.

[23] See above, n 16.

[24] Spittal, above, n 22. See the chapters by Ian Cameron and Alex Collie in this volume.

[25] See above, n 16. In the context of the UK see also Ipsos MORI Social Research Institute, *Personal Injury Discount Rate Research* (UK, Ministry of Justice, 2013) 42, which reported that claimants in the study typically reported housing and home modifications as an initial priority after settlement.

and contributes to positive long-term health outcomes.[26] However, as we discuss below, expenditure of lump sums on housing may not in fact be a 'safe' or appropriate way to spend a lump sum, once the complex interaction between tort system of common law compensation and social security, NDIS and NIIS legislation is more closely examined. In other words, the ability to purchase housing may often not be a justifiable reason to favour lump sums.

II. The Interaction between Social Security, NDIS, NIIS and Lump Sums

The interaction between social security law and personal injury law is a key factor in understanding why and how personal injury claimants may prematurely dissipate compensation.[27] Vines notes in her chapter in this book, that one of the lawyer factors which may drive premature dissipation of personal injury compensation is 'legal silos'.[28] In her study, Vines identified a 'profound' gap between social security lawyers and personal injury lawyers, with neither group necessarily understanding the processes associated with the other's work.[29] It may also be the case that personal injury lawyers may not have a comprehensive understanding of the intersection between common law personal injury claims and the NDIS and NIIS schemes. It is essential to understand the interaction between personal injury compensation, the social security system, the NDIS and the NIIS, given that there has been a deliberate government policy agenda to ensure that personal injury claimants cannot 'double-dip'.[30]

When an injured person receives lump sum compensation,[31] whether via settlement or via determination by a Court, the Social Security Act 1991 (Cth) (SSA) provides for a preclusion period from being able to receive compensation-affected social security benefits.[32] Where there is major or catastrophic injury, and larger settlements, these preclusion periods may stretch for many years.[33]

[26] Wright et al, above, n 8.

[27] See GM Grant et al, 'When Lumps Sums Run Out: Disputes at the Borderlines of Tort Law, Injury Compensation and Social Security' in K Barker et al, *Private Law in the 21st Century* (Oxford, Hart Publishing, 2017).

[28] Vines, above, n 12.

[29] ibid.

[30] P Vines et al, 'When Lump Sum Compensation Runs Out: Personal Responsibility or Legal System Failure? (2017) 39 *Sydney Law Review* 365, 373.

[31] Section 17(2) of the Social Security Act 1991 (Cth) (SSA) defines compensation as including a payment of damages, a payment under a State or Commonwealth insurance scheme, a payment in settlement of a claim for damages, and any other compensation or damages payment. The preclusion period can also apply to certain periodical payments, although these are not the focus of this chapter.

[32] SSA, Part 3.14, SSA, ss 1169–1170. For further discussion of social security preclusion see Vines et al, above, n 30, 381–84; Grant et al, above, n 27, 304–305.

[33] See eg *Tyropanis and Secretary, Department of Social Services (Social Services Second Review)* [2015] AATA 701 where a claimant with severe work injuries was precluded from benefits for almost 17 years.

Precluded social security benefits include the age pension, disability support pension, sickness allowance, parenting payment, carer payment, and Newstart (unemployment benefit).[34] The preclusion period is calculated by dividing the compensation part of a lump sum by the 'income cut-out amount'.[35] Importantly, the SSA provides for a presumption that 50 per cent of a gross settlement lump sum which includes any amount for loss of earnings or earning capacity is considered the 'compensation part of a judgment' (the 50 per cent rule).[36] This occurs regardless of whether 50 per cent of the settlement sum can actually be attributed to loss of income and occurs based on the gross lump sum without deduction of legal fees and medical fees.[37] The impact of these provisions is that a claimant may have a preclusion period from income support calculated based on compensation they did not actually receive for income support and based on compensation they never actually received in their pocket as it was deducted prior to payment for legal or medical fees. There are clear inequities in the application of the SSA, which itself contributes to premature dissipation of lump sum compensation.[38] For example, the 50 per cent rule significantly disadvantages seriously injured people whose future care awards constitute the majority of their lump sum settlement.[39] The situation is worsened where an injured person spends a large amount of a lump sum on housing, where the social security preclusion period has been calculated based on utilising those same funds for ongoing income support. In addition, recipients of compensation may be precluded from receiving the aged pension even where their lump sum only included an allowance for economic loss up to retirement age. Where 'special circumstances' exist, an injured person may apply for all or part of their compensation payment to be treated as not paid, thereby shortening or waiving their preclusion period.[40] This review discretion is initially exercised by the Secretary of the Department of Human Services (or delegate at Centrelink) with a two-stage administrative review of that decision through the Administrative Appeals Tribunal (AAT). However, as we discuss below expenditure of lump

[34] SSA, s 17; SSA, s 1161.

[35] SSA, s 17(8). As Grant et al, above, n 27, 304 fn 21 discuss, this amount is a set indexed amount which does not take into account factors personal to the claimant (for example the number of dependants). The amount utilised in the calculation is static – ie it is not updated to reflect changes in social security benefits or individual circumstances over the course of the preclusion period. The impact of this is to prejudice compensation recipients by lengthening their preclusion period which is calculated at the commencement of the preclusion period and not indexed over time.

[36] SSA, s 17(3). This is known as the 50 per cent rule.

[37] Legal fees are only excluded from the lump sum for the purposes of calculation of the preclusion period where they are yet to be determined at the time of settlement.

[38] Vines et al, above, n 30, 381–84.

[39] See for example *Welch and Secretary, Department of Family and Community Services* [2003] AATA 905, where the catastrophically injured claimant received $1,408,213 in lump sum settlement, of which $304,173 was in respect of past loss of earnings and future loss of earning capacity, but an initial compensation preclusion period of over 22 years applied based on 50 per cent of lump sum (ie $704,106).

[40] SSA, s 1184K.

sums on housing (where the housing is an asset that can be liquidated) is not generally considered by itself to be a special circumstance to waive a preclusion period.[41]

Similarly, supports available to injured people pursuant to the NDIS are not intended to replace funding for lifetime care and support costs which have been included in lump sum compensation.[42] Participant funding for reasonable and necessary supports from the NDIS can be reduced (the 'compensation reduction amount') where the participant recovered funding for supports in their compensation payment.[43] Similar to the social security arrangements, the NDIA can ignore or reduce the 'compensation reduction amount' where special circumstances exist.[44] There are potential implications of these provisions for claimants who would be eligible for NDIS support, but who have had the funding for those supports reduced due to their receipt of compensation. Where a significant amount of a lump sum provided (notionally) for lifetime care and support has been spent instead on housing, a claimant may find themselves with reduced or no entitlement to NDIS funding and with no personal funds to self-fund necessary support. The implications of this may be extreme for those with catastrophic injury who require extensive day-to-day care. Similar risks may arise in some state NIIS schemes. For example, in Queensland the relevant NIIS motor vehicle and work lifetime care and support schemes have retained an ability for claimants to take lifetime care and support costs as part of their lump sum and to choose to not participate in the NIIS scheme. This choice results in exclusion from the NIIS for at least five years.[45]

[41] Australian Government, *Social Security Guide*, Version 1.253, (20 March 2019), 4.13.4.10 guides.dss.gov.au/guide-social-security-law/4/13/4/10. Special circumstances must be 'markedly different to the usual run of cases', see *Beadle v Director of Social Security* (1985) 7 ALD 670. Factors which influence whether the discretion is applied include whether the applicant's circumstances are unusual, unforeseen or exceptional. See Australian Government, *Social Security Guide*, above, 4.13.4.20, guides.dss.gov.au/guide-social-security-law/4/13/4/20.

[42] National Disability Insurance Scheme (Support for Participants-Accounting for Compensation) Rules 2013 (Cth) (Compensation Rules); NDIS, *Compensation Operational Guideline*, www.ndis.gov.au/about-us/operational-guidelines/compensation-operational-guideline. For further discussion of the untidy interaction between tort compensation and the NDIS see H Luntz, 'Compensation Recovery and the National Disability Insurance Scheme' (2013) 20 *Torts Law Journal* 153.

[43] Compensation Rules 3.4–3.16. The calculation of the compensation reduction amount includes an allowance for an amount which represents any social security preclusion so that the NDIS participant is not prejudiced by both the existence of a social security preclusion period and a separate calculation of a compensation reduction amount.

[44] National Disability Insurance Scheme Act 2013 (Cth) (NDIS Act), s 116; Compensation Rule 3.10. The factors affecting whether or not special circumstances exist are undefined at this stage other than by reference to financial hardship. There are no current reported AAT appeals from NDIA determinations of whether special circumstances exist in relation to compensation reduction.

[45] National Injury Insurance Scheme (Queensland) Act 2016 (QLD), s 12, s 17(4); Workers' Compensation and Rehabilitation Act 2003 (QLD) s 232ZC, s 232ZD.

III. How Do Compensation Recipients Spend Lump Sums?

There is little reliable evidence in Australia (or internationally) about how much compensation is actually received by personal injury claimants, how money is spent or invested, and how long lump sum settlements last.[46] While some people may administer their lump sums effectively for a lifetime with good financial management, others dissipate their lump sum compensation very quickly.[47] It is unknown what proportion of compensation recipients overall spend their compensation prematurely.[48] It is evident that claimants with very serious injuries face a significant risk of under-compensation and premature dissipation of common law settlements.[49] Sometimes lump sums do run out, often with disastrous consequences for personal injury claimants.[50] We suspect, based on existing studies, that premature dissipation of compensation is a serious problem particularly for vulnerable individuals.[51]

A range of complex and inter-dependent factors have been found to contribute to premature dissipation of lump sums. A compensation lump sum is a once and for all payment, ostensibly deemed to deliver corrective justice, placing the claimant back into the position they were in (at least financially) prior to injury. However, statutory limits on heads of damages, discounts to lump sums to account

[46] Vines et al, above, n 30, 366–68; Grant et al, above, n 27, 302–303, 310. The Grant and Vines studies are amongst the first Australian studies to provide empirical evidence of lump sum dissipation.

[47] The Grant et al study, above, n 27, of compensation recipients appealing their social security preclusion appeals to the AAT found 248 AAT review decisions between 2004–2014 where a claimant claimed special circumstances after dissipating their lump sum. The average time of dissipation from common law resolution to AAT decision was 2.9 years (with actual dissipation likely to be much earlier).

[48] ibid. Lack of monitoring of financial management of lump sum settlements is not unique to Australia. In the UK there has been recent consideration of how people spend and invest lump sum compensation as part of an inquiry into discount rates in that country. The lack of reliable evidence base has been identified. See House of Commons Justice Committee, *Pre-legislative Scrutiny: Draft Personal Injury Discount Rate Clause, Third Report of Session 2017–19* (28 November 2017), publications.parliament.uk/pa/cm201719/cmselect/cmjust/374/374.pdf, 18.

[49] See Productivity Commission, above, n 7, 807–809; Vines et al, above, n 30. Grant et al, above, n 27, in review of 24 AAT preclusion period decisions involving claimants seriously injured in motor vehicle accidents (study 2) found that settlements for claimants with quadriplegia were substantially lower than the average lifetime care costs of $5.6 million for higher level quadriplegia cited in the Australian Productivity Commission Report, ranging from $165,750 to $1.8 million in the cases reviewed.

[50] See for example, Grant et al, above, n 27, 318–19 for discussion of *Secretary Department of Employment and Workplace Relations and Lloyd* [2007] AATA 26 involving a compensation recipient with quadriplegia.

[51] See Vines et al, above, n 30; Grant et al, above, n 27. Both of these studies identify groups of injured people who are probably the 'tip of iceberg'. For example, the Grant study considers social security preclusion appeals at the second review level of the AAT. It is clear that there probably were many more claimants who had grounds to appeal on the basis of special circumstances but did not do so; had appeals determined internally by Centrelink review officers or at the first level review by the AAT; or who settled or conciliated prior to final AAT determination. See Grant et al, above, n 27, 301–11 and fn 29. The Vines study included a file review of a group of 58 clients from the Welfare Rights Centre of New South Wales.

for projected investment returns, contributory negligence and deductions to reflect the vicissitudes of life, mean that damages often do not meet this requirement even at the time they are awarded.[52] Deduction of legal and medical fees, and repayment of any government benefits received prior to settlement, further reduce the amount of money actually received by injured claimants.[53]

In addition to the initial receipt of an inadequate lump sum, the severe and permanent nature of injury can make it unlikely that a claimant will be able to return to work.[54] Thus, there is limited potential to supplement lump sums with work-related income in the years following injury. Access to alternative sources of income may also be limited. As we note above, social security preclusion periods may significantly impact claimants and contribute to premature dissipation.[55] Rising care costs[56] and claimants outliving their projected life expectancy[57] may also contribute to early dissipation of settlement funds.

Vines, Butt and Grant identified inability to manage funds as the most notable 'personal' reason for early dissipation of settlement funds in their review of cases where the Welfare Rights Centre (WRC) of New South Wales acted for people subject to a lump sum preclusion period between 2012 and 2014.[58] While lump sum payments enable recipients to make their own choices regarding how to invest or spend their settlement funds, most are ill-equipped to manage large sums of money over a prolonged period of time.[59] Claimants may face pressures to give money away to relatives and friends[60] or may be legally required to do so in the advent of marital or de facto relationship breakdown.[61] Additionally, debts

[52] B Madden and T Cockburn, 'Full Compensation No Longer Sacrosanct: Reflections on the Past and Future Economic Loss "Cap" for High Earners' (2012) 20 *Torts Law Journal* 90, 91; Vines et al, above, n 30, 375–80; Grant et al, above, n 27, 311–13.

[53] See for example *Tyropanis and Secretary, Department of Social Security (Social Services Second Review)* [2015] AATA 701 where a claimant only received $649,000.00 of $1,494,492.43 settlement. For further discussion see Vines et al, above, n 30, and Grant et al, above, n 27.

[54] See Vines et al, above, n 30, where many claimants met eligibility requirements for disability support pension due to their existing level of disability.

[55] See for example *Welch and Secretary, Department of Family and Community Services* [2003] AATA 905 where the catastrophically injured claimant received $1,408,213.00 in lump sum settlement of which $304,173 was in respect of past loss of earnings and future loss of earning capacity, but compensation preclusion period of over 22 years applied based on 50 per cent of lump sum (ie $704,106). The preclusion period was varied based on claimant's personal circumstances including claimants 'medical conditions', 'inability to provide for himself physically or financially', 'his parent's aged and declining ability to care for him', and 'probable need for increasingly expensive care arrangements'. This judgment is in contrast to similar cases where the preclusion period was not varied – see for example *Jeffrey and Secretary, Department of Families, Housing, Community Services and Indigenous Affairs* [2009] AATA 471.

[56] See R Harrington, 'Meeting Lifetime Care Costs – Are Current Models Sustainable?' (2009) *Australia Policy Online*, www.apo.org.au/commentary/meeting-lifetime-care-costs. Real increases in care costs over time were also identified as a potential source of under-compensation in House of Commons Justice Committee, above, n 48, 14.

[57] ibid.

[58] Vines et al, above, n 30, 388.

[59] See *O'Neill and Secretary Department of Education Employment and Workplace Relations* [2009] AATA 919, [38]; Productivity Commission, above, n 7, 807.

[60] Grant et al, above, n 27, 317.

[61] ibid.

incurred during the pre-settlement period need to be repaid to friends, families and creditors.[62] Settlements awarded to cover lost income are understandably spent on daily living costs, bills, furniture, cars, equipment, entertainment and travel.[63] Faced with volatile financial markets and uncertain investment returns, some claimants take matters into their own hands and invest in share trading, business ventures or the property market, sometimes sustaining substantial losses.[64] Gambling, drug and alcohol addictions also contribute to early dissipation of compensation funds.[65]

Vines et al[66] argue that risks of early dissipation may be linked to social disadvantage, with 79 per cent of clients in their study reporting mental health problems as part of their presentation. Involvement in the compensation-seeking process itself has been found to adversely affect mental health,[67] and it is not unreasonable to suggest that those experiencing mental health issues may be more likely to accept inadequate and early settlements to minimise this impact. Additionally, recent research indicates that people with a history of mental illness may experience a heightened vulnerability to both injury[68] and its damaging impacts on mental health.[69] In this context, it is perhaps unsurprising that compensation recipients appear to most frequently spend lump sums on housing.[70] The purchase of housing can provide a sense of security for claimants dealing with the stressful sequelae of traumatic injury. Indeed, applicants in some AAT cases report

[62] Donations and debt repayments, and loans or gifts to others were reported expenditures from settlement funds in the majority of AAT preclusion period appeals involving claimants seriously injured in motor vehicle accidents reviewed by Grant et al, above, n 27, 317–18.

[63] Grant et al, above, n 27, 317.

[64] Grant et al, above, n 27, 317. See, for example, *Secretary Department of Employment and Workplace Relations and Lloyd* [2007] AATA 26; *Zhang and Secretary, Department of Social Services (Social Services Second Review)* [2015] AATA 668; *Whittal and Secretary, Department of Social Services* [2015] AATA 129.

[65] See Productivity Commission, above, n 7, 808. Gambling, and drug and alcohol addictions contributed to early dissipation in 50 per cent (8 of 16) of AAT preclusion period appeals involving claimants seriously injured in motor vehicle accidents in the Grant study (above, n 27), and 31 per cent (18 of 58) of WRC cases of early dissipation reviewed by Vines et al in 2017 (above, n 30).

[66] Vines et al, above, n 27.

[67] M O'Donnell et al, 'Compensation Seeking and Disability After Injury: The Role of Compensation-Related Stress and Mental Health' (2015) 76(8) *The Journal of Clinical Psychiatry* 1000; N Elbers et al, 'Do Compensation Processes Impair Mental Health? A Meta-Analysis' (2013) 44(5) *Injury. International Journal of the Care of the Injured* 674.

[68] M O'Donnell et al, 'Prior Trauma and Psychiatric History as Risk Factors for Intentional and Unintentional Injury in Australia' (2009) 66(2) *Journal of Trauma: Injury, Infection and Critical Care* 470.

[69] R Bryant et al, 'The Psychiatric Sequelae of Traumatic Injury' (2010) 167(3) *American Journal of Psychiatry* 312. See also Vines et al, above, n 30, 373 fn 25.

[70] Settlement funds were spent on property purchase in most AAT preclusion period appeals involving claimants seriously injured in motor vehicle accidents in the Grant study (above, n 27). Similarly, expenditure on housing was the most common way of using the lump sum among people who had run out of money in the Vines study (above, n 30). See also Ipsos MORI Social Research Institute (above, n 25) where purchase of housing was found to be the most reported initial priority for expenditure of compensation funds.

deliberately investing in housing to avoid frivolous spending of their remaining settlement funds[71] and ensure their dependants had 'a roof over their heads'.[72]

IV. Housing and Lump Sum Dissipation: A Content Analysis Study

As we note above, there is an absence of publicly available empirical data on how recipients of compensation spend their funds. One source of publicly available information about expenditure of compensation is reported AAT appeals involving compensation recipients appealing their social security preclusion periods to access social security when they have prematurely dissipated their compensation. Our previous review of AAT social security preclusion period appeals involving claimants severely injured in motor vehicle accidents revealed that many had purchased housing.[73] The preclusion period was not altered in many of these cases, due to the existence of a realisable asset – the claimant's home. It could reasonably be inferred that these claimants were subsequently placed in a position where they would need to sell, let, or effectively 'eat' their home via reverse mortgage arrangements, to fund their daily cost of living and care needs. In these cases, use of lump sums for home purchase appeared an unwise investment option. To investigate this issue further, we completed an additional study involving content analysis of all available AAT social security preclusion period appeals over a five-year time period.[74]

For this study, we searched the AAT database in AustLII[75] using the key term '1184K' for the calendar years 2013–2017. This is the section of the SSA which relates to waiver or reduction of preclusion periods in special circumstances. The initial search yielded 83 AAT cases which involved a lump sum compensation payment.[76] Cases which met the following criteria were included in the analysis: the claimant had been injured at work, in a motor vehicle accident or from other causes; they were applying for a reduction or waiver in their preclusion period for government benefits; and, they had spent some of their settlement funds on

[71] See *QHBN and Secretary, Department of Social Services (Social Services Second Review)* [2015] AATA 614 where the claimant invested in cabin and land to avoid gambling money away.

[72] *Seears and Secretary, Department of Social Services (Social Services Second Review)* [2015] AATA 656.

[73] Grant et al, above, n 27, 315–19 (Study 2).

[74] There are three levels of review of decisions made under the SSA. The initial level of review is an internal review within Centrelink. There are then two further levels of review within the AAT: the first by the Social Services and Child Support Division of the AAT; and a second review by the General Division of the AAT. This study concerns the AAT second review decisions which are the only review decisions publicly available.

[75] Australasian Legal Information Institute, *Administrative Appeals Tribunal database*, www.austlii.edu.au/cgi-bin/viewdb/au/cases/cth/AATA/.

[76] As we note above, n 51, AAT second review cases are likely the 'tip' of the iceberg where recipients of lump sums have prematurely expended their lump sums.

housing purchase. Thirty-nine of the initial 83 cases were excluded as they did not meet the inclusion criteria. We completed detailed content analysis of the remaining 44 cases (53 per cent of cases) which involved spending on housing, to determine whether preclusion periods were waived or varied due to special circumstances, and for what reason. Our finding that 53 per cent of the preclusion cases we identified involved spending on housing, supports findings from other studies which suggest that lump sums are frequently spent on housing and this may be a major reason for premature lump sum dissipation.[77]

Cases were coded[78] to record the sex of the claimants, type of injury sustained, type of claim (work, motor vehicle or other), the state or territory in which the AAT appeal was heard, the amount of lump sum settlement, the amount of money claimants reported receiving post settlement (where available), the amount spent on home purchase or to pay off the balance of a home loan, and whether or not special circumstances were found, and preclusion periods varied or waived. A summary of the results of this content analysis is presented in Appendix 1.[79] As illustrated in Appendix 1, the majority of claimants were males (36/44, or 82 per cent of claimants), with workplace injury being the most common claim type (27/44, or 61.4 per cent).[80] Lump sum compensation settlements ranged from $137,154 to $1.675 million, with a median settlement sum of $617, 500 and a mean settlement sum of $669, 567. These large median and mean settlement sums are indicative of the severity of injury sustained by claimants. However, insufficiency of lump sum compensation appeared, in itself, to be a major factor contributing to early dissipation of settlement sums. For example, the highest lump sum settlement of $1.657 million awarded to a man sustaining quadriplegia in a motor vehicle accident in Queensland (Case 36/2013) appeared quite low for this type of injury.[81] In addition, as can be seen in Appendix 1, the amount of money claimants reported actually receiving, after costs and other deductions, was often significantly less than the original lump sum. For example, a male claimant severely injured in a motor vehicle accident (Case 82/2016), notionally received a lump

[77] See above, n 70.

[78] We used a similar method to that adopted in the studies in Grant et al, above, n 27. The cases were coded independently by two coders applying coding instructions which were developed, piloted and refined on a sample of cases. An Access database was used to record and generate data on variables of interest. In relation to the use of content analysis to analyse judicial decisions see K Burns, 'The Australian High Court and Social Facts: A Content Analysis Study' (2012) 40 *Federal Law Review* 317, 322–26.

[79] Appendix 1 includes case reference, gender of applicant, nature of injury, amount of lump sum, amount of funds actually received by the claimant (where known), amount spent on housing (where known), whether special circumstances were found and whether the applicant had legal representation at the AAT review.

[80] There were 15 motor vehicle injury cases, one public liability case, and one case where the injury was of unknown origin. In the first Grant study of AAT appeals from 2004–2014, 69 per cent of claimants were male and work injury claims were also the most common (61 per cent of claims). See Grant et al, above, n 27, 307.

[81] *McCormick and Secretary, Department of Families, Housing, Community Services and Indigenous Affairs* [2013] AATA 36. As noted in Grant et al, above, n 27, 313 fn 46, in 2011 the Productivity Commission estimated average lifetime care costs for quadriplegic with high level needs at $5.6 million.

sum of $950,000, however reported to the AAT actually receiving after deductions and costs over $400,000 less.[82] Another claimant with a work-related back injury (Case 905/2015) notionally received a lump sum of $950,000 yet reported to the AAT actually receiving $500,000 less.[83] In one of the worst cases in our study, a claimant with severe work-related injuries (Case 701/2015), settled for a lump sum of $1.49 million, only to actually receive, after costs and deductions, $649, 000.[84] In all of these cases, the impact of the 50 per cent rule which calculated preclusion periods based on total lump sums (rather than the amount actually received by the claimant) was a likely source of injustice and contributed to premature dissipation.

As can be seen in Appendix 1, the amount spent on housing (where this could be identified) was frequently a large proportion of the overall lump sum and (consequently) of the actual amount of the compensation received by the claimant. The amount spent on housing ranged from only $35,617 (Case 680/2014)[85] to $665,000 (Case 337/2015).[86] For example, in Case 337/2015 the claimant settled for a lump sum of $550,000, actually received $500,000 of that sum in the hand, and spent $665,000 on housing. In Case 41/2015 the claimant settled for a lump sum of $1,025,000, actually received $516,236.65 and spent $409,000 on housing.[87] Overall, despite this the amount spent on housing (where known) might be considered to be relatively modest compared to the average cost of residential housing in Australia during the period.[88]

Preclusion periods were waived or varied on the basis of special circumstances in only 14 of the 44 cases (32 per cent) where compensation recipients had spent funds on housing. Only 7 of the 44 applicants had some form of legal representation at their hearings.[89] Analysis of the AAT decisions revealed an apparent lack of consistency in application of SSA, s 1184K in relation to what constitutes 'special circumstances'. This was to be expected due to the discretionary and multifactorial nature of the meaning of 'special circumstances'.[90] However, our findings highlight the inherent risks involved in using lump sum compensation for housing purchase for at least

[82] *Davis and Secretary, Department of Social Services (Social Services Second Review)* [2016] AATA 82.

[83] *Hammelswang and Secretary, Department of Social Services (Social Services Second Review)* [2015] AATA 905.

[84] *Tyropanis and Secretary, Department of Social Services (Social Services Second Review)* [2015] AATA 701.

[85] *Lind and Secretary, Department of Social Services* [2014] AATA 680.

[86] *Pakzad and Secretary, Department of Employment* [2015] AATA 337.

[87] *Cooper; Secretary, Department of Social Services and Housing* [2015] AATA 41.

[88] For example, the mean price of a residential dwelling in Australia in December quarter in 2013 was $539,400. See Australian Bureau of Statistics, *Residential Property Price Indexes: Eight Capital Cities, Dec 2013*, www.abs.gov.au/AUSSTATS/abs@.nsf/allprimarymainfeatures/D096F22C811A8AF2CA257CD60017CB90?opendocument. The mean price of a residential dwelling in Australia in the December quarter in 2017 was $686,700. See Australian Bureau of Statistics, *Residential Property Price Indexes: Eight Capital Cities, Dec 2017*, www.abs.gov.au/AUSSTATS/abs@.nsf/allprimarymainfeatures/427EF49AD5DE3757CA2582B000171F5A?opendocument.

[89] See Appendix 1. Note that despite legal representation, in only two of those cases was the claimant successful in arguing that special circumstances existed.

[90] See above, n 41.

some compensation recipients. While previous research has suggested that AAT applicants are generally not required to sell their home or a modest motor vehicle in order for preclusion periods to be waived,[91] in most of the cases we reviewed this was not the case. Surprisingly, cases with similar circumstances were often viewed differently, with preclusion periods varied in some, and not in others.

The Social Security Guide relating to factors to consider when determining special consideration provisions indicates that special circumstances would generally not be applied where a person has realisable assets to support themselves and their family, and 'where people choose to wantonly/irresponsibly spend all of their compensation proceeds and do not set aside sufficient funds to meet their living costs during the preclusion period'.[92] Mr N (Case 14/2015)[93] used $390,000 (the 'bulk' of the money he actually received) to purchase a house, together with a reverse mortgage of $130,000. He and his wife chose to purchase the house in full knowledge that a lengthy preclusion period would be applied. They reported making the decision to use the bulk of Mr N's settlement funds after careful consideration of their financial situation and Mr N's deteriorating health. At the time they anticipated Mrs N would be able to return to part-time employment to help fund their income needs. However, by the time of their preclusion period appeal, less than two years later they had minimal bank account savings, multiple debts owing, and Mrs N had not returned to work. The couple reported seeking financial advice to help manage their funds and maintained that they had never engaged in frivolous or unnecessary spending of funds. Additionally, Mr N's doctor reported that Mr N had experienced a recurrence of major depression, and that it would be potentially detrimental to his mental health, and the psychological wellbeing of his family, to be forced to sell his house. Mr N had acquired his injury at the age of 67 and claimed that his loss of income had been calculated based on a retirement age of 70. In view of this, the family's financial circumstances, and Mr N's ongoing health issues, the preclusion period was shortened to the time of Mr N's 70th birthday, which pre-dated the time of settlement.

Mr S (Case 656/2015)[94] also chose to spend the majority of his settlement funds on housing, but with a much less favourable outcome. He was awarded $550,000 for a workplace injury, and after paying $105,000 in legal costs, invested in a home at the cost of $310,000. He reported making the decision to purchase a home to ensure his children 'had a roof over their heads' after receiving financial advice that 'the lump sum would not generate sufficient income to live off'. Similar to Mrs N, Mrs S reported that she had given up employment to care for her family prior to settlement, as Mr S was suffering depression and having difficulty

[91] K Tranter and J Kelly, 'Private Motor Vehicle Ownership in Australian Social Security Law' (2014) 21 *Journal of Social Security Law* 32.

[92] See above, n 41. The guide does not bind the AAT, however regard can be had to it to the extent that it is consistent with the legislation. See *Drake and Minister for Immigration and Ethnic Affairs (No 2)* (1979) 46 FLR 409.

[93] *Nelson and Secretary, Department of Social Services* [2015] AATA 405.

[94] *Seears and Secretary, Department of Social Services (Social Services Second Review)* [2015] AATA 656.

coping. Mr S tried to return to work when his settlement funds ran out but was unable to do so. He maintained that he had not been informed by his legal advisers that a lump sum preclusion period would be applied, and that he would not have accepted the settlement offered had he known this at the time. There was no mention of Centrelink directly advising Mr S of his preclusion period prior to his home purchase. The AAT member in this case acknowledged that Mr S had 'acted responsibly at all times, seeking financial advice, investing in a home for his family, and avoiding unnecessary expenditure'. However, his home ownership tainted his claim of financial hardship and his preclusion period was not altered or varied. The existence of an unencumbered home and a wife willing to return to work, if a suitable position could be found, weighed against a finding of special circumstances sufficient to alter or waive his preclusion period.

In both cases the applicants had acted responsibly, sought financial advice and avoided unnecessary expenditure, but also intentionally deprived themselves of a means of financial support by spending the majority of their settlement funds on home purchase. Special circumstances were recognised in one case but not the other. While this variance in determination appears to be attributable to Mr N's senior years and ill health, it is relevant to note that the tribunal has not considered these reasonable grounds for special consideration in other cases, holding that preclusion from the aged pension post retirement age is an intended consequence of the legislative framework.[95] Instructions regarding what to look for in the case of straitened financial circumstances in the Social Security Guide include consideration of whether there are 'any other avenues of support, eg family/friends who are willing and able to provide the person with free board and lodging until the preclusion period expires'.[96] While Mr N's wife was willing to return to work, the tribunal acknowledged her limited capacity to do so in consideration of Mr N's care needs. By contrast, in Mr S's case the presence of a wife willing to return to work was cited as a reason for not exercising discretion to shorten the preclusion period. One could question Mrs S's capacity to do so, given she reported leaving work to care for her family due to concerns about her husband's depression and difficulty coping. One could assume that this was a decision not taken lightly, given the subsequent loss of income her family incurred during the pre-settlement period.

The wisdom of investing in housing for seriously injured claimants with future care needs appears questionable on the basis of the cases we reviewed. Mr E (Case 1733/2017)[97] received $1.585 million in compensation ($1.48 million which included a gratuitous care component of $184,850, in addition to weekly benefits prior to settlement) after sustaining a spinal cord injury at work. He also was of retirement age on settlement, and Centrelink subsequently informed him that his aged pension would be cancelled as a result of a 17-year preclusion period. Soon after

[95] See *Lind and Secretary, Department of Social Services* [2014] AATA 680; *Chamberlain and Secretary, Department of Family and Community Services* [2002] AATA 487.

[96] See above, n 41.

[97] *Erich and Secretary, Department of Social Services (Social Services Second Review)* [2017] AATA 1733.

settlement, Mr E and his wife purchased, renovated and sold in quick succession two houses, and purchased and sold a motor home, before finally buying a motorhome for around $217,000 which was modified to meet Mr E's needs. At the time of the AAT hearing, five years post settlement, Mrs E reported that apart from $5,000, all the money from the settlement was gone, and they had nothing left to sell other than the motorhome they lived in. Mrs E acknowledged that they had lived as if they were still working, spending money on a cruise and travelling extensively to visit family as they did not think they would live that long, and were determined to live to the fullest. With her husband's disability and her worry about ongoing expenses, Mrs E reported that she needed to travel for her mental health. However, due to the 'profligate' nature of the couple's spending (including $335,000 which was unaccounted for) and the presence of a realisable asset, no grounds for special circumstances were found. It was not considered unreasonable that the couple sell their home to fund Mr E's living expenses for the remaining nine years of the preclusion period. On face value, this decision appears reasonable given the nature of the couple's spending. However, the stated aim of the preclusion period summarised in the Guide to Social Security Law[98] is to ensure 'that people who are unable to work because of a compensable injury are prevented from receiving income support from both the social security and compensation systems for the same period'. It is unlikely that the economic loss component of Mr E's settlement covered a period of 17 years, given he was injured one year before retirement age and his settlement included a large award for gratuitous care. It is likely that a large proportion of his lump sum compensation was awarded for future care, significantly extending the preclusion period he would have been subject to in the absence of this head of damage. The AAT has highlighted that it is manifestly unjust to impose a lengthy preclusion period on age pensioners in other cases.[99] Additionally, while profligate spending was evident in Mr E's case, special circumstances have been found in other AAT appeals involving extravagant or reckless spending on the part of claimants.[100] Mrs E advocated on Mr E's behalf during the hearing, with no involvement of a legal advocate on the couple's behalf. As we discuss above, this was not unusual in the cases reviewed, with only 7 of the 44 cases involving legal representation for the applicant.

V. Implications and Conclusion

The provision of housing is an important aspect of ensuring improved long-term health outcomes for people with a significant disability because of injury.[101]

[98] See above, n 41.

[99] See *Secretary Department of Family & Community Services v Kelava* [2003] AATA 834; *Gulcan and Secretary Department of Family and Community Services* [2001] AATA 552; and *Senna and Secretary Department of Family, Housing, Community Services and Indigenous Affairs* [2008] AATA 240.

[100] See for example *Bergan and Secretary, Department of Social Services* [2014] AATA 109; *Byrnes and Secretary, Department of Social Services* [2014] AATA 197.

[101] Wright et al, above, n 8.

Expenditure of lump sum compensation on housing has been argued to be a justification for retention of lump sums, over other forms of periodic compensation delivery such as lifetime care and support schemes. In addition, the ability of an injured person to exercise self-determination and to exercise independent choice about how compensation funds are spent could be considered essential to the human dignity of an individual with disability. There may well be some injured people who can successfully manage a lump sum settlement and make it last, while at the same time using funds for housing. This seems more likely to occur where they receive large lump sums and have a very high standard of financial advice and/or competent financial management. In all cases, there seems to be a large element of luck which influences whether the long-term outcomes will be good and compensation will last long enough to ensure adequate lifetime care and support. However, the justifications for freedom to spend lump sum compensation in the common law collide uncomfortably with the underlying premises of Australian social security legislation, the NDIS and NIIS systems. Rather than individual choice and control about how to spend lump sums, including on housing, the social security and lifetime care and support schemes expect claimants not to 'double-dip' and punish claimants who fail to utilise funds awarded for income support and care and support for those purposes. In fact, as noted above, the impact of the 50 per cent rule and the calculation of preclusion periods based on total lump sum (as opposed to the amount received in the hand by the claimant) may be to unfairly force injured people to expend funds awarded for lifetime care and support for income support.

It is also apparent from our study, and other recent studies, that many recipients of lump sums who have found themselves in financial strife due to preclusion from social security benefits, have spent large amounts of their lump sums on housing. Expenditure of lump sums on housing has not always proved to be a 'safe' investment. Money spent on housing is not 'exempt' from the calculation of social security preclusion periods. In some cases, as our study shows, applicants who have utilised funds to purchase housing can successfully argue for waiver or reduction of their preclusion period, so they can access social security and retain their housing asset. However, in many more cases it appears preclusion periods are not waived, and an injured person's only choice may be to sell the housing asset to survive. In addition, it is unpredictable whether in any given appeal case Centrelink, and ultimately the AAT, will determine that special circumstances exist such that a preclusion period can be waived or varied. In our study, we identified similar cases with very different outcomes. This probably reflects the very discretionary nature of tests such as 'special circumstances', but also other factors such as lack of legal representation for applicants at the time of preclusion appeal.

Given that lump sum preclusion is a 'wicked' multifactorial problem,[102] there are no single solutions. As Vines has argued in her chapter in this book, there are 'lawyer' factors which could better manage to ameliorate or prevent issues

[102] Grant et al, above, n 27, 316.

caused by premature lump sum dissipation.[103] These include breaking down silos between personal injury lawyers and social security lawyers; identifying more carefully vulnerable clients who require financial management; a greater use of structured settlements; mitigating under-compensation; more realistic advice about likely settlement; more focus on appropriate settlements including whether it is appropriate to include economic loss claims[104] and avoidance of costs inclusive settlements;[105] and more detailed advice on the impact of lump sum preclusion periods. There is also an obvious need for compensation recipients to receive appropriate financial advice and perhaps even for the costs of financial management to be included in all large lump sum awards.[106] In addition, issues arise at the interface between damages rules and social security rules.[107] While a person's principal place of residence is an exempt asset for the purposes of all social security payments, housing purchased with compensation funds is not (ordinarily) exempt from the calculation of preclusion periods. As Vines et al argue, this an issue which requires closer attention, with a more nuanced approach, recognising that it is financially reasonable for a person to spend at least a proportion of economic loss compensation on housing costs, and entirely reasonable to spend non-economic general damages on housing.[108] In addition, funding from the NDIS for a person's lifetime care and support is not considered an asset for the purposes of reducing social security, however compensation funds for future care and support can, by virtue of the 50 per cent rule, be included within the amount used to calculate the social security preclusion period.[109] This creates inequities between vulnerable people dependent only on the source from which they received their funds.

The way Australian law deals with compensation for the injured has long been considered fragmented, contradictory and flawed in many ways. This chapter has identified one more piece in that puzzle. Lawyers support the existence of lump sums, at least in part, because they allow an injured person the autonomy to spend compensation on housing. Housing is considered 'secure' and 'safe'. At the same time, the way other systems – such as social security system, the NDIS and NIIS – treat compensation funds results in restrictions on (and sometimes punitive response to) injured people spending their compensation funds on the security of housing. Spending compensation on housing is not, it seems, 'safe as houses'.

[103] Vines, above, n 12.

[104] The inclusion of an economic loss claim, even if weak or minor, results in the settlement sum being considered 'compensation' and accordingly 50 per cent of the sum being used to calculate lump sum preclusion periods.

[105] The impact of costs inclusive settlements is to include legal costs received as part of the settlement in the calculation of the preclusion period. However, where costs are assessed post settlement, these are not included in the calculation of the preclusion period.

[106] At present, allowance for financial management of compensation lump sums are only included in damages awards where the claimant lacks cognitive capacity to manage their own funds. *Gray v Richards* [2014] HCA 40, (2014) 253 CLR 660.

[107] Vines et al, above, n 30, 387–89.

[108] ibid.

[109] SSA, s 1118(1D). See discussion in *Byrnes and Secretary, Department of Social Services* [2014] AATA 197.

Appendix 1: Content Analysis AAT Lump Sum Preclusion Housing Cases 2013–2017

AAT Case Ref	Gender	Nature Injury	Lump Sum ($)	Amount received ($)	Amount spent on housing ($)	Special Circ Found	Legal Rep
19/2013	M	Work	453, 750	unknown	360,000	No	No
36/2013	M	MV	1,657,500	1,657,500	unknown	No	Yes
167/2013	M	MV	325,000	unknown	unknown	No	No
505/2013	M	Work	399,584	unknown	250,000	No	No
586/2013	M	Work	378,941	180,000	100,000	No	No
660/2013	M	Work	395,000	unknown	200,000	No	No
831/2013	M	MV	778,560	unknown	471,725	No	No
109/2014	M	Work	650,000	unknown	unknown	Yes	Yes
172/2014	F	MV	310,000	135,231.53	unknown	No	No
197/2014	M	Work	1,650,000	unknown	542,000	Yes	No
389/2014	M	MV	650,000	481,210.85	400,000	No	No
481/2014	M	Work	733,000	unknown	200,000	No	No
516/2014	M	MV	265,750	unknown	147,000	No	No
657/2014	M	Work	360,000	294,000	306,000	Yes	No
680/2014	F	MV	281,875	172,938.56	35,617	No	Yes
763/2014	M	MV	250,000	121,258	88,483	No	No
825/2014	M	Work	775,000	638,619.22	280,000	Yes	No
41/2015	M	Other	1,025,000	516,236.65	409,000	No	Yes
129/2015	F	MV	725,000	413,000	261,000	Yes	No
165/2015	F	Work	775,000	500,700	315,000	Yes	No
277/2015	M	Work	700,000	576,000	295,000	Yes	No
337/2015	M	Work	550,000	500,000	665,000	No	No
389/2015	M	Work	389,500	286,032.90	50,000	Yes	No
405/2015	M	Work	731,769.97	unknown	390,000	Yes	No
417/2015	F	Work	137,154.72	42,000	unknown	No	No
582/2015	M	Work	1,426,442	unknown	unknown	Yes	No
614/2015	M	Work	330,600	unknown	78,484.88	No	Yes
629/2015	F	MV	780,000	unknown	319,684.25	No	No
656/2015	M	Work	550,000	423,345.82	310,000	No	No
668/2015	M	Work	977,292	528,737.20	200,000	Yes	No
694/2015	M	Work	500,010.	400,000	315,000	No	No
701/2015	M	Work	1,494,492.43	649,000	200,000	Yes	No
905/2015	M	Work	950,000	450,000	120,000	No	No
34/2016	M	Work	425,500	unknown	200,000	Yes	Yes
62/2016	F	MV	693,031.16	unknown	70,000	No	No
82/2016	M	MV	950,000	549,674.44	unknown	No	No
111/2016	M	MV	806,000	770,000	233,800	No	Yes

(continued)

(Continued)

AAT Case Ref	Gender	Nature Injury	Lump Sum ($)	Amount received ($)	Amount spent on housing ($)	Special Circ Found	Legal Rep
637/2016	F	MV	150,000	unknown	50,000	No	No
704/2016	M	Work	354,176.29	unknown	unknown	No	No
712/2016	M	MV	585,000	unknown	167,000	No	No
951/2016	M	Work	882,800	750,000	unknown	No	No
332/2017	M	Work	293,988	unknown	unknown	No	No
1384/2017	M	unknown	375,000	unknown	70,000	Yes	No
1733/2017	M	Work	1,584,850	unknown	unknown	No	No

7

Achieving a Just Culture that Learns and Improves

CHRISTOPHER HODGES*

Organisations where people fear that they will be criticised and in which vital safety information is withheld and not swiftly shared inhibit open cultures and inhibit learning and improvement. Thus, cultures involving blame and adversarial processes for resolving problems should be discarded in favour of open and just cultures, which have proved to be achievable and outstandingly successful in contexts such as aviation safety. The preferred cultures are based on open cooperation between all parties based on trust, which is in turn based on evidence that people can be trusted in the light of their values, purposes and behaviours. In the business context, these elements have been packaged as 'ethical business practice', supported by relationships of trust between businesses and regulators called ethical business regulation. The UK NHS has set the objective of having an open and just culture but faces serious barriers to its attainment. One important barrier is the system for compensating medical accidents, which should shift from negligence and adversarialism to a Nordic-style no-blame administrative compensation scheme model.

I. Overview

This chapter argues that the traditional approach to compensation law, based on a fault liability rule and an adversarial process, has two major disadvantages. First, it is a major barrier to the achievement of the culture that is desirable within the healthcare system and in society generally. Indeed, it is a driver of the wrong culture and behaviour, rather than driving ethical behaviour and culture, and improvements in them. Second, it is not an effective system in the core function of delivering compensation to those who deserve and need it. The traditional system is too slow and costly. It does not effectively deliver *care* (both physical and emotional) when it is needed.

* MA PhD FSALS; Professor of Justice Systems at Oxford University and a Supernumerary Fellow of Wolfson College; Head of the Swiss Re Research Programme on Civil Justice Systems, Centre for Socio-Legal Studies, University of Oxford; and Fellow of the European Law Institute. Research funding is received from the UK Department for Business, Energy & Industrial Strategy, the Swiss Reinsurance Company Limited and the European Justice Forum.

We have two deep systemic problems. First, two institutional systems are in conflict, rather than being aligned – the healthcare system and the legal system. Second, those two systems have different goals and outputs that are not mutually reinforcing (although we thought that they were). The legal system has been thought to support future improved conduct but in fact does not, and can actually impede it. The core assumption is that instances of failure and mistakes occur solely through individual conduct, and can be prevented by waiting until something goes wrong and then imposing a sanction that will deter future reoccurrence. The reality is that, in practice, individuals make mistakes for all sorts of reasons. Many mistakes occur as a result of systemic issues (people working together, or failing to do so, in groups). An approach to affecting future events that waits for an adverse event to occur and then ex post imposes a sanction (financial or otherwise, but based on finding fault and blaming someone) will *not* adequately address future behaviour or systemic issues.

We need to redesign these systems and approaches. This chapter does not state fresh evidence, but aims to take an overview of the currently available evidence on these important issues, so as to draw policy conclusions. The scientific evidence discussed should be of universal application, but the factual examples are from the United Kingdom. Section II first asks what patients want when they experience harm from a healthcare system. Research consistently identifies needs for care, concern, support, and reducing future risk. In section III, I analyse the legal system, its outcomes, and goals (providing money and deterrence). I then note the evidence on its lack of efficiency, and that its outputs (deterrence and an approach based on blame) are ineffective in achieving its goals and can be harmful. I also review discussions on introducing an alternative redress scheme to litigation in England and Scotland, and partial implementation in Wales. In section IV, I note wider developments in behavioural science on the causes of actions, and hence adverse incidents, and developments in applying that knowledge to regulatory systems. In section V, I turn to the public healthcare system in UK, the National Health Service (NHS), and analyse how investigations into repeated disasters have identified the importance of shifting to an 'open, just culture', and official statements stand by that effect, but, on critical analysis, how various aspects of current reality impede the development of such a culture. Section VI summarises the major conclusions, including critical steps that are indicated for creating an effective system.

II. What Do Patients Want the System to Do?

In setting the goals of a redress scheme, we should build on what patients say they want. There are many studies on this, which reveal 'a striking consensus'.[1]

[1] National Audit Office, *Handling Clinical Negligence Claims in England: Report by the Comptroller and Auditor General*, Session 2000–2001, HC 403, 3 May 2001. Note that the statistical data were

The outputs identified consistently in studies are an explanation and apology, an admission of fault, compensation, and the prevention of future accidents.[2]

I quote here just four particular studies, to give depth to the points. A 1994 study of 227 patients and relatives involved in medical negligence litigation found that although over 70 per cent were seriously affected by incidents that gave rise to litigation with long-term effects on work, social life, and family relationships, the decision to take legal action was determined not only by the original injury, but also by insensitive handling and poor communication after the original incident.[3] Intense emotions were aroused and continued to be felt for a long time. Where explanations were given, less than 15 per cent were considered satisfactory. Four main themes emerged from the analysis of reasons for litigation: concern with standards of care – both patients and relatives wanted to prevent similar incidents in the future; the need for an explanation – to know how the injury happened and why; compensation – for actual losses, pain and suffering or to provide care in the future for an injured person; and accountability – a belief that the staff or organisation should have to account for their actions.

A 2003 survey found that 4.8 per cent of a sample of 8,206 people believed that over the previous three years they had suffered some illness, injury or impairment that in their opinion was caused by their medical treatment or care, of which 15 per cent reported a temporary major disability and almost 30 per cent claimed that the event had had a permanent impact on their health.[4] The remedy most commonly considered appropriate was an apology or explanation (34 per cent), followed by an inquiry into the causes (23 per cent) or support in coping with the consequences (16 per cent). Only 11 per cent of respondents indicated that financial compensation would have been the most appropriate response.

A 2011 study involved 100 semi-structured, in-depth interviews with 39 patients and 80 family members who were involved in high severity healthcare incidents (leading to death, permanent disability, or long-term harm) and incident

criticised as 'deeply misleading': P Fenn et al, 'Current Cost of Medical Negligence in the NHS Hospitals: Analysis of Claims Database' (2000) 320 *BMJ* 1567; P Fenn et al, 'The Economics of Clinical Negligence Reform in England' (2004) 114 *The Economic Journal* 272.

[2] *Behavioural Insights into Patient Motivation to Make a Claim for Clinical Negligence. Final Report by the Behavioural Insights Team* (The Behavioural Insights Team and NHS Resolution, August 2018); S Lloyd-Bostock and L Mulcahy, 'The Social Psychology of Making and Responding to Hospital Complaints: An Account Model of Complaint Processes' (1994) 16 *Law and Policy* 123; C Vincent et al, 'Why Do People Sue Doctors? A Study of Patients and Relatives Taking Legal Action' (1994) 343 *The Lancet* 1609; A Simanowitz, 'The Patient's Perspective' in MM Rosenthal et al (eds), *Medical Mishaps. Pieces of the Puzzle* (Buckingham, Open University Press, 1999) 228; L Mulcahy, *Mediating Medical Negligence Claims: An Option for the Future* (The Stationery Office, 2000); National Audit Office, above, n 1; J Mellor, *Report on Selected Summaries of Investigations by the Parliamentary and Health Service Ombudsman. October to November 2014* (Parliamentary and Health Service Ombudsman, 17 June 2015); *RESOLVE News from the Ombudsman Service* (PHSO, December 2015).

[3] Vincent et al, above, n 2.

[4] Fenn et al (2004), above, n 1.

disclosure.[5] Most patients and family members felt that the health service incident disclosure rarely met their needs and expectations. They expected better preparation for incident disclosure, more shared dialogue about what went wrong, more follow-up support, input into when the time was ripe for closure, and more information about subsequent improvement in process.

A 2012 survey of 1,675 people into why they seek legal advice found that 'preventing something that had gone wrong from going wrong again' was a significant motivation.[6]

In 2016 the National Maternity review said:[7]

> **Litigious and blame culture**
>
> 3.32. Professionals also told us that the threat of litigation and the high costs associated with it could encourage obstetricians and midwives to practise in a risk-averse way, inhibiting their ability to support some of the choices that women may want to make, contributed to the administrative and data collection burden, and undermined multi-professional working. We also heard overwhelmingly from families whose baby died that litigation was a last resort, and that they only turned to litigation when they had failed to get answers about their baby's death through any other channels. They repeatedly told us that they were not motivated by the money, but they desperately wanted to make sure the same mistakes were not repeated with future families. The litigation process caused them considerable stress as it inhibited the clinicians from discussing openly what had gone wrong, and by needing to involve legal representatives, the process took longer to resolve, often many years.

In delivering the desired outputs, the system has to be designed to identify the true facts, to be open and respectful in sharing them with patients and their families, to resolve issues swiftly, to deliver support and care (including money), and to demonstrate that the system has digested relevant information and has improved practice. Some of these outputs need 'reparative gestures', including emotional support[8] and physicians who are able to establish rapport and communicate effectively.[9] The 'learning' component is the interesting one for current purposes. The system needs to be *capable* of collating the true facts, identifying the root causes, and making changes in practice and culture, as well as *demonstrating* that those features actually occur in an instant case.

[5] R Iedema et al, 'Patients' and Family Members' Views on How Clinicians Enact and How They Should Enact Open Disclosure: The "100 Patient Stories" Qualitative Study' (2011) *British Medical Journal* 343.

[6] *Evaluation: How Can We Measure Access to Justice for Individual Consumers? A Discussion Paper* (Legal Services Board, 2012).

[7] *Better Births: Improving Outcomes of Maternity Services in England: A Five Year Forward View for Maternity Care* (National Maternity Review, 2016) para 3.32.

[8] R Iedema and D Piper, 'Do Patients Want and Expect Compensation Following Harm?' (2013) 116 *Precedent* 48.

[9] GB Hickson et al, 'Patient Complaints and Malpractice Risk' (2002) *Journal of the American Medical Association* 2951.

III. The Legal System

A. Objectives of the Legal System

The compensation arm of the legal system has two principal objectives:[10] first, to deliver money, quantified so as to pay for the cost of care and to compensate for 'pain and suffering' or moral insult; second, to provide deterrence so that future actions similar to the action that was the cause of the harm that has been found to be caused by 'fault' will not recur. These two traditional objectives are *delivering compensation* and *providing deterrence*.

Speaking in 2010, Lord Neuberger, then Master of the Rolls, noting ongoing concern over personal injury litigation costs, agreed with the criticism of negligence as a basis for selecting those to whom compensation should be paid as a 'lottery', and that that view had been shared by William Beveridge in his 1942 report that presaged the founding of the NHS,[11] in 1967 by the founders of the New Zealand scheme,[12] and in UK 30 years later by Professor Patrick Atiyah.[13] He surmised that attention would turn to insurance-based schemes like that of New Zealand, which had been outside the remit of the review by Sir Rupert Jackson.[14] Recent decades have also seen discussions about whether a 'compensation culture' exists or not. Lord Falconer described the idea in 2005 as 'for every accident someone is at fault. For every injury, someone to blame. And, perhaps most damaging, for every accident, there is someone to pay'.[15] Ten years later, Lord Dyson MR commented:[16]

> 19. One consequence of this is the view that as a society we have undergone a cultural shift. No longer is British society characterised by a somewhat philosophical and accepting approach to life. On the contrary, the view is taken that we are becoming more

[10] Other objectives are sometimes claimed, such as vindication, upholding the law, restitution and retribution. Delving into that scholarly debate is outside the scope of this chapter. However, the scientific findings described later in this chapter are problematic for those goals, not least since they focus plaintiffs away from healing and reconciliation and towards adversarialism and money. Ian Cameron's chapter (see Ch 3) discusses a broad range of empirical evidence of the anti-therapeutic effects of compensation procedure that are contrary to liability law's intrinsic restitutionary goals: see B Laarman and A Akkermans, *Compensation Schemes for Damage Caused by Healthcare and Alternatives to Court Proceedings in the Netherlands – The Netherlands National Report to the 20th General Congress of the International Academy of Comparative Law*, Fukuoka, Japan, 22–28 July 2018, available at ssrn.com/abstract=3143320.

[11] W Beveridge, *Social Insurance and Allied Services* (1942) Cmd 6404, para 262.

[12] *Compensation for Personal Injury in New Zealand: Report of the Royal Commission of Inquiry* (Wellington, 1967) (the Woodehouse Commission) 19.

[13] P Atiyah, *The Damages Lottery* (Oxford, Hart Publishing, 1997).

[14] Lord Neuberger of Abbotsbury MR, 'Costs, Management, Proportionality and Insurance' speech to the Personal Injuries Bar Association Conference, Oxford, 26 March 2010.

[15] Lord Falconer, 'Compensation Culture', speech at Health and Safety Executive Conference, 22 March 2005, available at www.woodwardsolicitors.co.uk/lordfalconer.pdf.

[16] Lord Dyson MR, 'Magna Carta and Compensation Culture', The High Sheriff's Law Lecture, Oxford University, 13 October 2015, paras 17, 19, 20.

> American in our approach; more ready to rush into litigation. To borrow from Tony Weir, we have become a '*wondrously unstoical and whingeing society with (an) endemic neurosis*', and which rather than sees us '*grin and bear it*' sees us '*grit (our) teeth and sue*'.[17]
>
> 20. Perhaps even more dangerously, this shift in approach has been accompanied by a growing concern that an unjustified burden is now being placed on employers, businesses, schools, the NHS and local and central government (as regards payment of compensation and, even worse, legal costs which often substantially exceed the amount of compensation). …

In relation to the *delivering compensation* goal, it is widely accepted that many legal systems perform poorly in relation to duration, cost to access, and total transactional cost. That has certainly been an unsolved problem in England and Wales.[18] There is also a problem with the inherent mechanism, in that the output is money, but that does not necessarily address other desired outputs, such as immediate care, emotional support and timely reliable information. Providing money is a surrogate for other underlying and more important objectives.[19]

The cost of medical negligence to the NHS quadrupled from £400m in 2006/07 to £1.6bn in 2016/17.[20] Estimated liabilities for existing claims through the Clinical Negligence Scheme for Trusts, that involve future payments or are not yet settled, and potential clinical negligence claims for incidents that have already occurred but are not yet made, were £60 billion in 2016–17.[21] For some years these costs were described as being unsustainable. By 2020 the projected total for clinical negligence claims was £83 billion, including legal costs of £4.3 billion.[22]

The *deterrence* goal has reduced strongly in emphasis by tort law theorists in relation to its meaning of *affecting future behaviour*. The idea that imposing sanctions affects future behaviour has been significantly undermined by empirical evidence and in theorising.[23] The most influential theory has been that all

[17] T Weir, 'Governmental Liability' (1989) 40 *Public Law* 76.

[18] See successive major reports: Lord Woolf, *Access to Justice: Final Report to the Lord Chancellor on the Civil Justice System in England and Wales* (HMSO, 1996); Lord Justice Jackson, *Review of Civil Litigation Costs: Interim Report* (2009); Lord Justice Jackson, *Review of Civil Litigation Costs: Final Report* (2010); *Solving Disputes in the County Courts: Creating a Simpler, Quicker and More Proportionate System: a Consultation on Reforming Civil Justice in England and Wales – The Government Response* (The Stationery Office, 2012), Cm 8274; Lord Justice Briggs, *Civil Courts Structure Review: Final Report* (Judiciary of England and Wales, 2016). See also academic comments, eg C Hodges et al, *The Costs and Funding of Civil Litigation. A Comparative Perspective* (Oxford, Hart Publishing, 2010); J Peysner, *Access to Justice: A Critical Analysis of Recoverable Conditional Fees and No-Win No-Fee Funding* (Palgrave Macmillan, 2014).

[19] See I Cameron, 'Compensation and Health', Ch 3 above.

[20] *Annual Report and Accounts 2016/17* (NHS Resolution, 2017). This comprised £974 million on damages, £602 million on legal costs (£480 million on claimants' legal costs and £122 million on defence costs) and £10 million on claims operations.

[21] *Managing the Costs of Clinical Negligence in Trusts. Report by the Comptroller and Auditor General* (National Audit Office, 2017).

[22] K Burgess, '£4bn budget for legal fees in NHS negligence claims totalling £83bn' *The Times*, January 22, 2020.

[23] C Hodges and S Voet, *Delivering Collective Redress: New Technologies* (Oxford, Hart Publishing, 2018) Ch 7.

people who injure others are rational cost-avoiders, make decisions by calculating costs and benefits, and will be influenced in all future decisions (especially in choosing to avoid causing harm to others) by knowledge of the ex post imposition of financial or other sanctions on them or others.[24] Many objections have been tabled to that theory, not least from the findings of behavioural psychology on the reasons why humans act or fail to act. For example, behavioural studies suggest that a key tenet – that increasing a penalty will exert greater deterrent effect – is incorrect.[25] The concept of deterrence carries an assumption that imposition of a sanction (such as the cost of remedying the harm caused) will *completely* prevent similar behaviour or harm in future: there is little empirical evidence to support that assumption.

The empirical evidence that supposedly deterrent sanctions actually affect future behaviour is strikingly slim. Rather, there is plenty of evidence that 'deterrence' is not only ineffective but can also adversely affect compliance.[26] Decisions are taken for many reasons, and the supposed fear of legal penalties may have very limited or no effect on behaviour.[27]

Deterrence theory struggles to explain how harm can be avoided where it is caused by complex interactions between multiple people, systems and cultures. Medical practice was for some time subjected to the assumption that training and punishment would eliminate all medical error (the 'perfectibility' model).[28] Emphasis on the incompetent doctor shifts the focus away from the more fundamental questions about systemic approaches to mishaps.[29] Leape noted that reliance on inspection as a mechanism of quality control was discredited long

[24] Leading texts are AC Pigou, *The Economics of Welfare* (London, MacMillan, 1920); M Allingham, *Rational Choice* (New York, NY, St Martin's Press Inc, 1999); MS Archer and JQ Tritter, *Rational Choice Theory: Resisting Colonization* (New York, NY, Routledge, 2001); G Becker, 'Crime and Punishment: An Economic Approach' (1968) 76 *Journal of Political Economy* 169; GJ Stigler, 'The Theory of Economic Regulation' (1971) 2 *Bell Journal of Economics and Management Science* 3.

[25] LS Beres and TD Griffith, 'Habitual Offender Statutes and Criminal Deterrence' (2001) 34 *Connecticut Law Review* 55, 59; see I Ehrlich, 'Crime, Punishment, and the Market for Offenses' (1996) 10 *Journal of Economic Perspectives* 43 at 55–63; PW Greenwood et al, *Three Strikes and You're Out: Estimated Benefit and Cost of California's Mandatory New Sentencing Laws* (RAND Corporation, 1994) 16. But see D Kessler and SD Levitt, 'Using Sentence Enhancements to Distinguish Between Deterrence and Incapacitation' (1999) 42 *Journal of Law & Economics* 343.

[26] Accessible books are D Ariely, *Predictably Irrational: The Hidden Forces That Shape Our Decisions* (HarperCollins, 2008); MH Banaji and AG Greenwald, *Blindspot: Hidden Biases of Good People* (Bantam Books, 2016); R Barrett, *The Values-Driven Organization: Cultural Health and Employee Well-Being as a Pathway to Sustainable Performance*, 2nd edn (Routledge, 2017); MH Bazerman and AE Tenbrunsel, *Blind Spots: Why We Fail to Do What's Right and What to Do about It* (Princeton University Press, 2011); J Haidt, *The Righteous Mind. Why Good People Are Divided by Politics and Religion* (Penguin Books, 2012); M Heffernan, *Wilful Blindness. Why We Ignore the Obvious at Our Peril* (Simon & Schuster, 2011); D Kahneman, *Thinking, Fast and Slow* (Allen Lane, 2011).

[27] For a review see C Hodges, *Law and Corporate Behaviour: Integrating Theories of Regulation, Enforcement, Culture and Ethics* (Oxford, Hart Publishing, 2015).

[28] LL Leape, 'Error in Medicine' (1994) 272(23) *Journal of the American Medical Association* 851.

[29] L Mulcahy and MM Rosenthal, 'Beyond Blaming and Perfection: A Multi-dimensional Approach to Medical Mishaps' in MM Rosenthal et al (eds), *Medical Mishaps. Pieces of the Puzzle* (Buckingham, Open University Press, 1999) 8.

ago in industry,[30] because the technique is reactive. Product regulatory systems typically rely on continuous control and monitoring of design, manufacture, distribution and marketing functions by means of a permanent quality system. The typical pattern of medical mishaps is not caused by a sole individual, as a 2016 report made clear:[31]

> Safety issues and related incidents are often the result of complex local, organizational and system-wide processes, with similar events recurring repeatedly in different places across the healthcare system. The purpose of safety investigation is to understand the patterns of causality that produce harm, and to make recommendations that can address those causes across the healthcare system in order to improve the safety of all patients. …
>
> The vast majority of safety incidents are associated with inadvertent or unintentional errors on the part of caring and committed staff. These errors are typically provoked by poorly designed systems, equipment, or work contexts.[32]

Public regulators have experimented with different means of affecting future behaviour, increasingly informed by behavioural science, and a consensus is emerging amongst UK regulators on effective ways of affecting future behaviour and compliance by organisations. In brief, the tools that are relevant for most people are supportive of improvement and the 'harder' enforcement tools, historically associated with deterrence, are restricted to people who intentionally break the law: this is discussed below in section D. In other words, means of affecting future behaviour have now been identified that are nothing to do with compensation or dispute resolution systems.

If deterrence does not work with most people, it should logically be neither an objective nor a justification of liability law. The social goal that remains valid is to provide compensatory or corrective justice – a responsibility to make good harm caused – which has been asserted throughout modern history,[33] recently by contrasting theorists of private law[34] and rights-based analysis, based on basic

[30] Leape, above, n 28; citing DM Berwick, 'EM Codman and the Rhetoric of Battle: A Commentary' (1989) 320 *Milbank Quarterly* 262; WE Deming, *Quality, Productivity and Competitive Position* (Cambridge MA, MIT Press, 1982).

[31] *Report of the Expert Advisory Group; Healthcare Safety Investigation Branch* (Department of Health, May 2016) 21, available at www.gov.uk/government/uploads/system/uploads/attachment_data/file/522785/hsibreport.pdf.

[32] ibid, 25, 26, quoting National Advisory Group on the Safety of Patients in England, *A Promise to Learn – A Commitment to Act* (London, Department of Health, 2013).

[33] Aristotle, *Nichomachean Ethics, Book V* (T Irwin tr, Indianapolis, Hackett Publishing, 1999) paras 1131b–1134a; T Aquinas, *Summa Theologica* (Fathers of English Dominican Province trs, New York, Benziger Bros, 1947) part 2(2) question 62 arts 1–3; H Grotius, *De Jure Belli ac Pacis Libri tres* (FW Kelsey tr, Oxford, Clarendon Press, 1925) book 2 Ch 17 para I; S Pufendorf, *Of the Law of Nature and Nations* (HC Oldfather and WA Oldfather trs, Oxford, Clarendon Press, 1934) book 3 Ch 1 § 2; EJ Weinrib (ed), *Tort Law* (1991); EJ Weinrib, *The Idea of Private Law* (1995); EJ Weinrib, *Corrective Justice* (Oxford, Oxford University Press, 2012); A Beever, *Rediscovering the Law of Negligence* (Oxford, Hart Publishing, 2007); A Beever, 'Our Most Fundamental Rights' in D Nolan and A Robertson (eds), *Rights and Private Law* (Oxford, Hart Publishing, 2012) Ch 3.

[34] Weinrib (1991), above, n 33; Weinrib (1995), above, n 33; Weinrib (2012), above, n 33.

values of inter-personal morality, fairness and justice.[35] If providing compensation remains a valid objective and justification for those harmed, the issue that remains is how it is best achieved.

B. New Models of Delivering Redress

Traditional court systems have been replaced as means of delivering compensation in various situations.[36] For disputes between small companies and suppliers (eg over late payment), new intermediaries have been created such as a Small Business Commissioner[37] and Groceries Code Adjudicator.[38] For delivering redress to individuals and groups of consumers, some European states have developed sophisticated sectoral Ombudsmen and empowered regulatory authorities with redress powers. Those mechanisms have proved to be outstandingly successful, swift, cheap and efficient.[39] They have recently been approved by UNCTAD.[40]

Both consumer Ombudsmen and regulators can be effective in changing behaviours and systems of businesses. One advantage of these diverse mechanisms is that they promote a particular style of society, that identifies problems and solves them quickly and through cooperative engagement, rather than waiting for the litigation system to be invoked and to operate in a mode of conflict and adversarial legalism.[41]

A recent study has shown how many 'no blame' administrative compensation schemes exist around the world.[42] All Nordic states have 'no-fault' administrative compensation schemes for personal injuries.[43] Adjacent schemes cover patient, medicines, workplace and road traffic accidents. The patient schemes collate databases on all injuries and their causes, analyse these and feed them back to drive improvements in healthcare practice. The schemes are popular and efficient.

[35] R Stevens, *Torts and Rights* (Oxford, Oxford University Press, 2007); R Stevens, 'Rights and Other Things' Law' in Nolan and Robertson, above, n 33.

[36] C Hodges, *Delivering Dispute Resolution. A Holistic Review of Models in England and Wales* (Oxford, Hart Publishing, 2019).

[37] The Groceries Code Adjudicator Act 2013. See *Statutory Review of the Groceries Code Adjudicator: 2013–2016* (Department for Business, Energy & Industrial Strategy, 2017).

[38] Directive 2013/11/EU on consumer ADR. See C Hodges, *Delivering Dispute Resolution. A Holistic Review of Models in England and Wales* (Oxford, Hart Publishing, 2019); C Hodges et al, *Consumer ADR in Europe* (Oxford, Hart Publishing, 2012); J Zekoll et al (eds), *Dispute Resolution: Alternatives to Formalization – Formalization of Alternatives?* (Brill, 2014); P Cortes, *The New Regulatory Framework for Consumer Dispute Resolution.* (Oxford, Oxford University Press, 2016).

[39] Small Business Commissioners now exist in most Australian states, eg the Small Business Commissioner Act 2003, as amended, for Victoria. In UK, introduced by Enterprise Act 2016, s1.

[40] *Manual of Consumer Protection* (UNCTAD, 2017) Ch XI.

[41] RA Kagan, *Adversarial Legalism: The American Way of Law* (Boston, Harvard University Press, 2001); S Farhang, *The Litigation State: Public Regulation and Private Lawsuits in the US* (Princeton, Princeton University Press, 2010).

[42] S Macleod and C Hodges, *Redress Schemes for Personal Injuries* (Oxford, Hart Publishing, 2017).

[43] ibid, Chs 4–8.

A telling comment from the Medical Director of the Swedish Patient Compensation Scheme is that mistakes happen, and looking for scapegoats through a legal system for medical injuries based on fault is 'a very efficient way of killing more patients'.[44]

C. NHS Redress

No-fault compensation schemes have been considered and sometimes advocated by successive bodies, but never systematically introduced. In 1978 the Pearson Commission declared the tort system as costly, cumbersome, prone to delay, and too capricious in its operation to be defensible, but rejected a no-fault system for clinical negligence, because of perceived difficulty in overwhelming the tort liability system and the perceived difficulties in causation judgments.[45] A Swedish administrative system was proposed in 1988 by the King's Fund Institute.[46]

By 2001, concern was mounting over the sums spent and time taken on medical negligence litigation, as well as the need to change NHS culture so as to identify mistakes, record and learn from them, and so reduce the number of errors and the adverse consequences.[47] There was also concern that handling clinical negligence claims was too complex, slow and costly.[48] Debate was led by the Chief Medical Officer for England[49] which led to proposals in 2003[50] that included a redress scheme for harm caused by serious shortcomings in the standard of care provided, including an explanation and a care and/or compensation package, with the compensation element limited to £30,000. However, it was concluded that a general no fault scheme for medical injuries in England was unaffordable, and that awards would have to be significantly reduced from prevailing levels.[51] A statutory framework for a scheme was introduced in the NHS Redress Act 2006 but never implemented,[52] despite later Parliamentary support,[53] and was rejected by the Government in 2009 on grounds of cost.[54]

[44] ibid, 646. Quotation from Dr Pelle Gustafson.

[45] *Report of the Royal Commission on the Civil Liability and Compensation for Personal Injury. Chairman: Lord Pearson*, Cmnd 7054-1, 1978, para 1715.

[46] C Ham et al, *Medical Negligence: Compensation and Accountability* (London, King's Fund Institute and Centre for Socio-Legal Studies, 1988).

[47] *The NHS Plan, A Plan for Investment, A Plan for Reform* (Department of Health, 2000).

[48] See above, n 1.

[49] Sir Liam Donaldson, *Call for Ideas* (Department of Health, 2001).

[50] *Making Amends: A Consultation Paper Setting out Proposals for Reforming the Approach to Clinical Negligence in the NHS* (Department of Health, 2003).

[51] ibid.

[52] See criticism in C Foster, 'Pre-Trial Clinical Negligence Issues' in J Tingle and P Bark (eds), *Patient Safety, Law Policy and Practice* (Routledge, 2011).

[53] Response by Lord Darzi of Denham to a question by Lord Gregson, Hansard 18 March 2009: Column WA49; Health Committee – Sixth Report, *Patient Safety* (2009).

[54] *The Government Response to the Health Select Committee Report 'Patient Safety'* (2009) Cm 7709.

A major area of concern and cost, in terms of both litigation costs and damages, has been severely neurologically impaired babies. Litigation arises over whether the impairment was or was not caused by negligence at birth. In 2013/14 such cases accounted for 11 per cent of all cases where damage is paid and 35 per cent (the largest category) of all expenditure: such individual claims can be over £6 million.[55] It is difficult to prove negligence and causation, and the outcome is that one small group receives compensation and the larger group does not.

In 2013, a Report of the Department of Health looking primarily into reforms in the regulation of beauticians and cosmetic surgeons, following concern over unsafe treatment and the safety of cosmetic implants, included a recommendation that a single ombudsman system should cover all public and private sector health disputes.[56] The recommendation was that this could be achieved by extending the remit of the Parliamentary and Health Service Ombudsman (PHSO) in complaints against public sector health providers to private sector providers as well.[57]

Some progress was, however, made in Wales, where integrated arrangements for concerns, complaints and redress were introduced in 2011.[58] The arrangements include that if a Welsh NHS body is notified of 'concerns' with services provided, the body has a duty to investigate the matter and respond appropriately. The body must also consider whether the notification includes an allegation that harm has or may have been caused, and, if so, conclude whether it has a 'qualifying liability', in which case it must produce a written response leading to an offer of redress. The basis of the 'qualifying liability' remains tort law. The redress elements do not apply to primary care providers or independent providers. The redress may comprise:[59]

1 the making of an offer of compensation in satisfaction of any right to bring civil proceedings in respect of a qualifying liability;
2 the giving of an explanation;
3 the making of a written apology; and
4 the giving of a report on the action which has been, or will be, taken to prevent similar cases arising.

The compensation that may be offered can take the form of entry into a contract to provide care or treatment or of financial compensation, or both.[60] Guidance

[55] *NHS Litigation Authority Report and Accounts 2013/14* (NHS Litigation Authority, 2014) 24 and figs 16 and 17.

[56] *Review of the Regulation of Cosmetic Interventions. Final Report* (Department of Health, 2013), recommendation 34.

[57] The suggestion was made to the Department's Committee by C Hodges and S Macleod: see Meeting of the Review of the Regulation of Cosmetic Interventions Committee on 11 February 2013, available at webarchive.nationalarchives.gov.uk/20130402145952/http://transparency.dh.gov.uk/2013/02/11/rcci-11jan2013.

[58] The National Health Service (Concerns, Complaints and Redress Arrangements) (Wales) Regulations 2011, SI 2011/704 (W 108). See AL Ferguson and E Braithwaite, 'Putting Things Right in Wales' (2012) 18 *Clinical Risk* 6.

[59] ibid, reg 27.

[60] ibid, reg 27(2).

sets out a tariff for general damages.[61] There is a limit of £25,000 on the financial compensation element of redress in relation to special and general damages.[62] Redress is not available in relation to a liability that is or has been the subject of civil proceedings, and if civil proceedings are issued during the course of a Welsh NHS body's consideration of redress, the Welsh NHS body's consideration of redress must stop and the person who notified the concern must be so advised.[63] Limitation periods are suspended during the period in which a liability is the subject of an application for redress under the Regulations.[64] Free legal advice on the matter must be provided to the complainant.[65]

Despite various attractive features of this system (including a single point of entry, a commitment to openness and responsiveness) it is still based on tort, and in continuing to focus on the performance of the clinician, as opposed to the system as a whole, threatens efforts to encourage a culture of openness.[66] Decisions are also not made independently of the relevant NHS unit.

The Scottish Government has also considered whether to introduce a no-fault compensation scheme, after a manifesto commitment to do so in 2007.[67] However, nothing concrete has yet emerged despite statements to end the 'blame culture'.[68]

In 2016, the National Maternity Review proposed a 'Rapid Resolution and Redress' (RRR) scheme, strongly inspired by the Nordic models and incorporating elements of independent no-blame investigation, support for families and staff, an assisted open exchange, capture of relevant information for learning, and tariff-based compensation.[69] The proposed scheme would be administered by a distinct public body with expertise in medical indemnity insurance. Serious incident investigations would be triggered for all cases of severe brain damage, all stillbirths where the baby was alive at onset of labour, as well as all neonatal deaths and all maternal deaths. Payment would be triggered for harm occurring in full-term babies (37 weeks or more gestation) who were considered healthy when labour commenced, and to harm resulting in serious injury to the baby. It would not be necessary to establish negligence. The test would be one of causation: whether the

[61] A tariff is at *Putting Things Right: Guidance on Dealing with Concerns from the 1st April 2011* (3rd Version, Welsh Government, 2013) App Q. The guidance states that responsible bodies should 'avoid settling cases of doubtful merit, however small, purely on a "nuisance value" basis': para 8.22.

[62] The National Health Service (Concerns, Complaints and Redress Arrangements) (Wales) Regulations 2011, reg 29.

[63] ibid, reg 28.

[64] ibid, reg 30.

[65] ibid, reg 32.

[66] V Harpwood, 'Clinical Negligence and Poor Quality Care: Is Wales "Putting Things Right?"' in PR Ferguson and GT Laurie (eds), *Inspiring a Medico-Legal Revolution: Essays in Honour of Sheila McLean* (Farnham, Ashgate, 2015).

[67] See A-M Farrell et al, *No-Fault Compensation Schemes for Medical Injury: A Review* (Scottish Government Social Research, 2010); *No Fault Compensation Review Group: Report and Recommendations* (The Scottish Government, 2011); *A Public Consultation on Recommendations for No-Fault Compensation in Scotland for Injuries Resulting from Clinical Treatment* (The Scottish Government, 2012).

[68] *'No-Blame' Redress Scheme: A Public Consultation on Draft Proposals for a 'No-blame' Redress Scheme in Scotland for Harm resulting from Clinical Treatment* (The Scottish Government, 2016).

[69] *Better Births*, above, n 7.

harm was the probable consequence of the treatment provided or not provided during birth. An insurance assessor, working with appropriate professional and legal advice, would settle claims. The proposed scheme would be optional, existing alongside the tort system. The right to pursue a tort law claim for negligence would not be affected. If already successful under the scheme it would be expected that any subsequent payment made in respect of a successful negligence claim would deduct the payment previously made. Some clinical steps have been taken on implementation of the 'RRR' scheme.[70]

However, it appears that the redress elements of the 'RRR' scheme may not be implemented. Moreover, its proposed design would not be independent. That would be a fundamental mistake. A key design feature is that investigations and decision on the award of compensation must be made by an *independent* body. The need for independence has been consistently stated. Dame Janet Shipman's early-2000s inquiry identified a lack of fair procedures, failure to investigate complaints properly, failure to give adequate explanations, and lack of impartiality in organisations investigating their own conduct.[71] In 2015, the Parliamentary Ombudsman proposed that design principles that should apply to a new Public Ombudsman Service,[72] the first being that complaint handling should be 'independent, impartial and authoritative'. Sir Robert Francis concluded from his Mid-Staffordshire inquiry that there was a case for independent investigation of a wider range of complaints.[73] The need for the Healthcare Safety Investigation Branch to be independent was strongly emphasised by the advisory group who reviewed its proposed arrangements.[74] The need for an independent body was strongly emphasised by the National Maternity Review, as indeed was the need for speed.[75]

D. An Investigation and Redress Model

Macleod and Hodges recently analysed 40 compensation schemes for personal injuries from around the world.[76] They found that a quiet but notable shift has occurred away from adversarial court-based dispute resolution to administrative

[70] *Safer Maternity Care. Next Steps towards the National Maternity Ambition* (Department of Health, 2016); *A Rapid Resolution and Redress Scheme for Severe Avoidable Birth Injury: a Consultation* (Department of Health, 2017); *Department of Health Birth Injury Compensation Policy Research* (Ipsos Mori, 2017); *No-Fault Compensation Schemes. A Rapid Realist Review to Develop a Context, Mechanism, Outcomes Framework* (Department of Health, 2017); *A Rapid Resolution and Redress Scheme for Severe Avoidable Birth Injury: Government Summary Consultation Response* (Department of Health, 2017).

[71] *Fifth Report of the Shipman Inquiry*, 2004.

[72] Letter by Dame J Mellor to the Cabinet Office, 'Cabinet Office Consultation: A Public Service Ombudsman', 16 June 2015, see www.ombudsman.org.uk/news-and-blog/news/ombudsman-wants-no-wrong-door-complaining-after-government-launches-public.

[73] *Independent Inquiry into care provided by Mid Staffordshire NHS Foundation Trust January 2005 – March 2009. Volume I. Chaired by Robert Francis QC*, HC375-I (2010).

[74] *Report of the Expert Advisory Group*, above, n 31.

[75] *Better Births*, above, n 7, para 6.8.

[76] Macleod and Hodges, above, n 42.

compensation schemes. There was considerable diversity in such schemes, influenced significantly by their context (national cultures and legal systems) and the reasons why they were created. Such reasons included the need to avoid continuation of lengthy litigation (eg experience in Japan with SMON injuries or in UK with COPD, VWF, HIV and vCJD), to reduce the burden on the courts, to replace tort-based liability (schemes in New Zealand, France and Poland).

The administrative costs of all compensation schemes in the study are vastly lower than the tort litigation system in each country.[77] Economies of scale could be realised where schemes process a number of different injury types, even if different financial pools were operated for individual injury types. The schemes tend to be subject to defined time limits for processing matters, and provide relatively quick resolution.

Examples exist of both public and private bodies, demonstrating that private intermediaries could be effective and trusted if they operated with appropriate governance and transparency arrangements. Cost and duration were obviously affected by process design. The general observation was that administrative schemes drew on relevant medical and legal expertise (whether in-house or from external experts when required) in a manner that was more efficient that an adversarial and judicial procedure. Many administrative models were also able to innovate and introduce efficiency and technical reforms, provided their structures were not unduly rigid.

A major finding of the study was that the qualification criteria under schemes has evolved from the legal trigger of 'fault' on the part of a person who is held to have legally caused an injury, towards a set of factual criteria focused on the condition of the person harmed.[78] That shift is highly significant. First, the application of factual criteria[79] is a simpler, shorter and cheaper task than undertaking an extensive investigation into what was done by various staff over an extended period. It typically avoids a need to apply retrospective judgement on historical events. Second, it shifts the focus of the criteria from actions by a potential injurer to the condition of the injured and the circumstances of injury.

Macleod and Hodges concluded their study by proposing state-of-the-art parameters and outline model for an administrative compensation scheme, based on the following principles:[80]

1 unbiased and objective;
2 easily identifiable;
3 having expertise and authority;
4 efficient;
5 transparent;
6 fair;
7 supporting maintenance of and improvement in clinical performance.

[77] ibid, 628.
[78] ibid, 635.
[79] Eg for neonates who have suffered neurological damage, criteria might include birth weight, duration of pregnancy, vital statistics and signs at certain points, time of onset of symptoms after birth and so on.
[80] Macleod and Hodges, above, n 42, 647–48.

IV. Wider Developments in Science and Regulation

Having criticised the theory of deterrence as a regulatory technique, one may ask what other theories should be adopted to affect future behaviour. To answer this question, there is now a wealth of scientific and other empirical information, which has increasingly been applied by some regulatory authorities in various systems outside healthcare.

A. Blaming Prevents Learning

People will not volunteer information if they fear that they might be criticised, blamed, ostracised, sanctioned or subject to retaliation – whether by colleagues, employers, regulators, journalists, friends or family.[81] An example is where workers in cleaning businesses failed to raise concern over instances of poor treatment of workers where people feared risking their jobs.[82] Research into aviation safety clearly identified that a hard enforcement regime cut off the flow of information that is vital for safety.[83] It is universally accepted in relation to civil aviation that individuals will not share information if they fear potential adverse consequences, whether personal criticism, official investigations, criminal action, employment disciplinary action, social censure, embarrassment, or simply uncertainty over what will happen.[84] 'The sheer threat of judicial involvement is enough to make people think twice about coming forward with information about an incident that they were involved in'.[85]

Studies involving doctors have identified fear of litigation, damage to reputation and embarrassment as the main barriers to the practice of open disclosure.[86] Berlinger's interesting analysis of the morality and meaning of truth-telling in medical harm concluded that attempting to eliminate medical error is futile[87] and

[81] S Dekker, *Just Culture. Balancing Safety and Accountability* (Aldershot, Ashgate, 2007) 103; RL Helmreich, 'Building Safety on the Three Cultures of Aviation' in *Proceedings of the IATA Human Factors Seminar* (Bangkok, 1999) 39–43; D McCune et al, 'Safety Culture in Your Safety Management System' in AJ Stolzer et al (eds), *Implementing Safety Management Systems in Aviation* (Ashgate, 2011).

[82] W Sykes et al, *Coming Clean: The Experience of Cleaning Operatives* (Equality and Human Rights Commission, 2014) 16.

[83] M Tamuz, 'The Impact of Computer Surveillance on Air Safety Reporting' (1987) *Columbia Journal of World Business* 69; M Tamuz, 'Learning Disabilities for Regulators. The Perils of Organizational Learning in the Air Transportation Industry' (2001) 33(3) *Administration & Society* 276.

[84] *Report on Legal and Cultural Issues in Relation to ATM Safety Occurrence Reporting in Europe: Outcome of a Survey Conducted by the Performance Review Unit in 2005–2006* (Brussels, Eurocontrol Performance Review Commission, 2006).

[85] Dekker, above, n 81, 103.

[86] TH Gallagher et al, 'Patients' and Physicians' Attitudes Regarding the Disclosure of Medical Errors' (2003) 289 *JAMA* 1001; D Studdert et al, 'Legal Aspects of Open Disclosure II: Attitudes of Health Professionals – Findings from a National Survey' (2010) 193 *Medical Journal of Australia* 351.

[87] *To Err Is Human* (Institute of Medicine, 2000).

that fear is often at the root of failure to disclose.[88] He suggested that responses should be built around practices traditionally described as confession (encompassing truth-telling and apology), repentance and creating the appropriate conditions for forgiveness.

The 2015 Francis Report into whistleblowers in the NHS, arising after the Mid-Staffordshire Hospitals scandal, said that:[89]

> we have seen cases where a culture of blame leads to entrenched positions, breakdown of professional relationships and considerable suffering, utterly disproportionate to the nature of the problem from which this process originated. … The overarching principle is that every organisation needs to foster a culture of safety and learning in which all staff feel safe to raise a concern.

As noted above, the 2016 National Maternity Review was particularly clear about the adverse effects of litigation on creating a blame culture leading to the practice of 'defensive medicine'.[90]

B. The Scientific Basis for Ethical Behaviour and Regulation

Behavioural science has recently been enlisted as the basis of a new paradigm of ethical behaviour and effective compliance and regulation.[91] The basic idea is to regulate through culture. The major points are as follows. Organisational aspects are important to take account of inherent human mechanisms such as the following: to make decisions very quickly by instinct (or 'gut feel', using the 'fast brain' heuristic),[92] and then persuade ourselves that we comply, even when we obviously do not (cognitive dissonance),[93] discarding evidence or reasoning that does not support the decision taken;[94] and to see what we are focusing on and miss other things, however important, and to think that all we see is all there is.[95] It will be important to have time to reflect, to ask ourselves and others if our fact-base, analysis and judgement is correct, to check and be open to challenge.[96] We will

[88] N Berlinger, *After Harm. Medical Error and the Ethics of Forgiveness* (Baltimore, Maryland, The Johns Hopkins University Press, 2005).

[89] *Sir R Francis QC, Freedom to Speak Up: An Independent Review into Creating an Open and Honest Reporting Culture in the NHS* (Department of Health, 2015).

[90] *Better Births*, above, n 7.

[91] C Hodges, *Law and Corporate Behaviour: Integrating Theories of Regulation and Enforcement* (Oxford, Hart Publishing, 2015).

[92] Kahneman, above, n 26; Banaji and Greenwald, above, n 26.

[93] R Fairman and C Yapp, *Making an Impact on SME Compliance Behaviour: An Evaluation of the Effect of Interventions upon Compliance with Health and Safety Legislation in Small and Medium Sized Enterprises* (Health and Safety Executive, 2005) Research Report 366; M Syed, *Black Box Thinking. Marginal Gains and the Secrets of High Performance* (John Murray, 2015) 80.

[94] Haidt, above, n 26.

[95] C Chabris and D Simons, *The Invisible Gorilla* (Crown Books, 2010) ('they can't find what they're not looking for but they won't find what they're not looking for, no matter how dangerous it is').

[96] A Gawande, *The Checklist Manifesto. How to Get Things Right* (Profile Books, 2010).

make poor decisions when we are under stress, focus just on certain targets, or feel threatened.[97] We are particularly open to following the behaviour of the group in which we function.[98] Sociopaths and psychopaths are incapable of ethical social working.[99] All those factors need to affect our working culture. However, we can equally draw on our inherent ability to distinguish between right and wrong,[100] and the sense of social fairness that supports ethical behaviour[101] through sensing that fair rules are made and applied fairly.[102] All these aspects can support a fair and just system of behaviour in social groups, built on evidence of mutual trust. These ideas can be built on to construct more sophisticated systems that affect behaviour and culture (compliance and regulatory systems).

C. Developments in UK Regulatory Policy

Having occupied sole position as a theory of enforcement by regulatory authorities, deterrence has now made a surprising exit from the practice of many regulatory authorities. It is a change of major significance but one that has gone largely unnoticed by many tort lawyers and academics. The change accompanies the replacement of private law mechanisms and actors by public law mechanisms and actors in affecting behaviour in many situations.

The predominant current practice amongst UK regulatory authorities in relation to enforcement in response to identification of breaches of law has two components. First, public authorities differentiate infringers based on their motivations. Was their intent essentially deliberately anti-social and self-benefiting (criminal) or was it a mistake by someone or some organisation that essentially honestly intends to do the right thing and not harm others? Second, the tools to respond to people at those two extremes, and on a spectrum between them, need to be differentiated. You keep a hard enforcement tool (removal of liberty or licence to operate, disqualification, large fine) for criminals,[103] and you support

[97] D Gentilin, *The Origins of Ethical Failures. Lessons for Leaders* (Routledge, 2016); *Report of a Senior Practitioners' Workshop on Identifying Indicators of Corporate Culture* (International Corporate Governance Network, IBE, Institute of Chartered Secretaries and Administrators, held on 17 December 2015).

[98] Banaji and Greenwald, above, n 26, 130.

[99] P Babiak and RD Hare, *Snakes in Suits: When Psychopaths Go to Work* (HarperCollins, 2006).

[100] EO Wilson, *The Social Conquest of Earth* (Liveright Publishing, 2012); Haidt, above, n 26.

[101] LM Friedman, *The Legal System: A Social Science Perspective* (Russell Sage Foundation, 1975) 105–13; RA Kagan et al, 'Fear, Duty, and Regulatory Compliance: Lessons from Three Research Projects' in C Parker and V Lehmann Nielsen (eds), *Explaining Compliance: Business Responses to Regulation* (Edward Elgar, 2012).

[102] J Darley et al, 'Enacting Justice: the Interplay of Individual and Institutional Perspectives,' in M Hogg and J Cooper (eds), *The SAGE Handbook of Social Psychology* (Sage, 2003); TR Tyler, *Why People Obey the Law* (Yale University Press, 2006); TR Tyler and SL Blader, *Cooperation in Groups: Procedural Justice, Social Identity, and Behavioral Engagement* (Psychology Press, 2000).

[103] It is highly relevant that it is very rare that individuals in the NHS act criminally to harm others (such as Dr Shipman).

the well-intentioned to assist them to comply in future. If you use the wrong tool on the wrong person, not only will it be ineffective in achieving the desired outcomes, you may do more harm than good. For example, imposing a significant penalty on someone who was trying to do the right thing may lead to a reduction in compliance by them and others, since the action will be viewed as unfair. Although criminal law and hard penalties exist as a long-stop, it is unnecessary to remind people of their existence, and it is positively unhelpful in supporting a positive working culture for the vast majority to work in the context that they will be sanctioned.[104]

There has been a considerable evolution in practice, policy and theory on enforcement and hence on how to deliver regulation.[105] Steps in this development have included the concept of 'responsive regulation',[106] restorative justice in criminal law, and Better Regulation policy[107] including a risk-based approach towards securing compliance by business using advice and persuasion as the first step,[108] associated with Macrory's specification that the first aim of regulatory enforcement is to *change the behaviour* of the offender.[109]

[104] A striking example of this occurred after the conviction of Dr Bawa-Garba, which provoked widespread 'consternation and outrage' in the medical profession, described as 'toxic fear': see *Independent Review of Gross Negligence Manslaughter and Culpable Homicide* (General Medical Council, 2019).

[105] G Russell and C Hodges, *Regulatory Delivery* (Oxford, Hart Publishing, 2019). Of the six elements in the Regulatory Delivery Model for regulatory authorities recommended there, the concept of 'enforcement' has been replaced by 'intervention' where it is needed.

[106] Leading texts are I Ayres and J Braithwaite, *Responsive Regulation: Transcending the Deregulation Debate* (Oxford, Oxford University Press, 1992); K Hawkins, *Environment and Enforcement: Regulation and the Social Definition of Pollution* (Clarendon Press, 1984); K Hawkins, *Law as Last Resort* (Oxford, Oxford University Press, 2002); H Genn, 'Business Responses to the Regulation of Health and Safety in England' (1993) 15 *Law and Policy* 219; B Hutter, *Compliance: Regulation and Environment* (Clarendon Press, 1997); B Hutter, *Regulation and Risk: Occupational Health and Safety on the Railways* (Oxford University Press, 2001); P Grabosky, 'Beyond the Regulatory State' (1994) 27(2) *Australian and New Zealand Journal of Criminology* 192; N Gunningham and P Grabosky, *Smart Regulation. Designing Environmental Policy* (Oxford, Oxford University Press, 1998); F Haines, *Corporate Regulation: Beyond 'Punish or Persuade'* (Clarendon Press, 1997); F Haines, 'Regulatory Reform in Light of Regulatory Character: Assessing Industrial Safety Change in the Aftermath of the Kader Toy Factory Fire in Bangkok, Thailand' (2003) 12 *Social and Legal Studies* 461; B Hutter and C Jones, 'From Government to governance: external influences on business risk management' (2007) 1 *Regulation & Governance* 27; J Braithwaite and P Grabosky, *Of Manners Gentle: Enforcement Strategies of Australian Business Regulatory Agencies* (Oxford University Press, 1987); PJ May and S Winter, 'Regulatory Enforcement and Compliance: Examining Danish Agro-Environmental Policy' (1999) 18(4) *Journal of Policy Analysis and Management* 625; J Black and R Baldwin, 'Really Responsive Regulation' (2008) 71(1) *Modern Law Review* 59.

[107] See OECD texts: *Risk and Regulatory Policy: Improving the Governance of Risk* (OECD, 2010); *OECD Guidelines for Multinational Enterprises* (OECD, 2011); P Lunn, *Regulatory Policy and Behavioural Economics* (OECD, 2014); *OECD Best Practice Principles for Regulatory Policy: Regulatory Enforcement and Inspections* (OECD, 2014); *Corporate Governance and Business Integrity. A Stocktaking of Corporate Practices* (OECD, 2015); *G20/OECD Principles of Corporate Governance. OECD Report to G20 Finance Ministers and Central Bank Governors* (OECD, 2015); *Behavioural Insights and Public Policy. Lessons from Around the World* (OECD 2017); *Improving Regulatory Governance. Trends, Practices and The Way Forward* (OECD and KDI, 2017).

[108] P Hampton, *Reducing Administrative Burdens: Effective Inspection and Enforcement* (HM Treasury 2005).

[109] R Macrory, *Regulatory Justice: Making Sanctions Effective* (HM Treasury, 2006); reprinted in R Macrory, *Regulation, Enforcement and Governance in Environmental Law* (Oxford, Hart Publishing,

Under the Better Regulation approach of achieving better outcomes whilst saving resources for both public and private actors, a duty was imposed on many UK regulatory bodies[110] to observe statutory principles of good regulation, ie that 'regulatory activities should be carried out in a way which is transparent, accountable, proportionate, consistent, and that regulatory activities should be *targeted only cases in which action is needed*'.[111] Specified bodies are also under a duty not to impose or maintain unnecessary burdens in the exercise of regulatory functions.[112]

The 2014 UK Regulators' Code[113] stresses the need for regulators to adopt a positive and proactive approach towards ensuring compliance, requiring that:

1 regulators should carry out their activities in a way that *supports those they regulate to comply and grow*;[114] and
2 regulators should ensure clear information, guidance and advice is available to *help those they regulate meet their responsibilities to comply*.[115]

Sophisticated regulators now focus not on compliance but on outcomes.[116] In 2017, the UK Cabinet Office identified that the direction of travel of regulation is to recognise that the centre of gravity for responsibility of risk lies with those who create and can directly control it:[117] the primary role of regulators is to help, not to run things or mandate how they are run as long as the social and economic outcomes are achieved.

The findings from scientific research and from empirical research into regulatory practice outlined above have been used to support new understandings in business compliance and, regulation and 'enforcement'. The latest model involves the concepts of Ethical Business Practice (EBP) and Ethical Business Regulation

2010). Implementation was in the Regulatory Enforcement and Sanctions Act 2008. Subsequent codification occurred in the Consumer Rights Act 2015.

[110] See the Legislative and Regulatory Reform (Regulatory Functions) Order 2007, SI 2007/3544, which now applies to many national regulatory agencies such as the Civil Aviation Authority, the Environment Agency, the Financial Conduct Authority, the Food Standards Agency, the Health and Safety Executive, and the Pensions Regulator. See various subsequent amendments. Various regulators are specified in Legislative and Regulatory Reform Act 2006, s 24(5): the Gas and Markets Authority, the Office of Communications, the Office of Rail Regulation, the Postal Services Commission and the Water Services Regulatory Authority.

[111] Legislative and Regulatory Reform Act 2006, s 21. The government later claimed that the principles of good regulation were 'a widely accepted definition of best practice': S Vadera, *Government Response to the House of Lords Select Committee on Regulators: Report on UK Economic Regulators* (Department for Business Enterprise & Regulatory Reform, 2008) para 1.2.

[112] Regulatory Enforcement and Sanctions Act 2008, ss 72, 73(3)–(6).

[113] The Regulators' Code 2014. Introduced as the *Regulators' Compliance Code: Statutory Code of Practice for Regulators* (Department for Business Enterprise and Regulatory Reform, 2007), made under the Legislative and Regulatory Reform Act 2006, s 22(1).

[114] From 2017, UK regulators must 'have regard to the desirability of promoting economic growth': Deregulation Act 2015, s 108.

[115] Regulators' Code, provisions 1 and 5.

[116] The goal of achieving outcomes is specified in *Regulatory Futures Review* (Cabinet Office, 2017); M Butler, *Delivering Better Outcomes for Citizens: Practical Steps for Unlocking Public Value* (HM Government, 2017); *Primary Authority: Statutory Guidance* (Department for Business Energy and Industrial Strategy, 2017) para 1.27. See wide acceptance by regulators: Russell and Hodges, above, n 105.

[117] *Regulatory Futures Review* (Cabinet Office, 2017).

(EBR),[118] in which organisations ensure that they do the right thing and provide transparent evidence of this, thereby deserving trust and lower regulatory intervention since they are effectively self-regulating. Further, they should ensure that they have an ethical culture, since that responds to all eventualities, whether regulated, anticipated or not, and should drive the right responses. Organisational culture should be based on a single, simple social purpose and on espousal of ethical values in all behaviour by all staff. This approach principally acts ex ante, and constantly, so is preventative of breaches, but then aims to identify problems swiftly and rectify them.

We will now illustrate a successful regulatory regime that demonstrates some of the aspects identified above, and then demonstrate how a successful no-blame compensation scheme collects data and drives learning and improvement.

D. A Different Regulatory Paradigm: An Open Culture Delivering Safety in Civil Aviation

The safety outcomes in civil aviation are astoundingly good. Evaluation of data is undertaken constantly, so the flow of information is critical. The root cause of this is an 'open' and 'just' culture, in which all individuals constantly share all relevant information, however embarrassing it might be, in the knowledge that they do so in a 'safe space' environment. The concept of 'compliance' has been replaced by focus on *performance*: the approach is constantly to improve how people and the system are performing in a risk-based world. The issue is not to identify an individual and blame them, but to seek to learn and improve by asking 'Why would any human in that situation act in that way, so that we can reduce the risk of recurrence?'

Just culture in the European aviation industry is enshrined in EU legislation:

> The sole objective of safety investigations should be the prevention of future accidents and incidents without apportioning blame or liability.[119]
>
> The civil aviation system is based on feedback and lessons learned from accidents and incidents which require the strict application of rules of confidentiality in order to ensure the future availability of valuable sources of information. In this context sensitive safety information should be protected in an appropriate way.[120]
>
> The civil aviation system should equally promote a non-punitive environment facilitating the spontaneous reporting of occurrences and thereby advancing the principle of 'just culture'.[121]

[118] C Hodges and R Steinholtz, *Ethical Business Practice and Regulation. A Behavioural and Values Based Approach to Compliance and Enforcement* (Oxford, Hart Publishing, 2017).

[119] Regulation (EU) No 996/2010, recital 4. Even in 1994, it was provided that a safety recommendation shall in no case create a presumption of blame or liability for an accident or incident: Directive 94/56/EC, Art 10.

[120] Regulation (EU) No 996/2010, recital 22.

[121] Regulation (EU) No 996/2010, recital 24.

> The information provided by a person in the framework of a safety investigation should not be used against that person, in full respect of constitutional principles and national law.[122]

The legislation defines 'just culture' as meaning

> a culture in which front line operators or others are not punished for actions, omissions or decisions taken by them that are commensurate with their experience and training, but where gross negligence, wilful violations and destructive acts are not tolerated.[123]

Just culture draws a line between acceptable and unacceptable behaviour based on motivation. 'A wilful violation is not acceptable. An honest mistake is'.[124] Standards of behaviour require professional competence, openness, sharing, and taking responsibility for one's mistakes by correcting them and improving.[125]

It is critical that a just culture has to apply *throughout* the industry, in *all of* the regulatory, professional accreditation, commercial and social relationships. A risk of blame in any one of those relationships risks the entire enterprise of sharing and learning.

E. A Different Healthcare Redress Paradigm

We have referred above to Nordic administrative injury compensation schemes. Under these, no blame attaches to healthcare individuals involved, so staff encourage and assist patients to submit claim details. Some spectacular improvements have been achieved in health care practice by analysing the schemes' data. Examples will be given here from the Swedish Patient Compensation Scheme (LÖF). Certain authorised officers of employers can be authorised to access the data down to the level of individual patients. LÖF encourages self-analysis of data by care-giver organisations and individuals. It is introducing an online log-in facility. Data is not provided to the media below county level. Individual doctors are notified of a decision on award on compensation, but not of what sum is paid.

First, a dramatic improvement was achieved in serious birth injuries after the data identified some critical aspects, such as interpreting cardiograms, which led to intensive outreach with midwives, obstetricians and paediatricians: see Figure 1.

[122] Regulation (EU) No 996/2010, recital 25.

[123] Commission Regulation (EU) No 691/2010 of 29 July 2010 laying down a performance scheme for air navigation services and network functions and amending Regulation (EC) No 2096/2005 laying down common requirements for the provision of air navigation services, Art 2(k).

[124] Dekker, above, n 81, 15.

[125] McCune et al, above, n 81, 195.

Figure 1 LÖF data on settled claims involving serious birth injuries 2000–2015, per 100,000 babies born per quarter and per date of birth

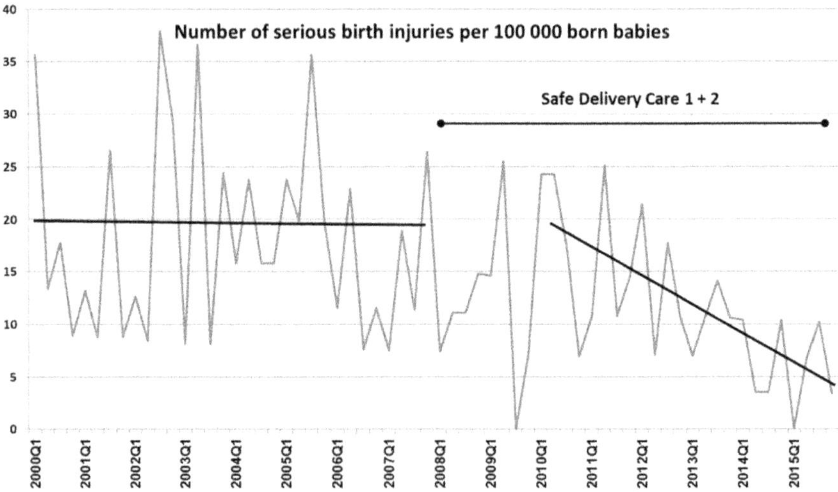

A second example of the same approach reduced joint infection after joint prosthesis surgery: see Figures 2 and 3 from hip and knee arthroplasties after retraining in a large orthopaedic department in 2010 and 2011.

Figure 2 Data on wound complications after hip arthroplasty in a large orthopaedic department 2006–2014

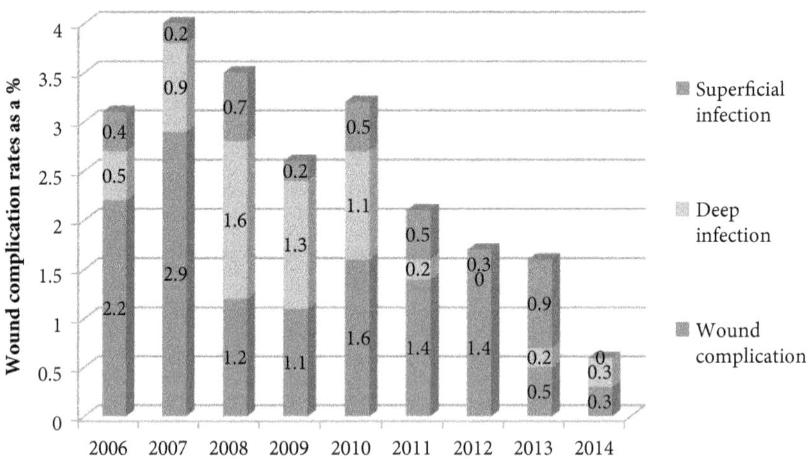

Examples of other smaller projects have included smoke-free operation, providing claims statistics to care-givers, marking of medication packaging, providing 100-point surgery checklists (SURPASS, invented in the Netherlands), crew resource management, and structured communications (SBAR).

Figure 3 Data on wound complications after knee arthroplasty in a large orthopaedic department 2006–2014

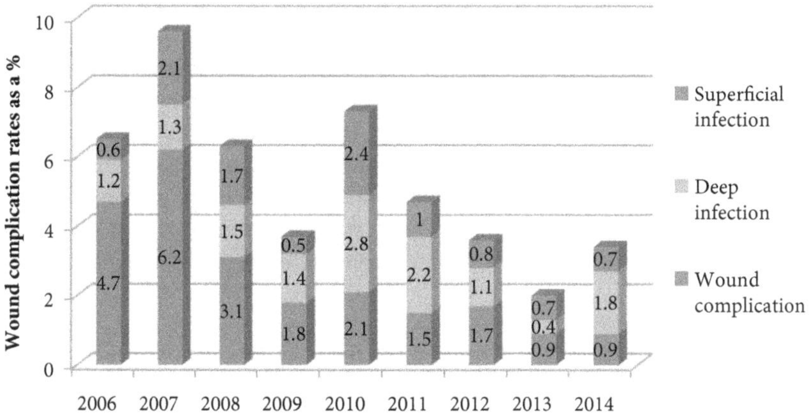

V. The NHS

We have so far identified that a system involving legal liability based on finding fault and a litigation system that is adversarial will present a barrier to the open and swift sharing of full information on medical mishaps. There are other available systems for delivering compensation, for example through administrative, non-adversarial schemes. This section summarises the state of attempts to create a no-blame culture in the NHS, and the impediments to this.

A. Regular Disasters Caused by Failures in Culture

It is striking not just that there have been so many major serious healthcare failures, occurring on a regular basis over recent decades, but also that subsequent inquiries have universally identified a failure in the *culture* of the organisations involved as a major underlying cause. Such cultural failures are in fact the consistent theme in different types of disasters.

The 2001 Bristol Royal Infirmary inquiry called for 'a new culture, of trust not blame' and 'the abolition of clinical negligence litigation, taking clinical error out of the courts and the tort system'.[126] The 2010 Francis Report into Mid-Staffordshire Hospitals found that complaints were poorly investigated, remedial action was often not applied, appraisal and professional development were accorded a low priority, the focus of the Board was on processes not outcomes, and its reaction to

[126] *Learning from Bristol: The Department of Health's Response to the Report of the Public Inquiry into Children's Heart Surgery at the Bristol Royal Infirmary 1984–1995*, (2002) Cm 5363, i and 367.

criticism was individually and collectively one of denial instead of searching self-criticism.[127] The 2015 Morecambe Bay hospitals maternity review, found a 'seriously dysfunctional' maternity service at Furness General Hospital, and distinguished between staff making individual errors and colluding in concealing the truth of what happened.[128] It found 'the repeated failure to examine adverse events properly, to be open and honest with those who suffered, and to learn so as to prevent recurrence' to be inexcusable.[129] The Parliamentary and Health Service Ombudsman made a clear call in 2016 for the establishment of a no blame culture in the NHS, following an investigation into avoidable deaths that indicated 40 per cent of internal investigations were inadequate in finding out what had happened.[130] Unless a no-blame culture is achieved, the NHS is doomed to experiencing a cycle of major disasters.[131]

B. Recognition that an Open and Just Culture is the Key

Strong emphasis has increasingly been placed in the last few years on improving performance by learning from mistakes and errors. In order to become a 'learning organisation' it has been accepted that the culture within the NHS has to change and, in particular, has to be based on a 'no-blame' policy.[132]

One of the watershed reports was that by Professor Norman Williams, President of the Royal College of Surgeons, and Sir David Dalton, Chief Executive of Salford Royal Hospital, who in 2014 emphasised the need to view human actions in the context of wider factors. They called for a 'duty of candour' to be re-emphasised in the NHS, through training and supporting staff, improving the levels and accuracy of reporting of patient safety incidents, and spreading and applying lessons learned into practice.[133] Those authors commented:

[127] *Independent Inquiry into Care Provided by Mid Staffordshire NHS Foundation Trust January 2005 – March 2009. Volume I. Chaired by Robert Francis QC*, HC375-I (2010).

[128] Dr B Kirkup CBE, *The Report of the Morecambe Bay Investigation* (Department of Health, 2015) para 11.

[129] ibid, para 8.3.

[130] *Learning from Mistakes. An Investigation Report by the Parliamentary and Health Service Ombudsman into How the NHS Failed to Properly Investigate the Death of a Three-year old Child* (Parliamentary and Health Service Ombudsman, 2016), also referring to *A Review into the Quality of NHS Complaints Investigations Where Serious or Avoidable Harm Has Been Alleged* (Parliamentary and Health Service Ombudsman, 2015).

[131] *Report of the Independent Inquiry into the Issues raised by Paterson*, House of Commons, 4 February 2020, HC 31.

[132] See *Learning not Blaming: The Government Response to the Freedom to Speak Up Consultation, the Public Administration Select Committee Report 'Investigating Clinical Incidents in the NHS', and the Morecambe Bay Investigation* (Department of Health, 2015), Cm 9113; *NHS England Serious Incident Framework (2015); Report of the Expert Advisory Group: Healthcare Safety Investigation Branch* (Department of Health, 2016).

[133] *Building a Culture of Candour: A Review of the Threshold for the Duty of Candour and of the Incentives for Care Organisations to be Candid* (Royal College of Surgeons of London, 2014). The authors recommended that the duty of candour should be extended from the initial limitation to events that caused death or serious injury to include harm defined as moderate: the issue had been disputed.

> 29 While there can be a degree of individual responsibility when something goes wrong (and that is certainly how it feels to the practitioners concerned) it is vital for investigations of harm to consider the human factors in the context of team, organisation and system factors. This is not only because it is a fair and balanced way of understanding individual responsibility, but also because it provides a far firmer basis for understanding why harm has occurred and therefore of preventing future harm. Individual cases of harm, rightly considered, can provide insights into wider organisational issues that can contribute to harm, such as loss of notes, the poor management of resource pressures, and shortcomings in discharge processes.
>
> ...
>
> 32 A compliance-focused approach will fail. If organisations do not start from the simple recognition that candour is the right thing to do, systems and processes can only serve to structure a regulatory conversation about compliance. The commitment to candour has to be about values and it has to be rooted in genuine engagement of staff, building on their own professional duties and their personal commitment to their patients[9].
>
> [9] For the impact of a lack of an enabling environment for candour /open disclosure, see Mazor et al, 'Communicating with patients about medical errors' (2004) 164 *Archives of Internal Medicine* 1690; Vincent, 'Understanding and responding to adverse events' (2003) 348(11) *New England Journal of Medicine* 1051.

These points were taken up in a major policy speech by the Secretary of State for Health, Rt Hon Jeremy Hunt MP, in 2016, called 'From a blame culture to a learning culture'.[134] He suggested using 'intelligent transparency' as the means to create 'the world's largest learning organisation'. He identified key components of achieving the change as:

> [a] new [Care Quality Commission] inspection regime; legislating for the statutory duty of candour; making progress – not always smoothly – towards a 7-day NHS; [asking] every trust to appoint independent freedom to speak up guardians so clinicians can relay concerns to someone other than their line manager; [launching] the Sign up to Safety campaign and recently the campaign to halve the number of stillbirths and neonatal deaths.
>
> But if we are really to tackle potentially avoidable deaths, we need culture change from the inside as well as exhortation from the outside. A true learning culture has to come from the heart. ....
>
> That means a profound change in culture. ....

If an Open Culture is the goal, let us now examine some aspects of whether that goal is capable of being attained, and the building blocks and barriers that might contribute to success or failure.

[134] Rt Hon Jeremy Hunt MP, Speech at Global Patient Safety Summit, Lancaster House, 10 March 2016, available at www.gov.uk/government/speeches/from-a-blame-culture-to-a-learning-culture.

C. Policy Objectives

The 2009 *NHS Constitution for England* commits to patients that when mistakes happen, it will 'acknowledge them, apologise, explain what went wrong and put things right quickly and effectively'.[135] The NHS Constitution states that:[136]

> any individual has the right to:
>
> - have any complaint they make about NHS services dealt with efficiently and have it properly investigated
> - know the outcome of any investigation into their complaint
> - take their complaint to the independent Health Service Ombudsman if they are not satisfied with the way the NHS has dealt with their complaint
> - make a claim for judicial review if they think they have been directly affected by an unlawful act or decision of an NHS body
> - receive compensation where they have been harmed by negligent treatment'.

This was further developed in the National Patient Safety Agency's 2009 *Being Open*[137] policy, which stated:

> *Being open* involves:
>
> - acknowledging, apologising and explaining when things go wrong;
> - conducting a thorough investigation into the incident and reassuring patients, their families and carers that lessons learned will help prevent the incident recurring;
> - providing support for those involved to cope with the physical and psychological consequences of what happened.
>
> *The principles*
>
> The following set of principles has been developed to help healthcare organisations create and embed a culture of Being open:
>
> 1 Acknowledgement
> 2 Truthfulness, timeliness and clarity of communication
> 3 Apology
> 4 Recognising patient and carer expectations
> 5 Professional support
> 6 Risk management and systems improvement
> 7 Multidisciplinary responsibility
> 8 Clinical governance
> 9 Confidentiality
> 10 Continuity of care.

[135] *The NHS Constitution for England* (London, Department of Health, 2009).

[136] The Health Act 2009 places a duty on NHS organisations (including contractors) to 'have regard to the NHS Constitution'.

[137] *Being Open – Communicating Patient Safety Incidents with Patients and their Carers* (National Patient Safety Agency, 2009).

In 2009, the Health Service Ombudsman published six Principles of Good Complaint Handling:[138]

1 getting it right;
2 being customer focused;
3 being open and accountable;
4 acting fairly and proportionately;
5 putting things right;
6 seeking continuous improvement.

NHS organisations are subject to legal,[139] contractual[140] and professional[141] obligations to provide an accessible and suitably responsive complaints procedure for service users. Since 2013, the Scottish Government has based its policies on fairness.

The *Being Open* policy states that the following should be communicated to a patient who has been harmed:[142]

- the chronology of clinical and other relevant facts;
- details of the patient's, their family's and carers' concerns and complaints;
- a repeated apology for the harm suffered and any shortcomings in the delivery of care that led to the patient safety incident;
- a summary of the factors that contributed to the incident;
- information on what has been and will be done to avoid recurrence of the incident and how these improvements will be monitored.

There has been recognition that both an open culture and a just culture are required in the NHS. Guidance has been issued on the concept of just culture in

[138] *Spotlight on Complaints: A Report on Second-stage Complaints about the NHS in England* (Healthcare Commission, 2009). See earlier, *Principles of Good Administration* (March 2007) and *Principles for Remedy* (October 2007).

[139] The Local Authority Social Services and National Health Service Complaints (England) Regulations 2009, SI 2009/308.

[140] From April 2009, all Primary Care Trusts (PCTs) are required to be registered with the Care Quality Commission, under the Health and Social Care Act 2008. As a condition of registration, a PCT is required to ensure that 'there are systems in place to ensure that patients, their relatives and carers:

- have suitable and accessible information about, and clear access to, procedures to register formal complaints and feedback on the quality of services
- are not discriminated against when complaints are made
- are assured that organizations act appropriately on any concerns and, where appropriate, make changes to ensure improvements in service delivery'. (Core standard C14, Standards for Better Health).

[141] For doctors: 'Patients who complain about the care or treatment they have received have a right to expect a prompt, open, constructive and honest response including an explanation and, if appropriate, an apology. You must not allow a patient's complaint to affect adversely the care or treatment you provide or arrange': *Good Medical Practice* (General Medical Council).

[142] *Being Open: Saying Sorry when Things Go Wrong* (National Patient Safety Agency, 2009), Stage 5: Process Completion.

the context of investigations,[143] based on identifying whether an individual who caused harm did so intentionally, or knowingly departed from protocols and other related factors. NHS Improvement has also started to issue materials on how to create a culture and leadership programme.[144] The latter includes 12 metrics cover three outcomes (quality and value; continuous improvement; and healthy, flourishing and engaged staff) and five cultural elements (vision and values; goals and performance; support and compassion; learning and innovation; and teamwork). The cultural change programme includes reliance on data, to be displayed in a dashboard, and is heavily management- and process-oriented. However, it appears complex and the simple message that staff should always 'do the right thing' appears lost in much detail. Further, the two concepts of open and just culture have not been connected together in a holistic manner.

Meanwhile, the retiring chair of NHS England, Lord Prior, referred to the NHS in 2019 as having chaotic organisation and that overuse of targets 'has led to a disempowered culture, a learned helplessness culture, a top-down looking-upwards culture, a very hierarchical culture'.[145] In July 2019, a Patient Safety Strategy repeated that blame prevented people 'admitting' errors, and proposed to create a 'patient safety culture', without saying how organisations should proceed to create open and just cultures other than by exhortation.[146]

D. Developments in Regulatory Enforcement Policy

The principal regulator of care activities in hospitals and GPs in the NHS is the Care Quality Commission (CQC). The central mode of operation of the CQC in overseeing safety in NHS units is based on carrying out inspections. In 2013, the CQC adopted language from the aviation sector in aiming to create a 'just and open culture in CQC, one that is open about what people think and believe, where we learn from mistakes to get better, and are encouraged to raise concerns that will be listened to'.[147] The CQC's 2016–2021 strategy adopted the following 'vision for quality regulation':[148]

- People trust and use expert, independent judgements about the quality of care.
- People have confidence that good and poor care will be identified and action taken where necessary so they are protected.

[143] *A Just Culture Guide* (NHS Improvement), available at www.improvement.nhs.uk/resources/just-culture-guide/#h2-what-do-we-mean-by-just-culture. See *Learning from Deaths. A Review of the First Year of NHS Trusts Implementing the National Guidance* (Care Quality Commission, 2019).

[144] A suite of documents includes: *Culture and leadership programme. Phase 1 Discover. Concepts and evidence* (NHS Improvement); *Culture and leadership programme. Phase 1 Discover. Culture and Leadership Programme Phase 1* (NHS Improvement), Version 2, May 2017.

[145] C Smyth, 'Health service is chaotic and dysfunctional, says NHS chief' *The Times*, 15 February 2019.

[146] *The NHS Patient Safety Strategy. Safer Culture, Safer Systems, Safer Patients* (NHS England and NHS Improvement, 2019).

[147] *Annual Report 2013/14* (Care Quality Commission, 2014).

[148] *CQC's Strategy 2016–2021: Shaping the Future: Consultation Document* (Care Quality Commission, 2016).

- Organisations that deliver care are encouraged to improve quality.
- Organisations are encouraged to use resources as efficiently as possible to deliver high-quality care.

The CQC stated in 2015 that an important part of its work is 'encouraging a culture of openness at all levels'.[149] One of the core aspects of the NHS' vision for success in 2020 is to rely on early intervention and prevention.[150]

However, there is anecdotal evidence from NHS units that the inspection regime can appear to be carried out so as to find fault, following which the attitude of inspectors might not be supportive of supporting improvements. A new Enforcement Policy came into force from April 2015,[151] which set out a backstop of criminal or civil enforcement actions but clearly prioritised softer actions to support and improve the performance of entities. Yet in 2017/18, although 72 per cent of services that were rated as 'inadequate' on their previous inspection improved their rating, and 51 per cent rated as 'requires improvement' improved their rating, 21 per cent of services previously rated as 'good' and 9 per cent of services rated as 'requires improvement' on their previous inspection deteriorated to a lower rating at their most recent inspection.[152]

In 2017/18 and 2018/19 the CQC carried out over 17,000 inspections. Table 1 shows that the number of enforcement actions has increased markedly in recent years. The vast majority related to regulated activities in adult social care (the sector with by far the most inspections). Most enforcement actions were warning notices, the purpose of which is to 'put providers on notice that legal action will be taken if they do not improve by a set deadline'.[153]

Table 1 Care Quality Commission Inspections and Enforcement Actions 2012/13 to 2018/19

	2012/13	2013/14	2014/15	2015/16	2016/2017	2017/18	2018/19
Enforcement actions	1,029	1,523	1,179	1,090	1,910	2,283	2,206
Of which Warning Notices	910	1,456	1,037	828	1,352	1,343	1,089

E. Duty of Candour

The 'duty of candour' has been referred to above. It came into force for providers, along with the fit and proper person requirement for directors for NHS bodies,

149 *Annual Report and Accounts 2014/15* (Care Quality Commission, 2015).
150 *Strategic Plan for the Next Four Years: Better Outcomes by 2020* (Public Health England, 2016).
151 *Enforcement Policy* (Care Quality Commission, 2015). See also *Enforcement Decision Tree* (Care Quality Commission, 2015).
152 *Annual Report and Accounts 2017/18* (Care Quality Commission, 2018).
153 *Annual Report and Accounts 2014/15* (Care Quality Commission, 2015).

in November 2014, and for all other services in April 2015.[154] Health and social care providers are *required* to be open and honest when things go wrong, and to hold directors (or their equivalents) to account when care fails'.[155] In 2016 the Secretary of State for Health announced the publication of a table that *grades* the openness and honesty of reporting cultures in hospitals.[156]

The mechanism is, therefore, authoritarian. It sends a message to people who thought that they were trying to do the right thing and be honest among themselves and with patients, that they will be treated as criminals if they are thought not to have been fully open in every situation. How would you feel if your employer imposed this duty on you? The empirical evidence is that reports of general adverse events in the NHS *declined* in England after it became clear that criminal enforcement of the duty of candour would be introduced, but continued to *increase* in Wales, where criminal enforcement was not introduced at the time.[157]

F. The Mode of Operation of the Healthcare Safety Investigation Branch

In 2016 the Secretary of State for Health announced the creation of a new Healthcare Safety Investigation Branch (HSIB) modelled on the Air Accident Investigation Branch.[158] It was claimed that the HSIB would be a support for staff through creating a 'safe space' within which to be entirely open. That way in which the message was formulated inherently sent a message that staff were not trusted to tell the full truth in any event. But the 'safe space' turns out not to be so safe after all.

The concept of the HSIB was set out by an Expert Advisory Group that reported in 2016.[159] The aims of the Expert Advisory Group were to design a new mechanism, operating in a new culture, which would deliver a number of different goals that were not fully compatible. A principal – but unstated – objective was to provide a forum for investigation of future major problems that was cheaper than inquiries such as the Bristol and Francis Inquiries (the cost objective). A second objective was to provide an expert investigation function that would identify the root causes of failures, so that the right correctives could be put in place to reduce the risk of occurrence (the investigation objective). A third function was to provide a forum in which harmed families and patients could feel involved,

[154] A contractual duty of candour was included in the standard NHS commissioning contract under *NHS Standard Contract 2014/15, Updated Technical Guidance* (NHS England) para 27.31, App 5.

[155] *Annual report and accounts 2014/15* (Care Quality Commission, 2015). See also *CQC's strategy 2016–2021: Shaping the future: consultation document* (Care Quality Commission, 2016).

[156] https://www.gov.uk/government/publications/learning-from-mistakes-league.

[157] It was proposed in the 2019 Health and Social Care (Quality and Engagement) (Wales) Bill. The duty of candour was introduced in Scotland from 1 April 2018 under the Health (Tobacco, Nicotine etc & Care) (Scotland) Act 2016.

[158] Speech at Global Patient Safety Summit, above, n 134.

[159] *Report of the Expert Advisory Group*, above, n 31.

so as to defuse their desire to campaign outside the system for expensive inquiries, to bring court cases, and generally be difficult to handle. The more humane way of stating that is to provide a forum in which patients and families would be treated with respect, honesty and dignity[160] (the involvement objective). This issue arose partly as a matter of respect between fellow human beings and partly since it was recognised that 'the way in which people are treated after adverse events can at times compound the distress and harm suffered'[161] and their desire to seek accountability and redress.

The Expert Advisory Group summarised its recommendations under the headings:

- independence, engagement and learning;
- system-wide investigation and improvement;
- just culture: trust, honesty and fairness;
- further actions required across the healthcare system.

The Report was clear that there were widespread, deep and long-standing problems in the NHS in relation to safety, and accident investigation, and they would not all be solved by the creation of a single new investigation body.[162] The Report made clear that responsibility for safety would remain with every individual NHS organisation, and that HSIB would not itself carry out the great majority of safety investigations.[163] Its primary goal would be to generate learning to support improvements in the safety of healthcare, which it would achieve by carrying out investigations into selected matters of highest risk, publishing investigation reports and making recommendations to prevent recurrence.[164] Recipients of HSIB recommendations would be required by legislation to publish a formal response setting out whether they accepted the safety recommendation or disputed it, and what actions they would take and by when.[165] The Report was clear that the purpose and remit of the HSIB would be limited to that of[166]

> an enabler, exemplar and catalyst for learning-oriented safety investigation. It is not to provide justice, or remedy, for patients and families. Nor are its purposes to determine liability, find fault or attribute blame. Those are important functions, but they belong elsewhere in the system, and they should not be undermined or diluted.

[160] ibid, 6: '… the way in which people are treated after adverse events can at times compound the distress and harm suffered. We recognise the distress and pain that result from serious safety failures, and acknowledge that this this can be amplified by poorly handled responses and investigations. In future, when the Branch identifies failings, it will describe and investigate them, and will provide patients and families with all relevant information'.

[161] ibid, 6.

[162] ibid, 12.

[163] ibid, 7.

[164] ibid, 23, 24.

[165] Ibid, 24.

[166] Ibid, 6.

One justification for creation of the HSIB lay in the need to ensure that healthcare personnel openly, voluntarily and swiftly shared information about their activities, acts and omissions that might expose them to criticism. The Report contained repetitive statements that a no-blame culture was the goal, still less blame of individuals, and it contained a section on 'Promoting a just culture' that referred to not blaming staff for honest mistakes and protecting them from 'unwarranted blame by others on the basis of the information provided during an investigation'.[167]

The approach outlined in the Report was a long way from the historical rhetoric of blame. However, there were some serious problems over the approach that was suggested. In fact, it was fatally flawed in three respects. First, the adoption of a just culture depended on action by every NHS unit in the country – not on statements or a small number of interventions by the HSIB. No plan was published for how that change might occur: the HSIB recommended that a Just Culture Task Force be established to 'determine the appropriate policies, practices and institutional arrangements that are required to move the healthcare system firmly towards a just culture of safety'.

Second, in particular, the HSIB was established only to investigate a handful of cases a year. It would be unclear to staff whether different 'regimes' of openness, protection and blame might apply under many circumstances. In aviation safety, important information is learned from speedy investigation into the causes of accidents, but this may only provide sparse learning.[168]

Third, there remains an unresolved and fundamental conflict in the proposed arrangements between, on the one hand, assuring staff that information they provide will be kept confidential within HSIB's investigation, thereby safeguarding them from criticism, ostracism or scapegoating, and, on the other hand, providing information openly to patients and families about what happened. In relation to the interests of patients and openness it was said:

> The Branch should encourage full and inclusive participation in a safety investigation, including by patients and their families, healthcare staff, commissioners, regulators, and educators. All knowledge should be valued equally; and all voices, including those of patients, of their families, and of staff, should be heard equally, in order to foster a genuine motivation to learn and to improve safety. … Those involved or harmed in safety incidents – whether patients, relatives or staff – must have the opportunity to be fully involved in investigations into what has happened. At the outset, the account of those involved or affected by the events should be sought, and their views as to what happened heard.[169]

[167] Ibid, 25, 26, 32: 'For staff, trust will depend principally on knowing that they will be treated fairly and not blamed for genuine mistakes. They must feel safe from unwarranted blame when taking part in an investigation. We are struck by work that has shown that the most effective learning takes place in conditions of psychological safety, characterised by a shared belief that participants will not be embarrassed, rejected, or punished for speaking up'.

[168] JG March et al, 'Learning from Samples of One or Fewer' (1991) 2(1) *Organizational Science* 1.

[169] *Report of the Expert Advisory Group*, above, n 31.

Some information would or could be provided to patients. All information on care and treatment would be provided, the job titles and roles of staff would be identified in reports, supposedly confidential information could in fact be made public by a court order – which is exactly what is normal and required practice in litigation – and information revealing potential intentional wrongdoing, gross negligence, or other concerns that constitute an immediate danger to present or future patients would be immediately passed on. A fair reconciliation between openness in making information available to patients and families and protecting staff from blame and potential retaliation was not established by these arrangements, because they do not address the totality of the 'real life' situation. The perpetuation of this conflict can be seen further in the following extract from the Report:

> During its investigations, a subset of information gathered by the Branch may not be relevant to the report findings but may directly relate to the care and treatment of a patient affected by a serious safety incident. This information must be shared with the patient and with the patient or patient's family, who are free to use this information as they wish. …
>
> In order to underpin a just culture that ensures the continued provision of safety information and the confidence of healthcare professionals, all other evidence collected solely for the purposes of safety investigation must be used solely for the purposes of safety improvement. It should not be made available to other bodies or admissible as part of another body's proceedings. …
>
> We stress that all information relevant to the care and treatment of a patient would be shared with the patient and their family, who are of course free to use it as they wish, and all information required to explain, fully and rigorously, the causes of a safety issue would be published in the public investigation report. We stress also that, should concern arise during a safety investigation over potential intentional wrongdoing, gross negligence, or other concerns that constitute an immediate danger to present or future patients, this would be notified to the relevant bodies for them to conduct their own investigation. These protections must not interfere with the proper administration of justice, and would not prevent any legal or professional regulatory proceedings in response to intentional wrongdoing or gross negligence. Appropriate co-ordination of any parallel investigations should be considered in the enabling legislation, and the Branch should draw up Memorandums of Understanding with other key bodies to facilitate co-ordination. …
>
> Information and reports published by the Branch will reflect the principle that all investigations are for the purpose of improving systems and practices, and not for holding individuals to account for past events. Therefore, the Branch must not identify the individuals involved in a safety issue or event under investigation. This is in order to avoid any perception that individuals are being found at fault, and instead to focus attention on the processes and mechanisms that cause a safety issue and that may be widely present across different parts of the healthcare system. While individuals will not be named or identified in reports beyond their job titles or roles, the purpose is not to provide any broader guarantee of anonymity to individuals, who may well be identified in other proceedings related to a serious safety event such as an inquest.

In summary, these HSIB arrangements would *not* remove a potential for blame arising through regulatory, professional, employment, patient, social media or media channels. The proposed 'safe space' that would apply in investigations would be porous, and not trusted by staff since it would exist in a daily sea of potentially unsafe space. From the staff perspective, there is too much uncertainty and risk. Accordingly, it would be inherently unlikely to maintain a just culture without *any* fear of blame in which staff will *always* volunteer *all* information. Hence, the critical culture that would support volunteering potentially embarrassing information, or prevent incomplete record-keeping or even falsification of records, would not be generated.

G. The Need to Educate Patients, the Media and Politicians Not to Ask "Who's to Blame?"

The Secretary of State for Health correctly identified a conflict between the new culture of openness and learning and the traditional regime of accountability through liability, blame and deterrence. Indeed, the latter attitude can be a knee-jerk reaction by the public, the media,[170] social media and politicians to respond to scandals by attributing blame, as a report into two Welsh hospitals warned:[171]

> The Review Team is concerned that this Report may be seen by some, and be reported by others, as evidence of failure and incompetence which should result in a search for 'the guilty' and for 'heads to roll'. This is the current bullying language frequently used to vilify those with responsibility for services and care in the NHS and other public services. … in every organisation providing services to the public, there will be lapses in standards and practice in some way. … It is very important to say this, in this report, which is about services provided by local people to fellow citizens in their own community. Local and national governance arrangements should provide the reassurance to the public that care and treatment issues … are routinely identified and action taken without recourse to one-off external reviews.

In 2015, the House of Commons Public Administration Select Committee noted[172] an 'unresolved tension between the desire for an open 'no-blame' culture and the

[170] A case that ran from 2011 to 2018 involved Dr Bawa-Garba, a paediatric registrar, who was convicted of manslaughter by gross negligence in circumstances where she was under considerable stress caused by overwork and inadequate support. Her erasure from the UK register 'made many doctors anxious and raised questions about what's next for the patient safety agenda': www.bmj.com/bawa-garba (accessed 13 February 2020).

[171] J Andrews and M Butler, *Trusted to Care. An Independent Review of the Princess of Wales Hospital and Neath Port Talbot Hospitals at ABMU* (Dementia Services Development Centre and The People Organisation, 2014) para 5.1.

[172] Public Administration Select Committee – Sixth Report: *Investigating Clinical Incidents in the NHS*, 24 March 2015, para 74. PASC noted an academic paper that had argued that 'Investigations should be focused on learning and improvement. They should not attribute blame or liability for the causation of safety issues and there should be clear agreements that punitive proceedings will not be

demand for the clear accountability the public is entitled to expect from a public service'. Similarly, the Secretary of State for Health, Jeremy Hunt, said:[173]

> And this means a fundamental rethink of our concept of accountability. Time and time again when I responded on behalf of the government to tragedies at Mid Staffs, Morecambe Bay, Winterbourne View, Southern Health and other places I heard relatives who had suffered cry out in frustration that no one had been 'held accountable'.
>
> But to blame failures in care on doctors and nurses trying to do their best is to miss the point that bad mistakes can be made by good people. What is often overlooked is proper study of the environment and systems in which mistakes happen and to understand what went wrong and encouragement to spread any lessons learned. Accountability to future patients as well as to the person sitting in front of you.
>
> The rush to blame may look decisive. It may seem like professionals are being held accountable. In fact, the opposite can happen. By pinning the blame on individuals, we sometimes duck the bigger challenge of identifying the problems that often lurk in complex systems and which are often the true cause of avoidable harm.

The way in which this issue is overcome in aviation is mainly through visible outcomes – flying on planes is overwhelmingly safe. Can the number and incidence of such 'safe' outcomes be achieved in healthcare, or is healthcare inherently risky? If the key to the achievement of the goal lies in a just culture, improvements in culture must be humanly possible in the healthcare system. Both aviation and healthcare are complex, with multiple actors and systems. Similar improvements in safety culture have been achieved in construction site safety in UK.[174]

It is important to note that aviation is blame-free but not accountability-free. Accountability comes through sharing information about failures and improvements, and a mutual desire to learn lessons. All operators are constantly socially accountable to their peers to be open, to share information, to question and to check, all in a non-hierarchical way.[175] Sidney Dekker, an expert in 'just culture', identifies critically contrasting viewpoints:

> Backward-looking accountability tries to find a scapegoat, to blame and shame an individual for messing up. Forward-looking accountability acknowledges the mistake and the harm resulting from it, should lay out the opportunities (and responsibilities!) for making changes so that the probability of such harm happening again goes down.[176]

taken against staff based on findings of any safety investigation'. C Macrae and C Vincent, 'Learning from Failure: the Need for Independent Safety Investigation in Healthcare' (2014) 107(11) *Journal of the Royal Society of Medicine* 439.

[173] Speech at Global Patient Safety Summit, above, n 134.

[174] M Webster and H Bolt (Frontline Consultants), *The Effectiveness of HSE's Regulatory Approach: The Construction Example* (Health & Safety Executive, 2016) RR1082.

[175] Hodges and Steinholtz, above, n 118.

[176] Dekker, above, n 81, 9.

H. The NHS Culture Deters Patients from Complaining

If patients are to trust the NHS, they will need to have evidence – from first-hand and anecdotal experiences – that support their giving of such trust. An important reason why a system may not succeed in learning is that it fails to capture information not just from its professionals but also from its customers (patients and families). Citizens generally seem to be reluctant to complain against many public bodies. However, a 2016 report by the NHS Ombudsman published data that GP services led the field of public services of whom people had had a poor experience (37 per cent), followed by local authorities (29 per cent) and hospitals (28 per cent): see Figure 4.[177]

Figure 4 Services people have had a poor experience with in the last two years

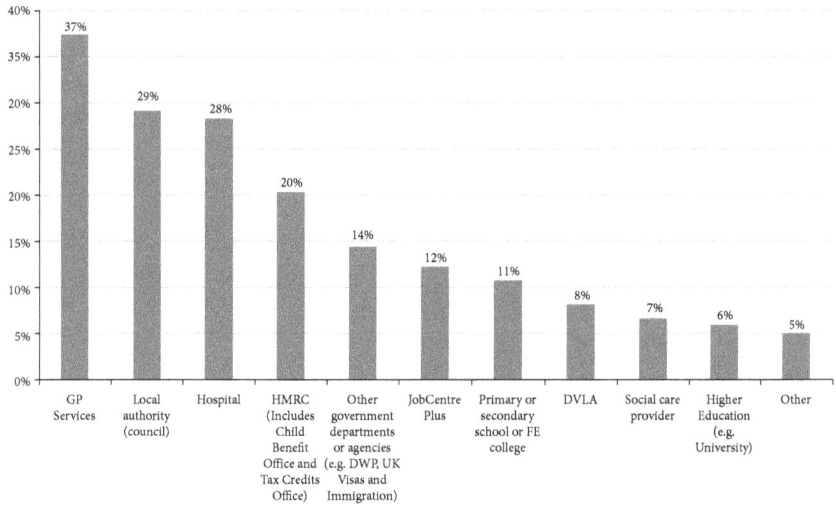

Fewer than one in four (22 per cent) of those surveyed who were unhappy about GPs had made a formal complaint. In relation to public services generally, 73 per cent had used informal channels to voice their frustrations, while 60 per cent exclusively used informal channels, whilst digital channels were emerging as popular methods of expressing frustration. By far the most common reason for not complaining was the belief that it would not change anything (52 per cent) and various other reasons related to fear of how they would be treated (19 per cent) or poor expectations of the process (too complicated 18 per cent, too long 15 per cent, not knowing how to complain 14 per cent): see Figure 5.[178]

[177] *Learning from Mistakes*, above, n 130.

[178] ibid. See also *What Do People Think About Complaining?* (Parliamentary and Health Service Ombudsman, 2015).

Similarly, over half (52 per cent) of respondents to a Complaints Survey carried out for Citizens Advice in 2015 said they did not complain because they 'didn't think it would change anything'.[179]

Figure 5 Reasons for not complaining after experiencing poor public service

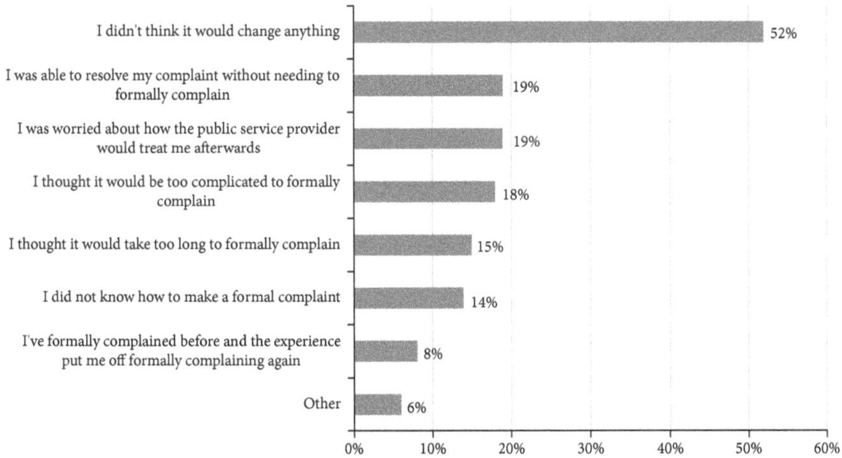

In the 1990s and 2000s, complaining about NHS service was rarely considered as an option by aggrieved patients.[180] People faced problems in getting a satisfactory response to a complaint and the NHS would fail to learn lessons from complaints, particularly thanks to the fragmentation of complaints systems across the NHS, private health-care, and social care.[181] One review found that many NHS complaints related to the fundamentals of good healthcare, such as effective communication with patients, the attitude of staff, record-keeping, privacy and dignity, plus in 19 per cent of cases a problem with the way in which a complaint was handled.[182] Recommendations for reforming the complaints system have included the need for a single point of access with integrated complaints and

[179] *Learning from Mistakes: How Complaints Can Drive Improvements to Public Services* (Citizens Advice, 2016) 15.

[180] L Mulcahy and JQ Tritter, 'Pathways, Pyramids and Icebergs? Mapping the Links between Dissatisfaction and Complaints' (1998) 20(6) *Sociology of Health and Illness* 825; Department of Health commissioned survey, 2005, referred to in *Listening, Responding, Improving: A Guide to Better Customer Care* (Department of Health, 26 February 2009); *Making Experiences Count: A New Approach to Responding to Complaints* (Department of Health, 2007).

[181] *Report: Making Things Better? A Report on Reform of the NHS Complaints Procedure in England* (Health Service Ombudsman for England, 2005). See previously H Wallace and L Mulcahy, *Cause for Complaint: An Evaluation of the Effectiveness of the NHS Complaints Procedure* (The Public Law Project, 1999); *Being Heard* (Department of Health, 1994) (the Wilson Report); *Cause for Complaint* (Public Law Project, 1999).

[182] *Feeding Back? Learning from Complaints Handling in Health and Social Care* (National Audit Office, 2008).

advice teams,[183] and the need for early discussions involving the patients and practitioners concerned.[184]

I. Conclusions on the Ability to Achieve an Open Culture in the NHS

An essential requirement of the open/just culture in aviation safety is that the same culture of trust applies in *every* relationship if it is to provide a comprehensive feeling that a person who shares difficult information would not thereby trigger adverse consequences. It has to exist throughout *social, operational, managerial, and regulatory and public* regimes. This chapter is not a comprehensive survey, but we have seen above various examples of where blame is still embedded in the system, or has not been completely removed. It is the basis of civil compensation liability; it is the default reaction of the traditional media and social media, and of politicians; it is unclear to what extent it exists in NHS units across the country; it is not removed from the HSIB; it exists in how many NHS units treat patients who make complaints. Unless blame is substantially removed from *all* of these situations, a just culture, and hence a learning culture, can never be created. Culture is built from the *bottom up* rather than by trying to impose it from the top down: the latter will fail. How can these issues be addressed?

VI. Conclusion: Building the Future

The proposition is that both a fault-based system and an adversarial process present strong barriers to clinical staff openly sharing information, and hence the achievement of both openness with patients about what happened and why, and medical learning so that future mishaps can be avoided on a wide scale.

The analysis in this short chapter is far from comprehensive, but does identify some major issues. Fault and adversarial systems are old technology.[185] More efficient mechanisms now exist for delivering compensation to those who qualify, and for delivering further functions, especially caring responses, explanations and apologies, aggregating data on adverse events and feeding back information on how to improve both practice and culture in healthcare. A system that only delivers money is functionally very limited. The fault and adversarial systems are inherently divisive (despite sometimes incorporating mediation techniques) and do not provide healing in terms of personalities or confidence in people and

[183] Lloyd-Bostock and Mulcahy, above, n 2; Health Select Committee report, *Complaints and Litigation*, July 2011.

[184] A Clwyd and T Hart, *A Review of the NHS Hospitals Complaints System. Putting Patients Back in the Picture* (Department of Health, 2013).

[185] C Hodges and S Voet, *Delivering Collective Redress: New Technologies* (Oxford, Hart Publishing, 2018).

systems. They can now be seen *not* to deliver deterrence, or support for an open, learning culture, whereas the approaches, systems and conditions that do support such a culture are now known. The traditional legal system is incapable of delivering the objectives that are needed.

Having the right culture is essential. The open (ethical) culture needs to exist between professionals themselves, and between them and patients. Relationships based on trust are essential, and trust is based on the sum of available evidence. We now know how to do this in various situations and sectors, so we know that it is possible.

The difficulty is in achieving the ideals set out here in practice. The NHS has recently adopted admirable rhetoric that it intends to create an open culture. But this will not succeed under current arrangements. People do not trust the NHS in their experiences of complaints and when things go wrong – as opposed to the day-to-day delivery of healthcare. The professionals will not trust their managers because an open culture is elusive and barriers to it still exist, such as fear of enforcement through imposition of the duty of candour and inconsistencies between inspection and enforcement practices. Mixed messages are being sent, when it is critical that consistently strong messages are required to underpin development of an open culture. One of the main barriers is fuelled by social media and other public comment that can scapegoat individuals and attract massive adverse publicity.

Some major impediments are: the sheer size of the NHS, which produces the impression in those on the front line that they are run by distant political masters who have limited understanding of what is needed to make things work in daily practice; the existence of several hierarchies, such as amongst different professions (eg surgeons, anaesthetists, nurses, pharmacists, auxiliaries) and managers (eg administrators, consultants, registrars, others); the extensive barrage of instructions and requirements being imposed on a top-down basis on care units, leading to their over-loading and inability to implement changes; the continued existence of unrealistic performance targets, rather than behavioural targets; and an ongoing fear of criticism and blame, whether from inspectors, employers, the press, or lawyers. These impediments prevent genuine collaborative teamwork in many NHS units.

Various indications follow for future changes in policy and practice.[186] An important consideration is whether the NHS should be reformed into smaller units that have less top-down authoritarian control, that give care units greater responsibility and free them from clogging bureaucracy, thereby enabling them to build greater operational trust between social groups that have more human scale in terms of size.[187] A second issue is a need to recognise that system

[186] See Hodges and Steinholtz, above, n 118.

[187] An understandable drive for integration of primary, secondary specialist and social care organisations involving NHS, private and local authority organisations, raises the issue of what size of organisation enables effective working between the people involved: see *Designing integrated systems (ICSs) in England* (NHS, 2019).

design is not the only element, and that the culture that operates in the system is equally – if not more – critical. Another vital reform is to switch from a legal mechanism involving blame and adversarialism to a no-blame administrative investigative and compensation scheme, that identifies problems quickly and resolves them swiftly and fairly.

PART III

Apologies

8

An Incentive-based Approach to Apologies and Compensation

NICOLA BRUTTI*

We can recall several examples in which law deals with certain social phenomena without regulating them directly: the increasing relevance of corporate codes of conduct, the use of reputational sanctions in social networks, the emergence of public apologies in tort law. In the last example, we may focus on many legal implications, such as the opportunity to provide safe harbour legislation, the acknowledgment of mitigating effects on non-material damages, the idea of judge-ordered apologies. According to law and economics thought, apologies can be deemed to fall within the category of 'merit goods': they allow people to reach the difficult goal of non-material compensation, giving voice to personal feelings without having to translate them into money. This chapter shows how behavioural incentives and mediation proceedings might be more appropriate than authoritative measures in order to gain benefits from apologies.

I. Introduction

In this chapter I suggest a different way of considering apologies and compensation in relation to civil liability. Where most studies of apologies within legal systems have focused on the evidential and remedial aspects of apologies, I take an economic approach, suggesting that apologies might be considered from the point of view of incentives. As a matter of unexpected consequences of compensation law, apologies may be seen as something that comes from outside the legal system but may affect outcomes and alter what we would naturally expect from the legal system.

We can examine the legal relevance of apologies through a conceptual pyramid. At the bottom, we find courtesy and day-to-day apologies which carry out a ritual role in our society. At the top of the pyramid we put all the cases in which apologies might be considered mandatory on a legislative or judicial basis. While civil law systems normally exclude this solution due to constitutional constraints

* Professor of Comparative Law, University of Padua, Italy.

and procedural guarantees, other legal traditions have allowed mandatory apologies, although the point raises a strong debate, as is discussed by Robyn Carroll in Chapter 9. In certain countries, especially those influenced by collectivist ideologies or religious concerns, an apology might be treated as a legal remedy because it is strictly connected with the principle of social harmony. This means that an individual must follow traditional norms to avoid litigation and seek social appeasement as the main goal in their life. Compelling someone to apologise might sound like a reputational sanction, but in exceptional situations it could be more effective than other options.

Sometimes judges manage a case through a 'consent order' based on a settlement in which the injurer agrees to apologise publicly. A consent order complies with the principles of fair trial and the rule of law as well as helping the parties to save some of the costs of litigation and compensation monies.

All this considered, we can say that the appreciation of the legal relevance of apologies is very varied. In between the two extremes, the total rejection of the legal relevance of apologies on the one hand, and the unreserved acceptance of apologies as a legal remedy on the other, lies a third, more gradual approach, that will be considered in this chapter. Denying legal relevance to apologies lacks realism and empathy, because in some cases the existence of apologies strongly influences a legal relationship. While it cannot be ignored, an apology does not seem to be economically measurable. The unreserved acceptance of apologies as a legal remedy is attempting to render artificially something that is intrinsically spontaneous.

According to Guido Calabresi's 'law and economics' thought,[1] it is preferable in most cases to follow an incentive-based approach rather than a mandatory and coercive one (pure command) or a 'pure-market'. This recalls the Latin 'in medio stat virtus'.[2] For this reason law cannot ignore benefits flowing from apologies, but it has to be careful not to impose them directly, giving them more space and stimulus while preserving their genuine nature. For the future, it could be useful to go on developing a complete and practical view of procedural mechanisms through which apologies can be properly encouraged. This might happen, for example, by awarding exemplary damages for lack of apologies, or issuing consent orders that reduce legal expenses, or mitigating damages as a consequence of appropriate spoken apologies etc.

II. Apologies and the 'Shadow Line' of Legal Relevance

The first point I would like to discuss is the problem of the legal relevance of apologies; that is, how apologies may or may not be used within the legal system.

[1] See G Calabresi, *The Future of Law and Economics. Essays in Reform and Recollection* (Cambridge, Cambridge University Press, 2016) Ch II (on merit goods).

[2] A literal translation would be 'the virtue is in the middle'.

Consider a recent decision[3] of the Italian Banking and Financial Ombudsman (the ABF).[4] The ABF is an alternative dispute resolution system for customer complaints about banks and other financial intermediaries. A man started proceedings before the ABF, complaining that a bank had refused to accept him as a client without any valid reason. He claimed an unusual remedy, asking the ABF to settle the matter by requiring the bank to offer him a public apology. The ABF decided that the bank had no obligation to accept him as a client, as this was just an expression of its own contractual freedom. Furthermore, the ABF stated that the remedy required could never be adopted because the latter falls within the rules of courtesy and is ontologically incompatible with the rules of law. That is, they took the view that apologies were not – and could not be – part of the law.

The ABF was probably worried about the fact that due to Article 128-bis of the Consolidated Law on Banking, it is bound only by statutory law or, at least, by deontological codes of conduct.[5] This makes this legislation one of those increasingly frequent cases in which a statutory law expressly refers to soft law as a minimum standard of conduct. For example, Article 9 (Courtesy) of the European Investment Bank's Code of Conduct prescribes that:

1. Members of staff shall act in a conscientious, correct, courteous and approachable manner. In replying to correspondence, telephone calls and e-mails, members of staff shall endeavor to be as helpful as possible and to answer enquiries.
2. If an enquiry does not fall within their area of responsibility, staff shall refer members of the public to the relevant Bank department.
3. They shall offer apologies in the event of error.

According to the above-mentioned source of law provision, is this a legal obligation or only soft law? Could it be considered a binding rule or only moral suasion?

Due to the existence of the above-mentioned provision, the claim of the ontological incompatibility of law and apologies should be rejected because there is a statute or a code of conduct stating a duty to apologise for banks. But sources like codes of conduct are not easy to monitor, as they are a widespread phenomenon and normally we do not regard them as having the status of law. However, it is notable that in a globalised world their legal implications are growing rapidly. And indeed, we must immediately stress that the abovementioned provision could

[3] ABF, *Collegio di Milano, 23 settembre 2010, n 959*, Presidente Antonio Gambaro, available at www.dirittobancario.it/node/2279/pdf.

[4] The ABF is regulated by Art 128-bis of the Consolidated Law on Banking (Legislative Decree No 385/1993). Participation in the ABF system is a legal obligation of banks, a condition for the exercise of banking and financial activities. Non-compliance is punishable by a fine. On the ABF, see Banca d'Italia, *The Banking and Financial Ombudsman Annual Report Abridged Version*, n 5 (2014) 5–6. See also G Alpa, 'ADR and Mediation: Experience from Italy' (2008) 19 *European Business Law Review* 5; M Pellegrini, 'Alternative Dispute Resolution Systems in Italian Banking and Finance: Evolution and Goals' in D Siclari (ed), *Italian Banking and Financial Law* (London, Palgrave Macmillan, 2015).

[5] See above, n 3.

make apologies mandatory as long as the bank has agreed to the code of conduct.[6] We shall return to this question shortly.

Another significant case in point occurred in Rome. Municipal police in the city are worried about getting little respect from citizens of Rome. People are typically very aggressive towards public officers who direct the chaotic Roman traffic. In Italy those who are reported by municipal police for contempt must write a letter of apology and pay a fine (usually around €200–250). This sanction is considered adequate to repair the damage at the pre-trial stage, thus cancelling the contempt.

In 2015, Roman municipal police decided to change their policy, and started to demand that videos of public apologies be published on YouTube, instead of a simple letter of apology.[7] The requirement was presented by the police as the only way to avoid a much more burdensome criminal trial. In fact, since insulting a public official is considered a criminal offence, those who refuse to repair the damage can be considered guilty of contempt.[8] The Heads of Police thought that a symbolic humiliation would deter people from being so disrespectful. The new procedure was criticised for bringing back mediaeval shaming sanctions like the pillory or the 'amende honorable', which some people associate with apologies. In the book *Discipline and Punish*, Michel Foucault described the amende honorable with reference to Robert-François Damiens' humiliation in front of the main door of the Church of Paris in 1757.[9] Here, the amende honorable is presented in its most violent and ancient version as a dominant technology of power.[10] Later in history, the amende honorable assumed different forms, similar to a reparatory/reconciliation tool or public apologies.[11] So the Municipal Police position aroused negative public reactions, focusing on the risk of reintroducing a sort of mediaeval practice. Some commentators have stressed that this sort of practice contrary to human dignity and should be opposed.[12]

Although the police in Rome require an apology video, the law does not provide explicitly for such a remedy. The judiciary is the only power allowed to decide about the effectiveness of reparation and thus to cancel the contempt. In doing so

[6] 'Code of good administrative behaviour for the staff of the European Investment Bank in its relations with the public', 2, available at www.eib.org/attachments/general/code_en.pdf. On codes of conduct, see EM Epstein, 'The Good Company: Rhetoric or Reality? Corporate Social Responsibility and Business Ethics Redux' (2007) 44 *American Business Law Journal* 207; EF Brown, 'No Good Deed Goes Unpunished: Is There a Need for a Safe Harbor for Aspirational Corporate Codes of Conduct?' (2008) 26 *Yale Law& Policy Review* 367.

[7] See T Kington, 'Rome Traffic Police Make Drivers Apologise on YouTube to Avoid Criminal Record' *The Times*, 22 December 2017.

[8] See Art 341-bis, Codice Penale (Criminal Code).

[9] M Foucault, *Surveiller et punir* (Paris, 1975) 2; for further considerations see GJ Van Niekerk, 'Amende Honorable and Ubuntu: An Intersection of Ars Boni et Aequi in African and Roman-Dutch Jurisprudence?' (2013) 19 *Fundamina* 397; E Descheemaeker, 'Old and New Learning in the Law of Amende Honorable' (2014) 36 *University of Edinburgh School of Law Research Paper* 3.

[10] D Hansen-Miller, *Civilized Violence: Subjectivity, Gender and Popular Cinema* (Routledge, 2016) 9–11.

[11] For a more detailed discussion, see J Hallebeek and A Zwart-Hink, 'Claiming Apologies: A Revival of Amende Honorable?' (2017) 5(2) *Comparative Legal History* 194.

[12] See, for example, C Bonini, 'La gogna su YouTube: "Hai offeso i vigili? Pubblica un video di scuse"' *La Repubblica*, 20 December 2017.

it cannot rely solely on the victim's desire for revenge, although it will certainly be influenced by the preference that the victim has expressed about it. It must also take into consideration other elements, including the protection of the constitutional rights of the offender, public policy objectives and – last but not least – the possibility of the insincerity of the apologiser.

After all, begging pardon in a video which can be disseminated across the internet is not the same thing as writing a letter of repentance. To be compelled to appear in a YouTube video is a humiliating threat to one's identity and privacy, whereas writing a letter would be a less publicly humiliating means of achieving the desired result: public repentance restoring the police honour. But is the letter published? If the letter is not published then it is not public, and is vastly different from a video on YouTube. But if the letter is published by the police, then the difference between the two scenarios is not so large.

In the two cases briefly described, each complaining party was searching for a specific and highly symbolic remedy, presumably without desiring anything else. In the Italian jurisdiction we can thus observe two completely opposite conceptions. On the one hand, the ABF said that using an apology as a legal remedy is out of the question. And even worse, law and apologies would be like oil and water, in other words absolutely incompatible with each other. On the other hand, the municipal police claim that a self-humiliating video is the best solution available to cancel out contemptuous behaviour towards them. In their opinion the injurer should not be able to influence the choice of remedy. So the victim is the only one who can decide the most adequate remedy to repair the offence. Who is right? The issue seems very uncertain.

Looking at the abovementioned cases, the reputation and credibility of the parties concerned are at stake, as well as the balance of power between them, and, not least, how greatly is the public concerned by the injury. All of this might make the difference between a reasonable request for an apology and a vexatious one.

It should be noted that the issue of legal relevance of apologies is addressed in many legal systems in ways very different from Italy.[13] According to one approach, apologies will always and inevitably be a mere act of courtesy between persons, and nothing more. However, this idea needs to be verified more thoroughly when the apologies take place within the context of a legal dispute or as an attempt to prevent potential litigation. In other words, a feasible distinction may be made between statements provided for courtesy and for purposes of good neighbourliness, and those provided for avoiding or resolving probable litigation. And I agree that there is a strong argument that it is a problem if law prevents the ordinary habits of apologising from happening. But notwithstanding the adversarial attitude of our adjudicative systems, in my view law cannot deal ordinarily with apologies that are completely inconsistent with litigation issues, so they are – in legal terms – absolutely worthless. In civil law countries we have quite a strong

[13] For further consideration, see Chapter 9 of this book, by Robyn Carroll.

separation between mere facts and juridical facts determined by the legislative power (especially civil codes).[14] But I think that similar reasoning works quite well in any jurisdiction, albeit with different boundaries fixed by customary law or case law (think about the strong legal value of certain customs in China or Japan,[15] and the judicial precedents in common law as a source of law).

On the other hand, we can find cases showing relevant legal implications. The hypothesis is that different effects can be attached to apologies according to the specific context in which they take place. In particular, apologies issued as a means for preventing or composing a potential legal dispute may be different from apologies used as a mere social habit or ritual,[16] or, to put it another way, daily occurrences that are not reasonably expected to turn into litigation, unless we want to bring to court even cases involving an involuntary push.[17] We can make such distinctions also on the basis that only in the first case can the apology definitively involve a substantial admission against interests.

According to such a method of analysis we can put at the 'base' of the pyramid an apology that conforms only to a social habit, and which is therefore without any legal significance. Conversely, we can place an apology at the 'top' of the pyramid when it is considered as a legal remedy.[18] However, the critical point is what happens in the middle of the pyramid. From a comparative perspective, I think that we can benefit from using the conceptual framework of gradual emergence of the legal meaning of apologies. This theoretical approach is borrowed from the *Durchbruchspunkte* theory by the German jurist Rudolph von Jhering since, from a literary and historical perspective, we are always dwarfs standing on the shoulders of giants (*nanos gigantum humeris insidentes*).[19] More specifically, this theory is useful in highlighting that legislators make laws for situations as they present themselves at the time, without, however, necessarily excluding other situations which have yet to arise.[20] Legislators often leave room for different interpretation

[14] JH Merryman and RP Perdomo, *The Civil Law Tradition: An Introduction to the Legal Systems of Europe and Latin America* (Stanford University Press, 2007) 71–72.

[15] For example, the essence of '*giri*' goes beyond simple social courtesy, reaching a very deep relationship of confidence in personal, social, or business relationships. See I Kitamura, 'The Role of Law in Contemporary Japanese Society' (2003) 34(4) *Victoria University of Wellington Law Review* 739.

[16] See E Goffman, *Relations in Public. Microstudies of the Public Order* (New York, 1971) 113.

[17] On apologies in social contexts, see WI Edmondson, 'On Saying You're Sorry' in F Coulmas (ed), *Conversational Routine. Exploration in Standardized Communication Situations and Prepattterned Speech* (The Hague, 1981) 273.

[18] For the concept-pyramid (*Begriffspyramide*), see GF Puchta, *Cursus der Institutionen* (Leipzig, 1841); K Larenz, *Methodenlehre der Rechtswissenschaft*, 6th edn (1991) 20–21.

[19] This concept was attributed in the 12th century to Bernard of Chartres by John Salisbury, and expresses the meaning of discovering truth by building on previous discovery. See DD Macgarry (ed), *The Metalogicon of John Salisbury: A Twelfth-century Defense of the Verbal and Logical Arts of the Trivium* (trans MacGarry, Daniel Doyle) (Berkeley, University of California Press, 1955) 167.

[20] See R von Jhering, *Geist des römischen Rechts auf den verschiedenen Stufen seiner Entwicklung, Teil 2, Bd. 2* (Leipzig, 1858) 359 ff. More recently see M Storme, 'Closing Comments: Harmonisation or Globalisation of Civil Procedure?' in XE Kramer and CH van Rhee (eds), *Civil Litigation in a Globalising World* (The Hague, 2012) 383. On anti-formalism, see also K Tuori, *Ratio and Voluntas: The Tension between Reason and Will in Law* (Routledge, 2016) 117.

of certain facts, as legally relevant or irrelevant, according to the emerging needs of society. As testified by Julius Stone's statement about the 'dynamic responsiveness of the substantive law to the needs of social and economic development',[21] the same concept can work quite well also in common law systems, although the role of legislators and judges is traditionally different. I think also that this methodological approach (gradual emergence of legal relevance) can fruitfully be used for all the topics that share the characteristic of being borderline between legal relevance and legal irrelevance – for instance, corporate codes of conduct. To put it another way, we can specifically focus on a shadow line standing between legal irrelevance and legal relevance of apologies.

III. Compensation of Non-pecuniary Losses: The Role of Apologies

It can be argued that law is strictly connected with (if not based on) the distribution of bad things and good things to people. In fact, this distribution often happens between more than the two parties normally involved in a litigation. After all, there is a systematic and consistent way that each community has developed over time to cope with the problem of scarcity of goods and surplus of social ills. In some cases there are remedies that perfectly counteract bad things: here we can find a perfect compensation. But there are other situations in which we cannot achieve, or can only partially achieve, such a counterbalance.

Take the issue of moral and psychological harm. In this case we can only try to reduce the impact of the losses, as it is very difficult to eliminate them: so the most important thing becomes a remedy that is good at mitigating the effects of the non-economic losses or negative outcomes flowing from a wrongdoing.[22] Otherwise, such a remedy is merely one way we try to pursue the 'lesser evil'. This also implies that to choose the lesser evil is not the same thing as mechanically determining a full compensation. Rather, we should speak of a repair function. The Romans said 'Factum infectum fieri nequit': 'what was done cannot be undone'. Consider a wrong that gives a bad example to society, for example violent behaviour by a famous football player, or a concealment of proof or information by an important physician. This bad example carries social costs, which in turn raises a complex debate about the deterrence function of torts.[23] Even more so, we can only get closer to the *status quo ante* when a non-economic value has been damaged.

[21] See J Stone, *Social Dimensions of Law and Justice* (Stanford University Press, 1966) 620–21. On a 'thicker idea' of the rule of law, see P Vines, 'Apologies, Liability and Civil Society; Where to from Here?' in R Levy et al (eds), *New Directions for Law in Australia* (ANU Press, 2017) 330.

[22] J Berryman, 'Mitigation, Apology and the Quantification of Non-Pecuniary Damages' (2017) 7(3) *Oñati Socio-legal Series* 528.

[23] See for further consideration S Hershovitz, 'What Does Tort Law Do? What Can It Do?' (2012) 47(1) *Valparaiso University Law Review* 99, 108–109.

In such a case there is no way for a perfect 'restitutio in integrum' and – in my opinion – the perfect compensation cannot exist when litigation arises.

Let us take a discriminatory act that is a proper example of a tort against human dignity. The remedy could be damages. But someone could express the concern that human dignity cannot be paid for with money. It is a very good point. So what is the correct amount of damages for a non-pecuniary loss? I doubt that a court, a victim and an offender will all have the same opinion about the economic value of moral suffering, but refusing to award any compensation to the victim would be a greater evil. So at some point we ought to find a synthesis. And this is what the legal system does all the time – awards less than perfect compensation because that is better than none. Given that monetary overcompensation or under-compensation is likely, a public apology coupled with a sum of money or with the publication of the judgment may be more appropriate.

In a recent case the Delhi High Court dismissed a defamation lawsuit against *Outlook* magazine and others.[24] The Opinion suggests some interesting findings about compensation and apologies in defamation cases. But they could be valid in most cases of non-pecuniary damages. The Court affirmed:

> Compensation in monetary damages can never set the record straight or restore the damaged reputation caused by a libellous news report.

In relation to reputational damages it stated that:

> Reputation of an individual is not something which can be measured or equated in money. It is only a written apology contained in the same media which may reach the same people who may have had access to the libellous material earlier published and that alone can restore the reputation.

The Court also added in respect of the prevention of high litigation costs: 'In cases where a court does decide damages, the magnitude of the damages can bankrupt a media company or at any rate affect the financial health of the media company'. And the court finally underlined that:

> [...] award of damages, particularly in large amounts, against media houses may also have a chilling effect on the media. In some cases, payment of such amount of compensation, if unable to [be] afford[ed], may compel the media to shut down or may make the media over conscious and thereby fail in its duty to report news on contemporaneous subjects of public interest.[25]

What is the benefit of a public apology over a pure compensation mechanism such as damages? Public (or private) apologies may have the advantage of avoiding

[24] *Bridgestone Corporation v Tolin Tyres Pvt Ltd*, CS (COMM) No 375/2016 www.mondaq.com/india/x/587674/Trademark/Delhi+High+Court+Takes+Strict+Action+Against+Tolin+Tyres+In+Bridgestone+V+Bridestone+Infringement+Case.

[25] Ibid.

another evil: having to go to trial. They can help the parties to join a settlement agreement. This added value should not be underestimated.[26]

The compensation function goes beyond adjudication and is only one, albeit the most important, of several functions typically attached to damages in tort law. Other important goals are deterrence, typically provided by punitive or exemplary damages; prevention and – last but not least – expressiveness.[27] The last of these is a very interesting topic. It takes place when the court focuses on sending a strong message to the public in order to protect some interests put at risk by the wrong-doing. For instance, the dissemination of apologies through a judicial order may restore some important social values in accordance with the needs and values of both society and private litigants.

One of the most curious cases I have ever seen was a case of environmental damage caused by massive oil pollution suffered by South American indigenous peoples: *Maria Aguinda v Chevron-Texaco.*[28] At the end of very complex litigation, a Tribunal of Ecuador awarded nine plus nine billion dollars (a total of $18 bn) in favour of environment and human rights groups. In this astonishing and creative judgment, which took place in a civil law country, half of the total amount was compensatory and the other half was punitive damages (*penalidad punitive*). Meanwhile the Tribunal issued an order to disseminate public apologies (*disculpas publicas*), and compliance with this order was a condition for the cancellation of punitive damages.[29] This seemed to be a sort of conditional remedy and – speaking from a civil law perspective – something similar to an 'alternative obligation'[30] when the debtor (or the obligated party) can choose between two alternative performances in order to comply with their legal duties.

In other words, the Tribunal ordered a public apology whose fulfillment by the defendant should have halved the total amount awarded. Chevron-Texaco – the oil company – chose not to apologise and appealed to the Supreme Court of Ecuador. The argument basically used for contesting the judgment was that the civil code of Ecuador does not provide any form of punitive damages at all, to say nothing of the violation of a due process clause for imposing on someone a duty to accuse himself (in latin *nemo tenetur se detegere*). At the end, the Supreme Court

[26] See JK Robbennolt, 'Apologies and Legal Settlement: an Empirical Examination' (2003) 102 *Michigan Law Review* 460; D Shuman, 'The Role of Apology in Tort Law' (2000) 83 *Judicature* 180; DL Levi, 'The Role of Apology in Mediation' (1997) 72 *New York University Law Review* 1165.

[27] For a seminal study, see M Galanter and D Luban, 'Poetic Justice: Punitive Damages and Legal Pluralism' (1993) 42(4) *American University Law Review* 1393; see also G Calabresi, 'Civil Recourse Theory's Reductionism' (2013) 88 *Indiana Law Journal* 451 and, more particularly, Hershovitz, above, n 23, 108–109.

[28] See A Pigrau, 'The Texaco-Chevron Case in Ecuador: Law and Justice in the Age of Globalization' (2014) 1 *Revista Catalana de Dret Ambiental*, vol V, 1 and K Payne, '*Aguinda v Chevron*: The Potential Rise or Fall of Mass Toxic Tort Claims Against US Companies' (2012) 46(4) *The International Lawyer* 1067.

[29] ibid.

[30] See *Black's Law Dictionary*, 6th edn (West Publishing, 1979) defining alternative obligation as: 'An obligation allowing the obligor to choose which of two things he will do, the performance of either of which will satisfy the instrument. A promise to deliver a certain thing or to pay a specified sum of money is an example of this kind of obligation'.

decided to overrule the part of the judgment concerning punitive damages and the attached conditional remedy.

Is it possible to provide an alternative to paying punitive damages for the defendant, if he prefers to omit apologies? I have no answer. And, to borrow from Socrates: 'I know that I know nothing'. Probably an insightful question is already quite something. But as far as it goes is not enough. The Tribunal of Ecuador may have avoided being overruled by the Supreme Court, if it had constructed the type of damages differently, as an alternative to public apologies.

Since there is no rule in the civil code concerning punitive damages, they are normally precluded in civil law jurisdictions. On the contrary, non-pecuniary damages are well established as a remedy specifically focused on criminal offences. Therefore, the Tribunal should have constructed the alternative to the 'public apologies' order as non-pecuniary damage, or moral damage. Might it have prevented the overruling? Once more I would like to focus on the 'alternative remedy', by asking a question. Do compelled public apologies properly carry out a moral repair function, or do they perform a different task, or a mixed one?[31] I think that the Ecuador case is more concerned with the promotion of public awareness and acknowledgment of wrongdoing at the expense of the defendant's reputation, rather than only on the moral repair goal. Public apologies here are probably better suited to deterrence and sanction than moral compensation, although these topics are not mutually exclusive. Can we say that achieving moral compensation through apologies is an irrelevant question for law? In civil law systems (with some remarkable exceptions) this question has not yet been completely examined.[32]

IV. Law and Economics Theory and Incentive-based Approach to Apologies

A. How Incentives Work

According to Guido Calabresi, 'merit goods' are those goods that cannot be allocated through the ordinary market or through pure command structures.[33] They would be better distributed in a number of other ways to avoid the moral costs that would flow from ordinary allocation.[34]

If our attributes are converted into actions and products that are desired by society for the common good, then incentives to develop and use these attributes

[31] See P Vines, 'The Power of Apology: Mercy, Forgiveness or Corrective Justice in the Civil Liability Arena' (2007) 1 *Journal of Public Space* 1.

[32] For an apology legislation analysis from a common law perspective, see R Carroll et al, *Apology Ordinance (CAP. 631): Commentary and Annotations* (Hong Kong, 2018).

[33] Id est: resource allocation system essentially based on public regulation: Calabresi, above, n 1, 42.

[34] ibid.

are needed.[35] We have positive incentives, like financial rewards, and negative incentives, like sanctions.

Generally speaking, what do I mean by an incentive-based approach? As taught by Tobin[36] and remarked by Calabresi as well,[37] incentives are represented by all those norms providing benefits or sanctions aimed at inducing someone to behave in a certain way. Normally incentives try to achieve the goal of facilitating a socially desirable choice from an individual or an undertaking. There are a lot of examples and different models.

If a sportsman charged with misconduct accepts an early plea, he can often receive a reduction from the base financial sanction.[38] Another example is when government uses green incentives, granting discounts to the advantage of people who decide to install solar panels. More clearly, take the example of leniency programs: the leniency policy is deemed 'a specialized form of the prisoner's dilemma game albeit with a few appreciable differences'.[39] As in the Prisoner's Dilemma,[40] cooperation is required, and an incentive like a safe harbor is necessary.

B. Incentivisation and Safe Harbour Legislation

The prisoner's dilemma can be also recalled to explain the function of safe harbour legislation with specific reference to apologies.[41] Such laws protecting apologies have been growing in importance in the common law world since the 1986 when the first apology act was enacted in Massachussets.[42]

What does an incentive-based approach through a safe harbour law mean? It creates an incentive to apologise so that the lawyers and parties change their mind about apologies: from suspicion and fear to a welcoming attitude. Apologies are facilitated by a safe harbour in order to grant them a performative function instead of consigning them to the confession/admission role that they would have within the ordinary hearsay rule.[43]

[35] ibid.

[36] In relation to investment transactions, Tobin notes that people are willing to assume more risk only if compensated by a higher level of expected return. One can thus think of a trade-off people are willing to make between risk and expected return. See J Tobin, *Money, 2, The New Palgrave Dictionary of Finance and Money* (1992) 770–79.

[37] Calabresi, above, n 1, 76.

[38] See for example, *Tribunal AFL* (Australian Football Association, 2015) p 4.

[39] See Editorial (2010) 1 *Indian Journal of Law & Economics* XV–XVI.

[40] See R Axelrod, 'Effective Choice in the Prisoner's Dilemma' (1980) 24(1) *Journal of Conflict Resolution* 3.

[41] See also B Ho, 'Apologies as Signals: with Evidence from a Trust Game' (2012) 58(1) *Management Science* 141.

[42] JC Kleefeld, 'Promoting and Protecting Apologetic Discourse through Law: A Global Survey and Critique of Apology Legislation and Case Law' (2017) 7(3) *Oñati Socio-legal Series [online]* 455.

[43] See JR Searle, 'A Classification of Illocutionary Acts' (1976) 5 *Language in Society* 12; J Ainsworth, 'The Construction of Admissions of Fault through American Rules of Evidence: Speech, Silence and Significance in the Legal Creation of Liability' in S Tomblin et al (eds), *Proceedings of The International Association of Forensic Linguists' Tenth Biennial Conference* (Birmingham, 2012) 29.

Turning finally to 'merit goods', we can underline that intangible values like altruism are normally considered as an end in themselves that is difficult to achieve through a pure command structure ('commandification'[44]) or through a pure market-based mechanism ('commodification').

Calabresi recalls the McKean paradox, where Roland McKean explained that it would be meaningless to ask: 'How much must I offer you to get you to love me for myself quite apart from my offer?' In other words, Calabresi observes that 'if we treat altruism or beneficence as an ordinary good and try to buy it in the market rather than increasing the amount of it that is produced, as occurs with most goods, we destroy it. And, significantly, it is equally meaningless to ask, 'How can I compel you to love me, for myself alone?' That is, just as use of a pure market destroys the good it seeks to increase, so too does pure command!'[45]

These questions do not make sense. But Calabresi notes that:

> [once] the issue is put in this way, quite a few interesting things follow. While it is true that I may not be able to get you to love me for myself alone by purchasing your love in a pure market … candy helps! And while it may be true that I cannot command you to be beneficent without destroying the beneficence that I value and desire, education – a mighty powerful form of command – may bring about just the result I want.[46] Put in other words: 'Flowers help!'[47]

We can use complex modified markets and less direct and less centralised command structures to increase goods like altruism (merit goods), such as apologies, instead of doing what we do through traditional markets and command structures for most goods.

Apologies can surely be an act of courtesy. But they can also influence the feelings and decisions of people affected by an unlawful act. In this way, apologies can deeply impact the consequences of such an unlawful act. Due to their effect on mediation and settlement of the dispute they can mitigate the quantification of non-economic damages in negligence cases too.[48] In addition, apologies can be relevant for the public interest, not only for interpersonal relationships. They can help the justice system to save money. This is all very well, but it hardly suffices for our purpose.

C. Apologies as Means or Ends?

What I would like to focus on is the following question: are apologies a means or an end? As well as altruism, we can look at apologies not as a means but as an end.

[44] Id est: the tendency to treat some matters through a command and control approach.

[45] Calabresi, above, n 15.

[46] ibid.

[47] ibid.

[48] See, recently, AM Zwart-Hink, 'The Doctor Has Apologised. Will I Now Get Compensation For My Injuries? Myth and Reality in Apologies and Liability' (2017) 7(3) *Oñati Socio-legal Series* 497; DJ Kaspar and LE Stallworth, 'The Impact of a Grievant's Offer of Apology and the Decision Making Process of Labor Arbitrators: A Case Analysis' (2012) 17(1) *Harvard Negotiation Law Review* 1.

More precisely, an apology statement could be considered as a means that has to be consistent with a specific end. We are speaking of a non-economic or emotional end, because we cannot measure the impact of apologies on someone's feelings or soul in economic terms.

According to a pure command critique, we cannot impose apologies except in rare cases where an order to apologise achieves in itself (ie is independently from its author's sincerity) a remedial goal, unless we want to overburden the social costs of the defendant. Why would we ever want to overburden their social costs? It may be that an apology could raise the social costs of the defendant in a way which helps to protect the social values of the plaintiff. For example, we might stress this social awareness in cases that involve facts which affect social fundamental values, such as racism or discrimination against women.

But we have to be careful if we extend such a remedy beyond this boundary. Let us look at the example of the municipal police in Rome, who attempt to make people apologise without having any statutory basis for their attempts. Misleading people about which is the correct legal procedure to follow before the trial begins could also amount to misconduct. In fact, the municipal police behave as if they have a great power (to impose limitations on privacy and personal dignity) that they simply do not have. In the Italian criminal code, the police have only the power to propose a settlement in a restorative justice framework, nothing more. For example, it would be better to allow the alternatives of uploading a YouTube video or sending a letter of apology plus the payment of a pecuniary sanction. The police would have done better to explain the steps to be taken in a fair way and possibly leave room for alternatives. As Calabresi said, 'education is a mighty powerful form of command'.[49] The most correct way to ask for an apology video would be on the basis of fair and transparent information that this is not the only way to comply, but simply one option among others (for example a letter of apology, or a letter plus a fine). That might also help to attach the correct reparatory value to the video.

Another issue I would like to point out is the commodification problem. The phenomenon of transforming merit goods into commercial goods is called commodification. As underlined by Calabresi, merit goods are 'pearl[s] without price'. If the merit goods are apologies, in this sense they are similar to inalienable rights involving freedom of speech and freedom of silence. We cannot buy apologies, because they reasonably do not have any price. Buying an apology fundamentally destroys its inherent value, since it is an intangible good that draws its strength from the free will and genuineness of the individual, among other things

Commodification or commandification of apologies, as a merit good, creates a real risk because it causes moral externalities. In other words, it may create a lot of insincere apologies, because people will choose this solution to gain a discount in damages or sanctions, or because they are ordered to do so. But courts commodify

[49] See above, n 33.

apologies when they decide to award punitive damages against a perpetrator who refuses to apologise to the victims. They put a price on this specific choice, not on the original violation. In doing so, they look beyond compensation towards other functions like deterrence, but that turns itself exactly into a hypothesis of commodification.

Let us take the case of environmental damages caused by a corporation. Public apologies expressed spontaneously by the corporation are an end in themselves. They can create interpersonal cooperation in order to repair moral damage. Quite differently, apologies mandated by the court or established by the state become a substitute, a means to achieve some further goals like public awareness and public vindication. This is more similar to a pure command approach. Contrarily, a pure market approach is like trying to exchange apologies for money, without doing anything from a legal point of view in order to facilitate a spontaneous apology, if it is not being paid for.

I would like to show that a mixed and more nuanced framework could be viable for both altruism and apologies. A more subtle interaction exists between apologies and compensation. When a plaintiff expresses his preference for apologies and the defendant answers with a proper statement, this may reduce the amount of liquidated damages. The incentive-based approach can work in both directions here. One way is satisfying the victim according to their preferences; the other is reducing the uncertainties about compensatory evaluation. But it should be understood that courts must take into account the preferences expressed by the plaintiffs. If they seek apologies and obtain them, the compensation-sanction should – albeit in part – be mitigated accordingly.

On the one hand, if courts reduce damages when apologies are issued, this may encourage more people to apologise. On the other hand, if the courts raise the amount of damages when the defendant does not comply with the apology preferences, they induce people to issue apologies. So moral externalities may be reduced accordingly. In these circumstances apology can gain a more independent function (facilitating settlement of disputes) which attaches authenticity to them.

Another important lever is represented by the liquidation of judicial costs. Here too, there is evidence of the structural relevance of an incentive-based approach. A main trend of many jurisdictions is to put the burden of judicial costs of the proceedings on the losing party. But it is not clear whether refusing to apologise can be deemed relevant in such a decision.

I would like to stress this point. How much money can be saved by issuing apologies as an alternative to litigation? Reasonably issuing apologies at a pre-trial stage can create a reduction in transaction costs, and particularly in both liquidated damages and judicial costs. The assessment of costs may depend on whether or not the dispute is successfully settled through apologies and damages, rather than being decided by a judgment awarding damages to the plaintiff.

I checked on this model in a specific Italian case of defamation committed conjointly by two journalists, one of whom settled with apologies, while the other preferred to go to trial.[50] Given the same type of wrongdoing, the total amount was more than doubled in the judgment. The additional burden accounted for approximately one third of damages and two thirds of judicial costs.

Similar conclusions can be reached when the tortfeasor refuses to make amends in defamation cases. Generally, the costs of the dispute can rise if the publication of the retraction is omitted by the injurer and a judicial order is then pursued by the defamed party.

A comparison between public apology and retraction could also be an interesting topic to explore with specific reference to their impact on compensation mechanisms. I think that in cases of defamation the consequences of an omission to publish a retraction should be more severe than the consequences of an omitted apology, because the first tends to be a core remedy while the latter is considered more incidental and ancillary. But an apology could probably add more value than a simple retraction according to its specific content. In fact, an early apology, including a retraction, can achieve full compensation even better than a simple retraction.

I would like also to underline that indemnity costs awards can work as an incentive to include apologies in settlement agreements. If one refuses an offer to settle and consequently decides to go to trial and is given a favourable judgment, the court can treat the previous refusal to apologise as a surplus of money to be paid by whoever had refused to settle. Since the judicial outcome is equal or worse than the hypothetical settlement offer, the court can decide to liquidate indemnity costs on the party that had previously refused the offer. According to this scenario, not all the circumstances of wrongdoing can be treated equally. It could be important to assess the chances of restoring a positive relationship between the parties. For example, a case involving personal and moral concerns would have to be treated differently from a case that lacks such characteristics.

V. Final Remarks

Can a court consider an omitted apology or the rejection of an offer including apologies relevant to the liquidation of damages or indemnity costs? Is it an interference with freedom of speech (freedom to remain silent) and with the rule of law that does not provide such a remedy?

I think that apologies cannot properly be treated as remedies in a technical sense, but rather as tools to facilitate mediation. Such reasoning is 'incentive-based' because pushing the parties to apologise can anticipate other remedies (for example an order to make a retraction, to publish the judgment, to pay punitive damages) without going to trial and at a lower cost. Given this framework an 'incentive-based approach' to apologies could make sense.

[50] App Milano Sez. II, 19-06-2008; for further references from a common law perspective, see also R Carroll, 'Apology as a Legal Remedy' (2013) 35 *Sydney Law Review* 325, about the case *Summertime Holdings Pty Ltd v Environmental Defender's Office Ltd* (1998) 45 NSWLR 291.

When we learn of an offence against the municipal police in Rome, we welcome the apologies of the offender. But we expect the offender to repair their wrongful act spontaneously. When we hear that the police tried to coerce, or mislead, the offender to publish apologies in a video, we may be puzzled, because a forced speech violates the fundamental right of free speech and – last but not least – it would probably lack authenticity. While some people have argued that coerced apologies have their merits, I think that only in limited cases of important narrative functions of apologies (such as restoring collective memories) will coerced apologies still have effect.

There is one big difference between the two situations: the non-coerced apology can be considered restorative as an end in itself, whereas the forced speech is like a means that can be used to achieve a different goal. In particular, such a goal could be restoring collective conscience and memory about mass violence and criminal acts against human dignity. An incentive-based approach seems to be more appropriate to pursue the goal of facilitating mediation outcomes (akin to moral compensation), whereas an approach focused on pure command is probably more suitable to reach a narrative goal (akin to deterrence).

Are apologies under safe harbour legislation admissible as a mitigating factor for damages? Generally, we can answer 'yes, they are' since an award of damages logically implies other evidence already achieved (elsewhere?). Safe harbour laws (which generally protect apologies from admissibility if they are prejudicial to the plaintiff) would not overlap with damages mitigation. Fundamentally, they are considered procedural rules, rather than substantive law.

I have tried to fix some points of reference to associate different incentives' effects with different scenarios of apology laws, and thus to apologies as well. Such an approach is based essentially on two main areas: incentives to cooperation between parties; and incentives to promote social goals of deterrence and public awareness (and indirectly compensatory goals). This is based on the assumption that the social benefits of apologising or the social costs of the omission to apologise have to be taken into account along with the private cost-benefits.

When apologies are given unreservedly but privately, a safe harbour law may help to protect the compensatory function and moral costs savings of apologies, with specific reference to moral damages. The extension of this protection can vary according to the extension of safe harbour law (admissions of facts can be included in this protection, for example in Hong Kong).[51] Accordingly, courts could better issue a mitigating effect on non-pecuniary damages (or non-economic damages as they are called in Italy), in order to facilitate moral costs savings. Conversely, no mitigating effects of this kind would lead to a reduction in case of punitive damages or exemplary damages, unless the apology is a public one and achieves the goals of public interest (like deterrence or public awareness goals). This is because a

[51] See Carroll et al, above, n 32.

private apology can reduce only private externalities, raising only the probability of a mediation. But it can do little for social negative externalities that can be better addressed by public apologies. Otherwise, in the case of apologies including such an admission of facts (that fall outside the protection of safe harbour legislation), courts would grant a reduction on exemplary damages.

The law could be depicted as the art of a permanent balancing of goods and evils, and as a method to manage the distribution of evils among people directly or indirectly involved in a dispute. The plaintiff would need more than the pursuit of judicial truth at all costs. Sometimes he would rather give to the defendant a chance to repent and reform, before going to court. Law can provide the right incentives to strengthen empathic reconciliation, in order to give more effectiveness to the rule of law. As observed by Bingham LJ:

> parties [to mediation] will not make admissions or conciliatory gestures, or dilute their claims, or venture out of their entrenched positions unless they can be confident that their concessions and admissions cannot be used as weapons against them if conciliation [or mediation] fails and full-blooded litigation follows.[52]

According to this perspective, a clear rule protecting apologies from being regarded as admissions against interests makes sense. In my opinion, the issue cannot be left to judicial discretion. In some civil law countries like Italy, France or Germany, courts are tempted to give apologies the value of a confession – the strongest type of prejudicial evidence we have. This may be quite different from common law countries (where the discretion of juries and courts is wider and they are not bound by such strict rules about the weight of evidence).

In my opinion, without safe harbor legislation, in most civil law countries apologies may be considered as admissions against interest (ie confession, given the different conception of evidence that exist in civil law countries) only if they objectively describe facts, and not if they consist in personal opinions or expressions of benevolence aimed at preparing an offer of settlement. But in civil law jurisdictions this point is far from clear and the issue is one underestimated by scholars, legislators and – above all – by courts.

More generally, I think that settlement agreement, mediation and all such preparatory acts play a prominent role in attaching a correct legal meaning to apologies. Above all, they should prevail over the adjudicative attitude that plainly equates apologies with admissions against interests, which has sometimes been the common law approach.[53]

There are plenty of cases in which the value of apologies can be appreciated as a non-economic remedy, ie as compensation. My first impression was that it is rather strange to assert that a victim can be compensated through apologies, because the ethical point of view must be kept separate from the legal one. However, the

[52] *Re D (Minors) (Conciliation: Disclosure of Information)* [1993] 2 WLR 721, 724.

[53] See P Vines, 'Apologies and Civil Liability in the UK: a View from Elsewhere' (2008) 12(2) *Edinburgh Law Review* 200.

reasonable argument of positivistic lawyers is: who can decide about alternative options to compensation, if not the victim? An apology becomes only cheap talk if you treat it like a legal remedy, as something similar to compensation. It may lose its peculiar moral value, becoming a matter of lawyers and adjudication, rather than a matter of ethics and empathy.

Reacting to this approach, I considered getting the ethical approach out of the way for the moment and asked myself: are we sure that apologies lack any legal meaning? Suddenly I found that there are a lot of grey areas and twilight zones to explore. Interdisciplinary methods can help us to focus on apologies and compensation without ideological bias such as the abovementioned challenge between ethicist and positivist theorists. The criticism is that the ethical perspective is used as a tool to pass tort counter-reforms. The 'Sorry works!' movement is regarded with some suspicion, as it could be a counter-movement against the principle of full compensation. This view, albeit not completely groundless, shows a hypercritical attitude especially in the work by Arbel and Kaplan that underestimates the emerging legal relevance of apologies.[54] It overlooks the reality: law is – and always will be – strictly interrelated with ethical issues. The problem is rather the balancing and nuancing of certain ethical concerns in the making of law.

So, what is the legal meaning of apologies? The question is a very challenging one: as well as being performative statements, we can detect all the characteristics of a speech act with specific legal effects. Apologies can communicate something (this is their expressive function) but at the same time they can do something that under certain circumstances deeply affects legal relationships (this is their performative function).[55] The performative function is very important in the study of legal language. If we consider apologies only as admissions against interests we underestimate their performative function, and we prevent apologies from achieving their proper goal. In other words, we prevent apologies from doing their work.

A more comprehensive approach to apologies could promote a change in litigation outcomes and a selection of efficient remedies. After all, we cannot overemphasise that it is largely a matter of interpretation and an issue to be focused on in specific contexts. Does an apology in Japan have the same meaning as in Italy? Not at all. And it is precisely because the meaning of an act is also inherent to a specific legal system, as a matter of comparative law, that the problem of the legal relevance of apologies (with its interferences with compensation) can be positively addressed if we move towards an incentive-based approach. The legal structures 'tell us a lot about what that particular society believes its incentive needs are, in comparison to how great its inequality moral costs are'.[56]

[54] See Y Arbel and Y Kaplan, 'Tort Reform through the Backdoor: A Critique of Law & Apologies' (2016–2017) 90 *Southern California Law Review* 1199. See also N Smith, *Justice through Apologies* (Cambridge, Cambridge University Press, 2014).

[55] JL Austin, *How to Do Things with Words*, The William James Lectures (Clarendon Press, 1962).

[56] G Calabresi, *The Future of Law and Economics, Essays in Reform and Recollection* (Cambridge, Cambridge University Press, 2016) 76.

9

Compensation for Intangible Loss: A Closer Look at the Remedial Function of Apologies

ROBYN CARROLL*

A tort system that makes compensation for personal injuries dependent upon fault-based liability inevitably limits the circumstances in which compensation is available to a victim. Further, the legal consequences of being at fault can affect the willingness of a wrongdoer to apologise to a victim. This chapter discusses three ways in which the law can contemplate a more expansive role for apologies and other non-monetary remedies alongside compensatory damages for negligently caused intangible loss. The potential benefits of apologies invite us to consider the interaction between law and apologies as a remedial response to wrongdoing and loss.

I. Introduction

The primary remedy for negligently caused loss is compensatory damages, which aim to put the injured party in the position that they would have been in had the negligence not occurred. One consequence of treating compensation as synonymous with damages is that it can distract us from asking whether there are non-monetary ways to compensate for intangible losses, including those resulting from personal injuries. Could a larger role be played by apologies and expressions of sympathy or remorse, acts of benevolence accompanying an admission of wrongdoing, corrections, disclosure of facts, and undertakings to reduce risk of future harm? This is a question that others, including tort experts, have asked for some time.[1] This chapter takes up this inquiry and focuses on apologies in the context of intangible loss caused by negligence.

* Professor, University of Western Australia Law School.

[1] Eg DW Shuman, 'The Role of Apology in Tort Law' (2000) 83 Judicature 180. See also Chapter 8 by Nicola Brutti in this edited collection.

Fault-based tort systems of compensation inevitably limit the circumstances in which compensation will be available. It is well known that these systems adversely affect the willingness of tortfeasors to apologise and offer amends to injured parties in other non-monetary ways. This, as Prue Vines says, is one of the unexpected consequences of a fault-based compensation system and is a consequence that needs to be addressed.[2] This chapter, in acknowledging this consequence, contemplates whether non-monetary remedies might play an expanded role alongside compensatory damages for negligently caused losses. The possibility of non-monetary remedies invites us to consider the interaction between the law and apologies as responses to wrongdoing and loss in three ways. One legal response is to limit the regard that can be given to apologies and their admissibility as evidence of fault or liability in civil proceedings. A second response is to allow evidence of apologies to be admitted as evidence that the amount of damages needed to compensate a tort victim's loss is less than would otherwise be the case because the tortfeasor has offered an apology to the victim. A third response, which supplements and potentially reduces the amount of damages awarded, is to compel a tortfeasor to apologise to their victim. Arguments that have been advanced in support of each of these are discussed in section III.

I discuss these responses in this chapter. In addition I consider three questions that call for consideration if we are to contemplate an expanded role for apologies to compensate for intangible losses. The first of these questions is whether both fault and intention are relevant to the circumstances in which the law might want to provide incentives for or compel a wrongdoer to apologise. A second question is whether it is helpful to think of the law's role relating to apologies as providing incentives for self-help by the parties, particularly in light of research that shows that an apology can provide some form of redress for mental and emotional distress. A third question is whether there are grounds to prefer any one of these three responses to the other. These questions are discussed in section IV with conclusions offered in section V.

The word 'compensation' is used in two ways here. The first way is in the sense of describing tort damages which perform a corrective function and aim to restore a person to the position they would be in but for the wrong. The compensation function is achieved by a monetary award. Within this – arguably narrow – meaning is an ongoing debate about the extent to which damages have solely a corrective function, as distinct from other functions including deterrence and distribution of loss. Debate also continues over the ability of damages to make good intangible losses, in large part because of the inability of money to restore an injured party to their pre-tort position. The second, broader sense in which 'compensation' is used (and is used here), is to describe as compensatory the function performed by various forms of redress that provide vindication, solace, and consolation for what has been lost and which might never be restored. This includes but is not limited

[2] P Vines, 'Apologies, Liability and Civil Society: Where to from Here?' in R Levy et al (eds), *New Directions for Law in Australia: Essays in Contemporary Law Reform* (ANU Press, 2017) 329, 335.

to an award of damages. Compensation for intangible loss, including mental and emotional distress, poses difficulties under either meaning.[3] It is within the broader meaning, however, that an act of benevolence, an expression of sympathy, and an apology that acknowledges fault and damage can be described as a form of compensation for intangible loss.[4]

The discussion in this chapter centres on loss resulting from personal injuries resulting from negligence for two reasons. First, it is the most common basis on which an injured party seeks compensation. Second, negligence is based on fault and this chapter concerns the relationship between fault, compensation, and apologies. Arguably, but not inevitably, we might want to contemplate a more expansive role for apologies as a non-monetary remedy for intangible losses resulting from personal injuries more so than damage to property. This could be based on the premise that mental and emotional distress resulting from personal injuries is generally foreseeable even if it is not recoverable at law, at least more so than negligent damage to property. However, I do not pursue that argument here.[5] In any case, many of the observations made in this chapter about the law's responses to apologies in the context of negligence are applicable to intangible loss howsoever caused – whether resulting from personal injuries or damage to property and from other torts or breach of contract. Suffice to say that the potential for an apology to provide redress for intangible loss extends beyond negligence.

I also distinguish between two categories of intangible loss caused by negligence. One category is loss for which damages are recoverable, for example pain and suffering from personal injuries including psychiatric injury, loss of amenity, and loss of consortium. Issues of incommensurability of loss to monetary

[3] There are difficulties in transposing the legal notion of 'compensation' onto a social interaction in the form of a speech act the functions of which are still not fully understood. An apology comes after harm – it cannot undo the loss or harm caused nor can it return the parties to their pre-harm position. In defamation law, non-pecuniary compensatory damages have been described as operating 'in two ways – as a vindication of the plaintiff to the public and as consolation to him for a wrong done. Compensation here is a solatium rather than a monetary recompense for harm measurable in money': see *Uren v John Fairfax & Sons Pty Ltd* (1966) 117 CLR 118, 150 (Windeyer J). In negligence, arguably an analogy can be drawn with the purpose of awarding non-pecuniary damages for personal injuries that 'must surely be based upon solace for a condition created not upon payment for something taken away': *Skelton v Collins* (1966) 115 CLR 94, 130 (Windeyer J). See further, agreeing with the views expressed by Windeyer J, H Luntz, 'The Purposes of Damages in Tort Law' in PD Finn (ed), *Essays on Torts* (Law Book Co, 1989) 262.

[4] See further Vines, who argues that, while damages are the central vehicle of corrective justice in that they operate to redress the balance between the parties by correcting the loss suffered by one party at the expense of the other who caused it, '[a]pologies can be part of this corrective justice mix if one considers compensation as practical reparation and apology as reparation for the emotional and moral pain suffered by the victim': see P Vines, 'The Power of Apology: Mercy, Forgiveness or Corrective Justice in the Civil Liability Arena?' (2007) 1 *Public Space: The Journal of Law and Social Justice* 1, 21.

[5] I note, however, that a recently published study which explores the nature and prominence of victims' material and nonmaterial needs in response to torts in simulated cases and their relationship to the remedies the victims desire resulted in the observation that 'nonmaterial needs were as prominent in the case of property loss as in the case of personal injury, as was the desire for apology': CP Reinders Folmer et al, 'Beyond Compensation? Examining the Role of Apologies in the Restoration of Victims' Needs in Simulated Tort Cases' (2019) *Law and Human Behaviour* 1, 6.

compensation and capping of damages lead to the question whether in this category apologies and other non-monetary remedies might provide an alternative remedial response to intangible loss. The issue here is whether and how best to expand the law's remedial response to recoverable loss beyond damages.

The other category of intangible loss is mental and emotional ('mere') distress resulting from personal injuries caused by negligence, which is not recoverable.[6] In the latter case the question of whether an apology might have an additional compensatory role arises but it will not be as an alternative to damages. Meanwhile, damages for intangible loss in the latter category is recoverable for some torts which protect intangible interests – in particular reputation, dignity, and privacy – by enforcing rights. In these cases, the remedial functions of damages include vindication of rights and compensation for loss caused by mental and emotional distress. Apologies have an established role in these torts as a factor relevant to the assessment of aggravated damages and is a factor in the assessment of exemplary damages where they are available.

This chapter proceeds on the basis that apologies can provide compensation in a broad sense for both categories of intangible loss caused by negligence. The question that arises in the context of personal injuries and negligence, however, is what role(s) the law should attribute to apologies with regard to the narrower category of recoverable intangible loss? The next parts address this issue after considering the significance of fault.[7]

II. Implications of Fault-based Compensation for Apologies

There is theoretical and empirical support for a meaning of 'apology' that recognises that there are multiple components to an apology. These components include expressions of emotion, admissions of wrongdoing, and a commitment to actions which might include repair, compensation for loss, and systems review and change.[8] Whether a particular apology will be acceptable to its recipient depends on many variables.[9] Psychological research tells us that what constitutes an apology for the recipient in any particular situation and context is a highly unique and subjective experience.[10] An act of benevolence – for example, sending flowers to

[6] Therefore, even if damages provide 'full' compensation for actionable losses resulting from negligent conduct, they will not necessarily compensate for all intangible loss.

[7] It is beyond the scope of the chapter to consider whether damages for 'mere' distress resulting from negligently caused personal injuries should be recoverable.

[8] See N Smith, *I Was Wrong: The Meanings of Apology* (Cambridge, Cambridge University Press, 2008); D Slocum et al, 'An Emerging Theory of Apology' (2011) 63 *Australian Journal of Psychology* 83.

[9] A Allan, 'Functional Apologies in Law' (2008) 15 *Psychiatry, Psychology and Law* 369.

[10] A Allan and R Carroll, 'Apologies in a Legal Setting: Insights from Research into Injured Parties' Experiences of Apologies' (2016) 24 *Psychiatry, Psychology and the Law* 1, 10.

someone who has been injured – and an expression of regret and sympathy – for example, saying 'I am sorry you have been injured' – are often referred to as apologies even though they are not accompanied by an admission of wrongdoing. There is a central difference, however, between an apology by which a person admits responsibility for their actions and the effect of their actions on another person in addition to expressing regret, remorse and sympathy (sometimes referred to as a 'full' apology), and an apology in which a person acknowledges the effect that their actions has had on another person in a way that does not admit responsibility (sometimes referred to as a 'partial' apology). I use 'apology' in this chapter to mean an expression of sympathy or remorse and acts of benevolence accompanied by admission of wrongdoing – that is, a 'full' apology by which a wrongdoer admits that they are at fault. With this said, I recognise that something less than this, or some other non-monetary response to loss, may have some remedial benefit to its recipient in a particular set of circumstances.[11]

Apologies are understood to serve a number of functions. Shuman refers to the theoretical benefits as being a way to adjust an imbalance of power in a relationship that occurs when a wrong is committed to one party to the relationship, clarifying responsibility for harm, helping to reduce the victim's anger or desire to see the wrongdoer punished, and helping a victim to forgive and move on with their life.[12] Empirical research confirms that people from most, if not all, cultures learn to use apologies as a mechanism to acknowledge their mistakes, repair their own reputation and the reputations of injured parties, and re-establish relationships where required.[13] Asking whether the law should regard an apology as compensation for intangible loss also raises questions about the remedial functions of apologies. As I have argued elsewhere, these include vindication, compensation, and expressive functions of the law.[14] How effective an apology will be in any particular case will depend on many factors, including the extent to which the injured party attributes responsibility for their injuries to the person offering the apology[15] as well as the sincerity, content, and focus of the apology.[16] We know that in social settings an expression of regret can suffice to remedy mental and emotional distress that might result from an accidental and unintended discomfort or injury – for example, speaking out of turn, bumping into someone, keeping someone waiting.

[11] The discussion of the role of apologies in the law could be broadened to include corrections, disclosure of facts, and undertakings to implement changes in the future that will help to prevent future personal injuries to the victim and other potential victims. These responses to wrongdoing are ways of addressing the needs of tort victims more comprehensively than damages and even apologies. Note, however, that these remedial actions also can be encompassed within a broad meaning of 'apology'.

[12] Shuman, above, n 1, 183.

[13] Allan and Carroll, above, n 10, 3.

[14] R Carroll, 'Beyond Compensation: Apology as a Private Law Remedy' in J Berryman and R Bigwood (eds), *The Law of Remedies: New Directions in the Common Law* (Irwin Law, 2010) 323, 352–69; and see generally R Carroll and N Witzleb, 'It's Not Just About the Money – Enhancing the Vindicatory Effect of Private Law Remedies' (2011) 37 *Monash University Law Review* 216.

[15] Allan and Carroll, above, n 10, 9.

[16] ibid, 14.

Even when there is fault an injured person might be willing to accept a partial apology as an end to a dispute, especially where there is minimal tangible loss.

In a legal setting, however, when the potential arises that one party is liable to compensate an injured party, whether or not an apology includes an admission of wrongdoing has evidential as well as psychological and social significance. An apology, therefore, may have legal significance beyond its social and psychological significance to a tort victim and for the relationship between a victim and tortfeasor. The fear that an apology will be admitted in evidence in civil litigation to prove liability that will result in a damages award is a common deterrent to apologetic behaviour by an alleged tortfeasor. For the victim, not receiving an apology from the person who has caused their personal injuries deprives them of the psychological benefits that may otherwise result from receiving an apology, as well as the forensic benefit of an admission of wrongdoing. More specifically, in personal injuries cases, financial compensation in the form of damages does not meet the need of some victims to have the wrongfulness of the tortfeasor's actions acknowledged in some other way. Recognising this shortfall, an apology is one way that this wrongfulness can be acknowledged.[17]

To the extent that the social and psychological benefits of an apology can provide compensation to a tort victim for injury to their person and feelings, how can a fault-based system respond? One obvious answer is to adopt a no-fault-based system of compensation. Arguably, the forensic disincentive to apologising that has been observed would be removed.[18] There are, of course, other reasons why a person who has injured another person might not offer an apology but at least the fear that it will have evidential implications for the determination of fault-based liability would be addressed. Short of this fundamental change to the tort system of most western legal systems, other ways to encourage apologetic behaviour have been proposed and, in some instances, adopted by the law. These are considered in the next section.

III. Ways to Provide a More Expansive Role for Apologies to Remedy Intangible Loss

This section discusses three ways in which apologies might play an expanded role in a fault-based tort system, as identified in the Introduction. These remedial roles

[17] Lord Justice Irwin, 'Can Compensation Bring Satisfaction? What Do Damages for Personal Injury Represent?' (Personal Injury Bar Association Annual Lecture, 15 November 2018), available at www.judiciary.uk/announcements/speech-by-lord-justice-irwin-personal-injury-bar-association-annual-lecture/.

[18] While this might be expected. it is not necessarily the case. For example, Khouri reports that in New Zealand – notwithstanding their no-fault accident compensation scheme – fear of liability remains a concern in personal injury claims, or at least in medico-legal personal injury claims: see N Khouri, 'Sorry Seems to be the Hardest Word: the Case for Apology Legislation in New Zealand' (2014) *New Zealand Law Review* 603, 613. Khouri examines the rationale and operation of apology legislation elsewhere and concludes that New Zealand would benefit from legislation that expands

of apologies in the legal context have been identified, discussed, and critiqued by some remedies scholars.[19] Each provides incentives for tortfeasors voluntarily to offer an apology that might reduce the intangible loss experienced by a tort victim and, potentially, a way to reduce reliance on damages as compensation for wrongdoing. This aim of this chapter is to consider how each of these roles might provide a non-monetary alternative to damages for personal injuries in negligence within the law of remedies, in the common law tradition.[20]

A. 'Apology-Protecting' Legislation

> I wanted to say sorry right from the start but my lawyer advised me not to because it might affect my case and my insurance claim.

The potential benefits of apologies being offered in the settlement of tort claims are well documented in the dispute resolution literature.[21] It is also well documented by proponents of law reform that the fear that an apology will be treated as an admission of liability can discourage apologies when there is potential for civil disputes to arise.[22] These concerns are addressed to a limited extent by legal rules that render inadmissible what is said in 'without prejudice' settlement negotiations and in facilitative dispute resolution processes, such as mediation. More specific exclusionary and inadmissibility rules are created by what is known as 'apology legislation', which operates in a similar way to exclude evidence of an apology offered, for example, in response to accidents.[23]

evidential protection beyond the existing without prejudice negotiations and mediation confidentiality for claims, including in personal injuries: see at 604.

[19] Eg R Carroll, 'Apologies as a Legal Remedy' (2013) 35 *Sydney Law Review* 317; K Barnett and S Harder, *Remedies in Australian Private Law*, 2nd edn (Cambridge, Cambridge University Press, 2018) Ch 15.A.

[20] Unquestionably, there are broader narratives which arise when a legal system attributes a role to apologies in order to address concerns about compensation in tort law. These include the roles attributed more broadly to apologies in civil dispute resolution and restorative justice processes, the ability of apology to repair moral damages, criticisms of the use of the apology in tort law and comparative legal systems perspectives. See N Brutti, 'Legal Narratives and Compensation Trends in Tort Law: The Case of Public Apology' (2013) 24 *European Business Law Review* 127.

[21] Eg JR Cohen, 'Advising Clients to Apologize' (1999) 72 *Southern California Law Review* 1009; D Pavlick, 'Apology and Mediation: The Horse and Carriage of the Twenty-first Century' (2003) 18 *Ohio State Journal on Dispute Resolution* 829, 853–55; E Latif, 'Apologetic Justice: Evaluating Apologies Tailored Towards Legal Solutions' (2001) 81 *Boston University Law Review* 289, 295–96; Vines, above, n 2.

[22] Eg British Columbia Ministry of Attorney General, *Discussion Paper on Apology Legislation* (Ministry of Attorney General, 2006); British Columbia Office of the Ombudsman, *The Power of an Apology: Removing the Legal Barriers* (Special Report No 27 to the Legislative Assembly of British Columbia, 2006).

[23] For a review and analysis of developments in apology legislation see P Vines and R Carroll, 'The Apology Ordinance: Bold Steps into Some Uncharted Areas of Apology-Protecting Legislation' (2018) 48 *Hong Kong Law Journal* 925. And, for an analysis of the potential role of apology legislation in civil jurisdictions, see W Vandenbussche, 'Introducing Apology Legislation in Civil Law Systems. A New Way to Encourage Out-of-Court Dispute Resolution' (2018) ssrn.com/abstract=3237528 (last accessed 13 February 2020).

Apology legislation offers evidential protection for an apology from the time an incident occurs and before settlement negotiations, mediation, and other dispute resolution processes are underway. This evidential protection continues until settlement or trial. This is unlike the temporally limited privilege attached to settlement negotiations which, generally speaking, will only cover apologies made in 'without prejudice' negotiations, and mediation. Apology legislation therefore offers wider protection to apologies than the protection of privileged communications during settlement negotiations and mediation. A key aim of apology legislation is to remove or at least lessen the 'chill' that prevents an early apology by a willing defendant. Since 1986, apology legislation has been introduced in more than 56 jurisdictions, including the USA, Australia, Canada, England and Wales, Scotland and Hong Kong. More often the legislation provides legal protection to partial, rather than full, apologies.[24] While the scope of apology legislation varies between jurisdictions there is a discernible trend towards the adoption of apology legislation that provides: (i) broader legal protection than merely rendering inadmissible an apology as evidence of fault or liability; and (ii) wider coverage in terms of the types of proceedings covered.[25]

There are benefits and disadvantages of attaching evidentiary protection to apologies and preventing them from being used as admissions to the prejudice of a potential wrongdoer. These benefits and disadvantages have been the subject of law reform and academic discussion.[26] Unfortunately, there is little empirical data on the extent to which behaviour involving apologies is influenced by apology legislation.[27] Despite this, the enactment of apology legislation supports the argument that this is one way that the law can provide incentives to parties to offer expressions of regret, sympathy, benevolence, and apologies. The offer of an

[24] JC Kleefeld, 'Promoting and Protecting Apologetic Discourse through Law: A Global Survey and Critique of Apology Legislation and Case Law' (2017) 7 *Onati Socio-Legal Series* 455; J Shing-ping Chiu, 'The Beginning of Apology Legislation in Asia' (2018) *Asian Journal on Mediation* 33.

[25] See in particular Apology Ordinance (Hong Kong) cap 631. For detailed commentary see R Carroll et al, *Apology Ordinance (Cap 631): Commentary and Annotations* (Sweet & Maxwell, 2018); P Vines and R Carroll, 'The Apology Ordinance: Bold Steps into Some Uncharted Areas of Apology-Protecting Legislation' (2018) 48 *Hong Kong Law Journal* 925 and JR Cohen, 'Legislating Apology: The Pros and Cons' (2002) 70 *University of Cincinnati Law Review* 819.

[26] The issues surrounding legislative protection of apologies are canvassed in detail in the Department of Justice, *Enactment of Apology Legislation in Hong Kong: Final Report and Recommendations Report* (2016), available at www.doj.gov.hk/eng/public/pdf/2016/apologyFinal_2016.pdf. See also Cohen, ibid. More recently see Vandenbussche, above, n 23, who critiques the academic commentary on apology legislation, including arguments that have been made for and against its adoption in common law jurisdictions, and argues that the case can be made for introducing apology legislation in civil law systems.

[27] In the area of medical malpractice see O Salem and C Forster, 'Defensive Medicine in General Practice: Recent Trends and the Impact of the Civil Liability Act 2002 (NSW)' (2009) 17 *Journal of Law and Medicine* 235; B Ho and E Liu, 'What's an Apology Worth? Decomposing the Effect of Apologies on Medical Malpractice Payments Using State Apology Laws' (2011) 8 *Journal of Empirical Legal Studies* 179; B Ho and E Liu, 'Does Sorry Work? The Impact of Apology Laws on Medical Malpractice' (2011) 43 *Journal of Risk and Uncertainty* 141; BJ McMichael et al, 'Sorry is Never Enough: The Effect of State Apology Laws on Medical Malpractice Liability Risk' (2019) 71(2) *Stanford Law Review* 341.

apology is no guarantee that this will be the outcome, of course, because a victim can choose to prosecute their claim in any case. I suggest, however, that it can be understood as a form of self-help in the process, potentially, of avoiding and settling legal claims and providing redress that meets the intangible needs of victims.

Another issue that arises in the context of apology legislation is whether the law should provide evidential protection for an apology for loss caused by intentional as well as negligent conduct. Some apology legislation applies only to personal injuries resulting from accidents and other negligent conduct. For example, the Australian civil liability legislation provisions largely apply only to negligent conduct. This is entirely the case in England.[28] The legislation enacted in Canada, and more recently in Hong Kong, applies to apologies made in connection with matters related to any civil proceedings, which includes intentional conduct. This means that, for example, an apology for institutional child abuse is afforded the same legal protection in civil proceedings as negligent conduct. It might be argued that limiting protection to apologies for negligent conduct only, and not intentional conduct, strikes a fairer balance between excluding evidence of an apology with the object of encouraging effective apologies and allowing a plaintiff to tender that apology as evidence of fault or liability. Two observations can be made at this point, however.

First, the legislation may be more effective to remove inhibitions to apologise for civil wrongdoing in general if it applies to all civil wrongs. The pros and cons of adopting apology legislation, including its application to intentional acts, were considered in the consultation process in British Columbia – the first province to enact apology legislation in Canada.[29] Arguably, this approach takes into account that the object of apology legislation is not to deter particular types of wrongdoing but more generally to remove disincentives to apologising for any civil wrongdoing.

Second, the effectiveness of an apology to provide redress for intangible loss and to contribute to the settlement of a dispute – and, therefore to further the objects of the legislation – will be influenced in any event by the seriousness of the wrongdoing, the sincerity of the apology, and multiple other factors. Recent studies raise important questions about the asymmetries between a victim's need for apologies and a wrongdoer's willingness to apologise against the remedial effectiveness of apologies. A study by Reinders Folmer et al tested what apology content victims desire and perpetrators provide in an apology in response to hypothetical personal injury incidents.[30] They found that perpetrators provide less comprehensive apologies than victims desire. This suggests that the subjectivity in victims' and perpetrators' perceptions of torts may undermine the remedial effectiveness

[28] Compensation Act 2002, s 2.

[29] British Columbia Ministry of Attorney General, *Discussion Paper on Apology Legislation* (Ministry of Attorney General, 2006) 5.

[30] C Reinders Folmer et al, 'Rethinking Apology in Tort Litigation Deficiencies in Comprehensiveness Undermine Remedial Effectiveness' (2019) 15(1) *Review of Law and Economics* 1.

of legal apologies. Less comprehensive apologies were associated with lower forgiveness. In another study, Leunissen et al found that victims mostly want to receive an apology after intentional wrongdoing whereas wrongdoers want to offer an apology particularly after unintentional wrongdoing.[31] This indicates that an apology is more likely to be wanted and less likely to be offered for intentional wrongdoing. In such a case, although the scope of the legislation may have little influence on whether an apology is offered or not, arguably the legislation is more likely to be effective if it applies to apologies for intentional, as well as unintentional, wrongdoing.

These studies provide insights into the effectiveness of apologies for people seeking and advising on apologies. They are not studies on the effectiveness of apology legislation but arguably the results provide support for apology legislation that has broad rather than narrow scope and application because of the extent to which it removes legal, if not other, disincentives to offering full apologies.

B. Creating Legal Incentives to Apologise

> I've said 'sorry'; does that count for anything?

The legislative initiatives adopted in some jurisdictions and discussed in the previous section go some way to removing legal disincentives for a wrongdoer to offer an apology to their tort victim. The law could create a further incentive for a wrongdoer to apologise by taking their apology into account as a loss-reducing factor when assessing damages for negligently caused intangible loss. Although this occurs in the assessment of damages for intentional and other torts that are actionable per se, it would be a novel development in the assessment of damages for negligence. This development has been raised for consideration by some torts and remedies scholars. I suggest that were the law to develop in this way, having regard to an apology as a factor that reduces a victim's intangible loss could be seen as another incentive to apologise and a second instance of remedial self-help by a negligent tortfeasor. In this section, I discuss these academic proposals after briefly overviewing the circumstances in which the law currently takes account of apologies in the assessment of damages.

i. Apologies as a Factor in the Assessment of Damages in Other Torts

Courts take apologies into account when assessing damages for torts which aim to compensate for indignity, mental suffering, disgrace and humiliation suffered by the plaintiff. Such torts include false imprisonment, assault, and defamation.[32]

[31] JM Leunissen et al, 'The Apology Mismatch: Asymmetries between Victim's Needs for Apologies and Perpetrator's Willingness to Apologize' (2013) 49(3) *Journal of Experimental Social Psychology* 315.

[32] Eg *Spautz v Butterworth* (1996) 41 NSWLR 1, 17–18 (Clarke JA). Section 38(1) of the Defamation Act 2005 (NSW) confirms that evidence is admissible on behalf of the defendant, in mitigation

Apologies can also be relevant to the assessment of damages for breach of privacy.[33] A court takes into account 'the whole of the conduct of the defendant to the time of verdict which may have the effect of increasing the injury to the person's feelings'.[34]

In defamation, the law is concerned with the effectiveness of an apology to mitigate damages which are awarded to compensate for pecuniary and non-pecuniary loss caused to the plaintiff by the publication, reparation for the harm done to the plaintiff's reputation, and to vindicate the plaintiff's reputation.[35] The extent to which a correction or an apology is effective in achieving these remedial objectives will be determined by the court, taking account of multiple factors, including timeliness of publication, the prominence given to the response, and the content of the correction or apology.[36] In defamation cases an apology is addressed both to the person defamed, in order to appease their injured feelings, and to those to whom the defamatory words were published, to undo the harm.[37]

Courts, tribunals, and administrative decision makers are also empowered to take account of apologies in assessing damages for loss or damage including emotional distress for claims arising from breach of privacy legislation,[38] unlawful discrimination,[39] and breach of the moral rights of an author under copyright legislation.[40]

ii. *Apologies as a Factor in the Assessment of Damages for Negligence*

The principles for assessment of damages for negligence do not provide for reduction or increase of damages based on the conduct of the defendant. Some torts and remedies scholars have argued that, in addition to granting an apology statutory protection from liability determinations, there may be justification for allowing it to be admissible as evidence of damages for intangible loss being less than they would be otherwise.

Shuman points to the fact that the law recognises the relevance of an apology to mitigate harm in other legal settings.[41] In addition to assessment of punitive

of damages for the publication of defamatory matter, that the defendant has made an apology to the plaintiff about the publication of the defamatory matter and/or the defendant has published a correction of the defamatory matter: see sub-ss (a) and (b).

[33] Eg *Jones v Tighe* (2012) 108 OR (3d) 241, [90]. See also R Carroll, 'Apologies and Corrections as Remedies for Breach of Privacy' in JNE Varuhas and NA Moreham (eds), *Remedies for Breach of Privacy* (Oxford, Hart Publishing, 2018).

[34] *Spautz v Butterworth* (1996) 41 NSWLR 1, 8 (Clarke JA).

[35] *Carson v John Fairfax & Sons Ltd* (1993) 178 CLR 44, 60, 66 (Mason CJ, Deane, Dawson and Gaudron JJ).

[36] Eg Defamation Act 2005 (NSW), s 18(2).

[37] *Cerutti v Crestside Pty Ltd* [2014] QCA 33 (28 February 2014), [44] (Applegarth J).

[38] See Privacy Act 1988 (Cth), s 52(1)(b)(ii).

[39] See Equal Opportunity Act 1984 (WA), s 127(b)(iii).

[40] See Copyright Act 1968 (Cth), s 195AZA(1)(d) (author), s 195AZGC(1)(d) (performer). See also *Perez v Fernandez* (2012) 260 FLR 1, [107] (Driver FM) (copyright).

[41] Shuman, above, n 1, 181; J Berryman 'Mitigation, Apology and the Quantification of Non-Pecuniary Damages' (2017) 7 *Oñati Socio-legal Series* 528.

damages and defamation actions, noted above, he points to criminal sentencing determinations in the US that formally acknowledge the mitigating impact of sincere expressions of remorse and acceptance of responsibility[42] and that remorse is taken into account in sentencing.[43] Courts and tribunals also regularly acknowledge the mitigating effect of an apology in disciplinary proceedings. He advocates that the sincerity of an apology and its impact can be considered on a case by case basis. Speaking of the US system, where damages are assessed by a jury, Shuman asks, '[w]ho better to determine whether an apology is an inadequate response to an intangible loss than the jury?' and advocates for affirmative, rather than indirect, encouragement of apologies by admitting them as evidence to mitigate damages. Essentially, Shuman's proposal is based on three rationales. First, cloaking apologies made in settlement negotiations and under apology legislation may protect a defendant but it does not affirmatively encourage apologies.[44] Second, awards of compensatory damages for intangible loss are already made and this proceeds on even less foundation than permitting a finder of fact to mitigate these damages based on the impact of an apology.[45] Third, an apology for a tort has the potential to help people who have suffered serious emotional harm through the wrongdoing of others in ways that monetary damages alone cannot.

More recently, Berryman has examined the research into how we experience pain, grief, and loss and how these experiences influence happiness.[46] He concludes that empirical evidence provides a reason to believe that a tort victim's subjective well-being will be improved on receiving an apology. He believes that moral, social, and economic policy arguments suggest that courts should alter common law doctrine and allow an apology to mitigate non-pecuniary loss in a larger number of actions than is currently practised.[47] While there are difficulties in monetising this improvement, Berryman concludes that providing the incentive of reduced damages for non-pecuniary damages as a result of making a sincere apology is a worthy objective aligned to the compensation goal of the common law.[48]

These are worthwhile efforts to explore the central question raised by this chapter, ie whether a larger role could be played by apologies as compensation for intangible loss caused by negligence. There are also a number of difficulties, in Australia at least, with the proposal for an apology to be treated as a mitigating factor in the assessment of damages in this context.

First, other tort reforms have been introduced by legislation, including limitations on the amount of non-pecuniary damages, to address the concern that intangible losses are incalculable and too high. There is a risk of undercompensating

[42] Shuman, above, n 1, 189.

[43] ibid.

[44] Shuman, writing in 2000, does note the limited potential for Federal Rule of Evidence 408 and its state law equivalents designed to exclude settlement negotiations as evidence as well as the effect of Massachusetts legislation that excludes benevolent gestures as evidence of liability: see Shuman, above, n 1, 188–89.

[45] Ibid, 189.

[46] Berryman, above, n 41.

[47] ibid, 542.

[48] ibid, 543.

a plaintiff in these circumstances if an apology is a further factor that can be taken into account to assess and reduce damages for intangible loss.

Second, apology legislation – particularly legislation that protects full apologies – offers incentives for a defendant to make a sincere apology for reasons other than to render it inadmissible as evidence, including the possibility that it might improve the dispute resolution process and increase chances of settlement.[49] It also allows for the victim rather than a court to assess the value of the apology. Shuman's question '[w]ho better to determine whether an apology is an inadequate response to an intangible loss … ?' than a jury is, essentially, answered by effective apology legislation as 'the tort victim'. This does not address the point that a court needs to assess damages when a matter proceeds to trial. Unlike in defamation cases, however, where an apology serves in part to restore the plaintiff's reputation in the eyes of the public, objectively assessed, the experience of intangible loss resulting from personal injuries caused by negligence is – by its nature – a subjective inquiry. I suggest that this brings into question the ability of a trier of fact to reliably assess the sincerity and effectiveness of an apology to reduce intangible loss.

Third, a distinction can be made between taking an apology into account in the assessment of torts which have an explicit remedial purpose of vindicating rights – for example defamation, assault, deprivation of liberty, breach of privacy – and negligence cases, where the primary purpose of damages is to compensate for loss.

Finally, there would be significant ramifications for the parties and courts if apologies routinely were taken into account in the assessment of intangible loss for negligence. As Shuman acknowledges, it would also require a bifurcated trial on liability and damages when evidence of the apology for liability purposes is excluded.[50] This has obvious attendant costs. To date there does not appear to have been any uptake of these suggested ways to reduce damages for intangible loss and increase the incentives for defendants to apologise.

A third possible way for apologies to play a larger remedial role to compensate for intangible loss is by an order to apologise, which is considered in the next section.

C. Compelling Apologies and Non-monetary Compensation

> If I pay compensation, does that mean never having to say 'I'm sorry'?[51]

Apology orders are rarely made by courts in common law jurisdictions. Even in defamation cases – where corrections and apologies feature prominently in

[49] Eg the objects of Apology Ordinance (Hong Kong) cap 631 include 'to promote and encourage the making of apologies with a view to preventing the escalation of disputes and facilitating their amicable resolution': see s 2.

[50] Shuman, above, n 1, 189.

[51] The line 'love means never having to say you're sorry' is spoken by Jenny, played by Ali MacGraw, in the film *Love Story* directed by Arthur Hiller (1970). The movie is based on Erich Segal's book *Love Story*. The phrase is a little different in the book: 'Love means not ever having to say you're sorry'.

settlements and assessment of damages – courts in the United Kingdom, Australia, Canada, and other common law countries generally do not regard these remedies as available to a plaintiff. A significant reason is that coercive remedies will not be awarded where compensatory damages would be adequate to compensate the plaintiff.[52] Another reason is the view that courts do not have the power to order a defendant to publish an apology under the common law due to constitutional protections of freedom of expression.[53]

i. Availability of Apology Orders by Legislation and Principles for Deciding Whether to Make an Order

Notwithstanding that apology orders are not widely regarded as a judicial remedy – in common law and civil law jurisdictions alike – there are a number of instances where courts and tribunals, along with other decision makers, have been conferred legislative power to order a defendant to apologise and have exercised that power. For example, in Australian copyright law a court has power to make an apology order as a remedy for interference with the moral rights of authors[54] and performers,[55] and for unlawful disclosure of private information.[56] Orders to apologise are also available under anti-discrimination legislation in Australia and some other countries.[57]

The Hong Kong Final Court of Appeal has said in the context of a statutory power to order an apology under the Disability Discrimination Ordinance (Hong Kong) cap 487:[58]

> … it will be a rare case where enforcement of an apology order will not be futile or disproportionate and contrary to the interests of administration of justice.

[52] See generally N Witzleb et al, *Remedies: Commentary and Materials*, 6th edn (Thomson Reuters, 2015) 25 [1.110].

[53] Eg in Australia see *Summertime Holdings Pty Ltd v Environmental Defender's Office Ltd* (1998) 45 NSWLR 291, 297 (Young J); *Cerutti v Crestside Pty Ltd* (2016) 1 Qd R 89, 110 [36] (Applegarth J); *VTS IT Pty Ltd v Russell* [2015] ACTSC 230 (14 August 2015), [41] (Refshauge J). And, in the UK see, eg, *Loutchansky v Times Newspapers Ltd (Nos 2, 3, 4 and 5)* [2001] EWCA Civ 1805, [2002] QB 783, 824, para [99] (Lord Phillips MR). With this said, some courts have endorsed the use of apology orders: eg, in Canada, see *Ottawa-Carlton District School Board v Scharf* [2007] OJ No 3030 affd 2008 ONCA 154 with leave to appeal refused: see [2008] SCCA No 285. See also *Moore v Canadian Newspapers Co* (1989) 69 OR (2d) 262 (HC) expressing the opinion in dicta that the Court did have the power to order an apology and that such an act would not violate the Canadian Charter of Rights and Freedoms. And in South Africa see, eg, *Le Roux v Dey* 2011 (3) SA 274 (CC), [206].

[54] See Copyright Act 1968 (Cth), s 195AZA(1)(d).

[55] ibid, s 195AZGC(1)(d).

[56] Eg Privacy and Personal Information Protection Act 1998 (NSW), s 55(2); Privacy Act 1988 (Cth), s 52(1)(b)(ii).

[57] The power to order apologies is conferred on courts and tribunals exercising anti-discrimination jurisdiction in a number of overseas jurisdictions. In Hong Kong, see Disability Discrimination Ordinance (Hong Kong) cap 487, s 72(4)(b). In the Republic of South Africa, see Promotion of Equality and Prevention of Unfair Discrimination Act 2000 (South Africa), s 21(2) which confers power on the Equality Court to make a wide range of remedies orders, including 'an order that an unconditional apology be made': see s 21(2)(j).

[58] *Ma Bik Yung v Ko Chuen* [2002] 2 HKLRD 1, 20-1, applying s 72(4)(b).

In making an order, the circumstances to be considered include:[59]

> … the nature and aim of the legislation, the interest of the community, the gravity of the unlawful conduct and the plaintiff's circumstances, including the extent of the loss and damage suffered.

Only then can the question be answered whether in the particular instance the guaranteed freedoms of the applicant justify the making of an order, notwithstanding the interference it constitutes with the guaranteed freedoms – including freedom of expression – of the defendant. One can foresee a court ordering a defendant to make an apology where the defendant has not already done so voluntarily but is willing to do so once they have been found to have acted unlawfully. Beyond this situation, the question narrows to what constitutes 'rare' and 'exceptional' circumstances for the purposes of ordering a defendant who remains unwilling to apologise for unlawful discrimination?

In *Wotton v State of Queensland (No 5)*, Mortimer J in the Federal Court of Australia stated:[60]

> The principal reason tending against ordering an apology in relation to an unwilling respondent is that the court has other remedies at its disposal that could better achieve the objectives of such an order. Nevertheless, in some cases it may well be appropriate to order an apology.

Her Honour identified the critical questions as 'whether a court-ordered apology is an act which the Court is satisfied would redress damage suffered by the applicants' and whether 'more appropriate methods of achieving that redress are available'.[61]

Many important issues arise when a court is contemplating making orders that compel a defendant to publish a correction or apologise for their wrongful conduct and other similar orders.[62] These include, amongst others, the (lack of) sincerity of a compelled apology, interference with a defendant's freedom of expression, and difficulties of enforcing an order to apologise. Each of these is significant on their own. Nevertheless, as courts have recognised and some commentators have argued, these are not insurmountable barriers to making an order in a suitable case.[63]

ii. Compelled Apologies and Negligence

Typically, apology orders are sought in cases involving torts that protect reputation and dignitary interests. None of these cases relate to tort claims in negligence

[59] ibid, [48].
[60] [2016] FCA 1457 (5 December 2016), [1577] (Mortimer J).
[61] ibid, [1584].
[62] Carroll, above, n 14, 232, 369–76.
[63] G van Dijck, 'The Ordered Apology' (2017) 37 *Oxford Journal of Legal Studies* 562; A Zwart-Hink et al, 'Compelled Apologies as a Legal Remedy: Some Thoughts from a Civil Law Jurisdiction' (2014) 38 *University of Western Australia Law Review* 100.

and as far as I am aware no orders of this nature have been made in any common law jurisdiction. This does not preclude the possibility of such orders, particularly if the power were conferred by legislation. Vines argues that it is time to order apologies along with damages for negligence for two reasons: first, to achieve the aims of compensation and corrective justice more comprehensively than a declaration of liability in a judgment; second, in recognition of the fact that the nature of loss is broader than the legal system usually allows.[64] Her proposal aims to ensure that the law maintains a balance of symbolic, emotional and monetary needs in response to civil wrongs.[65]

Apology orders are one possible way to address any gap between the damages recoverable for mental and emotional distress and the intangible loss experienced by a tort victim, and to acknowledge that loss. In order to serve remedial purposes, I argue that the apology order would need to be sought by the plaintiff – otherwise there is a risk that the apology would have no compensatory value. It should also be awarded only after consideration of the many issues that arise when an apology is compelled on an unwilling defendant and which already make this an uncommon remedy.[66] One area of fertile research, beyond the scope of this chapter, is the operation of redress schemes which require apologies to be made to victims who seek them as part of a compensation scheme that can be opted into by a victim and in which liability is admitted.[67] In this type of scheme, questions of remedial choice and compulsion are more party controlled as compared to where court orders are made. As a result, many of the concerns about compelled apologies will be avoided.

IV. Discussion

This chapter has identified three ways that the law can expand the role of apologies as a remedial response to negligently caused intangible loss. In relation to these responses three questions are asked. The first question asks whether fault is relevant not only to liability for negligence but also whether fault and intention are factors relevant to the circumstances in which the law might want to provide greater incentives for a wrongdoer to apologise. Beyond a substantial body of research that confirms that victims of torts often want to receive an apology from a

[64] Vines, above, n 2.

[65] ibid.

[66] For discussion of these issues see Carroll, above, n 14, 323, 369–76; van Dijck, above, n 63.

[67] Eg the recently introduced National Redress Scheme for Institutional Child Sexual Abuse Act 2018 (Cth) which provides, in addition to damages capped at $150,000, affected persons with a right to a 'direct personal response' from a participating institution. A 'direct personal response' is defined as one or more of an apology or a statement of acknowledgement or regret, an acknowledgement of the impact of the abuse on the person, and an assurance as to the steps the institution has taken, or will take, to prevent abuse occurring again, an opportunity for the person to meet with a senior official of the institution: see s 54(2).

wrongdoer, there is psychological research which also indicates that victims mostly want to receive an apology after intentional wrongdoing, whereas wrongdoers want to offer an apology particularly after unintentional wrongdoing.[68] Arguably, this finding has significance for the question posed here because it suggests that apology protection legislation might possibly be more effective if it removes legal disincentives to apologies for intentional as well as unintentional wrongdoing. This has implications for many jurisdictions which only offer legislative protection to apologies only in specified contexts, for example medical negligence cases.

As the law stands it is fault, not intention, that determines the law's remedial response once liability for negligence is established. The defendant's intention is not relevant to the assessment of damages for negligently caused personal injuries. Were the categories of recoverable loss for negligently caused personal injuries to be expanded to include 'mere' distress or apology orders to be made in such cases, however, the defendant's intention could become an important consideration, along with their conduct in relation to the tort and the seriousness of the wrongdoing more generally.

The second question asks whether it is helpful to think of the law's role relating to apologies as providing incentives for self-help by the parties. In my view it is helpful to think of the law's role in encouraging apologies as supporting self-help if it encourages parties and their legal advisers to address their non-monetary needs, particularly in light of research that shows that an appropriate apology can provide redress for mental and emotional distress and benefit both victims and wrongdoers. It was explained in section III that apology legislation aims to remove disincentives for a wrongdoer who is willing to apologise. Although not without evidential consequence for victims, this is a significant way in which the law supports this form of redress for emotional distress. This support very much depends on whether the legislation protects an apology which incorporates an admission of fault or liability and, more generally, the scope of application of the legislation. Importantly, the legislation does not require a tort victim to accept an apology or to accept less by way of monetary compensation if an apology is made. Nor does the legislation preclude a tort victim from rejecting the apology and pursuing the full amount of monetary compensation they are entitled to under the law. It does, however, recognise implicitly that apologies may be remedial and offers potential benefits to both parties. In this sense, apology legislation recognises the potential for apologies to compensate in some way for intangible loss as well as fulfilling other functions. If, unlike at present, an apology was relevant to the assessment of damages for negligence or available as a court order, this would further encourage a wrongdoer to apologise of their own volition and encourage wrongdoer self-help.

The third question asks whether there are grounds to prefer any one of the three legal responses over another. The first response, apology protecting legislation, does not compel a wrongdoer to apologise nor compel a tort victim to accept

[68] Leunissen et al, above, n 31.

an apology. It recognises that apologies can to some degree provide compensation for both recoverable and non-recoverable intangible loss caused by negligence. Whether or not the apology is effective as compensation or meets any of their intangible needs is for the victim to decide.

Conceptually, from the point of view of providing an incentive to apologise to a tort victim other than through apology protection legislation there is merit in the second response, which is to take account when assessing compensatory damages of an apology offered by the defendant for their negligence. There are also numerous practical·drawbacks to this approach, even putting to one side question of the need for a court to assess the sincerity of the apology in question. First, it would require evidence of the defendant's conduct in response to the tort in addition to evidence of the victim's loss and of the benefit to the victim of the apology. In doing so it would shift some of the focus of the inquiry from the victim's intangible loss to the reasonableness of the wrongdoer's conduct when quantifying the loss. Second, a reduction in the amount of compensation for intangible loss may compound the risk that victims of negligence who suffer personal injuries will be undercompensated for their loss by reducing the damages payable to a victim, especially once statutory bars, thresholds and caps on damages for intangible loss are factored in.[69]

There are different considerations when addressing the third response, namely for the law to allow judges to order a wrongdoer to apologise for the negligent infliction of personal injuries. There are arguments in support of making an apology order for negligence. First, as noted above, Vines argues that this could achieve the aims of compensation and corrective justice more comprehensively; and second, to recognise that the nature of loss suffered is broader than the legal system usually allows.[70] Ultimately, an order to apologise for intangible loss that is not recoverable as damages would expand the legal consequences of negligence. Accordingly, this expansion requires that the remedy is justified by reference to the rights and obligations created by the tort, not just the consequences of the wrongdoing. Second, an apology order supports a victim's remedial preference if they would refer this as a remedy or in reduction of their damages. The likelihood that any victim would prefer an apology to additional monetary compensation is a matter for speculation but cannot be ruled out entirely.

Even assuming an apology order is a victim's remedy of choice, the possibility that this order will be made in substitution for damages raise concerns as well as benefits of remedial flexibility. By making an apology order for negligent conduct the court would be imposing a coercive remedy on a defendant that is not generally available at common law even for torts that are actionable without proof of

[69] Two other chapters in this book discuss these and other causes of the difficulties encountered by tort victims whose personal injuries are not adequately compensated by a lump sum award of damages for personal injuries; see P Vines, 'Addressing the Problems of Lump Sum Compensation Dissipation and Social Security Denial: The Lawyer Contribution' Ch 11; K Burns and R Harrington, 'Safe as Houses? Lump Sum Dissipation and Housing' Ch 6.

[70] Vines, above, n 2.

loss, unlike negligence, and which have an established vindicatory purpose, for example, defamation and trespass. Can an apology order against a defendant who is liable for negligently caused intangible loss be justified if no such order would be available against them for the intentional infliction of the same loss for an assault, for example? There is also a risk that a victim will be undercompensated for intangible loss for negligence if a court decides the matter and the victim's willingness or otherwise to accept the apology is not determinative of whether damages are reduced or an apology order made.

This discussion reveals that there could be unintended consequence of treating apologies as a form non-monetary compensation in the assessment of damages or as a court order. A defendant has an opportunity at any point in time after their negligent conduct causes the plaintiff's intangible loss up to trial to 'self-help' by offering an apology and this is supported by apology protecting legislation where it applies. For these reasons I conclude that the answer to the third question is that the first response is to be preferred. At the same time I recognise that there are good reasons to continue to explore and debate the merits of the second and third responses.

V. Conclusion

There are at least three ways, discussed above, that a fault-based tort system can respond to unintended consequences of compensation and increase the potential for an apology to compensate for intangible loss. Three questions arising from these responses have also been discussed above. In response to the first question, whether intention as well as fault is relevant to the circumstances in which the law might want to expand the remedial role of apologies, I conclude that intention is an important factor influencing the parties' decisions about whether an apology will be made and its effectiveness as non-monetary redress. For this reason, it can be argued that apology legislation that applies to intentional as well as negligent conduct will be more effective to encourage self-help.

The second question is whether these responses can be understood as ways in which the law supports self-help by the parties to redress intangible loss caused by negligence. I conclude that all three can operate to varying degrees to indirectly support self-help, by creating incentives for a wrongdoer to offer an apology voluntarily.

The third question asks whether any of the three responses is a preferable way for the law to recognise apologies in response to intangible loss caused by negligence. I conclude that legislation that protects apologies which acknowledge fault has the greatest potential to encourage a response by a wrongdoer that can serve compensatory and other remedial functions. This is because it has broader application outside the litigation and trial process.

Apology protecting legislation also allows the parties themselves to decide whether an apology will be made and its scope, whether it will be accepted, and the remedial value of the apology. There might be a stronger argument for a remedial role for apologies in the assessment of damages or as orders in negligence cases where there is no apology legislation or the applicable legislation does not protect a full apology. Better first, however, to consider the rationale for strengthening apology legislation and its purpose. In respect of all three responses there is a danger that apologies will be instrumental rather than compensatory: I conclude that this risk is heightened when a court, rather than the victim, attributes a compensatory value to the apology. Even if the risk of under-compensation were addressed by compelling an apology only as an additional rather than as an alternative remedy to damages and only by choice of the victim, there are many other unexpected consequences of treating apologies as compensation that require careful consideration.

PART IV

Responsibilities of Lawyers

10

Exploring the Dynamics of Legal Service Use in Compensation Systems

CLARE E SCOLLAY*

Legal service use plays a critical role in compensation systems, given its associations with claimant access to entitlements, access to justice, health and recovery outcomes, and experiences and perceptions of compensation processes. In spite of this, the factors associated with legal service use are not well understood. This chapter maps the compensation system, legal practitioner, and legal services market factors that affect claimant decisions to use legal services. Compensation system factors include the existence of an established path for claiming; compensation scheme design; the complexity, length, and stressfulness of the claiming process; and the claimant-insurer relationship. Legal practitioner factors include the costs and perceived costs of legal services; client screening and selection practices; lawyer and law firm characteristics; and the transformation of complaints into legal issues. Legal services market factors include the availability of legal services and competitiveness of the legal services market; advertising and other client acquisition practices; the unbundling of legal services; and the development of new technologies. Findings suggest that the operation of schemes is closely connected to the development and functioning of the legal services market, which in turn contributes to the kinds of justice that schemes are able to deliver.

I. Introduction

In Australia, one of the more common legal problems faced by individuals is personal injury, or harm to a person for which compensation can be claimed.[1] Approximately one fifth of individuals who experience personal injury problems sustain their injuries in road traffic crashes.[2] Road traffic injuries are linked to adverse consequences beyond the initial trauma, including income loss and financial strain, stress-related illness, relationship breakdown, and moving house.[3]

* PhD Candidate in the Faculty of Law at Monash University.
[1] C Coumarelos et al, 'The Nature of Personal Injury' (2015) 50 *Updating Justice* 1, 1.
[2] ibid, 2.
[3] ibid, 3.

Accordingly, in most middle-income countries, compensation for personal injuries (including those sustained in road traffic crashes) is available through one or more mechanisms including private insurance, public compensation schemes, and tort liability systems.[4] Taken together, the compensation mechanisms in a given jurisdiction comprise the compensation system available to injured persons.

In compensation systems, claimants use legal services to navigate the claiming process, resolve disputes, access benefits, and establish negligence.[5] Legal services facilitate claimant access to legal entitlements, and, as a result, are associated with access to justice, or the extent to which people can enforce their rights through fair and open processes.[6] However, access to justice goes beyond legal service use, as it also focuses on building a culture in which fewer legal problems need to be resolved and, when problem resolution is required, the most appropriate method is selected.[7] Access to justice also emphasises the need for resolution methods to be accessible (affordable, certain, comprehensible, effective, efficient, fair, responsive, timely, well-organised, and well-resourced)[8] and for outcomes to reflect the merits of cases and be individually and socially just.[9] In addition to access to justice, legal service use is associated with claimant outcomes, including physical and mental ill-health, longer treatment times, delayed claim closure, and lack of claim closure,[10] although it is unclear whether legal service use predicts these outcomes,

[4] DR Hensler et al, *Compensation for Accidental Injuries in the United States* (RAND Corporation, 1991) vii; J Walsh, 'The ICF and Accident Compensation in Australia', *ICF Australian User Guide V10* (Australian Institute of Health and Welfare, 2003) 89.

[5] DF Murgatroyd et al, 'Understanding the Effect of Compensation on Recovery from Severe Motor Vehicle Crash Injuries: A Qualitative Study' (2011) 17 *Injury Prevention* 222, 224; E Kilgour et al, 'Interactions Between Injured Workers and Insurers in Workers' Compensation Systems: A Systematic Review of Qualitative Research Literature' (2015) 25 *Journal of Occupational Rehabilitation* 160, 177–78; NA Elbers et al, 'Differences in Perceived Fairness and Health Outcomes in Two Injury Compensation Systems: A Comparative Study' (2016) 16 *BMC Public Health* 658, 665.

[6] L Schetzer et al, *Access to Justice & Legal Needs: A Project to Identify Legal Needs, Pathways and Barriers for Disadvantaged People in NSW* (Law and Justice Foundation of New South Wales, 2002) 6–8; H Genn, *Judging Civil Justice*, 1st edn (Cambridge, Cambridge University Press, 2010) 115.

[7] BG Garth and M Cappelletti, 'Access to Justice: The Newest Wave in the Worldwide Movement to Make Rights Effective' (1978) 27 *Buffalo Law Review* 181, 222–27; C Parker, *Just Lawyers: Regulation and Access to Justice* (Oxford, Oxford University Press, 1999) 81–82; C Coumarelos et al, *Justice Made to Measure: NSW Legal Needs Survey in Disadvantaged Areas* (Law and Justice Foundation of New South Wales, 2006) 199–200; Access to Justice Taskforce, *A Strategic Framework for Access to Justice in the Federal Civil Justice System* (Commonwealth of Australia, 2009) 4.

[8] RA Macdonald, 'Access to Civil Justice' in P Cane and HM Kritzer (eds), *The Oxford Handbook of Empirical Legal Research* (New York, Oxford University Press, 2010) 509.

[9] Garth and Cappelletti, above, n 7, 182; Genn, above, n 6.

[10] JD Cassidy et al, 'Effect of Eliminating Compensation for Pain and Suffering on the Outcome of Insurance Claims for Whiplash Injury' (2000) 342 *The New England Journal of Medicine* 1179, 1181; JD Cassidy et al, 'Low Back Pain After Traffic Collisions: A Population-Based Cohort Study' (2003) 28 *Spine* 1002, 1004; RT Gun et al, 'Risk Factors for Prolonged Disability After Whiplash Injury: A Prospective Study' (2005) 30 *Spine* 386, 389; IA Harris et al, 'Predictors of General Health After Major Trauma' (2008) 64 *The Journal of Trauma, Injury, Infection, and Critical Care* 969, 970; SM Littleton et al, 'The Association of Compensation on Longer Term Health Status for People with Musculoskeletal Injuries Following Road Traffic Crashes: Emergency Department Inception Cohort Study' (2011) 42 *Injury* 927, 930; PP Casey et al, 'Associations with Duration of Compensation Following Whiplash Sustained in a Motor Vehicle Crash' (2015) 46 *Injury* 1848, 1851; B Gopinath et al, 'Predictors of Time

or these outcomes predict legal service use.[11] Legal service use is also associated with claimant experiences and perceptions of compensation processes.[12]

Legal service use plays a critical role in shaping claimant outcomes and experiences in compensation systems given its associations with claimant access to entitlements and justice. In spite of this, the factors associated with legal service use in compensation systems are not well understood. In particular, although a large body of international evidence has identified person-level factors that explain how individuals respond to legal problems, there has been little research attention paid to the systemic factors that shape legal service use in compensation settings. This is important, given that both internal and external enabling factors must be present for service use to occur.[13] External enabling factors include the facilities in which services are provided, and the broader system and environment in which service provision occurs.[14] To begin to remedy this gap, this chapter maps the compensation system, legal practitioner, and legal services market factors that affect claimant decisions about whether to engage legal services. It then explores the dynamics shaping the relationships between these factors, claimant legal service use, and claimant outcomes. By bringing together the strands of evidence exploring structural, service, and market-related explanatory factors, the chapter provides a framework for analysing legal service use in the diverse systems in which compensation is provided to injured claimants.

II. Compensation System Factors

The compensation system factors that influence claimant decisions to use legal services include structural factors, such as the existence of an established path for claiming, compensation scheme design, and the complexity, length, and stressfulness of the claims process; and practice factors, such as the nature of the claimant-insurer relationship.

A. Existence of an Established Path for Claiming

Legal problems differ based on the institutionalisation of remedy systems, or the extent to which there are established, routinised, readily available methods

to Claim Closure Following a Non-Catastrophic Injury Sustained in a Motor Vehicle Crash: A Prospective Cohort Study' (2016) 16 *BMC Public Health* 421, 425.

[11] NM Spearing et al, 'Research on Injury Compensation and Health Outcomes: Ignoring the Problem of Reverse Causality led to a Biased Conclusion' (2012) 65 *Journal of Clinical Epidemiology* 1219, 1220.

[12] Elbers et al, above, n 5, 667.

[13] RM Andersen, 'Revisiting the Behavioral Model and Access to Medical Care: Does it Matter?' (1995) 36 *Journal of Health and Social Behavior* 1, 3.

[14] ibid, 3–6.

for dealing with these problems.[15] Road traffic injuries have highly institutionalised remedy systems that facilitate claim lodgement by legitimising action as a response to these injuries.[16] These systems achieve this legitimisation by indicating that road traffic injuries are frequent and important enough to warrant the existence of redress systems, and that using such systems to respond to these injuries is appropriate.[17]

Although the institutionalisation of remedy systems facilitates claim lodgement, its effect on claimant legal service use is less clear. In theory, there should be less need for legal services in institutionalised systems given that the claiming process is largely routinised.[18] However, in practice, there are high levels of legal service use in road traffic injury claims relative to other types of claims.[19] This may in part be due to the financial attractiveness of road traffic injury claims to lawyers, as the established redress systems for these claims mean that they can be processed quickly and cheaply.[20] In addition, the high severity of road traffic injuries, combined with their acute, unambiguous, and well-documented onset, means that the legal cases associated with these injuries tend to be factually simple, require minimal input, and be resolved quickly.[21]

The relationship between institutionalisation and legal service use is likely to depend on the extent to which lawyers are embedded in remedy systems. Lawyers are frequently portrayed as adversarial parties who add complexity to cases, prolong conflict and strife, and take advantage of others in pursuit of their economic goals.[22] Such views are held so firmly in some settings that lawyers have been banned from particular processes altogether.[23] In contrast, in many compensation settings, lawyers play an appreciable role in the claiming process and, as such, there are institutionalised pathways for lawyer involvement in this process. For example, the role of lawyers is often delineated and communicated

[15] RE Miller and A Sarat, 'Grievances, Claims, and Disputes: Assessing the Adversary Culture' (1980–81) 15 *Law & Society Review* 525, 563.

[16] ibid, 564.

[17] ibid.

[18] JK Robbenholt and VP Hans, *The Psychology of Tort Law* (New York, NYU Press, 2016) 9.

[19] HM Kritzer et al, 'The Aftermath of Injury: Cultural Factors in Compensation Seeking in Canada and the United States' (1991) 25 *Law and Society Review* 499, 517–18; FC Dunbar and F Sabry, 'The Propensity To Sue: Why Do People Seek Legal Actions?' (2007) 42 *Business Economics* 31, 37. Note: these findings are from studies conducted in the US. This chapter includes findings from studies conducted in various countries, as well as multiple states and territories within these countries. However, care should be taken in transposing findings across countries, states, and territories, as findings from one setting might not be applicable to others. In particular, care should be taken in transposing findings between common and civil law settings, and between the US and other common law settings.

[20] R Lewis and A Morris, 'Tort Law Culture: Image and Reality' (2012) 39 *Journal of Law and Society* 562, 590–91.

[21] ibid.

[22] M Galanter, 'Predators and Parasites: Lawyer-Bashing and Civil Justice' (1994) 28 *Georgia Law Review* 633, 634–36.

[23] B Batagol, 'Fomenters of Strife, Gladiatorial Champions or Something Else Entirely? Lawyers and Family Dispute Resolution' (2008) 8 *Law and Justice Journal* 24, 27–30.

to claimants through scheme documentation.[24] In other compensation systems, however, lawyers are given restricted roles in, or are excluded from, such processes as the resolution of disputes relating to statutory benefits.[25]

The relationship between institutionalisation and legal service use is also likely to depend on the extent to which claimants understand redress systems. Qualitative studies report that compensation claimants often experience uncertainty regarding their entitlements and the process for accessing these, and frustration with the level of information provided by schemes, triggering the involvement of legal services.[26] Claimants also find insurer use of bureaucratic tools such as algorithms, limits, and rules to be depersonalising and insensitive, and engage legal services to communicate the impact of their injuries to insurers.[27]

Overall, although institutionalisation of remedy systems facilitates compensation claiming for road traffic injuries, it is less clear how it affects legal service use during the claiming process. It is probable that this depends on the design and management of compensation systems, as well as claimant understanding of, and experiences during, the claim lodgement process. Notably, institutionalisation might introduce inequalities in access to compensation, as it might enable more capable claimants to navigate schemes alone, whilst less capable claimants are compelled to rely on legal assistance. Institutionalisation might also introduce inequalities in outcomes, as it might encourage lawyers to approach all claims in a similar manner and expend limited time and energy processing them.[28] This is particularly likely to disadvantage claimants with complex claims and serious injuries.[29]

B. Compensation Scheme Design

Claimant decisions about legal service use are influenced by compensation scheme design, and in particular the types of benefits available within a scheme. One major aspect of scheme design is the basis on which benefits are provided; this may be no-fault or fault-based, or a combination of the two.[30] Compared to no-fault

[24] eg Transport Accident Commission, *Transport Accident Act Common Law Protocols – 1 July 2016* (Transport Accident Commission, 2016) 2.

[25] R Guthrie, 'Negotiation, Power in Conciliation, and Review of Compensation Claims' (2002) 24 *Law & Policy* 229, 229; Motor Accident Injuries Bill 2017 (NSW), pt 8 (8.3–8.11).

[26] D Murgatroyd et al, 'The Perceptions and Experiences of People Injured in Motor Vehicle Crashes in a Compensation Scheme Setting: A Qualitative Study' (2015) 15 *BMC Public Health* 423, 426; GM Grant, *The Claims, Advice and Decisions After Injury (CADI) Study: Final Report: Interviews with Claimants* (Monash University 2017) 29.

[27] GM Grant, 'Claiming Justice in Injury Law' (2015) 41 *Monash University Law Review* 618, 643–44.

[28] JE Carlin and J Howard, 'Legal Representation and Class Justice' (1965) 12 *UCLA Law Review* 381, 385.

[29] NF Engstrom, 'Sunlight and Settlement Mills' (2011) 86 *New York University Law Review* 805, 838–41.

[30] I Malkin, 'Victoria's Transport Accident Reforms – In Perspective' (1987) 16 *Melbourne University Law Review* 254, 255; Walsh, above, n 4, 89–90.

benefits, fault-based benefits may involve greater use of legal services due to the need to establish negligence; as such, schemes that primarily provide fault-based benefits are likely to encourage greater use of legal services than those that primarily provide no-fault benefits.[31]

Other aspects of compensation scheme design, such as the degree and duration of coverage and amount claimable, also affect claimant legal service use. The degree of coverage affects legal service use by influencing claimant decisions to seek legal services. In the Netherlands, for example, there is an integrated system of employee, health, and social insurances that provides no-fault benefits to injured workers; this system includes a tort overlay that enables claimants to sue for additional benefits. In the past, relatively few claimants sued or used legal services, as the comprehensive nature of the scheme ensured that their recovery needs were sufficiently met. However, as the level of protection of the social security system has decreased, resort to the tort system has increased.[32] The amount claimable also affects legal service use by influencing lawyer decisions to take cases. For example, since the 1970s, several United States (US) jurisdictions have introduced caps on non-economic (ie pain and suffering) damages in medical malpractice claims.[33] Qualitative interviews with medical malpractice lawyers find that they are less likely to accept cases where such caps exist, as these reduce the financial viability of cases.[34] This is a particular issue when economic damages are minor and lawyers operate under fee-shifting agreements.[35] These caps contribute to inequalities in access to legal services, as they increase the number of individuals with legitimate claims who are unable to secure legal representation and therefore justice (as legal services are central to success in medical malpractice claims).[36] Compensation caps result in the biggest reductions in damages among severely injured individuals and disadvantaged groups such as women, children, and the elderly.[37]

[31] N Allsop et al, 'To Fault or Not to Fault That is the Question?' (Institute of Actuaries of Australia 12th Accident Compensation Seminar) 5.

[32] K Armstrong and D Tess, 'Fault versus No Fault – Reviewing the International Evidence' (Institute of Actuaries of Australia 16th General Insurance Seminar) 14; SD Lindenbergh, *Arbeidsongevallen en beroepsziekten* (Deventer, Wolters Kluwer, 2016) 1.

[33] J Van Hoy, 'Markets and Contingency: How Client Markets Influence the Work of Plaintiffs' Personal Injury Lawyers' (1999) 6 *International Journal of the Legal Profession* 345, 347; S Daniels and J Martin, 'The Texas Two-Step: Evidence on the Link between Damage Caps and Access to the Civil Justice System' (2006) 55 *DePaul Law Review* 635, 636–37.

[34] Van Hoy, above, n 33, 346; United States General Accounting Office, *Medical Malpractice Insurance: Multiple Factors Have Contributed to Increased Premium Rates* (United States General Accounting Office 2003) 41–42; S Daniels and J Martin, 'Texas Plaintiffs' Practice in the Age of Tort Reform: Survival of the Fittest – It's Even More True Now' (2006–07) 51 *New York Law School Law Review* 286, 288.

[35] United States General Accounting Office, above, n 34; Daniels and Martin, above, n 33, 645–46.

[36] Daniels and Martin, above, n 33, 646.

[37] LM Finley, 'The Hidden Victims of Tort Reform: Women, Children, and the Elderly' (2004) 53 *Emory Law Journal* 1263, 1280–81; DL Rhode, *Access to Justice* (New York, Oxford University Press, 2004) 69; MN Trautner, 'Screening, Sorting, and Selecting in Complex Personal Injury Cases: How Lawyers Mediate Access to the Civil Justice System' (PhD thesis, University of Arizona, 2006) 112–13; Daniels and Martin, above, n 34, 313–14.

Overall, compensation scheme design increases legal service use where there is a requirement to establish negligence, there is minimal coverage in terms of the benefits provided, and there are no caps on the amount claimable in non-economic damages.

C. Complexity, Length, and Stressfulness of the Claims Process

In addition to scheme design, the complexity, length, and stressfulness of the compensation process affect both claimant legal service use and claimant outcomes. Factors that contribute to the perceived complexity, length, and stressfulness of the compensation process fall broadly into two categories: issues relating to benefits and entitlements, and issues relating to scheme administration and communication. Issues relating to benefits and entitlements include claimant sense of entitlement and perceived injustice;[38] the need to prove an injury or disability, including through numerous medical assessments that require reliving the trauma of the injury event;[39] difficulties accessing financial, treatment, or other entitlements;[40] and delays providing funds leading to financial difficulties.[41] Issues relating to scheme administration and communication include the adversarial nature of the claiming process;[42] inadequate communication by insurers;[43] and the quantity of paperwork required.[44]

The complex, long, and stressful nature of the compensation process can lead individuals to turn to legal services for assistance.[45] However, engagement of legal services can itself increase the duration of the claiming process. For example, in many jurisdictions, once a claimant has legal representation, insurers are required to communicate with that claimant solely through their lawyer, which can cause delays

[38] K Lippel, 'Workers Describe the Effect of the Workers' Compensation Process on their Health: A Québec Study' (2007) 30 *International Journal of Law and Psychiatry* 427, 433–34; Murgatroyd et al, above, n 5, 223–24; Kilgour et al, above, n 5.

[39] B Bryant et al, 'Compensation Claims Following Road Accidents: A Six-Year Follow-Up Study' (1997) 37 *Medicine, Science and the Law* 326, 331; Murgatroyd et al, above, n 5; GM Grant et al, 'Relationship Between Stressfulness of Claiming for Injury Compensation and Long-term Recovery: A Prospective Cohort Study' (2014) 71 *JAMA Psychiatry* 446, 449; Grant, above, n 27, 641–42; Kilgour et al, above, n 5; E Kilgour et al, 'Healing or Harming? Healthcare Provider Interactions with Injured Workers and Insurers in Workers' Compensation Systems' (2015) 25 *Journal of Occupational Rehabilitation* 220, 229–31.

[40] Murgatroyd et al, above, n 6; BJ Gabbe et al, 'Financial and Employment Impacts of Serious Injury: A Qualitative Study' (2014) 45 *Injury* 1445, 1449; Murgatroyd et al, above, n 26, 425–27; Kilgour et al, above, n 5, 173–74.

[41] Bryant et al, above, n 39, 326; Gabbe et al, above, n 40.

[42] Lippel, above, n 38, 436; Murgatroyd et al, above, n 5; Kilgour et al, above, n 39, 232.

[43] Lippel, above, n 38, 437; Murgatroyd et al, above, n 5; Gabbe et al, above, n 40; Murgatroyd et al, above, n 26, 425–26.

[44] NA Elbers et al, 'Factors that Challenge Health for People Involved in the Compensation Process Following a Motor Vehicle Crash: A Longitudinal Study' (2015) 15 *BMC Public Health* 339, 344.

[45] Murgatroyd et al, above, n 6; Murgatroyd et al, above, n 26; Elbers et al, above, n 5.

in information provision and decision-making.[46] Similarly, engagement of legal services can precipitate a series of medico-legal examinations, in which healthcare professionals furnish an opinion about claimant injuries, treatment, impairment, and disability to determine claimant eligibility for particular benefits.[47] Studies report intensive use of medico-legal examinations within claims as, for example, a study of road traffic injury claims that went through adjudication in court and tribunal settings in Victoria, Australia, reported an average of nine medical expert consultations per claim.[48] Although this high number of medico-legal assessments may be beneficial, as it may assist adjudicators to understand claimant injuries and make appropriate decisions,[49] it can also lead to significant delays in claim settlement, as well as claimant anxiety, frustration, stress, and inability to move on with life.[50] Medico-legal examinations can also lead to perceptions of unfairness, as examiners are engaged by insurer or claimant lawyers, and might thus feel pressure to provide a report that favours the case of the party that engaged them as opposed to an objective opinion.[51] If this is indeed the case, it introduces an access to justice issue, as it means that evidence is being selected based on favourability rather than ensuring a just outcome.[52] These and other delays can place financial pressure on claimants, leading them to abandon their claims or settle for less than they are entitled to.[53]

The complexity and length of the claims process also affect claimant outcomes, as they heighten feelings of anger, frustration, pessimism, powerlessness, sadness, and stress.[54] Stress can in turn lead to poor physical health outcomes, such as increased disability; poor mental health outcomes, such as increased anxiety and depression; and poor quality of life outcomes.[55] Some claimants may be particularly vulnerable to stressors in the compensation process, including those with poor mental health.[56]

Overall, the length and complexity of the compensation process is associated with increased legal service use and negative outcomes, particularly in vulnerable groups of claimants.

[46] Murgatroyd et al, above, n 26, 428.

[47] G Grant and DM Studdert, 'The Injury Brokers: An Empirical Profile of Medical Expert Witnesses in Personal Injury Litigation' (2013) 36 *Melbourne University Law Review* 831, 833–34.

[48] ibid, 850.

[49] ibid, 862.

[50] Bryant et al, above, n 40; Murgatroyd et al, above, n 5, 224–25; Grant and Studdert, above, n 47, 861; Grant, above, n 27, 641–42.

[51] B Braithwaite, 'Personal Injury Lawyers' Ethics' (2003) 6 *Legal Ethics* 7, 8; Elbers et al, above, n 5, 668.

[52] HD Sperling, 'Expert Evidence: The Problem of Bias and Other Things' (2000) 4 *The Judicial Review* 429, 431.

[53] Garth and Cappelletti, above, n 7, 190.

[54] C Roberts-Yates, 'The Concerns and Issues of Injured Workers in Relation to Claims/Injury Management and Rehabilitation: The Need for New Operational Frameworks' (2003) 25 *Disability and Rehabilitation* 898, 902; L Cacciacarro and B Kirsh, 'Exploring the Mental Health Needs of Injured Workers' (2006) 73 *The Canadian Journal of Occupational Therapy* 178, 184.

[55] Grant et al, above, n 39, 446.

[56] Casey et al, above, n 9, 1853.

D. Nature of Relationship between Claimant and Insurer

A final compensation factor that influences legal service use in compensation systems is the nature of the relationship between the claimant and insurer. The dominant feature of this relationship is a substantial power imbalance between parties,[57] which arises because the insurer controls the resources that the claimant is seeking to access,[58] whilst the claimant enters the relationship in the role of injury victim, a position with an inherent degree of powerlessness.[59] This power imbalance often leads claimants to engage legal services in an effort to bring both parties onto an equal footing.[60] However, it can carry over into the legal process, where claimants tend to be one-time participants whilst insurers are repeat players.[61] Their repeat player status enables insurers to hire expert lawyers, negotiate favourable retainers, absorb costs, withstand delays, recognise and pursue defences and, in situations where they have several cases opposite the same lawyer, trade off outcomes across cases (eg, by settling one case at the expense of another).[62]

This power imbalance also enables insurers to dictate the terms of settlement offers, as the risk of not obtaining a favourable outcome is substantially higher for claimants.[63] As a result, United Kingdom (UK) studies suggest that in two out of three cases, claimants accept the first offer that is made to them,[64] which is often less than would be awarded by a judge.[65] Insurers may pressure claimants to accept low settlement offers by withholding payments during pre-settlement periods,[66] adding time limits,[67] and falsely presenting offers as final.[68] Claimants who are not swayed by such tactics may seek legal assistance to increase the size of settlement offers.[69] Insurers also need to manage risk, and may choose to settle cases if the cost of litigating them would prove too high.[70] This dynamic results in insurers settling meritorious claims for less than their worth and paying off spurious

[57] Lippel, above, n 38, 435–36.

[58] Kilgour et al, above, n 5, 161.

[59] M Minow, 'Speaking of Silence' (1988) 43 *University of Miami Law Review* 493, 495.

[60] Murgatroyd et al, above, n 5.

[61] M Galanter, 'Why the "Haves" Come out Ahead: Speculations on the Limits of Legal Change' (1974) 9 *Law & Society Review* 95, 97.

[62] Galanter, above, n 61 98–101; R Davis, 'Negotiating Personal Injury Cases: A Survey of the Attitudes and Beliefs of Personal Injury Lawyers' (1994) 68 *Australian Law Journal* 734, 744; RL Abel, 'How the Plaintiffs' Bar Bars Plaintiffs' (2006–07) 51 *New York Law School Law Review* 345, 355; J Ilan, 'The Commodification of Compensation? Personal Injuries Claims In an Age of Consumption' (2011) 20 *Social & Legal Studies* 39, 47.

[63] Davis, above, n 62, 743; Lewis and Morris, above, n 20, 569.

[64] DR Harris et al, *Compensation and Support for Illness and Injury* (Oxford, Clarendon Press, 1984) 95.

[65] R Lewis, 'Insurance and the Tort System' (2005) 25 *Legal Studies* 85, 90.

[66] L Strunin and LI Boden, 'The Workers' Compensation System: Worker Friend or Foe?' (2004) 45 *American Journal of Industrial Medicine* 338, 342–43.

[67] Braithwaite, above, n 51, 8–9.

[68] Davis, above, n 62, 746.

[69] Grant, above, n 26, 29–31.

[70] Lewis and Morris, above, n 20, 569–70.

claims, leading to a disconnect between entitlement and award that bears little resemblance to justice.[71]

The claimant-insurer relationship is further characterised by suspicion on the part of the insurer, due to their focus on the identification and elimination of spurious claims.[72] This suspicion manifests in covert use of private investigators and overt questioning of families, friends, neighbours, and coworkers to determine whether claimants are engaging in activities that are supposed to be beyond their capabilities.[73] Although insurers need to prevent spurious claiming to ensure the just distribution of resources, use of such techniques is often seen as threatening and invasive by claimants.[74] As such, it can lead claimants to feel anger, injustice, and shame; that their relationship with the insurer is adversarial; and that legal services are required to restore their character and navigate this relationship.[75] It can also result in acceptance of low settlement offers even in legitimate claims.[76]

The extent to which the claimant-insurer relationship becomes adversarial and results in legal service use is also influenced by the quality of communication in the scheme. Claimants tend to forgo legal service use when their relationships with insurers are empathetic, positive, supportive, responsive, and characterised by frequent and helpful interactions.[77] In contrast, claimants tend to become dissatisfied and frustrated, and turn to legal services for support, when they feel that there is a lack of cooperation, information, and transparency regarding their entitlements on the part of the insurer, or that information is being purposefully withheld from them.[78] If this is indeed the case, it introduces inequalities in access to compensation, as claimants are unlikely to obtain their entitlements unless they know the correct questions to ask.[79] Claims management practices can enhance or diminish the quality of communication between the insurer and claimant as, for example, the rotation of claimant files across case managers can engender feelings of dissatisfaction and powerlessness as claimants are continually forced to re-explain the circumstances and details of their injury to new personnel.[80] Finally, insurer decisions to terminate treatments that are perceived as necessary by claimants often result in feelings of abandonment and anger, and engagement of legal services,[81] making the quality of decision-making within the scheme a critical determinant of legal service use.

[71] Lewis, above, n 65; Ilan, above, n 62.

[72] Ilan, above, n 62, 43.

[73] K Lippel, 'Therapeutic and Anti-Therapeutic Consequences of Workers' Compensation' (1999) 22 *International Journal of Law and Psychiatry* 521, 534–35; Lippel, above, n 38, 434–35; Braithwaite, above, n 51, 9; Strunin and Boden, above, n 66; Kilgour et al, above, n 5, 169.

[74] Lippel, above, n 38, 434–35; M Murray, 'Fish Harvesters with Injuries' Accounts of their Experiences with the Workers' Compensation System' (2007) 28 *Work* 47, 50; Kilgour et al, above, n 5, 169.

[75] Roberts-Yates, above, n 54, 903–904; Kilgour et al, above, n 5, 169.

[76] Braithwaite, above, n 51, 9.

[77] Murgatroyd et al, above, n 26; Grant, above, n 27, 639–40.

[78] Murgatroyd et al, above, n 26, 426–27; Grant, above, n 27, 637–39.

[79] Lippel, above, n 38, 437.

[80] Lippel, above, n 38, 437; Grant, above, n 27, 634–35.

[81] Cacciacarro and Kirsh, above, n 54, 182–83; Murgatroyd et al, above, n 26, 429; Kilgour et al, above, n 5, 173–74.

Overall, the relationship between the claimant and insurer is likely to facilitate legal service use when the claimant feels: the need to equalise a power imbalance; that there is an opportunity to increase a poor settlement offer; under suspicion from the insurer; that an adversarial relationship has developed; that interactions with the insurer are negative; and that their access to benefits has been unfairly terminated. It also influences the route claims take once legal services have been engaged, as power imbalances and use of surveillance can lead claimants to settle early and for small amounts.

III. Lawyer Factors

Legal practitioner factors also affect claimant decisions about legal service use. These include: the costs and perceived costs of legal services; client screening and selection practices; lawyer and law firm characteristics; and the transformation of complaints into legal issues.

A. Costs and Perceived Costs of Legal Services

If the costs of legal services are not covered by compensation schemes, these present a substantial barrier to lawyer engagement. Indeed, studies consistently find that one in four people cite the unaffordability of legal services as their reason for failing to seek legal assistance in response to a legal problem.[82] This constitutes an access to justice issue, as low- and high-income individuals are unable to resolve their problems through the same channels.

The extent to which costs and perceived costs act as barriers depends on the availability of legal aid and other cost-shifting mechanisms in the legal marketplace. In many jurisdictions, the amount of legal aid provided is woefully inadequate: in fact, one US study found that the combination of all legal aid and pro bono programs provided the equivalent of one full-time lawyer for every 5,000 people eligible,[83] forcing a choice between abandonment of a legitimate claim and self-representation. Legal aid programs also often limit the services that can be provided, and the groups that these services can be provided to,

[82] American Bar Association, *Legal Needs and Civil Justice: A Survey of Americans: Major Findings from the Comprehensive Legal Needs Study* (American Bar Association, 1994) 20–21; Task Force on Civil Equal Justice Funding and Washington State Supreme Court, *The Washington State Civil Legal Needs Study* (Washington State Supreme Court, 2003) 47; C Coumarelos et al, *Legal Australia-Wide Survey: Legal Need in Australia* (Law and Justice Foundation of New South Wales, 2012) 123; P Pleasence and NJ Balmer, *How People Resolve 'Legal' Problems: A Report to the Legal Services Board* (PPSR, 2014) 61.

[83] See RL Sandefur, 'Fulcrum Point of Equal Access to Justice: Legal and Nonlegal Institutions of Remedy' (2009) 42 *Loyola of Los Angeles Law Review* 949, 966.

disadvantaging prisoners, undocumented immigrants, and those just above the poverty line.[84]

In addition, legal aid is often unavailable in the personal injury sector, which instead relies on cost-shifting mechanisms. These include conditional fee agreements (CFAs), such as no-win-no-fee arrangements, in which some or all legal costs are contingent on the successful outcome of the matter to which those costs relate.[85] CFAs have been praised for reducing cost barriers and resource imbalances between claimants and insurers, and promoting efficient service delivery and access to justice.[86] However, they have been criticised for encouraging weak or dubious claims (as these can be pursued at no cost or risk to the claimant), exposing lawyers to income risk (as lawyers need sufficient resources to cover their own costs until the conclusion of a claim), and incentivising lawyers to settle cases when their clients might prefer to litigate (as settlement expedites the payment process).[87] CFAs are also often used to the exclusion of all other fee structures, including for claimants who might be better served by these structures.[88] For example, in the UK, the introduction of CFAs precipitated the abolition of legal aid for personal injury claims;[89] as a result, impoverished claimants can only lodge legal claims if they self-represent or find a lawyer willing to take their case on a no-win-no-fee basis.[90]

Claimants also often fail to understand how CFAs operate in practice, as one UK market analysis report stated that despite widespread awareness of no-win-no-fee practices, 25 per cent of people were concerned that they would need to pay legal costs if they brought and lost a case.[91] In addition, claimants display confusion, and require clarification, regarding what constitutes a win, circumstances other than a win in which lawyers can charge legal fees, how legal fees are calculated, and the disbursements that need to be paid even if a case is won.[92] Providing comprehensible information about legal costs is important in facilitating access

[84] DM Dale, *The State of Access to Justice in Oregon: Part I: Assessment of Legal Needs* (Oregon State Bar 2000) 2; Rhode, above, n 37, 30.

[85] Australian Law Reform Commission (ALRC), *Review of the Adversarial System of Litigation* (Commonwealth of Australia 2000) 312.

[86] Van Hoy, above, n 33, 348; Engstrom, above, n 29, 851; AC Hutchinson, *A Study of the Costs of Legal Services in Personal Injury Litigation in Ontario: Final Report* (Commissioned Reports, Studies and Public Policy Documents, 2016) 4–5; see also MC Regan and PT Heenan, 'Supply Chains and Porous Boundaries: The Disaggregation of Legal Services' (2010) 78 *Fordham Law Review* 2137, 2155.

[87] DE Rosenthal, *Lawyer and Client: Who's in Charge?* (New York, Russell Sage Foundation, 1974) 96–99; Van Hoy, above, n 33, 347–48; Daniels and Martin, above, n 34, 298–300; Baroness Hale, 'What's Wrong with the Compensation Culture?' (2007) 13 *Clinical Negligence* 60, 62; P Fenn and N Rickman, 'Personal Injury Litigation' in P Cane and HM Kritzer (eds), *The Oxford Handbook of Empirical Legal Research* (New York, Oxford University Press, 2010) 248–49; Lewis and Morris, above, n 20, 563.

[88] Engstrom, above, n 29, 877–78.

[89] Fenn and Rickman, above, n 87; Lewis and Morris, above, n 20, 579–81.

[90] See ALRC, above, n 85, 352.

[91] Datamonitor, *UK Personal Injury Litigation – The Compensation Culture Myth Exploded* (Datamonitor, 2002) 99.

[92] Victorian Legal Services Board and Commissioner, *'No Win – No Fee' Costs Agreements* (Victorian Legal Services Board and Commissioner 2015) 1–2; Grant, above, n 26, 54–55.

to justice, as it empowers claimants to make informed decisions about how to approach their legal problems.[93]

Overall, costs and perceived costs present a barrier to legal service use when legal aid and CFAs are either unavailable, or available but not well understood. In contrast, costs and perceived costs are unlikely to present a barrier where legal aid and CFAs are available and well understood, resulting in greater use of legal services. However, removing cost barriers does not always increase legal service use, as some individuals do nothing in response to legal problems even when taking action would cost no money or would be relatively inexpensive.[94]

B. Client Screening (Gatekeeping) and Selection Practices

The removal of real and perceived cost barriers does not necessarily increase legal service use because lawyers perform a gatekeeping function, screening out claims they are reluctant to pursue.[95] Lawyers perform this function even when cost barriers exist, as they are obligated to act only in cases with reasonable prospects of success,[96] and may be liable to costs orders if a court determines that no such prospects exist.[97] However, gatekeeping is likely to be more stringent under CFAs; this may be because individuals do not self-select out of the legal process, leading to an inflated number of potential claims.[98] Alternatively, it may be because financial risks are transferred from claimants to lawyers, leading lawyers to tighten their case selection criteria.[99]

Lawyers performing gatekeeping functions select cases by weighing the likelihood of success and expected damages against anticipated costs.[100] For a lawyer to take a case under a CFA, they must conclude that the legal fees paid out of the damages will be sufficient to cover their costs and turn a profit.[101] As such, lawyers favour cases where there is a strong likelihood of succeeding in the claim

[93] Access to Justice Taskforce, above, n 7, 125.

[94] RL Sandefur, 'The Importance of Doing Nothing: Everyday Problems and Responses of Inaction' in P Pleasence et al (eds), *Transforming Lives: Law and Social Process* (Norwich, Stationery Office, 2007) 112–15.

[95] M Galanter, 'Reading the Landscape of Disputes: What We Know and Don't Know (And Think We Know) About Our Allegedly Contentious and Litigious Society' (1983) 31 *UCLA Law Review* 4, 19; HM Kritzer, *Risks, Reputations and Rewards: Contingency Fee Practice in the United States* (Stanford, Stanford University Press, 2004) 67–68.

[96] Legal Profession Uniform Law Application Act 2014 No 16 (NSW), sch 2(2).

[97] ibid, sch 2(5).

[98] Kritzer, above, n 95.

[99] Van Hoy, above, n 33, 358; Daniels and Martin, above, n 34, 320; Fenn and Rickman, above, n 87.

[100] FK Zemans, 'Framework For Analysis Of Legal Mobilization: A Decision-Making Model' (1982) 7 *American Bar Foundation Research Journal* 989, 1046–47; Daniels and Martin, above, n 33, 651–53; GM Grant and DM Studdert, 'Poisoned Chalice? A Critical Analysis of the Evidence Linking Personal Injury Compensation Processes with Adverse Health Outcomes' (2009) 33 *Melbourne University Law Review* 865, 879; Robbenholt and Hans, above, n 18, 13.

[101] Kritzer, above, n 95; Trautner, above, n 37, 93–96; Daniels and Martin, above, n 33, 659; Grant and Studdert, above, n 100.

and achieving substantial damages.[102] In personal injury cases, this depends on the severity and (in some jurisdictions) permanence of claimant injuries, making these crucial for case selection.[103]

In contrast, lawyers screen out cases where there is a slim likelihood of succeeding or achieving substantial damages, or a high anticipated cost. Some lawyers also screen out economically or socially undesirable clients, such as the impoverished, previously imprisoned, and unemployed, perhaps because they lack lost current and future earnings to claim in damages, or are unlikely to elicit juror sympathy or pay legal fees.[104] Finally, some lawyers screen out claimants who might become dissatisfied and bring malpractice suits, including the emotionally volatile and those seeking revenge.[105] Importantly, gatekeeping does not always manifest in a flat refusal to take a case, as lawyers may dissuade claimants from legal action by brushing them off, convincing them that their problem is not serious, not amenable to legal remedy, or not worth pursuing.[106] Alternatively, if the case is not suited to legal intervention, a lawyer may divert it into a more appropriate channel.[107] Thus, lawyers act as gatekeepers to justice,[108] denying the legitimacy of cases they are reluctant to pursue.[109]

Although gatekeeping should prevent dubious claims, given their low probability of success, this does not necessarily occur in practice. Some lawyers might actually accept such claims on the assumption that opposing parties will settle to avoid the cost of defending them.[110] At the opposite end of the spectrum, gatekeeping can prevent individuals with legitimate claims from pursuing these if they are unable to find a lawyer to represent them.[111] In the personal injury sector, this is likely to occur when claimants are approaching the injury threshold that is required for some claims to be lodged. If claimants are clearly above or below this

[102] HM Kritzer, 'Holding Back the Floodtide: The Role of Contingent Fee Lawyers' (1997) 70 *Wisconsin Lawyer* 10, 10–13; EA Lind, 'Litigation and Claiming in Organizations: Antisocial Behavior or Quest for Justice?' in RA Giacalone and J Greenberg (eds), *Antisocial Behavior in Organizations* (Thousand Oaks, Sage Publication, 1997) 156; Trautner, above, n 37, 93–96; Robbenholt and Hans, above, n 18, 13.

[103] Grant and Studdert, above, n 100, 879–80; Robbenholt and Hans, above, n 18, 13.

[104] See findings from interview, observational, and survey studies conducted among personal injury and other plaintiffs' lawyers in China and the US, including: S Daniels and J Martin, 'It Was the Best of Times, It Was the Worst of Times: The Precarious Nature of Plaintiffs' Practice in Texas' (2002) 80 *Texas Law Review* 1781, 1817–18; Daniels and Martin, above, n 34, 654; E Michelson, 'The Practice of Law as an Obstacle to Justice: Chinese Lawyers at Work' (2006) 40 *Law & Society Review* 1, 27; Trautner, above, n 37, 96–99.

[105] L Mather et al, *Divorce Lawyers at Work: Varieties of Professionalism in Practice* (New York, Oxford University Press, 2001) 93; Michelson, above, n 104, 19.

[106] S Macaulay, 'Lawyers and Consumer Protection Laws' (1979) 14 *Law & Society Review* 115, 124–25; Zemans, above, n 100; Michelson, above, n 104, 22–24.

[107] Macaulay, above, n 106; Zemans, above, n 100.

[108] J Martin and S Daniels, 'Access Denied: 'Tort Reform' Rhetoric is Closing the Courthouse Door' (1997) 33 *Trial* 26, 26.

[109] Michelson, above, n 104, 22.

[110] A Morris, 'Spiralling or Stabilising? The Compensation Culture and Our Propensity to Claim Damages for Personal Injury' (2007) 70 *Modern Law Review* 349, 362.

[111] Kritzer, above, n 102; Lind, above, n 102, 159; Morris, above, n 110.

threshold, their requests for legal assistance are likely to be accepted or denied, respectively. However, if claimants are approaching this threshold, lawyers need to make a judgement about whether the threshold will be reached. As a result, lawyers screen out some claims that are legitimate, and pursue others that are not, causing a disconnect between entitlement and award.

Overall, gatekeeping reduces legal service use, particularly in certain groups. Indeed, US studies of personal injury plaintiffs' lawyers suggest that over 50 per cent of claimants seeking legal representation are routinely turned away;[112] however, the amount of gatekeeping engaged in in other settings is unclear. Gatekeeping is influenced by not only the merits of the cases being brought, but also by lawyer, law firm, and legal market characteristics.[113]

C. Lawyer and Law Firm Characteristics

One characteristic that might influence gatekeeping is firm size. Large firms might assume cases with higher risks and longer timeframes because they can use recoveries from other low-risk short-term cases to subsidise their costs.[114] In small firms, financial sustainability is dependent on fewer cases and, as a result, these firms might need to select cases with greater surety of success.

In the US, the plaintiffs' bar has a hierarchical structure, in which the top level consists of specialist lawyers who act in high-stakes, high-value, high-complexity cases (such as medical malpractice) whilst the bottom consists of non-specialist lawyers who act in low-stakes, low-value, low-complexity cases (such as road traffic injury claims).[115] Lawyers screen out cases that fall outside their niche specialisation; for example, lawyers at the top level screen out claims involving low values and minor injuries, whilst those at the bottom screen out claims involving catastrophic injuries, medical malpractice, and product liabilities.[116] In some cases, screened claims are referred to practitioners up or down the hierarchy;[117] however, claimants often fail to act on these referrals, instead becoming discouraged and abandoning their claims.[118] In other cases, lawyers' gatekeeping practices

[112] Kritzer, above, n 102; S Parikh, 'Professionalism and Its Discontents: A Study of Social Networks in the Plaintiffs' Personal Injury Bar' (PhD thesis, University of Illinois, 2001) 78; Kritzer, above, n 95, 71; Daniels and Martin, above, n 33, 651.

[113] Trautner, above, n 37, 75–84.

[114] For prior evidence of cross-subsidisation see DA Hyman et al, 'The Economics of Plaintiff-Side Personal Injury Practice' (2015) *University of Illinois Law Review* 1563, 1593.

[115] Daniels and Martin, above, n 104, 1788–95; S Parikh, 'How the Spider Catches the Fly: Referral Networks in the Plaintiffs' Personal Injury Bar' (2006–07) 51 *New York Law School Review* 243, 247–48; S Daniels and J Martin, 'Plaintiffs' Lawyers and the Tension between Professional Norms and the Need to Generate Business' in L Levin and L Mather (eds), *Lawyers in Practice: Ethical Decision Making in Context* (Chicago, Chicago University Press, 2012) 112.

[116] Kritzer, above, n 102; Daniels and Martin, above, n 104, 1788–95.

[117] Trautner, above, n 37, 79–81; Parikh, above, n 115.

[118] Macaulay, above, n 106.

persuade claimants that their claims are invalid, which can result in the abandonment of legitimate claims.[119]

In addition to influencing lawyer selection of clients, lawyer and law firm characteristics may affect both client selection of lawyers and claimant outcomes. In terms of client selection of lawyers, a small-scale qualitative study of road traffic injury claims in Australia found that claimants consider the ability of a firm to handle case complexities (with large and specialist firms favoured over small and non-specialist firms) and the personal approach of a firm (with small firms favoured over large firms) during the selection process.[120] In terms of claimant outcomes, a large-scale quantitative study of medical malpractice claims in the US found that top-tier firms have higher success rates and recoveries than lower-tier firms;[121] this introduces inequalities in access to justice, given that low socio-economic status claimants are more likely to be represented by lower-tier lawyers.[122] Clients of small firms also report receiving more attentive, informative, personalised service,[123] affecting their ultimate satisfaction with the outcomes of their claims.[124]

Finally, lawyer engagement is affected by access factors, as claimants often report difficulties reaching lawyers on the telephone, receiving timely responses, scheduling appointments, and accessing lawyers' physical offices due to distance, inconvenience, or limited opening hours.[125]

Overall, lawyer and law firm characteristics are likely to increase legal service use when these are well-matched to the needs of individuals seeking legal representation, and reduce legal service use when the reverse is true. Legal service use is also likely to be affected by access factors, which act as barriers where difficulties exist and facilitators where difficulties are absent.

D. Transformation of Complaints into Legal Issues

US studies indicate that whether legal services are ultimately engaged depends on the ability of lawyers (and clients) to transform complaints into issues that can be resolved through legal channels. Central to this transformation is the reformulation of a complaint to fit within a defined legal category.[126] Lawyers achieve this by listening to the initial complaint and imposing classifications on events and

[119] Michelson, above, n 104, 22. Note: the structure of the legal services market and its effect on gatekeeping practices in other countries remains unclear.
[120] Grant, above, n 26, 33.
[121] DA Hyman et al, 'Medical Malpractice Litigation and the Market for Representation: Evidence from Indiana' (2018) 6, available at papers.ssrn.com/sol3/papers.cfm?abstract_id=3205704.
[122] Parker, above, n 7, 23.
[123] Grant, above, n 26, 33.
[124] Bryant et al, above, n 39, 334.
[125] Coumarelos et al, above, n 82, 122–23.
[126] Galanter, above, n 95.

relationships, turning the complaint into a stock story with prescribed elements that is recognisable to other actors in the legal system and can be progressed in a particular way to achieve resolution.[127]

This reformulation may contract or expand the scope of the complaint to include a narrower or broader set of events and relationships.[128] Alternatively, it may change client expectations and goals in terms of the outcomes and remedies sought.[129] However reformulation occurs, its ultimate effect is to change the meaning of the original complaint; as a result, the cases that emerge in legal forums often bear little resemblance to the complaints that originally entered the legal system.[130]

The transformation of complaints has several benefits, as it allows individuals to enter the legal system, and identify, explore, organise, and negotiate their problems.[131] Lawyers facilitate this process by furnishing clients with information about the choices available to them and the consequences of these choices, reality-testing their expectations, and emotionally or socially supporting clients who are unsure of themselves or their objectives.[132] However, transformation of complaints may also be detrimental in that it may encourage lawyers to create a demand for their services by defining claimant problems in a way that suggests that legal recourse is their only option.[133] Lawyers have also been criticised for altering complaints to suit their own interests, and transforming complaints so much that the legal system is unable to address their underlying issues.[134] In doing so, lawyers deny the legal legitimacy of the original complaint and limit outcomes to those that they believe are reasonable rather than those that claimants are entitled to.[135]

These criticisms are concerning, given the procedural justice literature, which suggests that claimants are most likely to believe that justice has been achieved when they have an opportunity to tell their own stories, voice their concerns, and provide evidence to support their views.[136] Indeed, claimants who go to court and

[127] C Menkel-Meadow, 'The Transformation of Disputes by Lawyers: What the Dispute Paradigm Does and Does Not Tell Us' (1985) *Journal of Dispute Resolution* 25, 31–32.

[128] L Mather and B Yngvesson, 'Language, Audience, and the Transformation of Disputes' (1980) 15 *Law and Society Review* 775, 778–79; DM Engel, 'Legal Pluralism in an American Community: Perspectives on a Civil Trial Court' (1980) 5 *American Bar Foundation Research Journal* 425, 450–51; WLF Felstiner et al, 'The Emergence and Transformation of Disputes: Naming, Blaming, Claiming …' (1980) 15 *Law and Society Review* 631, 641–42; Galanter, above, n 95; Menkel-Meadow, above, n 127.

[129] Engel, above, n 128; Felstiner et al, above, n 128, 642–43; Galanter, above, n 95; A Sarat and WLF Felstiner, 'Law and Strategy in the Divorce Lawyer's Office' (1986) 20 *Law and Society Review* 93, 107; A Sarat and WLF Felstiner, 'Law and Social Relations: Vocabularies of Motive in Lawyer/Client Interaction' (1988) 22 *Law and Society Review* 737, 762; A Sarat and WLF Felstiner, 'Lawyers and Legal Consciousness: Law Talk in the Divorce Lawyer's Office' (1989) 98 *The Yale Law Journal* 1663, 1684.

[130] Galanter, above, n 95.

[131] Felstiner et al, above, n 128, 646.

[132] ibid.

[133] ibid, 645.

[134] Felstiner et al, above, n 128, 645; Zemans, above, n 100, 1049.

[135] Michelson, above, n 104, 8.

[136] Lippel, above, n 73, 541; NA Welsh, 'Disputants' Decision Control in Court-Connected Mediation: A Hollow Promise Without Procedural Justice' (2002) *Journal of Dispute Resolution* 179, 180;

lose still view the process as beneficial as it provides them with an opportunity to have their experiences and feelings acknowledged by an unbiased person in a position of authority.[137] In transforming complaints to the point where they are unrecognisable, lawyers may prevent their clients from telling their stories in legal settings, which may in turn affect their perceptions of whether justice has been achieved.

Overall, transformation is likely to increase legal service use where complaints have the elements required to connect them to stock stories, and lawyers are able to recognise these connections.

IV. Legal Services Market Factors

Legal services market factors that affect claimant decisions about legal service use include: the availability of legal services and competitiveness of the legal services market; advertising and other client acquisition practices; the unbundling of legal services; and the development of new technologies.

A. Availability of Legal Services and Competitiveness of the Legal Services Market

The number of lawyers in the legal marketplace has increased steadily and substantially over the past several decades.[138] At the same time, the legal services market has transformed from one characterised by few firms, assured tenure, minimal lateral movement of lawyers across firms, and a loyal clientele, to one characterised by many firms, substantial lateral movement, mergers and divestments, and an inconstant clientele.[139] In addition, new and disruptive technologies have automated several functions previously performed by lawyers.[140] As a result, the legal marketplace is becoming increasingly competitive as law firms vie for clients and

B McAdoo and NA Welsh, 'Look Before You Leap And Keep on Looking: Lessons from the Institutionalization of Court-Connected Mediation' (2004) 5 *Nevada Law Journal* 399, 405.

[137] DW Shuman, 'The Psychology of Compensation in Tort Law' (1994) 43 *Kansas Law Review* 39, 64; Lippel, above, n 38, 438.

[138] M Galanter and T Palay, *Tournament of Lawyers: The Transformation of the Big Law Firm* (Chicago, University of Chicago Press, 1991) 110–11; ALRC, above, n 86, 248; J Flood, *Will There Be Fallout from Clementi? The Global Repercussions for the Legal Profession after the UK Legal Services Act 2007* (Jean Monnet/Robert Schuman Paper Series, University of Miami, 2008) 5; Law Society of England and Wales, *The Future of Legal Services* (The Law Society of England and Wales, 2016) 25.

[139] According to US studies, including: Galanter and Palay, above, n 138, 54–55; M Galanter, 'The Faces of Mistrust: The Image of Lawyers in Public Opinion, Jokes, and Political Discourse' (1998) 66 *University of Cincinnati Law Review* 805, 831; TJ Replogle, 'The Business of Law: Evolution of the Legal Services Market' (2017) 6 *Michigan Business & Entrepreneurial Law Review* 287, 292–94.

[140] RE Susskind, *Tomorrow's Lawyers: An Introduction to Your Future*, 2nd edn (Oxford, Oxford University Press, 2013) 35–36.

employees, and lawyers compete for clients within and outside their own firms.[141] This competitiveness is being intensified by a decline in the demand for legal services,[142] and the entry of well-resourced international firms into local markets due to globalisation.[143] Competitiveness increases legal service use by expanding both the number of services available and the accessibility of these services.[144] However, it can also lead lawyers to retain rather than refer out cases beyond their capabilities, disadvantaging claimants.[145]

Lawyers and law firms are also facing increasing competition from non-legal entities.[146] In the UK, for example, reforms have authorised non-lawyer ownership of law firms and eliminated traditional restrictions on the practice of law,[147] enabling consumer-oriented organisations such as supermarkets to provide legal services.[148] Other non-traditional purveyors of legal services include real-estate firms that offer conveyancing or leasing services;[149] companies that supply self-help and do-it-yourself legal kits;[150] education centres that run law courses for non-lawyers;[151] community, government, internet, and library agencies that proffer legal information and advice;[152] and artificial intelligence (AI) technologies that provide customised assistance with specific legal problems or tasks.[153] As a result, use of traditional legal services is decreasing, with almost two-thirds of individuals now preferring to receive legal help from high street brands than conventional law firms.[154]

[141] According to US studies, including: CF Epstein, 'Book Review: The Betrayed Profession: Lawyering at the End of the Twentieth Century' (1997) 34 *Society* 88, 89; Daniels and Martin, above, n 115, 117; Replogle, above, n 139, 291.

[142] L Ribstein, 'The Death of Big Law' (2010) 2010 *Wisconsin Law Review* 749, 751; Melbourne Law School and Thomson Reuters Peer Monitor, *2016 Australia: State of the Legal Market* (Melbourne Law School and Thomson Reuters Peer Monitor, 2016) 9; TS Clay and EA Seeger, *Law Firms in Transition: An Altman Weil Flash Survey* (Inc Altman Weil, 2017) ii.

[143] Ribstein, above, n 142, 765–67; DB Wilkins, 'Some Realism about Legal Realism for Lawyers: Assessing the Role of Context in Legal Ethics' in LC Levin and L Mather (eds), *Lawyers in Practice: Ethical Decision Making in Context* (Chicago, The University of Chicago Press, 2012) 38–39; Replogle, above, n 139.

[144] Zemans, above, n 100, 990.

[145] S Daniels and J Martin, '"Its Darwinism – Survival of the Fittest": How Markets and Reputations Shape the Ways in Which Plaintiffs' Lawyers Obtain Clients' (1999) 21 *Law and Policy* 377, 395–96.

[146] L Mather and LC Levin, 'Why Context Matters' in LC Levin and L Mather (eds), *Lawyers in Practice: Ethical Decision Making in Context* (Chicago, The University of Chicago Press, 2012) 9; Clay and Seeger, above, n 142, 4–5.

[147] D Clementi, *Review of the Regulatory Framework for Legal Services in England and Wales: A Consultation Paper* (Department for Constitutional Affairs, 2004) 68–69.

[148] Flood, above, n 138, 8–9.

[149] Melbourne Law School and Thomson Reuters Peer Monitor, *2015 Australia: State of the Legal Market* (Melbourne Law School and Thomson Reuters Peer Monitor, 2015) 13.

[150] J Giddings and M Robertson, 'Large-Scale Map or the A-Z? The Place of Self-Help Services in Legal Aid' (2003) 30 *Journal of Law and Society* 102, 103.

[151] G Renouf et al, 'Pro Bono Opportunity in Discrete Task Assistance' (2003) 41 *Law Society Journal* 54, 54.

[152] Schetzer et al, above, n 6, 10.

[153] GE Marchant, 'Artificial Intelligence and the Future of Legal Practice' (2017) 14 *The SciTech Lawyer* 20, 22.

[154] According to a UK study; see R Susskind and D Susskind, *The Future of the Professions: How Technology Will Transform the Work of Human Experts*, 1st edn (Oxford, Oxford University Press, 2015) 67.

Market competitiveness is also being affected by lawyer migrations across case types and jurisdictions in pursuit of profitable claims.[155] These migrations result from legislative changes that decrease or increase the appeal of particular areas of practice. For example, in the US, capping non-economic damages in medical malpractice claims has led personal injury lawyers to diversify into divorce and nursing home cases in order to maintain their income.[156] Notably, lawyers who remain in less profitable areas once others have left tend to be highly specialised, making it difficult for claimants with legitimate but modest cases to obtain representation.[157]

Overall, when the legal marketplace is competitive due to high numbers of lawyers operating in the market, traditional legal service use is likely to increase. However, when the legal marketplace is competitive due to the availability of alternative legal services, traditional legal service use is likely to decrease. In both situations claimants' odds of resolving their legal problems are enhanced.

B. Advertising and Other Client Acquisition Practices

The competitiveness of the market has led lawyers and firms to explore new revenue generation methods, including advertising. Advertising increases legal service use by raising awareness about the possibility of engaging legal services and the process for doing so, as well as addressing barriers to, and reinforcing benefits of, use.[158] In terms of addressing barriers, advertising may assuage fears about meeting with lawyers by giving lawyers an approachable image or providing options for remote contact; portray legal claiming as an easy, fast, stress-free process; and remove cost barriers through no-win-no-fee promises.[159] In terms of reinforcing benefits, advertising may highlight the financial value of pursuing a legal claim; imply that legal claims are frequently successful; and create feelings of entitlement to compensation.[160] In addition, by routinely exposing consumers to the suggestion that compensation claiming and legal service use are natural consequences of injury, advertising creates a cultural link between injury, legal service use, and compensation over time, institutionalising it as a remedy system.[161]

Advertising increases access to justice by educating claimants about available legal services and their costs, enabling them to make informed decisions about

[155] CS Alexander, 'Litigation Migrants' (2018) 2–3, available at ssrn.com/abstract=3230195.

[156] S Daniels and J Martin, '"The Impact That It Has Had Is between People's Ears": Tort Reform, Mass Culture, and Plaintiffs' Lawyers' (2000) 50 *DePaul Law Review* 453, 488–91.

[157] Daniels and Martin, above, n 104, 1825.

[158] AJ Hudec and MJ Trebilcock, 'Lawyer Advertising and the Supply of Information in the Market for Legal Services' (1982) 20 *University of Western Ontario Law Review* 53, 54; Lewis and Morris, above, n 20, 586.

[159] Morris, above, n 110, 373–75; Lewis and Morris, above, n 20, 586.

[160] ibid.

[161] HM Kritzer, 'Propensity to Sue in England and the United States of America: Blaming and Claiming in Tort Cases' (1991) 18 *Journal of Law and Society* 400, 420; Morris, above, n 110, 374.

how to resolve their legal problems.[162] This is particularly important for disadvantaged groups such as: the impoverished, uneducated, and young;[163] those who may be ignorant, or hold misconceptions, about legal services;[164] and those who lack familial or social contacts to connect them to legal representatives.[165] However, the volume of advertising can make it difficult for claimants to differentiate between legal service providers based on competence, responsiveness, and suitability,[166] particularly as many advertisements focus on image-building rather than information provision.[167] This can lead claimants (and especially disadvantaged claimants who are more susceptible to advertising) to select firms whose services are a poor fit to their needs.[168] In addition, advertising might encourage contact from claimants with weak or non-existent cases, causing lawyers to expend substantial resources on gatekeeping activities, and increasing the risk of spurious claiming.[169]

Negative perceptions also surround the advertising of legal services, although these are held primarily by lawyers. Lawyers fear that advertising erodes the legitimacy of, and contributes to public cynicism towards, their profession.[170] In contrast, US studies show that consumers who receive information through legal advertising have high opinions of the legal profession and lawyers who advertise.[171] Concerns about legal advertising have resulted in regulatory controls and restrictions in several jurisdictions.[172] Although these are designed to prevent false and misleading advertising,[173] they can also impede competition, efficiency, innovation, and information flow.[174] Thus, lawyers' concerns about, and resistance to, advertising can inhibit claimants from accessing competitive, cost-effective services.[175]

Despite the rise of advertising, the main method of client acquisition by some lawyers remains referral.[176] As a result, these lawyers do not advertise to the public

[162] MG Bolocan, *Professional Legal Ethics: A Comparative Perspective* (Central European and Eurasian Law Initiative, 2002) 11.

[163] RJ Cebula, 'Does Lawyer Advertising Adversely Influence the Image of Lawyers in the United States? An Alternative Perspective and New Empirical Evidence' (1998) 27 *Journal of Legal Studies* 503, 504–505.

[164] Hudec and Trebilcock, above, n 158, 79.

[165] Bolocan, above, n 162, 22; Engstrom, above, n 29, 853.

[166] Abel, above, n 62, 357.

[167] RH Brock, 'This Court Took a Wrong Turn with Bates: Why the Supreme Court Should Revisit Lawyer Advertising' (2009) 7 *First Amendment Law Review* 145, 201.

[168] Engstrom, above, n 29, 853–54.

[169] HM Kritzer and J Krishnan, 'Lawyers Seeking Clients, Clients Seeking Lawyers: Sources of Contingency Fee Cases and Their Implications for Case Handling' (1999) 21 *Law and Policy* 347, 354.

[170] JK Van Patten, 'Essay: Lawyer Advertising, Professional Ethics, and the Constitution' (1995) 40 *South Dakota Law Review* 212, 212–13; Bolocan, above, n 162, 22; W Hornsby, 'Clashes of Class and Cash: Battles from the 150 Years War to Govern Client Development' (2005) 37 *Arizona State Law Journal* 255, 256–61.

[171] American Bar Association, *The Impact of Advertising on the Image of Lawyers* (Commission on Advertising 1995) 20; Cebula, above, n 163, 513; Rhode, above, n 37, 152.

[172] Bolocan, above, n 162, 22.

[173] ibid.

[174] See Hudec and Trebilcock, above, n 158, 56.

[175] Rhode, above, n 37, 117.

[176] According to US studies, including: Daniels and Martin, above, n 115, 113–14.

but to other lawyers who might refer cases to them.[177] Other more dubious client acquisition practices include obtaining or purchasing injured persons' information from tow truck drivers, crash repair workshops, emergency services workers, healthcare practitioners, and funeral parlours.[178] In the UK, claims management companies also began 'farming' claims in the late 1990s by recruiting injured persons and selling their claims to lawyers at a profit.[179] Although such contacts might increase access to justice among those who otherwise would not pursue claims, they can result in stress and worry, as claimants are left unsure about the commitments they have made.[180]

Overall, advertising and other client acquisition practices are likely to increase legal service use. However, despite the proliferation of advertising, many claimants fail to seek legal assistance.[181] This may be because claimants doubt the ethics of personal injury law, are dubious about no-win-no-fee advertising, or view legal claiming as illegitimate or undesirable.[182]

C. Unbundling

In addition to new revenue generation methods, lawyers and firms are exploring cost-cutting mechanisms to retain their edge in the competitive market. One such mechanism that has risen in popularity since the mid-1990s is unbundling.[183] Unbundling refers to the division of legal services into discrete components, some of which are completed by lawyers, whilst the remainder are completed by clients using self-help strategies, near-sourced to legal practitioners in low-cost cities in the same country, or outsourced to legal practitioners in different countries.[184] Tasks completed by lawyers range from providing an opinion (eg about the viability of a case or settlement offer), to preparing documentation, or representing a client at a dispute resolution conference or court hearing.[185]

Unbundling increases the manageability and predictability of legal costs.[186] In doing so, it facilitates both legal service use and access to justice by enabling

[177] Kritzer and Krishnan, above, n 169, 358; DA Hyman et al, 'Medical Malpractice Litigation and the Market for Plaintiff-Side Representation: Evidence from Illinois' (2016) 13 *Journal of Empirical Legal Studies* 603, 604.

[178] Daniels and Martin, above, n 145, 390–91; Rhode, above, n 37, 114; Abel, above, n 62, 358.

[179] Lewis and Morris, above, n 20, 579–80.

[180] S Marks, *Door to Door: CAB Clients' Experience of Doorstop Selling* (National Association of Citizens Advice Bureaux, 2002) 16–17.

[181] Lewis and Morris, above, n 20, 586.

[182] Morris, above, n 110, 376.

[183] FS Mosten, 'Unbundling of Legal Services and The Family Lawyer' (1994) 28 *Family Law Quarterly* 421, 424–26; Rhode, above, n 37, 157.

[184] Mosten, above, n 183, 422–24; Regan and Heenan, above, n 86, 2139; Wilkins, above, n 143, 35.

[185] Mosten, above, n 183, 423; B MacDermott, 'Unbundling: A Risk Profile' (2003) 41 *Law Society Journal* 60, 60; H Macken, 'Step-In, Step-Out Litigation' (2003) 41 *Law Society Journal* 48, 48–49; Renouf et al, above, n 151, 55; Rhode, above, n 37, 157–58.

[186] Productivity Commission, *Access to Justice Arrangements: Productivity Commission Inquiry Report* (Commonwealth of Australia 2014) 20.

claimants to receive assistance with some components of their legal problems, even if they cannot afford or obtain full representation.[187] In addition, it allows lawyers to focus on legal rather than administrative activities as the most efficient person performs each task.[188] Finally, unbundling empowers claimants to contribute to problem resolution, which can lead to satisfaction, self-respect, and a sense of control.[189] This is particularly important in personal injury cases, where claimants may be disempowered by both the initial trauma and the compensation claiming process.[190]

However, client completion of tasks using self-help strategies is not appropriate in all situations. Self-help strategies are best suited to tasks that are stand-alone, routinised, standardised, well-defined, and unlikely to require judgement calls.[191] Self-help strategies are also best suited to clients that have the skills required to complete these tasks, including high levels of education, articulation, and legal capability.[192] Self-help is thus unsuitable for clients with limited language, literacy, or communication skills; poor legal capability; and complex, multiple, or substantial legal problems.[193]

In addition, unbundling limits the time available for lawyers to engage in research, analysis, and reflection.[194] This means that lawyers may not be able to accurately assess the facts of a case or likelihood of a positive outcome, which is an issue given their obligation to act only in cases with a reasonable prospect of success. Time constraints also mean that lawyers may provide legal advice based on an incomplete understanding of the facts,[195] which exposes lawyers to the risk of malpractice suits, and claimants to the risk of unjust outcomes.[196] Finally, there are concerns about the quality of unbundled services, particularly when tasks are near or outsourced, as this creates lapses in oversight that suppliers

[187] Renouf et al, above, n 151, 55; Productivity Commission, above, n 186.

[188] MacDermott, above, n 185; JS Dzienkowski, 'The Future of Big Law: Alternative Legal Service Providers to Corporate Clients' (2014) 82 *Fordham Law Review* 2995, 3015; L Wortham, 'The Future of the Legal Profession and Legal Services Delivery' in L Wortham et al (eds), *Learning From Practice*, 3rd edn (St Paul, West Academic Publishing, 2016) 764.

[189] MacDermott, above, n 185; Susskind and Susskind, above, n 154, 35.

[190] DA Alexander et al, 'Personal Injury Compensation: No Claim Without Pain?' (2006) 30 *Psychiatric Bulletin* 373, 374–75.

[191] J Giddings and M Robertson, '"Lay People, for God's Sake – Surely I Should be Dealing with Lawyers?" Towards an Assessment of Self-Help Legal Services in Australia' (2002) 11 *Griffith Law Review* 436, 453; Renouf et al, above, n 151, 55.

[192] M Robertson and J Giddings, 'Legal Consumers as Coproducers' (2002) 40 *Family Court Review* 63, 71.

[193] S Scott, 'Law Online' (2000) 25 *Alternative Law Journal* 24, 25–26; H Genn and A Paterson, *Paths to Justice Scotland: What People in Scotland Do and Think About Going to Law* (Oxford, Hart Publishing, 2001) 247; Robertson and Giddings, above, n 192; EA Spieler, 'The Paradox of Access to Civil Justice: The Glut of New Lawyers and the Persistence of Unmet Need' (2013) 44 *University of Toledo Law Review* 365, 388.

[194] F Mosten, 'The Unbundling of Legal Services: Increasing Legal Access' in R Smith (ed), *Shaping the Future: New Directions in Legal Services* (London, Legal Action Group, 1995) 52.

[195] Mosten, above, n 194; ALRC, above, n 85, 402; V Shirvington, 'No Unbundling for Ethical Obligations' (2003) 41 *Law Society Journal* 58, 59.

[196] Mosten, above, n 183, 430–33; ALRC, above, n 85, 402; Shirvington, above, n 195.

might exploit.[197] However, studies find unbundling to be as effective as full representation for some (housing-related) legal problems.[198]

Overall, unbundling is likely to increase legal service use, particularly among claimants who cannot afford or obtain full representation. However, its limitations may decrease the number of claimants who can access unbundled services, and the quality of services received.

D. Technology

New revenue generation and cost-cutting mechanisms are being powered by new technologies. In terms of revenue generation, the Internet and social media are becoming common advertising mediums,[199] whilst chat and other software applications (apps) are enabling lawyers to diversify and unbundle their product offerings[200] and differentiate themselves from competitors.[201] In terms of cost-cutting, sales support and other technologies are improving case selection, contract development, cost estimation, and resource planning practices;[202] customer relationship management, data search, document composition, document review, file sharing, file storage, and workflow tools are streamlining account and activity management;[203] and AI apps are automating legal research, document identification, and document analysis activities.[204] New technologies are also changing the product offerings available by automating and routinising tasks historically performed by lawyers.[205] For example, a host of websites now provide downloadable legal documentation and automated assembly,[206] whilst legal robots provide customised assistance with specific tasks and legal questions.[207]

[197] Dale, above, n 84, 49; Regan and Heenan, above, n 86, 2156.

[198] DJ Greiner et al, 'How Effective Are Limited Legal Assistance Programs? A Randomized Experiment in a Massachusetts Housing Court' (2012) 37, available at ssrn.com/abstract=1880078.

[199] Law Institute of Victoria, *Advertising Guidelines* (Law Institute of Victoria, 2016) 1; Victorian Law Reform Commission, *Access to Justice – Litigation Funding and Group Proceedings* (Victorian Law Reform Commission, 2018) 146.

[200] Susskind and Susskind, above, n 154, 117; GJ Glover, 'Online Legal Service Platforms and the Path to Access to Justice' (2016) 90 *The Florida Bar Journal* 88, 88–89.

[201] Melbourne Law School and Thomson Reuters Peer Monitor, above, n 142, 7.

[202] Melbourne Law School and Thomson Reuters Peer Monitor, above, n 149, 14; Melbourne Law School and Thomson Reuters Peer Monitor, above, n 142, 8; D Remus and F Levy, 'Can Robots Be Lawyers? Computers, Lawyers, and the Practice of Law' (2017) 30 *The Georgetown Journal of Legal Ethics* 501, 514.

[203] Melbourne Law School and Thomson Reuters Peer Monitor, above, n 149, 14; Melbourne Law School and Thomson Reuters Peer Monitor, above, n 142, 8.

[204] Law Society of England and Wales, above, n 138, 39; Replogle, above, n 139, 295–96.

[205] DM Katz, 'Quantitative Legal Prediction – or – How I Learned to Stop Worrying and Start Preparing for the Data-Driven Future of the Legal Services Industry' (2013) 62 *Emory Law Journal* 909, 910.

[206] C Johnson, 'Leveraging Technology to Deliver Legal Services' (2009) 23 *Harvard Journal of Law and Technology* 259, 261; Susskind, above, n 140.

[207] Law Society of England and Wales, above, n 138, 39; Marchant, above, n 153.

Adoption of these technologies is being driven by internal desires to cut costs and accommodate the working preferences of millennial employees, as well as external pressures from clients who are seeking novel solutions to problems, market entrants who are conducting business differently, and judicial and regulatory bodies who are introducing their own technological innovations.[208] New technologies disseminate legal advice, documentation, education, information, and self-help tools that can be used alone or in conjunction with services provided by a lawyer.[209] Thus, they increase use of legal services and alternatives to legal services, as well as access to justice, by enhancing service accessibility, affordability, convenience, and efficiency.[210] This is particularly important for claimants who face access barriers (such as difficulties reaching lawyers during office hours), communication barriers (such as speaking a different language), geographic barriers (such as incarceration or isolation), and impairment barriers (such as blindness, deafness, or immobility).[211]

There are, however, challenges associated with use of new technologies. First, digital solutions are limited to those with access to the technologies used, which can exclude the elderly, impoverished, uneducated, unemployed, and those in remote communities.[212] Second, those with access often experience difficulties navigating the volume of information available and selecting advice appropriate to their situations;[213] this is a particular issue for those with complex problems or poor language, literacy, and communication skills.[214] Third, there are concerns about whether AI can decide disputes in an accurate, fair, legal, transparent, and unbiased manner.[215] Fourth, technological service delivery often relies on unlicensed and untrained laypersons, which can result in incomplete or

[208] A Stanfield, 'Online Courts: The Way of the Future?' (2015) 9 *Law Society of NSW Journal* 50, 50; Law Society of England and Wales, above, n 138, 40; Wortham, above, n 188, 773–84; Melbourne Law School and Thomson Reuters Peer Monitor, *2017 Australia: State of the Legal Market* (Melbourne Law School and Thomson Reuters Peer Monitor, 2017) 2.

[209] M Legg, 'Limiting Lawyers' Liability in the Brave New World Wide Web' (2000) 38 *Law Society Journal* 48, 50; J Giddings and M Robertson, '"Informed Litigants with Nowhere To Go": Self-Help Legal Aid Services in Australia' (2001) 26 *Alternative Law Journal* 184, 184; Giddings and Robertson, above, n 191, 448.

[210] Johnson, above, n 206, 259; Susskind, above, n 140, 61; Replogle, above, n 139, 295–96.

[211] National Alternative Dispute Resolution Advisory Council, *Dispute Resolution and Information Technology: Principles for Good Practice* (National Alternative Dispute Resolution Advisory Council, 2002) 7.

[212] Scott, above, n 193; Access to Justice Taskforce, above, n 7, 81; Australian Bureau of Statistics (ABS), '8146.0 – Household Use of Information Technology, Australia, 2016–17' (2018) available at www.abs.gov.au/ausstats/abs@.nsf/mf/8146.0.

[213] Access to Justice Taskforce, above, n 7, 77; M Fitzharris et al, *Factors Associated with Common Law Claims Lodged to the Transport Accident Commission* (Monash University, 2013) 9; Law Society of England and Wales, above, n 138, 57–58.

[214] Coumarelos et al, above, n 82, 215; P Pleasence et al, *Causes of Action: Civil Law and Social Justice*, 2nd edn (Norwich, Stationery Office, 2006) 159–60.

[215] M Legg, *The Future of Dispute Resolution: Online ADR and Online Courts* (University of New South Wales Law Research Series, University of New South Wales, 2016) 12–14; Remus and Levy, above, n 202, 548–51; T Rostain, 'Robots Versus Lawyers: A User-Centered Approach' (2017) 30 *The Georgetown Journal of Legal Ethics* 559, 564.

incorrect advice.[216] Finally, digital solutions can create a false impression that self-representation is appropriate, and technological tools sufficient, to resolve legal problems.[217]

Overall, new technologies are likely to increase access to, and use of, legal services despite these challenges. However, this is not occurring to the extent predicted, particularly in the field of personal injury. This may be because some new technologies are streamlining processes for existing clients rather than reaching new clients.[218] Alternatively, it may be because personal injury lawyers play a counselling role that cannot be easily supplanted by digital solutions.[219]

V. Discussion and Conclusion

Compensation system, legal practitioner, and legal services market factors affect claimant decisions to use legal services. Factors that increase legal service use include the complexity, length, and stressfulness of the compensation process, the claimant-insurer relationship, transformation of complaints into legal issues, advertising and other client acquisition practices, and unbundling. Factors that decrease legal service use include costs and perceived costs of legal services, and client screening and selection practices. Factors that can increase *or* decrease legal service use include compensation scheme design (eg legal service use increases when benefits are provided on a fault basis, but decreases when benefits are provided on a no-fault basis), lawyer and law firm characteristics (eg legal service use increases when these are well-matched to the needs of claimants seeking representation, but decreases when the reverse is true), and emergence of alternative legal services and new technologies (eg these can be used as a gateway or supplement to, or a replacement for, legal services). Factors whose relationship with legal service use remains unclear include the existence of an established path for claiming.

Several of these relationships appear to be mediated in part by claimant experiences and perceptions. This is particularly the case for the compensation system factors, as insurer communication (lack of cooperation, information, and transparency), case assessment (use of bureaucratic tools and surveillance techniques), claims management (rotation of claimant files across case managers), and decision-making (termination of treatment) practices can result in claimant feelings of depersonalisation, dissatisfaction, frustration, injustice, powerlessness, uncertainty, and vulnerability which in turn trigger engagement of legal services.[220]

[216] CJ Lanctot, 'Scriveners in Cyberspace: Online Document Preparation and the Unauthorized Practice of Law' (2002) 30 *Hofstra Law Review* 811, 848.
[217] ALRC, above, n 85, 653–54.
[218] Marchant, above, n 153, 21–22.
[219] Rostain, above, n 215, 571.
[220] Grant, above, n 27, 634–45; Murgatroyd et al, above, n 26, 426–29.

In contrast, the dynamics of the relationships between the legal practitioner and legal services market factors and legal service use, including how these play out in practice from the claimant perspective, remain unclear. Notably, these factors do not operate in isolation, but interact to influence overall levels of legal service use. For example, compensation scheme design factors (such as the capping of damages) affect the profitability of particular claims; this can lead to more stringent gatekeeping practices and lawyer migration into other case types, affecting market competitiveness and specialisation.

Compensation system, legal practitioner, and legal services market factors also interact to influence overall levels of access to justice. Many developments that have been introduced to enhance access to justice have not applied to the most disadvantaged groups. For example, no-win-no-fee arrangements were introduced to facilitate access to legal services among those who could not afford them.[221] However, this has not occurred for all claimants, as some lawyers screen out undesirable groups such as the impoverished, imprisoned, and unemployed.[222] Similarly, unbundling tasks for claimants to complete using self-help strategies is not effective for those with limited communication, language, or literacy skills; poor legal capability; and complex, multiple, or substantial legal problems.[223] Finally, new technologies exclude claimants with access barriers (such as the elderly, impoverished, uneducated, unemployed, and those in remote areas) and competence barriers (such as those with limited communication, language, or literacy skills).[224] Thus, there is substantial overlap between claimants who are gatekept from no-win-no-fee arrangements, cannot afford to pay for legal services, and lack the skills to implement unbundled or digital solutions and resolve their problems alone.[225]

In part, this might be because these developments aim to increase the accessibility and affordability of legal services and alternatives to legal services in groups that already have some level of access, rather than to bridge the gap for those that have none. As such, there is value in these developments. However, there is still a need to increase the accessibility of legal services and alternatives to legal services, for example by making existing resolution strategies more affordable, certain, comprehensible, effective, efficient, fair, responsive, timely, well-organised, well-resourced,[226] and available to underserved groups of claimants. There is also a need to look beyond the engagement of legal services and support claimants to select the most appropriate method of problem resolution: this might not be legal

[221] Hutchinson, above, n 86.

[222] Daniels and Martin, above, n 104; Daniels and Martin, above, n 33, 654; Michelson, above, n 104; Trautner, above, n 37, 96–99.

[223] Scott, above, n 193; Genn and Paterson, above, n 193; Robertson and Giddings, above, n 192; Spieler, above, n 193.

[224] Scott, above, n 193; Access to Justice Taskforce, above, n 7, 81; Coumarelos et al, above, n 82, 215; ABS, above, n 212.

[225] Law Society of England and Wales, above, n 138, 45.

[226] Macdonald, above, n 8.

services, as lawyers are not always the most appropriate source of guidance for claimants.[227]

This chapter does not provide a comprehensive overview of all factors that affect claimant decisions to use legal services in compensation systems. However, it does discuss the principal compensation system, legal practitioner, and legal services market factors that influence this outcome. It suggests that the operation of schemes is closely connected to the development and functioning of the legal services market, which in turn contributes to the kinds of justice that schemes are able to deliver.

[227] Susskind, above, n 140, 59.

11

Addressing the Problems of Lump Sum Compensation Dissipation and Social Security Denial: The Lawyer Contribution

PRUE VINES*

When a person is injured and given a lump sum package, their compensation may run out faster than envisaged at the outset. When they turn to social security for support they may find that the rules of social security preclude them from support. This chapter considers the factors concerning lawyers which contribute to both the low level of compensation which tort law often gives to plaintiffs and to the consequent dissipation of the monetary awards and failure of social security to support those who run out. Factors considered include the silos of specialisation of lawyers, their failure to push hard enough for compensation in courts, which means that in settlements sums often are even less, and a lack of sufficient care in advising about legal costs and the consequences in social security law to a group of people who may be vulnerable in a number of ways, not least in their ability to manage money, which creates a situation where lump sum awards may be extremely problematic.

I. Introduction

When a person is injured and given a lump sum compensation package, compensation may run out faster than envisaged at the outset. In many cases such injured persons may turn to social security for support only to find that the rules of social security preclude them from being given financial support for some considerable period. This appears to be true not only in Australia, but also elsewhere.[1] Wherever social security systems exist, rules for the protection of the public purse will rightly

* Professor and Co-director of Private Law Research and Policy Group, Faculty of Law, University of New South Wales, Australia.

[1] R Lewis et al, 'Loss of earnings following personal injury: do the courts adequately compensate injured parties?' (2003) 113 *The Economic Journal* F-568; R Lewis, *Deducting Benefits from Damages for Personal Injury* (Oxford, Oxford University Press, 2000); R Lewis, 'Politics and Economics of Tort

also exist.[2] In Australia some of these rules appear to create injustice for people who have suffered a personal injury and received lump sum compensation for it.[3] In this chapter I highlight the role of lawyers in both creating and possibly solving this problem. The process of getting compensation is mostly guided by lawyers, and it is lawyers who may be able to advise, warn and behave in ways which will reduce some of the problems that have been identified in seeking compensation after lump sums have dissipated. People run out of compensation for a range of reasons, including that they have been undercompensated in the first place. This chapter draws on an earlier study[4] of this issue which included case studies of people who sought help from social security after their compensation had run out, only to be told that their lump sum preclusion period had a great deal more time to run.[5]

In this chapter I briefly recount the basic findings already reported and move the focus of attention to the role of lawyers in creating and solving these problems.

II. The Study

In this study we considered the position of people who had run out of their lump sum compensation and been denied social security. We examined the law relating to damages assessment, settlement and social security law as it applied to them. A second aspect of the study involved case studies of people who had come to the Welfare Rights Centre (WRC) for help because they had run out of compensation and not been able to get social security. In most cases people were seeking disability benefits because they were unable to work. We studied some 36 cases where the Centre represented people in appeals to various tribunals including the Social Security Appeals Tribunal (SSAT). These had the advantage that often the files included a great deal of information about the initial compensation case. The third aspect involved an analysis of approximately 15 decided cases from the Administrative Appeals Tribunal of Australia (AAT), which were appeals from the SSAT. These latter cases had less information available about the initial process of compensation

Law: Judicially Imposed Periodical Payments of Damages' (2006) 69(3) *Modern Law Review* 418–22; see the Social Security (Recovery of Benefits) Act 1997 (UK) and similarly, the Health and Social Care (Community Health and Standards) Act 2003 (UK) Pt 3.

[2] Most Western countries have some type of social welfare or social security system which acts as a safety net for the poor. These range from comprehensive (eg Sweden, the Netherlands) to minimal (eg United States). In developing countries social security is much less available. Australia has Social Security Agreements with some 31 countries: www.dss.gov.au/about-the-department/international/international-social-security-agreements/current-international-social-security-agreements.

[3] P Vines et al, 'When Lump Sum Compensation Runs Out: Personal Responsibility or Legal System Failure?' (2017) 39(3) *Sydney Law Review* 365; M Butt and P Vines, 'Running out of Compensation Money: Whipping Away the Security Blanket?' (2013) 7 *Court of Conscience* 17; G Grant et al, 'When Lump Sums Run Out: Disputes at the Borderline of Tort Law, Injury Compensation and Social Security' in K Barker et al (eds), *Private Law in the 21st Century* (Oxford, Hart Publishing, 2016).

[4] Vines et al, above, n 3.

[5] Vines et al, above, n 3. Note the WRC study had Ethics Approval from UNSW: HC13176.

but were also treated as case studies. In all these cases we looked to see what had happened to the compensation monies and how the law of social security considered these dealings with the money. We also looked at the processes the clients had gone through in gaining their compensation in the first place where that was possible. For example, in some cases we could determine whether there had been litigation or settlement, the billing structure in place, the advice given by lawyers before or at the time of the compensation payment and so on. Not all these matters could be determined. We also interviewed a number of personal injury lawyers.

A brief summary of those findings shows that the clients received lump sums which were typically between $AUD 300,000–500,000. Only two of the matters involved catastrophic injury. The median gross lump sum received was $415,875 and the median length of the preclusion period set by social security was 278.5 weeks (five years and four months). These were not huge sums and they did not last for a long time. Median legal costs were $77,500, which is 18.6 per cent of the gross lump sum. The vast majority (95 per cent) of the cases were settled on a 'costs inclusive' basis, that is, without taking out the amount known to be owed for legal fees.

A. How Much Money Clients Actually Received

Table 1 shows the sums received by the WRC clients and, where possible, the amount of the legal fees. Table 2 shows the same received by parties in the AAT. What became clear is that legal fees were often quite a high proportion of the lump sum awarded.

Table 1 Welfare Rights Centre cases

Client (de-identified and given letter)	Settlement (S) or court award (C)/ or workers comp (WC)	Compensation lump sum $	Legal fees $	Legal fee as % of lump sum	Amount remaining to client after legal fees taken out
A	S	550,000	55,000	10	
B	S	431,750	75,000		
C	S	475,000			
D	S	350,000			
E	WC	204,375			
F	S	312,500	42,000	13.44	270,000
G	S	126,000			
H	S	1,020,733.70			597,348.01
I	S	268,100			206,100

(continued)

Table 1 *(Continued)*

Client (de-identified and given letter)	Settlement (S) or court award (C)/ or workers comp (WC)	Compensation lump sum $	Legal fees $	Legal fee as % of lump sum	Amount remaining to client after legal fees taken out
J	S	800,000	263,000	32.88	
K	S	476,303			
L	S	851,455	251,455	29.5	600,000
M	S	218,400			
N	S	352,000			
O	S	211,692	52,228	24.67	159,464
P	S	142,58			
Q	C?	1,180,000			
R	S	580,000			
S	S	280,000	94,000	33.57	186,000
T	WC	240,000			
U	WC	294,000			
V	S	478,750			
W	S	899,000	359,000	39.93	540,000
X	C?	338,469			
Y	S	425,000			
Z	ONGOING				
AA	C?	187789.60			
AC	S	100,000			
AD	ongoing	45,000 so far			
AE	S	140,000			
AF	S	150,000			
AG	C? not PI	1,400,000	877,000	62%	523,000

Table 2 AAT cases (where legal fee information available)

Name	Lump sum amount	Legal fees	Legal fee as % of lump sum	Remainder
Johansen[6]	325,000	60,000	19	265,000
Gifford[7]	244,000	44,000	18	200,000

(continued)

[6] *Johansen and SDEEWR* [2014] AATA 941.
[7] *Gifford and SDSS* [2014] AATA 873.

Table 2 ***(Continued)***

Name	Lump sum amount	Legal fees	Legal fee as % of lump sum	Remainder
Morison[8]	775,000	125,000	16	650,000
Barba[9]	1,500,000	400,000	26.6	1100,000
Lind[10]	275,000	25,000	9	250,000
Taleb[11]	360,000	66,000	18	294,000

B. What Clients Did with their Money

Table 3 WRC clients' spending

Paid for a holiday	Bought house Paid off mortgage Renovated a house	Paid money to other family members or friends	Bought a business	Bought a car	Gambling	Addiction to alcohol or other drugs
1	16	12	1	12	8	5

N = 30

Table 4 AAT decided cases plaintiff spending

Paid for a holiday	Bought house Paid off mortgage Renovated a house	Paid money to other family members or friends	Bought a business	Bought a car	Gambling	Addiction to alcohol or other drugs
3	12	4	0	6	1	0

N = 15

[8] *Morison and SDSS* [2014] AATA 825.
[9] *Barba and SDSS* [2010] AATA 403.
[10] *Lind and SDSS* [2014] AATA 680.
[11] *Taleb and SDSS* [2014] AATA 657

Figure 1 What clients did with their money as percentage of all clients

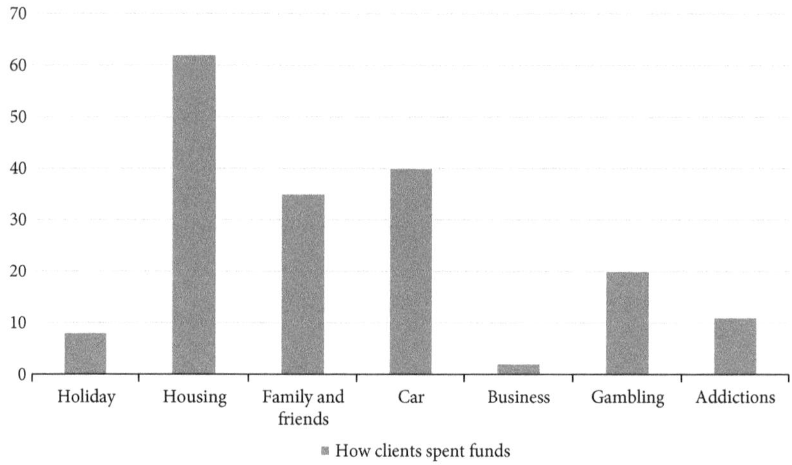

Of 36 plaintiffs who had run out of compensation in our study, 16 spent money on paying off a mortgage, buying a house or renovating a house. This was the most common use of large sums of money. Twelve loaned money to friends which was not paid back, or gave money to family members. This issue of the relationship between housing and lump sum preclusion in social security is discussed in Chapter 6 by Kylie Burns and Ros Harrington.

III. What Happens when the Compensation Runs Out? The Law

A. Social Security

In many cases the plaintiff will not be entitled to social security because the lump sum preclusion period calculated under the Social Security Act 1991 (Cth) (SSA) prevents them from accessing benefits. The rationale for the imposition of preclusion periods is said to be to prevent 'double dipping', that is, the receipt of both compensation and social security in respect of the same injury.[12]

The SSA sets out a formula for calculating the length and start date of the preclusion period.[13] The formula for calculating the length of the period in weeks is the compensation part of the lump sum divided by the income cut out amount.[14]

[12] *SDSS v a'Beckett* (1990) 2 FCR 349.

[13] Section 1170. For some of the complications this can give rise to see *Jackson v SDSS* [1997] FCA 1111; *Re Allan and SDFaCS* [2002] AATA 612.

[14] Section 1170(4).

The compensation part of the lump sum is a reference to the part of the lump sum which is, or is taken to be, the amount received for lost income or lost earnings capacity. When it is divided by the income cut out amount, this gives the number of weeks for which social security is precluded.[15] Obviously the higher this amount is the shorter the lump sum preclusion period is. This is an indexed figure, as the pension rate is indexed for cost of living changes. But the calculation of the preclusion period is fixed when the money is received, so the length of the preclusion period is not adjusted for that period. The potential unfairness of this has been discussed by the AAT, and will be considered further below.[16]

The SSA determines the compensation part of the lump sum differently depending on whether the amount was determined by: (i) settlement or consent judgment, where matters have been determined by the parties themselves; and (ii) court judgments made after hearing evidence.[17] In the case of settlements (the vast majority of cases, and 95 per cent of our sample) or consent judgments, 50 per cent of the total lump sum is deemed to be the compensation part.[18] In the case of court judgments, the amount is the amount that the court or tribunal specifies to be for past and future economic loss.

The rationale for the 50 per cent rule is said to be to prevent manipulation of the heads of loss by the parties to settlements to obtain a social security advantage (that is, agreeing on a global sum and attributing most of that figure to non-economic heads of loss).[19]

Lump sums for the one injury cannot be split into separate parts to avoid the application of the preclusion period, but are aggregated when the final part is paid.[20] This seems to lead to confusion for people affected, as well as incorrect advice from legal advisers or Centrelink.[21]

Similarly, the medical costs component of inclusive settlements is included in the lump sum.[22] Other sums awarded in a single total amount are also captured.[23]

The Act allows the Department of Social Security (now Department of Human Services/Centrelink) to recover money directly from compensation payers, usually insurers, if a debt arises because of the imposition of a compensation preclusion

[15] The income cut-out amount is the amount of weekly income at which the pension paid at the single rate is no longer payable, as at the date compensation is received: ss 17(1), 17(8) and 1064 (pension rate calculator).

[16] Eg *Re Coxon and SDFaCS* [2001] AATA 294.

[17] Sections 17(3)(a), 17(3)(ab), 17(3)(b).

[18] In NSW, it is worth noting that acceptance of a damages assessment by the Claims Assessment and Resolution Service under the Motor Accidents Compensation Act 1999 is not a 'settlement'. See *Kezchek and SCFHCSIA* [2009] AATA 604.

[19] *SDSS v Banks* (1990) 23 FCR 416; *SDSS v Smith* (1991) 30 FCR 56.

[20] Section 1171.

[21] *Re Alavanja and SDFHCSIA* [2008] AATA 286; possibly *Re Banicek and SDEWR* [2006] AAT 435.

[22] *SDSS v a'Beckett* (1990) 2 FCR 349.

[23] For example, the interest component. See *Mourilyan and SDFaCS* [20000] AATA 1026; also past and future lost superannuation: see *Re Nathan and SDFACHSIA* [2009] AATA 263.

period.[24] The insurer is under an obligation to tell Centrelink if it becomes liable to pay compensation.

B. Special Circumstances and Reducing the Preclusion Period

i. The Meaning of 'Special Circumstances'

Under s 1184K of the SSA, the Secretary (or on review, an Authorised Review Officer, the SSAT or the AAT) has a discretion to disregard some or all of the compensation money if there are special circumstances. In practice, this is approached more directly as the issue of whether the preclusion period should be reduced or ended early.[25] Generally, 'special circumstances' is said to be a phrase which bears its ordinary meaning, which is circumstances which are unusual or uncommon.[26] It is impossible to define the situations which will count as special, and the discretion must be applied flexibly. Special circumstances do not have to be unique, but must be markedly different from the usual.[27] It may also include situations where the strict application of the law would be unfair or inappropriate.

Discussions of the discretion in the area of compensation often say that the decision-maker must consider the particular circumstances of each case and decide whether there is something that makes the case special, so that strict enforcement of the compensation rules would be unjust, unreasonable or inappropriate, keeping in mind the purposes and objects of the Act and whether exercising the discretion would further those objects or frustrate them. This includes the purpose of avoiding 'double dipping'.[28]

Because 'special circumstances' is so broadly defined and has to be determined against the particular facts of the case the jurisdiction is highly discretionary. The determinations in many of the cases in the SSAT and the AAT can lead to the conclusion that the area is extremely uncertain. The factors that might contribute

[24] Sections 1182–1184.

[25] This discretion can also be applied to receipt of periodic compensation, but in practice this is very rare. See *Zarvalis and SDSS* [1989] AATA 603, *Gutierrez and SDSS* [1993] AATA 756, *Groth and SDSS* (1995) 40 ALD 541 – upheld on appeal, *Martinez and SDFCS* [1999] AATA 955.

[26] *Re Beadle and Director-General of Social Security* (1984) 6 ALD 1, per Toohey J (handicapped child's allowance backdating rule); *Beadle v Director-General of Social Security* (1985) 7 ALD 60, Full FC; *Dranichnikov and DIMA* [200] AATA 830. The weight of authority is that the word 'exceptional' sets the bar too high. See *Ryde and SDFaCS* [2005] AATA 130; *Angelakos and SDEWR* [2006] AATA 220.

[27] *Randall and SDFHCSIA* [2011] AATA 922, *Re Shinwari and SDFHCSIA* [2009] AATA 317: it is sufficient if there is something that takes the matter out of the usual ordinary case, (see *Haidar v Secretary Department of Social Security* [1998] FCA 994; (1998) 52 ALD 255 at 264; [1998] FCA 994; 28 AAR 288 at 297, in which Hill J cited the earlier Federal Court cases of *Groth v Secretary, Department of Social Security* [1995] FCA 1708; (1995) 40 ALD 541 and *Secretary, Department of Social Security v Ellis* (1997) 24 AAR 535, 46 ALD 1).

[28] *SDSS v Hulls* (1991) 22 ALD 570, citing *Beadle* and *Ivovic and DGSS* [1981] AATA 57; *SDSS v Smith* (1991) 30 FCR 56 (includes impact of rules on the person).

to the existence of special circumstances include the use of the lump sum to purchase an asset or pay down a mortgage because of a special need for housing; existence of an addiction, and later unexpected ill health. In many cases a selection or all of these factors exist. Other arguments made include arguments about the appropriateness of the 50 per cent rule and changes to the pension since the lump sum preclusion period was calculated which would have altered the length of the preclusion period.

Evidence in the various studies – including our own – suggests that the most notable reason people ran out of funds was because of an inability to manage the funds. This will be discussed more later, but there can be two reasons people cannot manage – either because they are vulnerable in the first place through lack of capacity or some other matter such as illness (this is relevant to lawyers' handling of them) or they cannot handle money because the compensation process has actually harmed them.[29]

The mental health issues that commonly arise when injured people go through the compensation process will not be discussed here. There is also an obvious incongruity between the damages rules which aim to put a person back into the position they would be in if the accident had not happened, and the social security rules which are imposed when people run out of this compensation.[30]

IV. Lawyer Factors Contributing to Early Dissipation

It seems that some of the issues which create the loss of compensation and failure to get social security could be managed better by the personal injury lawyers running the compensation cases. In her chapter in this volume, Clare Scollay discusses the importance for the use of legal services that lawyers are embedded in the remedial system. This is certainly true for the compensation processes embedded in the law of negligence, workers' compensation and motor accidents, but it is far less true in relation to social security. Lawyers involved in compensation law may have nothing at all to do with social security, and their ignorance may compound the inabilities of those needing social security to access its services.

Here I consider some possible ways in which this could be done. There are a range of issues which may be within the power of the lawyer to either alert the client to or to manage themselves. We suggest that uneducated and ill or injured people may be regarded as vulnerable, with all that that entails. In my view lawyer factors which may contribute to the problem include legal silos, failure to recognise the vulnerability of some clients, management of settlement and how it derives

[29] For an analysis of the literature considering adverse health outcomes from compensation processes see G Grant and D Studdert, 'Poisoned Chalice? A Critical Analysis of the Evidence Linking Personal Injury Compensation Processes with Adverse Health Outcomes' (2009) 33 *Melbourne University Law Review* 865.

[30] These issues are discussed in Grant and Studdert, above, and in the sources cited in n 3, above.

from cases argued in court, arguments about damages in litigation, the process of reporting compensation to social security, the high cost of legal assistance and the failure of lawyers to ensure that clients understand legal costs agreements.

A. Legal Silos

It became clear when discussing the issues with lawyers that the gap between personal injury lawyers and social security lawyers is profound. This 'silo' effect means that lawyers managing the compensation process may be unaware, or only partially aware, of the factors which might affect their clients' eventual treatment under social security law. Similarly, social security lawyers did not necessarily understand the processes of compensation law and therefore did not understand some of the reasons for clients running out of funds. But more important, perhaps, is that personal injury lawyers, while being aware that there was a lump sum preclusion period and advising clients that it existed, were sometimes mistaken in their knowledge of how the lump sum preclusion period was calculated, and appeared to have little knowledge of the actual processes used by social security to deal with clients. This may be a necessary consequence of specialisation and the change from the generalist solicitor to the specialist in the mega-firm.[31] With the advent of the late twentieth century and increased globalism, large firms frequently became mega-firms. As Marc Galanter says in relation to American lawyers, 'Mega-law firms are not mere aggregations of lawyers who do similar work. A high degree of specialisation is cultivated within such firms.'[32]

There is no reason to think that this is not the case elsewhere and it is also true in Australia. This is relevant because the level of specialisation means that personal injury lawyers may never see what happens to their clients after they receive their award of compensation. They therefore do not see the process of premature

[31] To give some background, legal practice in Australia was highly localised until the 1960s. Indeed, even until 1972 in New South Wales any solicitor whose address was more than one mile from the centre of Sydney had to have a city agent. Many of these local, formerly family-controlled firms became corporate law firms in the 1960s. These firms became the high-status end of the solicitors' profession, eventually challenging (though not quite toppling) the barristers' pre-eminence in the profession. As in many other legal systems in the world, a major change to legal practice in the late 1960s and 1970s came with the advent of new consumer legislation and the huge growth in corporate activity which accompanied it. Leading law firms had often had relationships with large banks or insurance companies, but the advent of multi-nationals investing in Australia in manufacturing, mining and finance created a different ambience and some of the leading firms benefited greatly from this and grew enormously. These movements in corporate finance, consumer legislation, mining and closeness to major corporations applied not only to Australia, but also to most other Western countries, and solicitors' firms suddenly grew.[31] Instead of firms with two to five partners, firms had 20 or 30 partners. David Weisbrot in *Australian Lawyers* (Longman Cheshire, 1990) refers to 'the decade of merger frenzy (1979–1988)'. In the twenty years after that a number of barriers dropped, including the prohibition against corporations and against combining with other professions such as accounting.

[32] M Galanter, 'Mega-Law and Mega-Lawyering in the Contemporary United States' in R Dingwall and P Lewis (eds), *The Sociology of the Professions; Lawyers, Doctors and Others* (St Martin's Press, New York, 1983) 155.

dissipation and may not advise well about the risks.[33] Our data strongly suggest that this is happening.

B. Recognising Vulnerable Clients

Most of the clients in our sample could be regarded as vulnerable. They tended to have low levels of education and low levels of social or family support. Of the WRC cases we considered, the education level was mostly a maximum of Year 12. Sixteen per cent had a post-secondary qualification and 57 per cent had completed year 10 or less. It is impossible to know how representative the sample is of people who run out of compensation and whether this is just more likely to happen when people are vulnerable, or whether it is really a factor of compensation being too low. The majority of clients were single men. This is not a random sample, of course, and it is not argued that the compensation process necessarily causes this vulnerability. However, the education levels of many of these clients alone may indicate a lack of ability to communicate what has happened to them and to articulate its impact on their life in such a way that it could lead to better compensation. It also seemed, when we looked at the sums of compensation they received, that they had been awarded low levels of compensation. For a man at the age of 45 to be awarded $400,000 in compensation for the rest of his working life does not, at first glance, appear to be equivalent to what he would have earned had he been able to work, nor does it seem like enough to last the 20 years to the standard retirement age of 65.

For example, Mr B was very severely and permanently injured in his arms, hands and shoulders in a workplace accident in 2003. The injuries led to permanently limited capacity in both arms and reduction in his ability to self-care. He developed serious substance abuse problems post injury. A Centrelink assessment awarded him 30 points for loss of use of his arms and 30 points for substance abuse, when only 20 points is needed to qualify for the disability support pension. That is, he was regarded as severely disabled. Mr B had worked continually since leaving school at 14 in labouring jobs. At the time of the injury he was 39; that is, he had about 26 years working life left. It took 10 years to settle his workers' compensation claim. He received a total of $399,500 made up of two interim payments of $107,000 paid four years earlier and $292,000 as a final payment. He was subject to a four-year preclusion period from the date of settlement.

He spent almost all the money buying and repairing a house in a small country town for himself and his wife. There was evidence of possible poor advice from Centrelink officers, but also about Mr B's cognitive impairment from substance abuse. Mr B was very unlikely to be able to manage his funds because of his

[33] K Burns, 'Submission to Education, Tourism, Innovation and Small Business Committee Workers' Compensation and Rehabilitation (National Injury Insurance Scheme) Amendment Bill 2016' (RECOVER Injury Research Centre, Griffith University, 2016) 3, available at www.parliament.qld.gov.au/documents/committees/ETISBC/2016/WorkersComp/submissions/001.pdf.

cognitive impairment, but Mr B also was given an award which was only $400,000 for severe injuries that rendered him permanently unfit for work. This does not seem equivalent to the roughly quarter century of working life which he lost. Mr B may be an example of the kind of person who is under-compensated *and* not very capable of managing his money.

Mr Vecchi had very low levels of cognitive capacity and was clearly an extremely vulnerable client.[34] He had the reading comprehension of a 6-year-old and the listening comprehension skills of a 7-year-old. He said he did not understand the settlement process he went through and he was advised to settle, so he did. The tribunal held that even if Mr Vecchi was not properly advised about the settlement or did not understand this would not give rise to special circumstances. Evidence was accepted that Mr Vecchi had been abused as a child and before the accident managed the after-effects of this trauma by physical activity. This was no longer possible after the accident. Mr Vecchi bought a house almost immediately after he received his lump sum in an attempt to feel secure. Unfortunately the house could not be let and was largely unusable. There was evidence that if he was made to sell it this would affect his mental state even more. The circumstances of his abuse, and the fact that his accident made it impossible for him to continue his way of managing, along with his low level of comprehension were taken by the tribunal to be special and his lump sum preclusion period was altered.

Amongst our plaintiffs many appear to have had their decision-making affected by a range of circumstances. Sometimes these are unconnected with the injury – for example, they have limited experience with financial planning because they have had a low income or have limited formal schooling, and sometimes because they have cognitive impairment. This suggests that they may have difficulty in managing large sums.

It is not usual to award the costs of managing a lump sum in a personal injury compensation claim unless the negligence caused the inability to manage. Whether this principle reflects an assumption that the ordinary plaintiff who receives a lump sum can manage their money or not, there is certainly no reason to think that this is correct. Managing a lump sum appropriately may require a considerable amount of judgement and knowledge. It may require a person to assess different investment options or, where it is unclear what the extent of their injury is or when they might recover from it, to predict when they might be able to return to work and have another income source. Recent alarming findings about the training and competence of financial managers in Australia[35] suggest that competence in managing money is uncommon, even among professionals. The global financial crisis galvanised Australia into developing a National Financial Literacy Strategy, run by ASIC. The aim is to enhance financial literacy levels, which were perceived

[34] *Secretary, DFHCSIA and Vecchi* [2012] AATA 346.

[35] 'Completion of an 8-day diploma known as RG 146 is all it takes to qualify as a financial planner' in A Ferguson and B Butler, 'Cheating Rife in Financial Planning' *Sydney Morning Herald*, 18 August 2014.

as so low in Australia that even if many people were given significant levels of information their financial literacy might not be sufficient for them to evaluate the information.[36]

When the accident causing the problem also causes brain damage, awards may be made to cover the costs of financial advice.[37] The evidence from our study and the general findings from financial advice surveys suggest that an award for financial advice for many people who are given compensation should be sought, not only for those who are brain damaged by the wrong. This may be seen as a departure from the general principle of returning the injured person to the position they would have been in had the accident not happened, on the basis that the person lacked that capacity originally and still lacks that capacity. Against this view, it could be argued that a true application of the principle would recognise that unless financial advice is paid for in the damages, then the returning of the person to their original position will not be effective.

C. Recognising a Lack of Financial Capability as a Reason to Seek a Structured Settlement

All participants in our study had been awarded lump sum compensation. Given that the Civil Liability Act 2002 (NSW) provides for structured settlements this might be somewhat surprising.[38] Section 25 places an obligation on legal practitioners to advise their clients about the possibility of a structured settlement and to get independent financial advice about it. Several accredited specialists in personal injury were asked about the obligation in s 25 only to find that none of them had heard of it. This is clearly an obligation that needs to be taken seriously. Whether or not there is a legal direction on lawyers to advise their clients about structured settlements, the evidence of vulnerability and lack of ability to manage money strongly suggest that many clients should be advised to consider them.

Structured settlements are extremely rare in NSW and in Australia generally. Solicitors questioned about this said first that lump sums gave plaintiffs more freedom and the possibility to create a business or buy property. When challenged on the basis that we know that the vast majority of small businesses fail,[39] they also said that insurers did not like structured settlements and that the tax structure was

[36] P Ali et al, 'The Financial Literacy of Young Australians: an Empirical Study and Implications for Consumer Protection and ASIC's National Financial Literacy Strategy' (2014) 32 *Company & Securities law Journal* 334; A Worthington, 'Financial Literacy and Financial Literacy Programmes in Australia' (2013) 18(3) *Journal of Financial Services Marketing, Suppl special Issue: Financial Product Complexity and the Limits* 227.

[37] *Gray v Richards* [2014] HCA 40, (2014) 253 CLR 660.

[38] Sections 22–26.

[39] The Commonwealth Department of Industry, Innovation, Science, Research and Tertiary Education says 59.7% of small businesses (with less than 20 employees) survived from 2008–2011: *Australian Small Business Key Statistics and Analysis* (2012) Table 14, 42, available at static.treasury.gov.au/uploads/sites/1/2017/06/AustralianSmallBusinessKeyStatisticsAndAnalysis.pdf.

antithetical to annuities. It is also worth noting that annuities are rare in Australia generally, so advice to a client to buy an annuity is not easily followed. However, structured settlements would eliminate the problem of an inability to manage a lump sum. In the light of our knowledge of how few people are really able to manage a large sum of money, the lack of use of structured settlements seems problematic and puzzling.

The United Kingdom has a stronger regime of structured settlement,[40] showing that these problems can be solved. The Courts Act 2003 provides that a court can award a periodical payment of damages even if one party does not agree. Annuities based on compensation are protected by the Financial Services Compensation Scheme (by the Damages Act 1996) so that if the provider becomes insolvent the claimant is indemnified. The National Health Service is also encouraging structured settlements for amounts awarded over £250,000.

Burns and Harrington discuss in Chapter 6 above why lawyers like lump sums. They suggest that lump sums may be attractive to lawyers partly because they provide a fund from which lawyers' fees will be paid, but they doubt that this is the major attraction of lump sums for lawyers. The fact that this is an area where many claimants simply do not have the resources to fund their own litigation means lawyers cannot be blamed for using lump sums to allow access. Another suggestion is that lawyers may like lump sums because of the possibility that they will allow people to buy their own home, but as Burns and Harrington's chapter shows, this may not be a safe way for people to use their compensation money.

These factors suggest that lawyers need to rethink at least some of their opposition to structured settlements, particularly where they are dealing with those who are relatively vulnerable to incapacity to handle financial matters. Our study showed that the inability to manage funds was one of the most serious factors contributing to premature dissipation of lump sum compensation.

D. Mitigating the Consistent Under-compensation of the Tort System

Far from over-compensating personal injury plaintiffs, tort law significantly under-compensates them, and then compounds that by dealing with their social security claims in a way which ignores or contradicts the initial rules of compensation to their detriment. A lack of realism about employment prospects appears to be one significant factor. Some of the clients we considered had been assessed on the basis

[40] This was investigated by The Law Commission in No 224: *Structured Settlements and Interim and Provisional Damages* (London, HMSO 1994). This gave rise to amendments to the Damages Act 1996, which provides for periodical payment orders with or without the consent of the parties. See also the use of some structured settlements in Canada: eg British Columbia Insurance (Vehicles) Act, RSBC 1996 cl 231 s 99 which provides for structured settlements for motor vehicle accidents where the court feels they are warranted.

that they would physically be able to go back to work at some time, but this proved impossible for most because by the time they were physically improved they encountered age discrimination in the work place,[41] or other factors intervened and they never got better. This shows that the compensation was not adequate because it was based on unrealistic assumptions, as well as because of the systematic process of reducing the compensation amounts in order not to damage the defendant.

The assessment of damages awards was well known to be inadequate as far back as 55 years ago, when the case of Gillian Thurston was decided.[42] Despite this knowledge, the Australian Tort Reforms of 2002 and following were passed, and their major effect was to reduce damages by a series of caps and reductions in liability.[43] Similar processes have occurred in other parts of the common law world, notably in the United States.[44]

Plaintiff lawyers are well aware that the system consistently under-compensates tort plaintiffs. A brief outline of the process will be a useful reminder at this point.

The basic rule is that the plaintiff is to be put back in the position they would have been if the accident had not happened: *restitution in integrum*.[45] However, the combination of the courts' concern not to punish the defendant ('the question is not what are the ideal requirements but what are the reasonable requirements of the respondent')[46] and the caps and limits in the Civil Liability Act 2002 (NSW) reduce the compensation a great deal.

Economic loss for lost earnings and capacity to earn is awarded but capped at 3 times average weekly earnings (at present maximum damages per year is thus approximately $190,000). This is reduced by the expenses which won't be needed during the years the claimant is unable to work (such as uniforms and so on), in order to avoid over-compensation. Awards for gratuitous services (economic needs created by an injury needing nursing care) are not available unless they are needed for more than six months, and for more than six hours per week. The rate of payment has been capped at average weekly earnings, again reducing the amount from the common law rate. Lost earnings and economic expenses are

[41] Age discrimination in workplace hiring appears to begin at about age 45 (see www.abc.net.au/news/2018-12-02/ageism-rampant-discrimination-problem-in-the-workplace/10550704); B Pocock et al, *Work Well, Retire Well: Findings from the Work, Care, Health and Retirement 'Ageing Agenders' Project* (Centre for Workplace Excellence, University of South Australia, 2017). See also RA Posthuma and MA Campion, 'Age Stereotypes in the Workplace: Common Stereotypes, Moderators, and Future Research Directions' (2009) 35(1) *Journal of Management* 158.

[42] Thurston received a record award of £69,000 in 1965 in New South Wales. By 1973 it was already proving inadequate: NSW Law Reform Commission, *Issues Paper: Accident Compensation* (1982) 26.

[43] Civil Liability Acts in Australia: Civil Law (Wrongs) Act 2002 (ACT); Civil Liability Act 2002 (NSW); Personal Injuries (Liabilities and Damages) Act (NT); Personal Injuries (Civil Claims) Act (NT); Civil Liability Act 2003 (Qld); Personal Injuries Proceedings Act 2002 (Qld); Civil Liability Act 1936 (SA); Civil Liability Act 2002 (Tas); Wrongs Act 1958 (Vic); and Civil Liability Act 2002 (WA).

[44] See legislation in n 43 for Australia; Canada: eg Injury Regulation -Insurance Act (NB) Reg 2003–20 s 4; Automobile Insurance Tort Recovery Limitation Regulations (NS) Reg 182/2003 s 3; US: eg California Civil Code s 3333.2; Colorado Rev Stat s 13-21-102.5(3)(a).

[45] *Todorovic v Waller* (1981) 150 CLR 402.

[46] *Arthur Robinson (Grafton) Pty Ltd v Carter* (1968) 122 CLR 649.

then discounted at a standard of 15 per cent for the vicissitudes of life[47] and then discounted again at a rate of 5 per cent for the present value of money,[48] even though the rate of inflation has been between 1–2 per cent for several years.

In the past, compensation for non-economic loss was often used to make up the lack which the calculation of damages for economic loss often resulted in, but this too has been capped at (presently) $572,000 for the most severe case (eg quadriplegia). All other losses must be proportionately less. No interest can be paid for non-economic losses, but they are not discounted. As noted above, the difference between economic loss and non-economic loss is extremely important for the way social security preclusion is calculated.

What can the lawyer do about this? They might argue harder for a higher and more realistic assessment of the loss than many of our plaintiffs received, and be less willing to accept a great deal less on settlement. They might argue more strongly about the discount rates based on vicissitudes of life, currently 15 per cent in NSW. Hodgson JA in *Macarthur Districts Motorcycle Sportsman v Ardizzone*[49] observed:

> The usual allowance of 15 per cent is not on the basis that there is a 15 per cent possibility that even without the injury, the plaintiff would not have achieved the most likely economic situation, but on the basis that this is a reasonable discount having regard to a myriad of possibilities each of which could have meant that the plaintiff fell short of this situation to various degrees. … there is the added difficulty that s 1392 does not seem to deal with the situation, contemplated in *Blake*, where there is a significant chance that the plaintiff's economic circumstances but for the accident might have been far better than the most likely circumstances.' … it may be that, consistently with a purposive interpretation of s 13(2), positive vicissitudes can be taken into account in reaching the appropriate figure for adjustment, and perhaps even completely balance out negative vicissitudes …'

Blake[50] concerned an actor who, it was argued, was on the verge of huge financial success at the time of the accident which put him in a vegetative state and whose award was greatly increased because of this possibility. There may be room for arguing more strongly in favour of less negative or even positive vicissitudes of life, as in *Blake*. The former discount used against a 'marriageable' – ie attractive – widow, was abolished as unsuitable.[51] Such arguments can be made in particular cases as well as generally.

E. Advising about Likely Compensation More Comprehensively

One factor which came up often in our study was clients reporting that they had been told by the lawyer in early meetings that they were likely to get a certain sum

[47] Civil Liability Act 2002 (NSW), s 13.
[48] Civil Liability Act 2002 (NSW), s 14.
[49] [2004] NSWCA 145.
[50] *Norris v Blake (No 2)* (1997) 41 NSWLR 49 (CA).
[51] *De Sales v Ingrilli* (2002) 212 CLR 338.

in damages and then the matter was settled for a great deal less. Of course, there was usually no record available of what the client stated had been said to them, so there is no way of verifying this. However, the complaint is reasonably common. Indeed, some clients asserted that they had borrowed money in anticipation of a certain sum being achieved. Whether this is naïve may be debated; but it may be that some reliance has occurred. It is vital to ensure that advice is clear, and sometimes it will need to be in writing, which raises other comprehension issues.

F. Dealing with the Settlement Issues

The vast majority of cases of personal injury settle and, consistent with that, in our sample, some 95 per cent of the cases involved a settlement, all of which were settled on a costs-inclusive basis. A number of issues are created by the fact that the award is in a settlement. One major issue is the fact that there is no available record of what the heads of damages were, including how long the damages were expected to last. This means that when the client turns to social security there is no statement to say whether the sum was for non-economic loss or for economic loss or income support, the latter being the proper basis for determining lump sum preclusion.

Are settlements are being made on the basis of incorrect or over-optimistic assessments of the impact of the injury on future employment? It is worth noting that when competent lawyers are involved, settlement is affected by the known outcomes for matters that go to trial. *This means that the systematic undercompensation by the courts feeds into the settlement outcome*s for the vast majority of cases which are resolved in that way. And it is assumed that settlement sums should be less than compensation by the court because the cost of litigation has been avoided. Are lawyers and insurers, who also have an interest in being paid and therefore avoiding the risks of a trial, settling for too little for clients?

The interaction of settlement and costs is discussed below. One of the lawyers I interviewed said:

> … unless the judge has been specifically assigned in advance, you don't find out which Judge is going to hear the matter until at earliest 4 pm the day before the hearing …
>
> It is always very amusing to see one party (be it the insurer or the injured person) become all of a sudden extremely interested in talking settlement on the 'footsteps of the court' as they say once they realise the Judge who has been allocated to the case may not be such a good 'draw' (an expression often used to describe whether you have 'drawn' well or poorly in the lottery that is how cases are assigned for hearing) when it comes to the Judge who has been allocated to hear the case.[52]

Lump sum damages is only 'compensation' for social security purposes if it has an economic loss component. Lawyers will often include a weak claim for a future

[52] L1 transcript p 1.

economic loss in a pleading to bolster the settlement negotiations. If settlement is reached, even though in substance there was no basis for the economic loss claim, Centrelink and most decision-makers will place great weight on what is in the pleadings in deciding whether the amount should be treated as compensation because it included an amount for economic loss. A prudent adviser will weigh up the possible increase in the eventual settlement against the lost income support from the preclusion period before drafting such pleadings.

G. Taking Legal Costs into Account in Settlement and Reporting to Social Security

Legal costs were a significant burden on our plaintiffs. Generally the actions were done on a no-win-no-fee basis so that the plaintiff had to pay when they won, subject to a costs order. That is, clients entered into a costs agreement with their lawyer under which they did not have to pay legal fees, including disbursements such as filing fees, counsel's fees or expert witness fees, and the fees of their solicitor, while the matter was progressing (or at all if unsuccessful) but would have to pay if the matter was resolved in their favour. This, as discussed above, is a way of ensuring that an action can be run when otherwise the plaintiff could not pay the costs. Where there is a costs order after litigation, although the rule is that the loser pays the costs, this does not mean there is nothing left to pay even if the plaintiff wins. However, where there is a settlement there is no order for costs[53] and generally each party will bear their own costs and the no-win-no-fee contract will mean the plaintiff has to pay their own costs.

The evidence from our clients suggested that many of them did not understand either the settlement process or the costs agreement. When this was put to Lawyer 1 he observed

> … 99% of clients fail to understand costs agreements. It's not because they are dumb. It's because you need to be Einstein to work it out …. I would love a dollar for every time I have sent a costs agreement to a client and received a phone call to the effect 'Mate, what does all this mean?' Invariably my answer is 'please understand that if I didn't have to send you this document I wouldn't. The legislation requires me to send you the document'.

He is referring to the fact that the NSW Legal Profession Act 2004 requires solicitors to use mandatory words and cover mandatory issues in the costs agreement[54] where a conditional fee is agreed. This is not supposed to be a contingency fee (these are prohibited)[55] but a fee worked out on an itemised basis. However, the

[53] As a general rule in Australia, as in the UK and Germany, costs follow the event, so that the person who loses the case pays the costs.

[54] Section 324.

[55] Legal Profession Act 2004 (NSW) s 325. Now replaced by Legal Profession Uniform Law (NSW), s 183. The Uniform Law applies to the legal profession across Australia.

pattern observable in the cases suggests that what is happening looks a great deal like a contingency fee, since the larger the damages amount the greater the fee appears to be – that is, the percentage appeared to be steadier than one might have expected. The proportion many clients pay out of their lump sum is as high as 40 per cent and 30–40 per cent is common. Table 1 showed WRC clients' situation and Table 2 showed the decided cases percentages. In one of those the legal fees were 62 per cent of the lump sum.

It is very difficult to assess how difficult it was to run any of these cases (in terms of the work required of the lawyers), as they come to the WRC some time after being run and often that information is not available. However, the percentage for legal fees seems quite high. This is significant when one thinks that the court does not allow for legal fees in their compensation assessment, and clearly the award of costs does not relieve the plaintiff of legal fees.

In a climate where access to justice is a big issue, one of the major hurdles is cost.[56] It is clear from the data that legal costs are a massive incursion into compensation amounts which are not currently taken account of. The legal costs in many of our clients' cases were counted as an amount the client received in the calculation of lump sum preclusion including being part of the economic compensation. Settlement can be done exclusive of costs or inclusive of costs. It is settled that the legal costs component of settlements inclusive of costs is included as part of the lump sum.[57] However, where legal costs are paid separately on a 'plus costs' basis, with costs not determined at date of settlement, Departmental policy is to exclude this amount from the lump sum.[58] This means it is possible for a lawyer to pay the client and notify social security in such a way that the amount on which the lump sum preclusion period is based does not include fees and costs, which the client has never received.

Although often clients no longer had copies of costs agreements, as they came to the WRC years after their matters were settled, in many cases we have copies of the final trust statement accounts and bills from their lawyers. These show that, in all cases, two things occurred:

- their cases were settled on a costs inclusive basis – that is, the insurer agreed to settle on a global basis with no extra specified amount for the plaintiff's legal costs, which were to be paid out of the global sum; and
- the plaintiff's legal fees were mostly attributable to time-based general fees of their solicitor, rather than to disbursements, billed on an itemised basis.

Because the rule is that if the court has not determined otherwise 50 per cent of the lump sum will be deemed to be economic loss, costs inclusive settlements mean that 50 per cent of the legal costs also become part of the sum used to define

[56] See Productivity Commission, *Access to Justice Arrangements: Overview*, Inquiry Report No 72 (Canberra, 2014).

[57] *SDSS v a'Beckett* (1990) (1990) 2 FCR 349; *SDSS v Hulls* (1991) 22 ALD 570.

[58] *Guide to Social Security Law* at 4.12.2.30.

the lump sum preclusion period. The median amount of legal costs paid by our plaintiffs was $77,500 so 50 per cent of this amount, or $38,750 was included in the amount the person was deemed to have received as economic loss. This added an extra 41 weeks (calculating at July 2015) (that is, about 10 months) to the lump sum preclusion period, which would not have been there if the settlement had been done on a costs-exclusion basis. The cases have gone both ways in considering whether this should be something leading to shortening the lump sum preclusion period.[59]

Quite apart from the question of the level of lawyers' fees, lawyers could assist clients by doing settlements on a costs-exclusive basis and have costs to be agreed at a later date. The costs would then not be regarded as part of the lump sum and would not increase the lump sum preclusion period. It is only this form of settlement that, under government policy, sees legal costs excluded from the preclusion period calculation.[60]

H. Advice about the Lump Sum Preclusion Period

Lastly, our study showed that many clients, especially those who had not had social security while waiting for compensation, felt they had not been warned that they would be subject to a lump sum preclusion period. This meant that it was a terrible shock when they discovered that they were not entitled to social security when the money ran out. General advice in written form (a brochure, for example) might help with this. It may be that lawyers have told them, but our study showed that sometimes the lawyers got it wrong and sometimes clients did not understand what they had been told. People under stress comprehend badly; when they are injured they probably comprehend even more badly, and vulnerable clients will have real difficulty in retaining new information at such times.

It is worth considering that a similar thing was said by several clients about the costs agreement. It seems that for many clients what they are told – including what is given to them in writing about future likely events – may be very difficult for them to understand and/or retain unless real effort at effective communicating is made.

V. Conclusion

This chapter has considered how the significant unaddressed problem of undercompensation in our legal system, and the interaction of the tort system and the

[59] eg *Re Panetta and SDFHCSIA* [2009] AATA 873: seen as unfair and supports waiver of preclusion period vs *Re Sard and SDFHCSIA* [2011] AATA 106 where it was rejected as a basis for exercising the discretion to waive.

[60] See the table at guides.dss.gov.au/guide-social-security-law/4/13/2/30.

social security system, is seriously compromised by mismatched objectives and assumptions. Although mainly NSW has been considered here, findings from other states – such as those of Burns and Harrington – show this problem is Australia-wide and may be replicated or occur in some similar form elsewhere.

This chapter has attempted to focus on the possible role of lawyers in ameliorating and preventing this problem. It is not just a matter of law reform, although some law reform should be carried out. It is also a matter of reducing the silos between lawyers and developing strategies based on the understanding of the interaction of damages law and social security so that the real interests of clients can be better protected.

12

Lawyers' Responsibility for Claimant Health in Injury Compensation Schemes: Developing an Ethical Response

GENEVIEVE GRANT* AND CHRISTINE PARKER**

This chapter explores how claimant lawyers might ethically respond to evidence of the negative health impacts of stressful claims on their clients. It begins by providing a profile of the lawyers involved and the compensation schemes they work in. It then turns to consider the underexplored question of whether and to what extent lawyers might contribute to the claim-related health impacts some clients experience. Parker and Evans' framework of ethical approaches to lawyering and an ethics in context approach are used to examine the explanations and justifications for various aspects of lawyers' work in this setting, and the ethical issues that arise. The chapter identifies the challenge in balancing the various possible roles of the claimant lawyer, which may indeed be in tension. We conclude that a more nuanced approach to ethics is required to enable lawyers to formulate a multi-dimensional and sustainable response to stressful claimant experiences.

I. Introduction

This chapter reflects on the ethical implications for lawyers of empirical research demonstrating that stressful claims experiences are associated with poor health outcomes amongst injury compensation claimants. Do lawyers have any responsibility for claimants' stressful experience and resulting poor health outcomes? Is it possible for lawyers in this practice context to see and understand the way claimants experience compensation schemes, and to take responsibility for improving their experience? As Mather has put it, what is a good lawyer to do?[1] The chapter

* Associate Professor, Faculty of Law, Monash University.
** Professor, Melbourne Law School, The University of Melbourne.
[1] L Mather, 'What Do Clients Want? What Do Lawyers Do?' (2003) 52 *Emory Law Journal* 1065, 1065.

addresses these questions by considering the application of Parker and Evans' framework of four ethical approaches to lawyering[2] and socio-legal research on personal injury lawyering following an ethics in context approach.[3] It explores the ways lawyers might contribute to stressful claimant experiences and the degree to which they might help address this problem. We conclude that a multidimensional ethical approach incorporating a range of perspectives is required, rather than over-reliance on any one approach in isolation. In particular, we argue the predictable, knee-jerk emphasis on an ethics of care response is inadequate to properly account for the lawyer's role and the opportunity to improve claimants' experiences and outcomes.

Our analysis focuses on the Australian context, in light of the country's status as a hotbed of compensation schemes and research interest in their health and social impacts.[4] We begin by clarifying the nature and parameters of compensation schemes in Australia, and present a snapshot of legal practice and its relationship with client experience in these settings. We then set our focus on empirical evidence of the negative health impacts of stressful claims processes. Drawing on tools of legal ethics, we explore the kinds of responses lawyers might be expected, and ultimately encouraged, to make.

II. Contemporary Injury Compensation Schemes in Australia

At the outset it is useful to set out the legal practice context of Australian statutory injury compensation schemes. The origins of statutory compensation schemes can frequently be found in a desire to overcome the many inadequacies of tort law (and its associated processes) as a mechanism for justly compensating injured people.[5] Historically, much of the legal scholarship has neatly categorised arrangements for compensating injured claimants as 'no-fault' (administrative) or 'fault-based' (common law, or damages-based). In recent decades, however, the landscape of injury law in Australia has become decidedly more complicated, making it harder to conclusively establish the parameters of what counts as a compensation scheme.

[2] C Parker and A Evans, *Inside Lawyers Ethics*, 3rd edn (Cambridge, Cambridge University Press, 2018) Chs 1 and 2; C Parker, 'A Critical Morality for Australian Lawyers and Law Students' (2004) 30(1) *Monash University Law Review* 49.

[3] LC Levin and L Mather (eds), *Lawyers in Practice: Ethical Decision Making in Context* (University of Chicago Press, 2012).

[4] See Chapter 3, 'Compensation and Health', by Ian Cameron; and Chapter 4, 'Apples, Oranges and Bananas: Comparative studies of Australian Injury Compensation Schemes', by Alex Collie.

[5] See, for example, the New South Wales Law Reform Commission Report that led to the establishment of a motor crash compensation scheme for New South Wales (NSWLRC, *Accident Compensation: A Transport Accidents Scheme for New South Wales* (NSWLRC, report no 43, 1984). See also the Royal Commission into Institutional Responses to Child Sexual Abuse and its recommendation of the National Redress Scheme (Royal Commission, *Final Report Recommendations* (2015) 73–90).

To illustrate the difficulty, consider the dominant statutory schemes of Australian injury law: those for work and transport crash injury. These schemes are the most institutionalised and overt about their objective of returning injured people to work and health through rehabilitation and compensation.[6] These are also the schemes in relation to which we now have the most research evidence about claimants' experiences of claiming. Even with the defined subject matter of work and transport crash injury, the hallmark of these schemes is their diversity, both within and between sub-national jurisdictions.[7] The matters on which schemes may differ include: the range and type of benefits available; the qualifying criteria and process; the time within which a claim (or claims for specific benefits within a claim) must be brought; the involvement of private actors in the claims management process; the way disputes are resolved; and the extent of legal representation of claimants.[8] State-based injury schemes also have thorny interactions with other public and private mechanisms of financial support and protection, including those operated at the Commonwealth level, such as social security.[9]

The characteristic feature of statutory compensation schemes is their detailed legislative architecture, setting the parameters of such matters as claimant eligibility and the benefits available under the scheme. These are not entirely statutory schemes, however. Australian compensation schemes for work and transport crash injury increasingly blend elements of administrative, no-fault compensation with tort-based damages claims.[10] Though aspects of damages claims are regulated by statute, common law principles also play their part. Additionally, the practices of the scheme participants are often shaped by dedicated policy and protocol frameworks, which operate around the scheme and affect such matters as the way particular benefits are claimed and disputes are resolved.[11] Beyond work and transport crash injury, standing statutory schemes also provide compensation for victims of crime,[12] and

[6] See, for example, Transport Accident Act 1986 (Vic), s 8; Victims of Crime Compensation Act 1996 (Vic), s 1; Work Injury Rehabilitation and Compensation Act 2010 (Vic), s 10.

[7] H Luntz et al, *Torts: Cases and Commentary*, 8th edn (Chatswood, Lexis Nexis, 2017) Ch 1.

[8] G Grant, 'The Australian Work Disability Patchwork' in E MacEachen (ed), *The Science and Politics of Work Disability Prevention* (New York, Routledge, 2019) 72.

[9] P Vines et al, 'When Lump Sum Compensation Runs Out: Personal Responsibility or Legal System Failure?' (2017) 39 *Sydney Law Review* 365; GM Grant et al, 'When Lump Sums Run Out: Disputes at the Borderlines of Tort Law, Injury Compensation and Social Security' in K Barker et al (eds), *Private Law in the 21st Century* (Oxford, Hart Publishing, 2017).

[10] For example, in 2017 the NSW motor crash compensation scheme was reformed to introduce more extensive administrative income replacement and treatment benefits, regardless of fault, whilst imposing a new 'minor injury' threshold to limit the number of damages claims. See Motor Accident Injuries Act 2017 (NSW).

[11] See, for example, the Transport Accident Commission Protocols, a series of agreements made by the Transport Accident Commission, the Law Institute of Victoria and the Australian Lawyers' Alliance about the preparation and processing of disputes claims for lump sum impairment benefits, serious injury (tort threshold) certification and common law damages claims, as well as Joint Medical Examinations: see www.tac.vic.gov.au/providers/type/legal-professionals/for-legal-professionals/tac-protocols.

[12] Victims Rights and Support Act 2013 (NSW); Victims of Crime Assistance Act 2009 (Qld); Victims of Crime Act 2001 (SA); Victims of Crime Assistance Act 1976 (Tas); Victims of Crime Assistance Act

limited-term schemes (whether legislative or based on *ex gratia* payment policies) are periodically established to provide benefits to specific groups of injured persons, such as members of the Stolen Generations[13] and survivors of institutional child sexual abuse.[14]

For the purposes of the discussion that follows, we define a statutory compensation scheme inclusively as a program established to receive, process and determine claims for compensation from a defined category of injured persons. Beyond that starting point, a non-exhaustive list of other common scheme characteristics includes:

- detailed legislative architecture setting out who is eligible to claim and for what benefits, which is frequently supplemented by policy guidance or protocol agreements between major scheme stakeholders;
- the compensation payable may include a level of no-fault or administrative benefits, which may be a prelude to a fault-based or common law damages claim;
- the state is an active stakeholder or participant, whether as an institutional defendant receiving and managing claims, acting as a principal for claims management agents, or as a regulator of private insurance actors;
- claimant entry to the scheme is through a bureaucratic gateway, involving an application or claim form (which may be initiated online, over the phone or in hard copy);
- claimant entry most often occurs soon after the injury is sustained, reflecting the fact that many schemes require initial claims to be made within a year of injury;
- claimants' engagement with the scheme occurs through a bureaucratic claims management process operated by decision-making personnel; and
- there is some degree of public transparency and accountability about the operation of the scheme, through mechanisms including parliamentary oversight, independent complaints processes and annual reports.

This is a deliberately expansive list, but several kinds of organised mechanisms for distributing compensation fall outside of it. One is a private settlement program employed by a powerful, institutional defendant to resolve claims against it. Confusingly, such private arrangements may self-describe as a 'compensation

1996 (Vic); Criminal Injuries Compensation Act 2003 (WA); Victims of Crime (Financial Assistance) Act 2016 (ACT); Victims of Crime Assistance Act 2006 (NT).

[13] The Tasmanian Government established a statutory scheme with the Stolen Generations of Aboriginal Children Act 2006 (Tas). South Australia and NSW instead established redress arrangements based on policies supporting *ex gratia* payments: see Aboriginal Affairs NSW, *Guidelines for the Administration of the NSW Stolen Generations Reparations Scheme* (September 2019); Government of South Australia, *Report of the South Australian Stolen Generations Scheme Independent Assessor* (July 2018), available at www.dpc.sa.gov.au/__data/assets/pdf_file/0020/45704/Report-of-the-south-australian-stolen-generations-reparations-scheme.pdf.

[14] National Redress Scheme for Institutional Child Sexual Abuse Act 2018 (Cth).

scheme', acquiring a consequential veneer of credibility and independence, but without the necessary transparency and accountability. A useful example of such a program is the discredited 'Melbourne Response', the private arrangement put in place by the Melbourne Archdiocese of the Catholic Church to deal with compensation claims arising out of child sexual abuse by clergy.[15] Another appropriate exclusion is settlement distribution schemes established to allocate proceeds of successful class actions to members of the group of claimants, such as the $495 million settlement in the Kilmore East Kinglake Bushfires action in the Supreme Court of Victoria, settled in 2014.[16] Though the distribution of such settlements is supervised by the Court and highly regulated,[17] it differs from a compensation scheme in that settlement schemes are only established once a class action has been resolved and the terms of the agreement are known. Consequently, they lack pre-claim transparency about compensation eligibility and assessment found in scheme settings. Other exclusions include the routine negotiations in sub-fields of personal injury law where settling individual damages claims remains the main activity of legal practice, such as medical negligence and public liability actions. While in some contexts the negotiated settlement of tort damages claims may take on a systematised, mill-like quality,[18] the absence of dominant institutional defendants in these claims in Australia[19] and the resultant lack of consistent claims processes and transparency mitigate against classifying these as compensation schemes according to the criteria set out above.

III. Legal Practice in Australian Compensation Schemes

By 2018 there were 76,303 solicitors practising in Australia, a number that had grown by a third since 2011.[20] In New South Wales, Australia's most populous

[15] See Royal Commission into Institutional Responses to Child Sexual Abuse, *Report on Case Study 16: The Melbourne Response* (July 2015).

[16] Supreme Court of Victoria, 'Kilmore Bushfire Class Action': Settlement Distribution Scheme (10 November 2014), available at www.supremecourt.vic.gov.au/sites/default/files/assets/2017/09/a5/aa2765adb/settlement%2Bdistribution%2Bscheme.pdf. See M Legg, 'Kilmore-East Kinglake Bushfire Class Action Settlement Distribution Scheme: Fairness, Cost and Delay Post-Settlement' (2018) 44(3) *Monash University Law Review* 658.

[17] See, for example, Supreme Court Act (Vic), s 33V and Supreme Court of Victoria, *Practice Note SC GEN 10 – Conduct of Group Proceedings (Class Actions)* (2017), available at www.supremecourt.vic.gov.au/law-and-practice/practice-notes/sc-gen-10-conduct-of-group-proceedings-class-actions. See further Victorian Law Reform Commission, *Access to Justice – Litigation Funding and Group Proceedings: Report* (VLRC, March 2018) 97–107.

[18] N Freeman-Engstrom, 'Sunlight and Settlement Mills' (2011) 86 *New York University Law Review* 805.

[19] Unlike the National Health Service in the United Kingdom, for example, which acts as the institutional defendant in the majority of medical negligence claims involving hospitals in that jurisdiction. See R Goldberg, 'Medical Malpractice and Compensation in the UK' (2012) 87 *Chicago-Kent Law Review* 131.

[20] Urbis, *2018 National Profile of Solicitors* (Prepared for the Law Society of New South Wales), 17 July 2019, available at www.lawsociety.com.au/sites/default/files/2019-07/2018%20National%20Profile%20of%20Solicitors.pdf.

state, personal injury lawyers accounted for around 10 per cent of all solicitors in the decade 2006/07 to 2016/17.[21] If the proportion of solicitors specialising in personal injury law in New South Wales is reflected in other Australian states and territories, there would be around 7,630 personal injury lawyers in Australia. Industry reports estimate that in 2018 there were 2,061 businesses in personal and workplace injury law practice for claimants in Australia, which generated annual revenue of $1.6 billion.[22] That revenue was close to evenly split across three major practice sectors of transport crash injury, workplace injury and other injury claim types.[23] The three largest plaintiff firms accounted for 27.1 per cent of market share, with a large number of small and sole-proprietor firms continuing to undertake a significant proportion of work in this field.[24] Importantly, lawyers also act for compensation payers (defendants, insurers and schemes); they may be located in commercial law firms or work in-house with an insurer or scheme organisation. Lawyers representing claimants or compensation payers may act in relation to individual claims, and may also play a role in contributing to the monitoring and evaluation of scheme performance, as well as scheme design and reform.

Beyond this broad characterisation of the injury law legal services market, there is strikingly little research evidence about the nature of plaintiff or defendant (compensation payer) personal injury practice in Australian compensation schemes. Statutory schemes do not regularly report on the prevalence of legal representation amongst claimants, nor the proportion of claims for which compensation payers engage lawyers, and there is little empirical legal scholarship exploring lawyer use and the factors contributing to lawyer engagement.[25] Scollay et al report that amongst the 49,602 persons who made claims in the Victoria transport crash compensation scheme from 1 January 2007 to 31 December 2009, 15.5 per cent used a lawyer in the six years following their crash.[26] Similarly, analyses based on the Law and Justice Foundation of New South Wales' *LAW Survey* identified that among people who had experienced a personal injury problem in the previous 12 months, 16.1 per cent had consulted a lawyer.[27] Far less is known about the prevalence or nature of lawyer use by compensation payers. There is also a dearth of empirical research exploring the work practices of

[21] Urbis, *NSW Profile of Solicitors 2016: Final Report* (prepared for the Law Society of New South Wales), 19 July 2017, available at www.lawsociety.com.au/sites/default/files/2018-04/NSW%20PROFILE%20OF%20SOLICITORS%202016%20FINAL%20REPORT.pdf.

[22] Kim Do, *Personal and Workplace Injury Lawyers in Australia* (IBISWorld Industry Report OD5519, June 2019) 3.

[23] ibid, 11.

[24] ibid, 21.

[25] See Chapter 5, 'Exploring the Dynamics of Claimant Legal Service Use in Compensation Systems' by C Scollay; P Casey et al, 'Associations with Legal Representation in a Compensation Setting 12 Months after Injury' (2015) 46(5) *Injury* 918; CE Scollay et al, 'Claimant Lawyer Use in Road Traffic Injury Compensation Claims' (2020) 43(1) *University of New South Wales Law Journal*.

[26] Scollay et al, above, n 25.

[27] C Coumarelos et al, 'Personal Injury Problems: New Insights from the Legal Australia-Wide Survey' (2017) 22 *Justice Issues* 1.

Australian plaintiff and defendant injury lawyers,[28] particularly compared with the rich tradition of socio-legal research on this topic in comparable Anglo-American legal systems.[29]

Research about claimants' experience of lawyer use is a valuable source of insight into how legal services are received and understood by consumers;[30] however, it, too, is thin on the ground, particularly in relation to injury schemes as opposed to tort-based litigation settings.[31] A recent Australian study explored claimants' experiences of making decisions, seeking advice and legal services in the course of motor crash injury compensation claims in New South Wales.[32] The Claims, Advice and Decisions after Injury (CADI) Study interviewed five key informants (spanning lawyers, insurers, and the scheme regulator) and 20 motor crash compensation claimants recruited from a longitudinal cohort study of survivors' health and social outcomes. The study identified that claimants experience the claims process as dynamic and uncertain with respect to their health, recovery and the likely future impacts of injury; what the claims process entails; the role of key personnel, such as lawyers and insurers; how different systems of support fit together; and how their claims are assessed. The study findings revealed differing

[28] The exceptions include M Robertson and L Corbin, 'To Enable or to Relieve? Specialist Lawyers' Perceptions of Client Involvement in Legal Service Delivery' (2005) 12(1) *International Journal of the Legal Profession* 121; O Rundle, 'Lawyers' Perspectives on 'What is Court-Connected Mediation for?" (2013) 20(1) *International Journal of the Legal Profession* 33; T Popa, 'Criticising Current Causation Principles: Views from Victorian Lawyers on Medical Negligence Legislation' (2017) 25(1) *Journal of Law and Medicine* 150; M Popa, '"No One Gets Closure In the End": Non-Adversarial Justice and Practitioner Insights into the Role of Emotion in Medical Negligence' (2018) *Journal of Judicial Administration* 148; T Popa, 'Righting Wrongs: Lawyers' Reflections on the Amendments to the *Wrongs Act 1958* (Vic) on Medical Negligence and Mental Harm Claims' (2017) 24 *Torts Law Journal* 64.

[29] See, for example, HM Kritzer, *Risks, Reputations, and Rewards: Contingency Fee Legal Practice in the United States* (Stanford University Press, 2004); Freeman-Engstrom, above, n 18; DE Rosenthal, *Lawyer and Client: Who's in Charge* (Russell Sage Foundation, 1976); MN Trautner, 'Tort Reform and Access to Justice: How Legal Environments Shape Lawyers' Case Selection' (2011) 34(4) *Qualitative Sociology* 523; A Boon, 'Ethics and Strategy in Personal Injury Litigation' (1995) *22 Journal of Law & Society* 353; A Boon, 'Client Decision-Making in Personal Injury Schemes' (1995) 23 *International Journal of the Sociology of Law* 253; A Morris, 'Personal Injury Compensation and Civil Justice Paradigms' in R Halson and D Campbell (eds), *Research Handbook on Remedies in Private Law* (Edward Elgar, 2019) 47; R Lewis, 'Tort Tactics: An Empirical Study of Personal Injury Litigation Strategies' (2017) 37(1) *Legal Studies* 162.

[30] See Ch 9, 'The "Lawyer was an Angel": New Zealand and American Patients' and Family Members' Experiences of The Role of Lawyers in "Resolution" Processes After Medical Injuries', by Jennifer Schultz Moore, discussing how patients' experience of responses to medical malpractice sometimes evoked the phrase in the title.

[31] See, for example, GK Hadfield, 'Framing the Choice between Cash and the Courthouse: Experiences with the 9/11 Victim Compensation Fund' (2008) 42(3) *Law & Society Review* 645 (on the 9/11 fund claims); G Grant, 'Claiming Justice in Injury Law' (2015) 41 *Monash University Law Review* 618 (on Australian transport crash and workers' compensation schemes). On the broader data gaps in relation to claimants' experiences and objectives in litigation-based claims in the US, see T Relis, 'Civil Litigation from Litigants' Perspectives: What We Know and What We Don't Know About the Litigation Experience of Individual Litigants' (2002) 25 *Studies in Law, Politics and Society* 151. See also NA Elbers et al, 'Exploring Lawyer-Client Interaction: A Qualitative Study of Positive Lawyer Characteristics' (2012) 5(1) *Psychological Injury and Law* 89.

[32] GM Grant, *The Claims, Advice and Decisions After Injury (CADI) Study: Final Report – Interviews with Claimants* (Monash University, 2017).

claimant preferences and approaches for managing advice sources – including lawyers – over the course of the claim. This diversity was closely connected to the varying levels of personal skills, experiences, capabilities and resources claimants brought to their claim. Claimants took a wide variety of pathways to the use of legal services. A number of interviewees were able to identify factors that were highly influential in their decision, including:

- lack of familiarity with or information about process and entitlements;
- preconceived impressions of the reputation or complexity of the process;
- perceived time pressure associated with lodging a claim;
- the seriousness of the injury and its immediate or projected life impacts;
- a lack of alternative support mechanisms (such as from a spouse or family);
- a negative encounter with the compensation payer, or an adverse decision;
- an offer of help from a lawyer in the claimant's social network;
- a suggestion about representation from a trusted person (for example, a health care provider, police officer or friend); and
- scepticism about the insurer's interests, particularly with respect to lump sum compensation and whether the insurer's offer would reflect an accurate assessment of claimant injuries.

Interestingly, the key stakeholders interviewed for the study tended to focus more on insurer-based catalysing events in explaining the conversion of claims from 'direct' (unrepresented) to legally-represented status, such as an adverse decision with respect to liability or treatment funding. Evidence from the claimant perspective demonstrates that a recommendation from a trusted contact at any stage in the claim can have be an important influence on the decision to consult a lawyer, despite the nature of any relationship the claimant has with the compensation payer.

The CADI Study identified that lawyers were an important resource for claimants as they navigated the process of claiming compensation. Claimants identified the service lawyers provided as including clarifying and explaining the law, process and claimants' entitlements; keeping claimants informed about claim progress; mediating interactions with the compensation payer; and negotiating the ultimate claim outcome. Establishing whether the claim was worth pursuing was also a valuable aspect of the lawyer's assistance, as was guidance for the claimant on the injury-related losses and impacts that were relevant to their claim. Claimants valued the way lawyers were able to identify impacts of injury that might otherwise have been overlooked, and their advice about ensuring a claim wasn't 'closed off' prematurely, before the likely course of injuries and their appropriate compensation was clear.

The most prominent approaches claimants described to dealing with their claim once the lawyer was acting were disengagement (including by 'leaving it to their lawyer', whether by active choice or not), or taking a more proactive and involved stance. Some claimants adopted a mixed approach, making strategic use of their 'lurking lawyer' to intervene when they encountered difficulty in the process they felt they could not manage themselves. Nonetheless, interactions with their own lawyer could be a source of stress for some claimants. Some reported the perception that communication with their lawyer did not seem to speed up the claims process. Fear and confusion about legal costs were reported as operating as a barrier to claimants seeking assistance from lawyers where it was desired. A number of claimants indicated they felt as though they lacked understanding about the legal costs agreements they had entered into. This dissatisfaction was magnified in the context of the explanation of the way legal costs operated in connection with settlement with respect to the fees and costs that were deducted from settlement monies.[33]

IV. The Health Impact of Claimants' Experiences in Injury Compensation Schemes: A Research Snapshot

Over the last two decades, a growing body of research about Australian work and transport crash compensation schemes has generated a valuable evidence base about claimants' experiences of, and outcomes associated with, engaging with claims processes. This research has been very effectively facilitated by large epidemiological cohort studies, together with analyses of administrative claims and health service payment data. Qualitative and quantitative research has established that there is considerable diversity in claimants' experiences: some have straightforward, relatively trouble-free engagements, while for others claiming is a protracted and negative ordeal. A small proportion of claimants have highly challenging experiences of injury compensation claims processes.

The dominant characterisation of lawyer involvement in this literature is as a risk factor for poor client outcomes. It is common to find a variation of lawyer presence (ranging from speaking with, or consulting, a lawyer, through to being formally represented) as a predictor variable in studies exploring a range of health and social outcomes. Such research often speculates that the findings can be explained by plaintiff lawyers instructing their clients to exaggerate,[34] a practice that would be in breach of the lawyer's professional obligations and remains difficult to prove or disprove. More nuanced explanations have considered the complexity of the reasons why claimants engage lawyers, and the possibility that those who are legally represented differ in systematic ways to those without lawyers.

[33] Legal costs are a common cause of complaints to legal profession regulators. In Victoria, for example, lawyer overcharging in relation to costs or bills was the subject of between 28% and 31% of complaints to the regulator by consumers in each year from 2016/17 to 2018/19 (Victorian Legal Services Board and Commissioner, *Annual Report 2018–19* (VLSB, 2019) 53).

[34] See, for example, LJ Ioannou et al, 'Traumatic Injury and Perceived Injustice: Fault Attributions Matter in a "No-Fault" Compensation State' (2017) 12(6) *PLoS One* e0178894 12.

Relatively few studies have linked analysis of claimants' experiences in compensation schemes – that is, how stressful or challenging the claimant perceived the process to be – to their health outcomes.[35] By seeking to unpack the way the process of claiming may itself negatively impact upon claimants' health, this strand of research has raised important questions that go to the heart of the purpose of compensation schemes in the restoration and compensation of injured persons. One such study explored the claiming experiences and health outcomes of a cohort of 332 Australian claimants in a longitudinal study over six years.[36] It combined validated health and quality of life measures with a survey about the stressfulness of claiming. Just over half of claimants reported experiencing moderate-to-high levels of stress in connection with one or more elements of the claims experience. The most frequently-reported sources of stress were understanding what the claimant needed to do for the claim (34 per cent of claimants); the delay associated with dealing with the claim (30 per cent of claimants); and the number of medical assessments or examinations required (27 per cent of claimants). The prospective nature of this study – in that claimants were recruited in hospital, shortly after their injury occurred and before their 'exposure' to the claims process – enabled the research to explore the relationship between stressful experiences of the claims process, and claimants' long-term health outcomes. This analysis found that claimants who reported high levels of claim-related stress were at heightened risk of poor long-term recovery (with higher levels of anxiety, depression and disability, and poorer quality of life). These associations between stressful claims experiences and poorer health and quality of life outcomes remained significant after adjustment for a range of clinical and demographic factors that may have predisposed claimants to experiencing the claims process as being stressful.

These findings build upon a range of health and medical research that has explored the relationship between claiming compensation and health outcomes. Usefully, they advance the evidence base by moving from identifying poorer outcomes amongst claimants to identifying potential mechanisms of the effect, focusing on the way differential experiences of the claims system are associated with claimants' outcomes. We now turn to exploring how legal practitioners might respond to these findings.

[35] See ML O'Donnell et al, 'Compensation Seeking and Disability After Injury: The Role of Compensation-Related Stress and Mental Health' (2015) 76(8) *The Journal of Clinical Psychiatry* e1000-5; NA Elbers et al, 'Factors that Challenge Health for People Involved in the Compensation Process Following a Motor Vehicle Crash: A Longitudinal Study' (2015) *15 BMC Public Health* 339; NA Elbers et al, 'Differences in Perceived Fairness and Health Outcomes in Two Injury Compensation Systems: A Comparative Study' (2016) 16 *BMC Public Health* 658; SE Gray et al, 'Association Between Workers' Compensation Claim Processing Times and Work Disability Duration: Analysis of Population Level Claims Data' (2019) 123(10) *Health Policy* 982.

[36] GM Grant et al, 'Relationship between Stressfulness of Claiming for Injury Compensation and Long-term Recovery: A Prospective Cohort Study' (2014) 71 *JAMA Psychiatry* 446.

V. An Ethical Framing for the Lawyerly Response

For the lawyer, as for other scheme stakeholders, the suggestion that the way claims processes are experienced by claimants may contribute to poor health outcomes is alarming. Participating in, and even facilitating, processes that are damaging to clients' health runs contrary to the plaintiff lawyer's conception of their professional role in assisting with supporting the claimant to seek a legal remedy through their claim.[37] There is an inherent contradiction in a legal process that has the overt, legislative objective of restoring injured persons to work and health but in practice may have the opposite effect. The lawyer's potential contribution to this impact adds another problematic dimension to existing understandings of the tension between the lawyer's professionalism and the furtherance of their economic interests through their work.[38]

Against this backdrop, legal ethics frameworks help us to understand and develop the range of ways lawyers might respond to the research evidence, and their limitations. In taking this stance, we bring to the practice context of Australian compensation schemes an approach previously applied to injury litigation to understand lawyers' work.[39] Situating lawyers in their routine practice is critical for understanding the factors that shape their ethical judgments and decision-making.[40] There is a considerable degree of overlap between injury litigation practices and lawyer work in compensation schemes. The structure of many Australian schemes sees administrative, no-fault claims operate as a precursor to a litigated dispute or damages claim. Previous ethical analyses have emphasised court-based work rather than the administrative making and processing of claims. Accordingly, we focus on the more routinised nature of work in injury schemes. We also concentrate on two of the chief sources of claim-related stress for claimants in claims processes: the delay associated with claims processing and the number of medical assessments claimants are required to undergo in the building and assessment of their claim.[41] Importantly, we also limit our analysis to lawyers acting on behalf of claimants. While there are clear reasons to be interested in the practices of compensation payer-side lawyers,[42] we lack sufficient empirical insight into their work to include them.

We draw on Parker and Evans' four ethical approaches to lawyering to analyse the potential responses lawyers might make.[43] These are the Adversarial Advocate,

[37] See, for example, Robertson and Corbin, above, n 28.

[38] See, for example, S Daniels and J Martin, 'Plaintiffs' Lawyers and the Tension between Professional Norms and the Need to Generate Business' in Levin and Mather, above, n 3.

[39] ibid; HM Kritzer, 'Betwixt and Between: The Ethical Dilemmas of Insurance Defense' in Levin and Mather, above n 3; M Keet et al, 'Anticipating and Managing the Psychological Cost of Civil Litigation' (2017) 34(2) *Windsor Yearbook of Access to Justice/Recueil annuel de Windsor d'accès à la justice* 73.

[40] L Mather and LC Levin, 'Why Context Matters' in Levin and Mather, above, n 3, 4.

[41] Grant et al, above, n 36.

[42] See V Holmes, 'Compounding the Abuse: Lawyers for the Catholic Church in the Ellis Case' (2014) 17(3) *Legal Ethics* 433.

[43] Parker and Evans, above, n 2.

the Responsible Lawyer, the Ethics of Care and the Moral Activist. These ethical approaches are a way to organise the literature and common debates and insights in scholarly and practitioner discussion about lawyers' ethics. Parker and Evans put them forward as a practical way to help imagine the range of potential ethical responses lawyers can make to a situation, and come to a conclusion as to what response is appropriate. The ethical approaches can be seen in terms of different but complementary attitudes or responses lawyers can make to their traditional role in the legal system in relation to clients, the courts and the law. We can think of them as responses to the traditional role-oriented conception of the ethics of lawyers as non-accountable partisans in the adversarial system.

A. Adversarial Advocacy and Responsible Lawyering

The first of Parker and Evans' approaches is the most familiar, that of the Adversarial Advocate. In this model, the lawyer's actions and decisions are guided by their advocacy role in an adversarial system, with a duty to zealously argue for their client's position within the bounds of the law. It is a conception that emphasises the client's autonomy, and the lawyer's loyalty to them.

Plaintiff lawyers' accounts of their work highlight their sense of contributing to the achievement of just outcomes for their clients. The socio-legal literature indicates that this kind of justice seeking through maximising return to an underdog client against a large corporate or institutional defendant is central to many lawyers' self-identity and perception of their role.[44] The limited empirical evidence does tend to suggest that the involvement of a plaintiff lawyer generates better monetary claim outcomes for claimants,[45] an effect that is likely to be explained in large part by the case (and client) selection practices lawyers employ.[46] Using the Adversarial Advocate frame, a lawyer might see themselves as justified in taking the necessary steps to extract the greatest settlement possible for a claimant, by amassing as much medical evidence as possible to identify the relevant impacts of injury, and to prosecute the claim for as long as required to maximise the settlement achieved.

Other professional and institutional stakeholders in compensation schemes do not share lawyers' enthusiasm for their Adversarial Advocate role, however.

[44] S Daniels and J Martin, 'Plaintiffs' Lawyers: Dealing with the Possible but Not Certain' (2010) 60 *DePaul Law Review* 337 at 354–58.

[45] See, for example, C Silver and D Hyman, 'Access to Justice in a World without Lawyers: Evidence from Texas Bodily Injury Claims' (2008) 37 *Fordham Urban Law Journal* 357. See also evidence from the NSW motor crash compensation scheme indicating that in 2015 the average claim size for minor severity injuries was $15,000 for non-legally represented claimants and $95,000 for legally-represented claimants (Ernst and Young, *Review of Selected Performance Indicators in the NSW CTP Scheme, May 2016* (2016, on file with authors)).

[46] MN Trautner, 'Tort Reform and Access to Justice: How Legal Environments Shape Lawyers' Case Selection' (2011) 34(4) *Qualitative Sociology* 523.

Qualitative studies in the compensation health research field have identified that lawyers are sometimes perceived by other scheme stakeholders – including insurance claims managers,[47] policy makers[48] and health care practitioners[49] – as contributing to poor claimant experience and outcomes through their work. The perception of lawyer involvement as a marker of increased adversarialism, cost and delay in claims processing seems to play a prominent role. These characterisations are consistent with Galanter's 'taxonomy of anti-lawyer themes',[50] including the vision of lawyers as 'corrupters of discourse', 'fomenters of strife' and 'economic predators'. The conundrum Galanter identifies, however, is that there are similarities in these common critiques of lawyers and the attributes for which lawyers are esteemed by their clients.[51] Indeed, several of the positive lawyer characteristics Elbers et al report[52] that clients identify – decisiveness, independence and expertise – reflect the client's preference for the Adversarial Advocate's commitment to zealous advocacy for the client's interests.

The second of Parker and Evans' approaches, the Responsible Lawyer, tempers the lawyer's client advocacy with attention to their role as a trustee of the legal system and officer of the Court – that is, the lawyerly responsibility to 'make law work as fairly and justly as possible', which may even necessitate acting as a 'gatekeeper of law and advocate of legal system' against the client in some cases.[53] In interpreting the formal rules and obligations lawyers are bound by, the responsible lawyer does not seek to exploit shades of grey, instead promoting the operation and effectiveness of the substantive law, maintaining autonomy from clients in representing the law to the client.

Legal ethics scholars have long identified the gaps between the formal prescriptions of professional responsibility in the law of lawyering, and the lived experience in practice. The Australian Solicitors' Conduct Rules regulate lawyers' conduct but shed little light on how a lawyer might best deal with a client's stress in a claims process.[54] A solicitor is required to act in their client's best interests,[55] but the precise meaning of 'best interests' is elusive. As Wolski has identified, 'lawyers are afforded a measure of discretion in deciding how to interpret and apply the rules and fill any gaps', and the objectives and values of the processes they are

[47] S Newnam et al, 'Stuck in the Middle: The Emotional Labours of Case Managers in the Personal Injury Compensation System' (2016) 55(2) *Work* 347 at 354–55; MA Trippolini et al, 'Beyond Symptom Resolution: Insurance Case Manager's Perspective on Predicting Recovery after Motor Vehicle Crash' (2019) *Disability and Rehabilitation* 1 at 5–6.

[48] P Zardo et al, 'External Factors Affecting Decision-Making and Use of Evidence in an Australian Public Health Policy Environment' (2014) 108 *Social Science & Medicine* 120 at 123–24.

[49] E Kilgour et al, 'Procedural Justice and the Use of Independent Medical Evaluations in Workers' Compensation' (2015) 8(2) *Psychological Injury and Law* 153 at 159.

[50] M Galanter, 'Predators and Parasites: Lawyer-Bashing and Civil Justice' (1993) 28 *Georgia Law Review* 633.

[51] Parker and Evans, above, n 2, 37.

[52] Elbers et al, above, n 31.

[53] Parker and Evans, above, n 2, 37.

[54] On the Canadian equivalent, see Keet et al, above, n 39, 75.

[55] ASCR r 4 ('Other Fundamental Ethical Duties').

involved in are relevant to the exercise of the discretion.[56] Where proceedings are commenced in court, lawyers increasingly owe additional obligations that seek to temper adversarial lawyer behaviour by binding the advocate to operate as a responsible lawyer.[57] In the practice context of injury compensation schemes, claims management guidelines and protocols for claim processing and appropriate dispute resolution seek to achieve similar effects, promoting non-adversarial and collaborative approaches.[58] A lack of evaluation means it is unclear how much these kinds of initiatives impact on the stressfulness of the experience from the client's perspective, given that it is to some degree mediated through their contact with their lawyer.[59]

B. Ethics of Care and the Therapeutic Response

The approach Parker and Evans characterise as the ethics of care points to the lawyer's responsibility to preserve relationships and avoid harm as superseding an impersonal idea of justice, with the nurturing of relationships and communities as the dominant guiding principles.[60] There is a tendency to respond to evidence of the harmful effects of legal practices and actions via a particular conception of the ethics of care. The ethics of care recognises that the adversary system must be tempered with humanity and relational ethics that incorporates moral, emotional and health aspects and implications of clients' legal problems. It is associated with Carol Gilligan's idea that women reason by reference to care, not rights.[61]

At the same time as the compensation health research evidence base has been amassing, law as a profession and academic discipline has increasingly turned its attention to the health, welfare and wellbeing of participants in legal processes. Some of this attention has come through the profession's reflections on its own members, and the toll of mental health problems on law students and practitioners.[62] There has been a turn toward non-adversarial justice and therapeutic jurisprudence for their emphasis of law's health-related externalities, or costs. Other scrutiny has been generated through analysis of the impact of

[56] B Wolski, 'On Mediation, Legal Representatives and Advocates' (2015) 38(1) *University of New South Wales Law Journal* 5, 13; *cf* Castles' suggestion that best interests means what the client instructs their lawyer to mean, rather than what the lawyer decides: M Castles, 'Mind the Gaps: Ethical Representation of Clients with Questionable Mental Capacity' (2015) 18(1) *Legal Ethics* 24–45.

[57] See, for example, Civil Procedure Act 2010 (Vic) and Civil Procedure Act 2005 (NSW).

[58] See, for example, the Transport Accident Commission Protocols, above, n 11; NSW Government, *Motor Accident Guidelines* (2019) (which regulate matters including claims management, communication between insurers and claimants and aspects of legal costs in the NSW motor crash compensation scheme).

[59] Grant, above, n 32, 35–41.

[60] Parker and Evans, above, n 2, 38.

[61] C Gilligan, *In a Different Voice: Psychological Theory and Women's Development* (Harvard University Press, 1982).

[62] C Parker, 'The Moral Panic over Psychological Wellbeing in the Legal Profession: A Personal or Political Ethical Response' (2014) 37 *University of New South Wales Law Journal* 1103.

compensation claims processes on claimants in settings such as Royal Commissions,[63] Ombudsman reports[64] and parliamentary committee inquiries.[65]

Instinctively it makes sense to embrace the ethics of care response when considering the health impact of a legal process. This approach helps us to understand the ways actors, practices and systems might contribute to participants' health. As Pryor has identified,

> [a]lthough the lawyer is not doctor or therapist, his or her representation will intersect with and sometimes influence the client's suffering and loss process. The lawyer is a key player in many of the ways in which the claiming process could fold into and influence the client's suffering and recovery process.[66]

In compensation schemes, which have a legislated focus on restoring claimants' health, negative health impacts and the opportunity to do better have a pressing urgency. The ethics of care perspective has underpinned calls for lawyers in litigation settings to modify their practice to improve claimants' experiences, often framed by therapeutic jurisprudence. Keet and colleagues, for example, suggest lawyers can prevent 'litigation stress' in their clients through adopting client-centred and collaborative practices, open communication with the client, giving consideration to appropriate dispute resolution processes, monitoring clients for stress and 'decision fatigue' and preparing clients for evidentiary processes, such as cross-examination.[67] Other studies have used this approach to identify practices occurring in compensation scheme settings that impede or act against claimant recovery or quality of life.[68]

Despite its intuitive appeal, there are dangers in over-emphasising the caring response as a means to address the health impacts of compensation claims processes. Such an approach can be unduly individualistic and have politically conservative implications. There is a risk that the focus on procedural and interactional justice entailed by the caring response may denigrate other dimensions of justice afforded by compensation schemes, such as substantive and distributive justice. Consider, for example, the claimant who, on the advice of her lawyer,

[63] See, for example, Royal Commission into Institutional Responses to Child Sexual Abuse, *Final Report: Recommendations* (2017).

[64] Victorian Ombudsman, *Investigation into the Management of Complex Workers Compensation Claims and WorkSafe Oversight* (2016); Victorian Ombudsman, *WorkSafe 2: Follow-up Investigation into the Management of Complex Workers Compensation Claims* (2019).

[65] See, for example, Australian Parliament, Senate Foreign Affairs, Defence and Trade References Committee, *The Constant Battle: Suicide by Veterans'* (2017) (investigating the contribution of the military compensation scheme to suicides by veterans and ex-service personnel).

[66] ES Pryor, 'Noneconomic Damages, Suffering, and the Role of the Plaintiff's Lawyer' (2006) 55 *De Paul Law Review* 563, 598.

[67] Keet et al, above, n 39.

[68] K Lippel, 'Therapeutic and Anti-Therapeutic Consequences of Workers' Compensation' (1999) 22(5–6) *International Journal of Law and Psychiatry* 521; M King and R Guthrie, 'Using Alternative Therapeutic Intervention Strategies to Reduce the Costs and Anti-Therapeutic Effects of Work Stress and Litigation' (2007) 17 *Journal of Judicial Administration* 30; WE Wilkinson, 'Therapeutic Jurisprudence and Workers' Compensation' (1994) *Arizona Attorney* 28; TC Ison, 'The Therapeutic Significance of Compensation Structures' (1986) 64 *Canadian Bar Review* 605.

elects not to pursue a lump-sum benefit to which she might be entitled because of the additional medical examinations and delay that claiming the benefit would require. Is such a claimant better off having claimed or not claimed? The long-term outcomes of claimants in compensation schemes have not been the subject of a significant amount of study – that is, we lack good data about the extent to which schemes actually achieve their economic restoration objectives.[69] In the absence of that key information, it is hard to assess whether promoting the caring response might translate into under-compensation.

There is also potential for compensation schemes, insurers and claims management agents to make self-serving use of evidence of the negative health impacts of stressful claims processes. Reforms or practice modifications that purport to reduce the stressfulness of the process could foreseeably also reduce access to benefits, legal representation, avenues of review or appeal, or public dispute resolution mechanisms. Such changes could reduce the stress of the claims process, and scheme costs, but in ways that diminish the substantive support claimants are able to access. Interestingly, plaintiff lawyers have a complex symbolic and social capital in reform debates in relation to compensation schemes. They are perceived in policy development and law reform processes as having a deeply vested interest in protecting claimant access to benefits and therefore the lawyer's own profits[70] – but injury claimants often lack an alternative effective and knowledgeable representative voice, particularly beyond the workers' compensation context.

There is further complexity in the likelihood that different claimants have different preferences about claims processes and what it means to resolve a claim in a way that minimises stress for them.[71] A truly claimant-centred approach should accommodate different claimant preferences for how a claim is resolved: it might not be as simple as generically making the experience as 'low stress' as possible. For example, should the priority be to resolve a claim as quickly as possible, drawing on the lawyer's experience with previous like claims (which may reduce the opportunity for client participation, and result in claim resolutions discounted for imperfect evidence)? Or to ensure that the most accurate evidence is collected to support the client's claim (which may take longer and cost the client more)? Should it be to maximise client participation and voice in the process (which again, may take more time and cost more)?[72] Or to truly tailor the way legal services are delivered to the needs and preferences of claimants – that is, to make them more human-centred?[73] The diversity of claimant views on these matters is not likely to be well accommodated by the economies of scale and consistency of approach that underscore practice in plaintiff law firms. Many claimants are not highly informed consumers of legal services (particularly at the point at which legal services are

[69] The few examples of this kind of work include Vines et al, above, n 9; Grant et al, above, n 9.

[70] M Galanter, 'Why the "Haves" Come out Ahead: Speculations on the Limits of Legal Change' (1974) 9 *Law & Society Review* 95 at 118–119.

[71] Grant, above, n 32, 35–41.

[72] Boon, above, n 29.

[73] See M Hagan, 'Participatory Design for Innovation in Access to Justice' (2019) 19 *Daedalus* 120.

first engaged),[74] so it is unlikely that a firm offering such differentiated services would acquire a significant market advantage.

Finally, taken to its extreme, an ethics of care response to the health impacts of the stressful compensation claims processes could result in advice that an injured person not pursue a claim to 'protect' them from a potentially damaging claims experience. Evidence suggests this advice is already being provided by some health care practitioners dealing with patients with work-related mental health and musculoskeletal conditions.[75] Such an approach is problematic for a range of reasons: it could result in systematic underclaiming by groups with particular conditions or demographic profiles, and impact on the data used to make decisions about scheme performance and to understand the burden of injury. It is also questionable whether the lawyer has what Pryor describes as the 'therapeutic competence' to assess whether or how each aspect of their management of a claim will impact upon a client.[76] By focusing on the individual claim level, the lawyer concentrating on such a 'caring response' misses the opportunity to contribute to the development of improved processes at the level of the compensation scheme and legal system. We now turn our attention to the lawyer's role in this work.

C. Building a Complete Picture with Moral Activism and the Sociological Imagination

The final approach, the lawyer as Moral Activist, sees them as capable of acting as an agent of justice, agitating for change to enhance substantive justice through public interest lawyering, law reform activities and counselling clients to pursue the moral course.[77] Moral activism is a necessary complement to the other approaches to make them meaningful. Our analysis here is one part of a broader project on lawyers' ethics and the sociological imagination.[78] The central contention of the project is that lawyers' ethics – including the dimensions represented by Parker and Evans' four approaches – should not be a matter of purely private, individual morality and were never developed to be so. Rather, as the sociologists of law and the legal profession recognised in the past, at their best professional ethics are precisely about connecting the individual's practice of their profession with public interest.[79] 'Sociological citizenship' offers the vehicle for understanding how individuals' behaviours and actions can shape social structure and culture, while the

[74] Grant, above, n 32, 31–33.

[75] B Brijnath et al, 'Is Clinician Refusal to Treat an Emerging Problem in Injury Compensation Systems?' (2016) 6(1) *BMJ Open* e009423, 5.

[76] Pryor, above, n 66, 598–99.

[77] Parker and Evans, above, n 2, 37–38.

[78] See, for example, C Parker and T Rostain, 'Law Firms, Global Capital, and the Sociological Imagination (2011) 80 *Fordham Law Review* 2347; S Kerr and C Parker, 'Making Climate Real: Climate Consciousness, Culture and Music' (2019) 30(2) *King's Law Journal* 185.

[79] Parker and Rostain, above, n 78.

social structure concurrently shapes individuals' consciousness.[80] By connecting the actions of individuals to broader system change, sociological citizenship casts light on how the lawyer might work to improve claims systems and processes for the benefit of claimants whose health might be negatively affected by the stressfulness of the process.

Each of Parker and Evans' four approaches is necessarily distilled in its description: in practice, they are multidimensional, consistent with the shape of law and justice, and so should be the lawyer's ethical response to research findings of the kind under consideration here. There is a need for lawyers to exercise imagination to ensure legal processes and systems can be caring but also just. They can do this by working as a profession to have and take responsibility for collective action to keep improving the system at hand. This drive should be kept in balance with the other approaches already considered. The empirical research findings about the health impacts of stressful claims processes should prompt our sociological imagination as lawyers responsible for legal justice in a number of ways. Consider, for example, the highly variable nature of claimants' experiences: the majority have straightforward, trouble-free passages through compensation systems, while a small proportion have protracted, stressful and difficult interactions.[81] The way a lawyer interacts with a client may influence their experience of procedural justice for better or for worse. Evidence of claimant perspectives suggests that much of these clients' stress and dissatisfaction appears to come from a basic desire to get justice, that is, to be heard, believed and compensated in a timely and effective manner. This indicates that some clients' experiences of compensation systems, and especially their sense of procedural justice, relates to their experience of legal services and systems. That is, claimants want to engage with the legal system to obtain just compensation and want their lawyer to be their guide, advocate and expert representative, in line with fairly traditional notions of adversarial advocacy and responsible lawyering. Of course, they need their lawyer to do so sensitively and with humanity and care – and this need for an ethics of care ought not to be any great revelation.[82]

We suggest that in addition to implementing aspects of the canvassed ethics of care approach, lawyers need to take responsible lawyering and moral activist responsibility for justice of the existing system and its accompanying institutions. Recognising the multiple roles plaintiff lawyers have in injury compensation schemes is a key part of formulating the optimal response to the health-related research evidence. In the context of compensation schemes, a key focus for this

[80] S Silbey et al, 'The "Sociological Citizen": Relational Interdependence in Law and Organizations' (2009) 59 *L'Année Sociologique* 201; see also C Wright Mills, *The Sociological Imagination*, 2nd edn (Oxford, Oxford University Press, 2000).

[81] Grant, above, n 31, 631.

[82] See Pryor, above, n 66, 588–97 (indicating ways that a lawyer might engage in a practice informed by awareness of the claimant's process of suffering and loss, but still respecting the boundaries of the lawyer's competence); RE Rosen, 'And Tell Tchaikovsky the News: The Wedding of Therapeutic Jurisprudence and Preventive Lawyering' (1999) 5(4) *Psychology, Public Policy, and Law* 944.

work should be the opportunity to work collaboratively with schemes, insurers and regulators to implement improved cultures and practices. While attention is often drawn to the lawyer as advocate for the individual client, lawyers also contribute to system design, change, reform and evaluation, through advocacy by peak bodies, liaison and reference groups, having input into policies and protocols that shape how claims are managed and processed and the compensation system is implemented as a matter of practice, in addition to the formal law on the books in compensation scheme statutes. These opportunities could be used to promote initiatives such as dispute resolution system that are about a more integrated and holistic sense of justice – including restorative justice and apology where appropriate, for example. Lawyers could also consider the more widespread implementation of systems for public interest activism and lobbying to support these efforts. Such steps are likely to generate a more sustainable response for the benefit of claimants, compensation schemes and their stakeholders, including the legal profession and the broader community.

VI. Conclusion

Recent research evidence suggesting that stressful experiences of legal processes are associated with poor health outcomes adds an empirical bite to lawyers' understanding of their work in injury compensation systems. Our analysis, while necessarily only focused on lawyers acting for claimants, rather than for compensation schemes or payers, indicates that a more nuanced reaction than one based solely on the ethics of care instinct is preferable. A range of ethical resources are available, as illustrated by Parker and Evans' four approaches and encapsulated by sociological citizenship, to enable lawyers to formulate a multidimensional and more sustainable response.

13

The 'Lawyer was an Angel': New Zealand and American Patients' and Family Members' Experiences of the Role of Lawyers in 'Resolution' Processes after Medical Injuries

JENNIFER SCHULZ MOORE*

This chapter uses empirical data about New Zealand and American patients' and family members' experiences of the role of lawyers in non-litigation approaches to medical injuries. What does the New Zealand and American empirical data reveal about the role of lawyers in 'resolution' after medical injury? How can plaintiff lawyers help resolve medical injuries and restore trust in medical practitioners? These questions are important because the role of lawyers in alternative resolution processes after medical injury is under-researched. These knowledge gaps complicate health systems' efforts to develop patient-centred responses to medical injuries. By drawing from in-depth interviews with injured patients and family members, this chapter contributes to our understanding of the lawyer's important role in facilitating resolution. In contrast to depictions of lawyers as 'devils', the data suggest that competent lawyers, who approach resolution as a collaborative process, should be considered 'angels'. These legal 'angels' facilitate fairness, create opportunities for injured patients to be heard and restore trust in provider-patient relationships.

I. Introduction

The well-known shortcomings of medical malpractice have led organisations in various countries to develop non-litigation resolution alternatives to meet

* Associate Professor Jennifer Schulz Moore is the Director of Learning and Teaching at the Faculty of Law and an Associate in the Department of Public Health and Community Medicine, Faculty of Medicine, University of New South Wales, Australia. From 2015–2016, she was a Harkness Fellow in Health Care Policy and Practice at Stanford Law School in the United States.

patients' needs following medical injuries. For example, in the United States (US), communication-and-resolution-programs (CRPs) seek to make disclosure of injuries, explanation, apology and other remedial gestures such as compensation, routine. New Zealand has long operated a no-fault compensation scheme for medical injuries. Despite the burgeoning investment in these alternatives to medical malpractice litigation, patients' experiences with these processes are not well understood. While the role of lawyers in medical malpractice litigation has been analysed,[1] the role of lawyers in alternative resolution processes after medical injury is under-researched. These knowledge gaps complicate health systems' efforts to develop patient-centred responses to medical injuries.

Research, and media reports, suggest that public trust in lawyers is low in many jurisdictions.[2] Commentators argue that lawyers 'encourage their clients to think with selfish defensiveness, to imagine and prepare for the worst from everyone else' and to 'add suspicion and unnatural caution to all our relationships, whether personal or professional'.[3] The overwhelmingly poor public perception of lawyers is often attributed to lawyers who have violated the rules of professional conduct, committed crimes, abused substances, ignored legal matters entrusted to them, and engaged in unethical behaviour. In popular culture, lawyers have been depicted as akin to devils.[4] The literature about plaintiff lawyers in medical malpractice litigation emphasises that these attorneys are also unfavourably portrayed and the focus of 'considerable criticism'.[5] A common refrain from health practitioners who participated in our research was that lawyers should be excluded from resolutions on the basis that one should 'feed a cold, starve a lawyer'.

By contrast, in the specialised field of medical injury resolution, two studies have revealed that injured patients and family members often describe their lawyers as 'angels'.[6] This chapter considers possible explanations for these starkly different portrayals of lawyers. Mello, Bismark and I have argued that in the US, United Kingdom and Australia, involving lawyers may help ensure that patients'

[1] CT Harris et al, 'Who Are Those Guys? An Empirical Examination of Medical Malpractice Plaintiffs' Attorneys' (2005) 58 *SMU Law Review* 225. A Netherlands study about lawyer-client interaction in traffic accident personal injury cases found that the five desirable characteristics for lawyers were communication, empathy, decisiveness, independence, and expertise: NA Elbers et al, 'Exploring Lawyer-Client Interaction: A Qualitative Study of Positive Lawyer Characteristics' (2012) 5 *Psychological Injury and Law* 89, research.vu.nl/en/publications/exploring-lawyer-client-interaction-a-qualitative-study-of-positi.

[2] M Galanter, 'The Faces of Mistrust: The Image of Lawyers in Public Opinion, Jokes, and Political Discourse' (1997) 66 *University of Cincinnati Law Review* 805.

[3] D Denby, 'A Motion to Suppress' (1994) *New York Magazine* 51, 52.

[4] G Morris, 'Devils Down Under: Perceptions of Lawyers' Ethics in New Zealand Fiction' (2013) 44 *VUWLR* 609.

[5] Harris et al, above, n 1, 226.

[6] JS Moore et al, 'Patients' Experiences with Communication-and-Resolution Programs after Medical Injury' (2017) 177(11) *JAMA Internal Medicine* 1595; JS Moore and MM Mello, 'Improving Reconciliation Following Medical Injury: A Qualitative Study of Responses to Patient Safety Incidents in New Zealand' (2017) 26 *British Medical Journal Quality and Safety* 788.

interests are protected, but could make the tenor of discussions more adversarial and provoke anxiety in clinicians.[7]

In this chapter I use empirical data about New Zealand and American patients' and family members' experiences of the role of lawyers in non-litigation approaches to medical injuries. In earlier work, Mello, Bismark and I explored the experiences of patients and family members with medical injuries, and non-litigation approaches to 'resolution', to understand the different aspects of health care organisations' responses to injury that facilitated and impeded resolution.[8] In this chapter, I will highlight the role of lawyers in resolution processes after medical injury. What does the New Zealand and American empirical data reveal about the role of lawyers in 'resolution' after medical injury? In particular, I focus on how plaintiff lawyers can help resolve medical injuries and restore trust in medical practitioners.

In the following section, I outline the research designs of the New Zealand and American empirical studies. Section III highlights the results that are relevant to the chapter's focus on the role of lawyers. The final section discusses the implications of those results for the role of lawyers in non-litigation approaches to the resolution of medical injury.

II. Research Designs of the New Zealand and American Studies about Non-Litigation Approaches to Medical Injury

I have described the research designs of these studies in detail elsewhere.[9] This section highlights the research design aspects that are pertinent to this chapter's focus on the role of lawyers in the resolution of medical injury.

A. Aims

The overarching aims of our projects in New Zealand and the US were:

1 to further explore patients' and family members' experiences with medical injuries and reconciliation processes in order to understand aspects of institutional responses to injury that promoted and impeded reconciliation;
2 to make recommendations about how institutions can better meet injured patients' needs.

[7] Moore et al, above, n 6.
[8] Moore et al, above, n 6; Moore and Mello, above, n 6.
[9] ibid.

The specific aim of this chapter is to analyse the data about the role of lawyers in 'resolution' processes following medical injuries.

B. Study Settings and Sites

New Zealand is an island nation where the government provides and finances health care services. Functioning alongside the health system is a government-operated entity, the Accident Compensation Commission (ACC). The ACC scheme, which came into effect in the 1970s,[10] extinguished New Zealanders' right to bring civil claims for personal injuries. Instead, injured persons can apply to ACC for compensation and rehabilitation. The ACC functions alongside New Zealand's healthcare system. It is a government-operated, tax-funded entity which is accountable to a parliamentary minister. In 1992, the ACC legislation was amended. With the introduction of 'medical error', fault appeared in the otherwise no-fault scheme. ACC was obliged to report all findings of medical error to the Medical Council and compensation claims could result in discipline for practitioners. This created delays and made some practitioners unwilling to participate in the claims process. In 2005, further law reform was undertaken which included removing 'medical error' and replacing it with 'treatment injury'. This change signalled a shift away from identifying error or fault and instead providing treatment and rehabilitation. A key impetus for these reforms was to improve patient safety.

Research is currently being undertaken to assess whether the ACC should be extended to cover both accidents and sickness.[11] If this proposed extension is implemented, it may have implications for the legal causation tests for treatment injury. At present, the law constrains awards for treatment injury if the injury was caused wholly or partly by an underlying health condition.[12] If the ACC is amended to cover sickness, legal debate about this causation issue may be obviated.

All of New Zealand's 20 public hospitals, governed by District Health Boards, were approached to participate in the Moore, Bismark and Mello study. In the US, dissatisfaction with medical malpractice litigation has led a small number of health care organisations to introduce alternative dispute resolution programs. Among the programs receiving attention are communication-and-resolution programs (CRP).[13] In the US an injured patient may go through the hospital-led

[10] Accident Compensation Act 1972.

[11] T Pullar-Strecker, 'ACC Should Cover Sickness and Disability, Says Sir Geoffrey Palmer' (2018) *Stuff NZ*, available at www.stuff.co.nz/business/industries/106959952/acc-should-cover-sickness-and-disability-says-sir-geoffrey-palmer; 'Research fellow to look at extension of ACC scheme', 11 December 2017, available at www.lawsociety.org.nz/news-and-communications/latest-news/news/research-fellow-to-look-at-extension-of-acc-scheme.

[12] Accident Compensation Act 2001 (NZ), s 32(2)(a).

[13] It is usual to distinguish 'open disclosure' or 'incident disclosure' from CRP because, strictly speaking, incident disclosure is only the first part of the process. However, sometimes in the UK and Australia the term' open disclosure' is used to denote a CRP.

CRP instead of filing a suit in court. A goal of CRPs is to resolve the cases early and to avoid medical malpractice suits or reduce costs of litigation. Patients can choose to appoint a lawyer even though the CRP is not an adversarial process. The CRP process can be started by the injured patient, their family, or clinicians who contact patient complaints services or risk management.

Not all hospitals implement CRPs in the same way. Typically, however, the CRPs involve an initial disclosure shortly after the medical injury, then a formal meeting, or (and more typically) a series of formal meetings with the clinicians and risk management staff such as claims managers and lawyers. Depending on the injury, some of these formal meetings may occur after the patient is discharged. After the CRP, some patients may still decide to sue, but this is rare. If the case is 'resolved', patients sign a release, which means they cannot sue. Only a handful of US hospitals operate CRPs, but the Agency for Healthcare Research and Quality (AHRQ) recently invested $23 million in improving patient safety, reducing medical liability and in scaling up the CRP approach nationwide.[14]

In the Moore, Bismark and Mello study, we approached three sites to participate in the study: (1) Stanford University Medical Center, Stanford, California; (2) Baystate Medical Center, Springfield, Massachusetts; (3) Beth Israel Deaconess Medical Center (BIDMC), Boston, Massachusetts. These institutions were selected because they operate CRPs that maintain patient contact information. BIDMC and Baystate collaboratively implemented a similar CRP.

C. Recruitment of Participants

Because injured patients are a difficult population to reach for research purposes,[15] in New Zealand, two approaches were used to recruit patients: first, we invited members of Acclaim Otago (a national support group for injured patients); second, we used snowball sampling.[16] The hospital administrators, ACC staff and practising plaintiff lawyers who specialise in ACC were recruited by sending invitation letters.

In the US, the CRP administrators identified participants and sent them invitation letters which outlined that university researchers would undertake the interviews and analyse the data.

[14] AHRQ, *Request for Task Order: Comprehensive Patient Safety and Medical Liability Communication and Resolution Program Educational Toolkit* (Rockville, MD, AHRA, 2013); Agency for Healthcare Request and Quality, 'AHRQ Toolkit Helps Health Care Organizations and Providers Communicate with Patients and Families When Harm Occurs' (2016).

[15] R Iedema et al, 'Patients' and Family Members' Views on How Clinicians Enact and How They Should Enact Incident Disclosure: The "100 Patient Stories" Qualitative Study' (2011) 343 *BMJ* d4423.

[16] R Atkinson and J Flint, 'Accessing Hidden and Hard-to-reach Populations: Snowball Research Strategies' (2011) 33 *Social Research Update* 1.

D. Interview Methods

In 2015 and 2016, we conducted in-depth, semi-structured interviews in New Zealand and the US. In New Zealand, we undertook interviews with 62 patients injured by healthcare, as well as administrators of 12 public hospitals, five lawyers specialising in ACC claims, and three ACC staff. In the US, we conducted interviews with 30 patients and 10 staff involved with CRPs in the three health organisations that participated in our research and run CRPs – Stanford's CRP 'PEARL', BIDMC's CRP 'CARe' and Baystate's CRP 'CARe'. From PEARL, we recruited 11 patient and family members and five healthcare institution staff and insurers. From BIDMC and Baystate (which both operate CARe), we recruited 19 patients and family members and five healthcare institution staff and insurers. Interviews with patients and family members lasted 60–180 minutes. Questions focused on the patients' injury experiences, the hospitals' responses, the relationships between patients and individual clinicians as well as hospitals after the injury, and the role of support people (such as lawyers) in the resolution process. Interviews were audio recorded and transcribed.

E. Data Analysis

Transcribed interview data were managed using NVivo and analysed by applying grounded theory.[17] Grounded theory is often used in qualitative health research which is exploratory and/or sensitive.[18] Glaser and Strauss (the developers of grounded theory methods) blur the divisions between theory and practice by advocating theory which is grounded in research data. The two key aspects of grounded theory are: (1) the role of pre-existing theory and literature in the analysis of data; and (2) the techniques of grounded theory such as coding. According to the methods of grounded theory, concepts, categories and themes are identified, developed and 'coded' while the research is being undertaken. Concepts are the basic units of analysis. Theory building 'occurs in an ongoing dialogue between pre-existing theory and new insights generated as a consequence of empirical observation'.[19]

Using transcripts from a small sample, two of us (Schulz Moore and Bismark) used thematic content analysis[20] to independently identify the main concepts and themes that became a coding scheme. The coding trees were discussed by all members of the research team. I then coded the remaining interview transcripts and generated initial theories and compared those against newly-coded data.[21] Frequencies of responses were tabulated for some questions.

[17] B Glaser and A Strauss, *The Discovery of Grounded Theory* (Chicago, IL, Aldine, 1967).
[18] PL Rice and D Ezzy, *Qualitative Research Methods: A Health Focus* (Oxford, Oxford University Press, 2001) 193–95.
[19] Rice and Ezzy, above, n 18, 194.
[20] Glaser and Strauss, above, n 17.
[21] H Becker, *Tricks of the Trade: How to Think About Research as You're Doing It* (Chicago, IL, Chicago University Press, 1998).

III. Results

A. Participant Characteristics

In New Zealand, the 82 participants comprised 56 patients, six family members, three ACC staff, 12 District Health Board administrators and five lawyers. In the US, the participants comprised 27 injured patients, three family members, and 10 CRP staff. The participant demographic tables, which are published elsewhere,[22] provide further details about the participants' characteristics.

B. Summary of Key Findings from the New Zealand and US Studies

Interview responses converged on five facilitators of more effective reconciliation following medical injuries:

1 involve the people who patients want involved in the disclosure discussion, including practitioners involved in the harm event;
2 engage the support of lawyers, mediators, and patient relations staff as appropriate;
3 ask, rather than assume, what patients and families need from the process and recognise that, for many patients, being heard is important and should occur early in the disclosure process;
4 support timely, sincere, and meaningful apologies, avoiding forced or tokenistic quasi-apologies; and
5 choose words that promote reconciliation.

C. The Plaintiff Lawyer's Role in Resolution after Medical Injury

In New Zealand, an injured patient does not need to engage a lawyer to file a claim. Instead, a patient who is injured by health care may file a claim with the ACC free of charge through a health care provider (often a general practitioner). The District Health Board administrator who participated in our research reported that patients do not typically involve their own lawyers in medical injury cases unless the case is complex. In New Zealand injured patients cannot litigate, so patients and families are told by lawyers that they are statute barred from doing so, but may, if desired, file a complaint with the Health and Disability Commissioner and/or be assisted by counsel through the hospital open disclosure process and ACC process.

[22] See above, n 6.

In the US CRPs, injured patients are not required to instruct a lawyer to handle their cases. However, CRP staff sometimes advise injured patients that they may consider whether to engage a lawyer. In the US, the patients and family members who we interviewed, and who instructed lawyers, told me during interviews that the lawyers explained the options to them, ie, broadly, CRP or litigate. According to the patients' accounts of these explanations, the lawyers outlined the benefits of alternative dispute resolution from the patient perspective (such as quicker resolution and apology) versus litigation which can take years, and an apology is rarely offered.[23]

The New Zealand and American injured patients and family members in our study who instructed lawyers reported the benefits of involving attorneys in resolution after medical injury. All of the patients who chose not to engage lawyers reported that they 'regretted' that decision.

The New Zealand and US data about lawyers revealed that experienced attorneys who approach resolution as a collaborative process are most likely to provide patients with the support they need while facilitating timely, appropriate resolution. Patients and family members reported that they valued their lawyers' roles in the process and that attorney participation tended to help the process. In the US research, 35 of the 40 participants reported that including plaintiff's attorneys in the resolution discussions was helpful. In the New Zealand research, 78 of the 82 participants believed that the involvement of lawyers in ACC treatment injury cases was beneficial.

In the following sections, I discuss the following four main ways that lawyers play important roles in resolution after medical injury: (1) ask; (2) being heard; (3) fairness; (4) trust.

D. Ask

Almost all injured patients in New Zealand and the US reported that health care providers should not assume that they know their needs and, instead, ask about their needs and then listen carefully. As a New Zealand lawyer explained:

> There has to be a window of vulnerability on the part of the hospital and doctor, where they relinquish control, and *ask* the patient which remedy they want. (Participant's emphasis).

Similarly, patients and family members reported positive experiences of the disclosure conversations when the health care providers asked how they could meet their needs. The main reason for patients' desire to be asked about their needs was to ensure that the response could be tailored to their individual needs. Patients were particularly unforgiving when health care providers made assumptions about patients' needs and 'read from a script designed for any patient, but not me'. For

[23] It is fair to say that there are a number of medical injury lawyers, particularly in Boston, who work a lot in the CRP space, so they are well-versed in these narratives. It is possible that patients would be told very different stories by lawyers who are accustomed to litigation and believe that it is better than alternative dispute resolution.

example, a mother who lost her baby to a preventable error explained that she wanted a hospital room named after her baby, rather than the traditional responses to medical injury such as disclosure, an apology and compensation.

Patients and family members in New Zealand and the US reported that lawyers can facilitate a resolution process which values asking about patients' needs and how to meet them. The following comments from a NZ injured patient capture the sentiments of many participants:

> I really appreciated that my lawyer said to the hospital, up front, before our meeting – 'hey, you guys need to make sure you ask my client want he needs and wants. Don't assume that you already know. Put your checklist away and listen to my client.' That is what the hospital did in the end and it worked well for me.

E. Being Heard

There was widespread agreement among New Zealand and US participants that being heard was an important, but often unmet, need after medical injury. Being heard is more than listening. It involves prioritising the patient's needs and allowing those concerns to lead the discussions. The patient's needs should be prioritised and heard, even if those needs are deemed clinically immaterial. For instance, many patients reported frustration when they wanted to discuss the impact of the injury on their daily lives and the health care practitioner 'constantly interrupted'. According to a patient:

> I wanted to discuss how the mistake meant I couldn't do my house work anymore. And I hate an untidy house. But the doctor kept interrupting and telling me that wasn't relevant. Well, it's important to me!

Patients and family members in New Zealand and the US reported that lawyers play a vital role in being heard in two ways: (1) lawyers can provide opportunities for their clients to be heard during the client-lawyer consultations; (2) lawyers can create space during the health care provider-patient resolution process.

Many of the lawyer participants were well aware of their role in facilitating opportunities for injured patients to be heard. One lawyer, for example, described these opportunities as the 'crying chair sessions'. He explained that his injured patient clients would canvass 'all manner of issues, none of which were legally or clinically relevant, but all of which were immensely important to the client'. A US patient described her experience as follows:

> My lawyer spent lots of time hearing what I'd been through … He helped me through it all and gave me good advice. He's wonderful, very kind … And he's an expert on this subject. I was so pleased he was in the meeting with me.

These findings are consistent with the legal therapeutic jurisprudence literature that recognises the 'therapeutic value of telling one's story and being heard and of a procedure that values the ongoing, continuous relationship between the parties'.[24]

The lawyers explained that creating space for patients to be heard is particularly important because those who felt that they were not heard were 'more likely to go on a crusade', including filing a medical malpractice claim or, in New Zealand, complaining to the Health and Disability Commissioner.

F. Fairness

There was agreement across the participant groups, and the two participating countries, that lawyers play a vital role in ensuring that the resolution process is fair and protects patients' rights. Health care provider participants emphasised that they often encourage patients to consult with lawyers because the lawyer is able to advise the client if the compensation offer is fair and reasonable. Patients reported similar experiences:

> My thinking was – you nearly killed me and my heart is damaged and can't be returned to normal. Surely that's worth millions! But my lawyer explained we wouldn't get that much money. He told me the hospital's offer was fair.

Lawyers are able to ensure that patients' interests are protected. Our data also suggests that lawyers can provide important emotional and practical support. As a New Zealand patient explained:

> I know we don't need a lawyer in NZ because we have ACC. But I was so pleased I decided to get a lawyer because the process would have been so scary. I didn't know what was going on or how to find my way through the maze-like system. I would have felt lost without my lawyer. I just feel like I was treated more fairly because my lawyer was there. I have a friend who went through the same process but didn't have a lawyer and he said it was just horrendous and he ended up with nothing.

This finding echoes an earlier study from Canada which concluded that injured patients who do not seek legal representation frequently feel unsupported and that their rights are being usurped.[25] Therefore, patients could benefit from engaging lawyers in resolution processes after medical injury.

G. Trust

Patients and family members also reported that their lawyers played a role in facilitating restoration of the therapeutic relationship by asking the right questions

[24] DB Wexler, 'Therapeutic Jurisprudence in the Appellate Arena' (2000) 24 *Seattle University Law Review* 217 at 219; N Des Rosiers, 'From Telling to Listening: A Therapeutic Analysis of the Role of Courts in Minority-Majority Conflicts' (2000) *Court Review* 54 at 56.

[25] KB Kovacs, 'Canadian Patient Safety Champions: Collaborating on Improving Patient Safety' (2008) 11 *Healthcare Quality* 3.

when families were overwhelmed and by providing another outlet for patients to be heard. Several participants (four in New Zealand and six in the US) were particularly happy with their lawyers' work and described them as 'angels'.

One metric for evaluating the success of non-litigation approaches to the resolution of medical injuries is patient satisfaction. Another marker is whether the injured patient is willing to continue receiving care from the same provider. Can the displaced trust between the patient and provider be restored so that the patient feels comfortable receiving care from the provider who was involved in the harm event? In the US, 18 of the 30 patients reported that they continued to receive care from the provider who harmed them. Many of these patients specifically credited their attorney for facilitating restoration of trust in the patient and provider therapeutic relationship and facilitating resolution. The following explanation from a US patient captures the sentiments of others:

> I saw the hospital as my enemy and the doctor as evil. My attorney asked how I'd like the outcome to look and how I saw the relationship with the hospital as part of that. It made me realise that they didn't go into work that day to hurt me and it was the mistake that needed fixing, because they weren't evil people. I was able to trust them again and get more treatment there. I don't know if I'd have got to that point without my attorney, or it'd probably take a lot more time.

The New Zealand and US research participants reported that another way that lawyers were able to facilitate the restoration of trust in the therapeutic relationship was by encouraging effective apologies from health providers. Lawyers demonstrated their view of how coerced apologies could further damage displaced trust in the therapeutic relationship:

> The doctor says 'sorry' at the appropriate, predetermined time, but only when jabbed by his boss, or the HDC [Health and Disability Commissioner]. My experience is that clients do not appreciate those types of 'apologies'.

Lawyers who were experienced in alternative dispute resolution processes also had a good understanding of how effective well-executed and well-tailored apologies can be in restoring trust in the therapeutic relationship. Similarly, patients reported on the role of lawyers in ensuring that they created opportunities for health care providers to consider apologising during resolution processes. As one patient put it:

> I really wanted the doctor and nurse to apologise. They just didn't get it. I talked to my lawyer. She said she'd already spoken to the doctor about this. About a week later, I went to a meeting. They did a really nice job of listening to how I was feeling. Afterwards, they explained how sorry they were for the parts that they played in my bad outcome. I just know that wouldn't have happened without my lawyer nagging them about it. It meant that I was able to see that same doctor again. I'm not unwell any more, but, if I was, I'd see that doc again.

The findings outlined in this chapter, and this section in particular, suggest that, contrary to conventional wisdom, 'good' lawyers, who are sympathetic to the resolution principles, play an important role in facilitating timely resolution and restoration of the therapeutic relationship. These outcomes are important and encouraging for all parties who are involved in improving the safety of healthcare and committed to meeting patients' needs after medical injuries.

Connecting patients with lawyers who understand the 'resolution' process, and who excel in these roles, may be challenging. Mello, Bismark and I have argued elsewhere that US CRPs could surmount this challenge by partnering 'with attorney organisations to provide education on the CRP approach and develop a list of qualified, interested lawyers'.[26] Such partnerships may allay the fears held by many US torts lawyers that they will lose their livelihoods if the system shifts entirely towards CRPs. The data in this chapter suggest that there is a strong argument for including competent, collaborative lawyers in CRPs.

IV. Study Strengths and Limitations

The main strengths of the study were: (1) the candour with which the New Zealand and American participants shared their experiences; (2) the inclusion of 62 patients and family members in New Zealand and 30 patients in the US, given that injured patients are a hard-to-reach population for research; (3) the nuanced insights into the complexity of injured patients' experiences of institutional responses to medical injury; (4) the diversity of participants, including key informants such as ACC law specialist practitioners and CRP managers.

The main limitations of the study were: (1) the study sample was not representative and the results may not be generalisable; (2) there may have been selection bias, particularly in the US where the sites identified injured patients and family members; (3) selective recall may have affected participants' accounts.

V. Conclusion

This chapter analysed empirical data about New Zealand and American patients' and family members' experiences of the role of lawyers in non-litigation approaches to medical injuries. The role of lawyers in alternative dispute resolution processes after medical injuries is under-researched and not well understood. This chapter contributes to our understanding of how lawyers can play an important role in facilitating resolution after medical injury. In contrast to the overwhelming literature which depicts lawyers as 'devils', the data analysed in this chapter reveal that competent lawyers, who approach resolution after medical injury as a collaborative process, may play a vital role in facilitating fairness, creating opportunities

[26] Moore et al, above, n 6.

for injured patients to be heard, and restoring trust between injured patients and health care providers. This narrative is encouraging for lawyers, injured patients, family members, and health care providers. The data highlights the valuable role of lawyers who promote resolution and restore trust in the therapeutic relationship. As health care organisations strive to provide care that meets patients' needs, an opportunity exists to include competent and collaborative lawyers in resolution processes after medical injury.

INDEX

www.ingramcontent.com/pod-product-compliance
Ingram Content Group UK Ltd.
Pitfield, Milton Keynes, MK11 3LW, UK
UKHW020243290926
15470UKWH00002B/714

9 781509 927999